INSPIRE / PLAN / DISCOVER / EXPERIENCE

CANADA

DK EYEWITNESS

CANADA

CONTENTS

DISCOVER 6

EXPERIENCE 72

NEED TO KNOW 378

Left: Snow-dusted red canoes in storage
Previous page: Banff National Park at sunset

DISCOVER

Toronto skyline at dusk

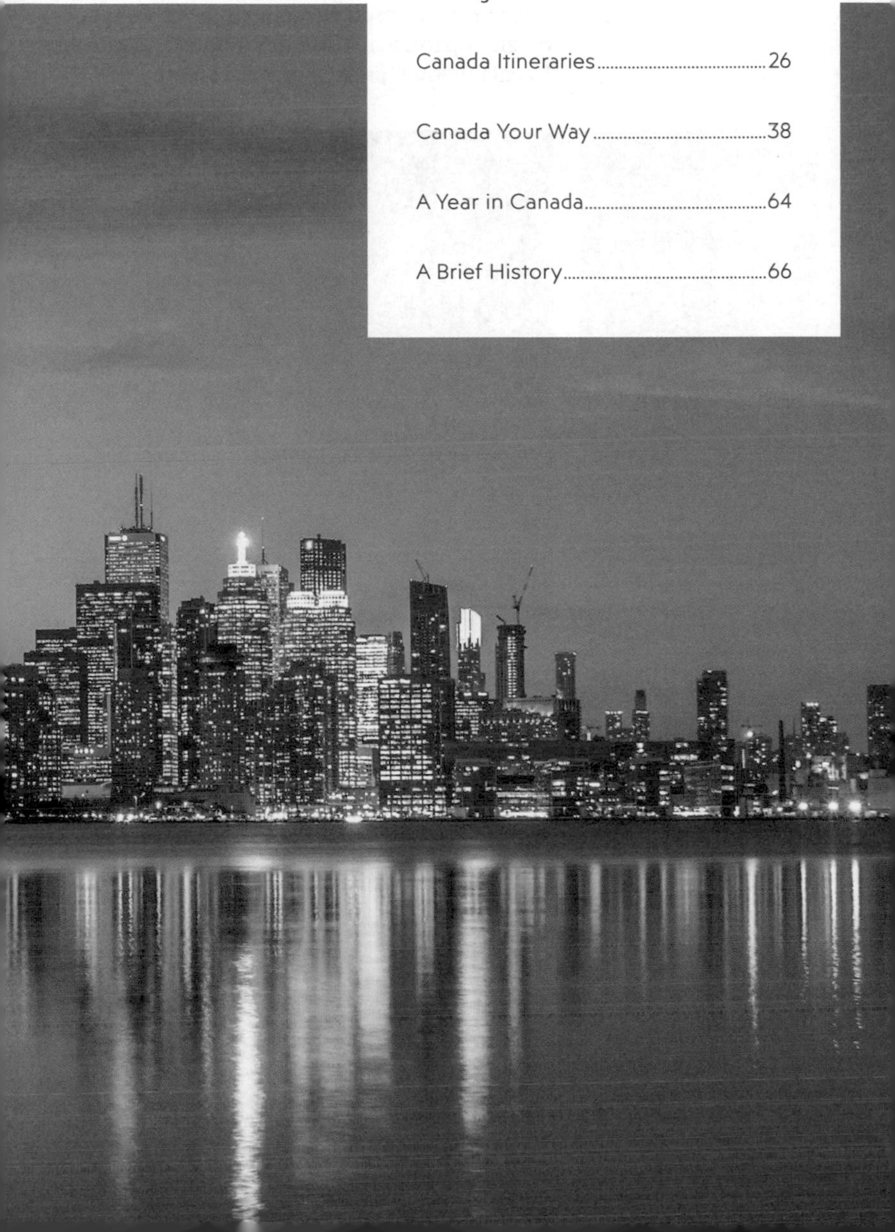

WELCOME TO
CANADA

Soaring snow-capped mountains and rugged coastlines. Vast stretches of pristine Arctic wilderness. Vibrant cosmopolitan cities, furious ice hockey games, and dollops of maple syrup: this enormous country has it all. Whatever your dream trip to Canada includes, this DK Eyewitness Travel Guide will prove the perfect companion.

1 Female grizzly bear in the rainforest in BC.

2 Soaring skyscrapers in downtown Toronto.

3 Rugged mountains reflected in Moraine Lake, Banff National Park.

Sprawling across the northern end of the American continent and stretching up into the Arctic Ocean, Canada is unimaginably vast. Only 10 percent of the country is populated – the rest is untamed wilderness, where shimmering glaciers, dramatic ocean vistas, and forests of fiery maple trees will leave you awestruck. Hike exhilarating trails beneath snowy peaks, paddle a canoe on backcountry rivers, or head to the Arctic for the greatest light show on earth: the Northern Lights. Everywhere there is wildlife as amazing as the land it inhabits – from breaching whales to grizzly bears.

Canada's urban areas, too, will not disappoint. There's delightful diversity across the country's main cities, from French-speaking Quebec City's European ambiance to Montreal's bustling multicultural neighborhoods, and from the gleaming skyscrapers of Toronto to the dynamic buzz of Vancouver. Farther afield, you'll find pretty French-style towns, small indigenous communities, and charming fishing villages. In every place you stay, you'll receive a famously warm and polite Canadian welcome.

The sheer scale of Canada, and the endless number of breathtaking experiences on offer, can seem overwhelming. We've broken the country down into easily navigable chapters, with detailed itineraries, expert knowledge and colorful, comprehensive maps to help you plan your visit. Whether you're staying for a weekend, a week, or longer, this Eyewitness guide will ensure you see the very best of Canada. Enjoy the book, and enjoy Canada.

REASONS TO LOVE
CANADA

Vast, vibrant and breathtakingly beautiful, the world's second-largest country offers endless possibilities for travelers. Ask any Canadian and you'll hear a different reason why they love Canada. Here, we pick some of our favorites.

1 THE ROCKIES

With soaring peaks, crystal-clear lakes and acres of forests, the beauty of the Canadian Rockies *(p128)* is spellbinding. Ski the slopes, hike the trails or take in the amazing views.

THE NORTHERN LIGHTS *2*

Seeing these eerie and elusive ribbons of light tops many a bucket list. Churchill *(p177)*, the Yukon *(p350)* and the Northwest Territories *(p360)* are some of the top viewing spots.

3 WHALE WATCHING

The thrill of seeing a breaching whale gushing out of the water or a mother and calf plying the waves is incredible. Tour boats sail off both the Atlantic and Pacific coasts.

CAPTIVATING CITIES 4

The French flair of Montreal *(p238)*, the cosmopolitan cool of Vancouver *(p74)* and the multicultural energy of Toronto *(p178)* make a dynamic contrast to Canada's scenic landscapes.

SPECTACULAR TRAIN JOURNEYS 5

Marvel at dazzling fall colors on the Algoma Central Railway, pristine wilderness on the Polar Bear Express, or stunning snow-capped peaks on the Rocky Mountaineer *(p384)*.

POUTINE 6

Hot, crispy french fries, topped with cheese curds and salty brown gravy: it's easy to crave this simple comfort food that hails from Quebec but is loved right across the country.

NIAGARA FALLS 7
The thunderous torrent plunging over Horseshoe Falls (p204) is one of North America's greatest natural spectacles. Take a boat cruise into the mist at the bottom of the falls to truly feel their power.

LIFE ON THE LAKES 8
Paddle a canoe, cast a fishing line or catch the wind in your sails. From the bustling Great Lakes to the quiet backcountry, Canada is dotted with lakes to enjoy a wealth of watersports.

9 INDIGENOUS ART
The phenomenal skills of Inuit and First Nations artists can be seen in intricately carved totem poles, sensuous sculptures and vibrant paintings across the country.

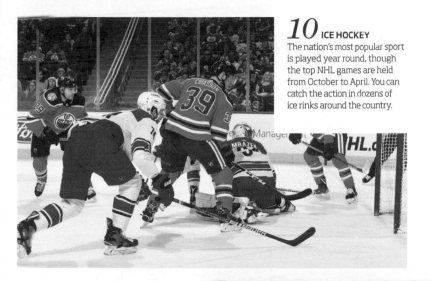

10 ICE HOCKEY

The nation's most popular sport is played year round, though the top NHL games are held from October to April. You can catch the action in dozens of ice rinks around the country.

DISCOVERING DINOSAUR FOSSILS 11

Explore some of the world's richest fossil beds at Dinosaur Provincial Park, then follow the Dinosaur Trail through badlands studded with bizarre hoodoo rock formations (p168).

HIKING OFF THE CABOT TRAIL 12

Amazing trails through Cape Breton Highlands National Park (p316) capture all the beauty of Atlantic Canada: sandy beaches, green highlands, dense forests, and marvelous ocean views.

EXPLORE
CANADA

This guide divides Canada into
14 colour-coded sightseeing areas,
as shown on the map below.
Find out more about each area
on the following pages.

Ellesmere
Island

Bathurst
Island

Devon
Island

Somerset
Island

Inuvik

Victoria
Island

Dawson City

Great
Bear Lake

YUKON
p350

**NORTHWEST
TERRITORIES**

**NORTHWEST TERRITORIES
AND NUNAVUT**
p360

Whitehorse

Yellowknife

NUNAVUT

Juneau

Great
Slave Lake

**BRITISH
COLUMBIA
INTERIOR**
p110

Fort St. John

Prince George

ALBERTA

SASKATCHEWAN

MANITOBA

Edmonton

**VANCOUVER
ISLAND**
p92

**CANADIAN
ROCKIES**
p128

Kamloops

VANCOUVER
p74

THE PRAIRIES
p148

Lake
Winnipeg

Saskatoon

Victoria

Calgary

Seattle

Regina

Winnipeg

Portland

Helena

Fargo

Bismarck

St Paul

0 kilometers   400

0 miles   400

N

UNITED STATES

Casper

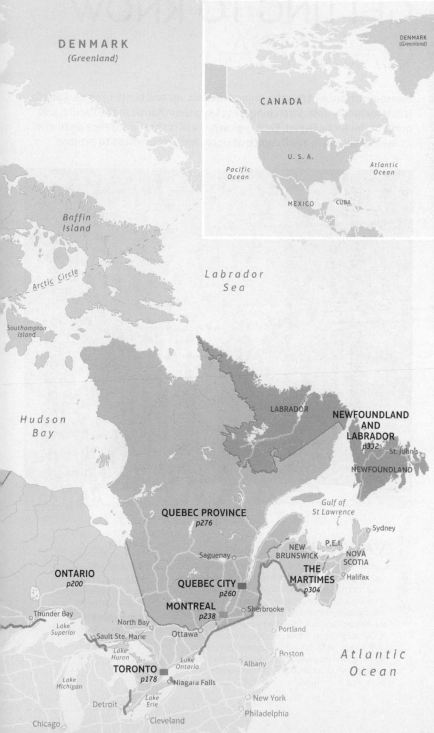

NORTH AMERICA

DENMARK
(Greenland)

CANADA

U.S.A.

Pacific
Ocean

Atlantic
Ocean

MEXICO   CUBA

DENMARK
(Greenland)

Baffin
Island

Arctic Circle

Labrador
Sea

Southampton
Island

Hudson
Bay

LABRADOR

NEWFOUNDLAND
AND
LABRADOR
p332

St. John's

NEWFOUNDLAND

QUEBEC PROVINCE
p276

Gulf of
St Lawrence

Sydney

Saguenay

NEW
BRUNSWICK

P.E.I.

NOVA
SCOTIA

ONTARIO
p200

QUEBEC CITY
p260

THE
MARTIMES
p304

Halifax

Thunder Bay

MONTREAL
p238

Sherbrooke

North Bay

Lake
Superior

Sault Ste. Marie

Ottawa

Portland

Lake
Huron

Albany

Boston

Atlantic

TORONTO
p178

Lake
Ontario

Ocean

Lake
Michigan

Niagara Falls

Detroit

Lake
Erie

New York

Chicago

Cleveland

Philadelphia

GETTING TO KNOW
CANADA

Blessed with ancient forests, rugged mountains, and bustling cities, Canada is astonishingly vast, stretching west from the Atlantic to the Pacific, and north to the Arctic Ocean. Each region has a history and essence distinctly its own, resulting in a rich choice of sights and experiences to explore.

VANCOUVER

PAGE 74

Canada's cosmopolitan western seaport enjoys a stunning location, tucked between an island-studded strait and rugged coastal mountains. The shimmering glass skyscrapers of its buzzing downtown sit alongside trendy restaurants, art galleries, and boutiques in the historic Gastown district. Vancouver is also home to Canada's largest Chinatown, where mouthwatering eateries can be found on every corner. Beyond the center, abundant parks and gardens call out to be explored, and outstanding First Nations art can be viewed at the University of British Columbia.

Best for
Ethnic restaurants and vibrant nightlife

Home to
Stanley Park, Granville Island, and the Gastown district

Experience
A bike ride around the perimeter seawall in Stanley Park

VANCOUVER ISLAND

PAGE 92

This mountainous island has a wild beauty and a relaxed pace of life. The towns of its southeastern corner offer a lively food and arts scene, while Victoria, the pretty provincial capital, has a charming harbor and fine museums packed with the works of First Nations artists. To the west of the island lies the Pacific Rim National Park Reserve, which features miles of lush coastal rainforest and rugged surfing beaches. It is a renowned whale-watching spot, with these popular visitors often venturing so close to the shore that they can be glimpsed from land.

Best for
Cold-water surfing and hiking the coastal rainforest

Home to
Pacific Rim National Park Reserve, Royal British Columbia Museum, and Victoria

Experience
A whale-watching excursion in the island's busy local waters

→

PAGE 110

BRITISH COLUMBIA INTERIOR

Thundering waterfalls, majestic rivers, and mineral hot springs are among the beautiful landscapes that lie between the western Coast Mountains and the Rockies to the east. Thanks to British Columbia's mild climate, orchards and vineyards flourish here in the southern Okanagan Valley. In sharp contrast, the dramatic wilderness of the northern parks includes ice fields, tundra, and volcanic terrain, while the Haida Gwaii islands preserve ancient rainforest.

Best for
Skiing and snowboarding against a spectacular backdrop

Home to
Whistler Blackcomb, Okanagan Valley, and the Kootenays region

Experience
A vineyard tour and wine tasting in the Okanagan Valley

PAGE 128

CANADIAN ROCKIES

Jagged snowy peaks, luminous glaciers, and shimmering turquoise lakes are strung across Canada's stretch of the Rocky Mountains. Both stunning natural features and a wealth of wildlife – from grizzly bears to bison – are protected in a series of national and provincial parks, which are populated by splendid scenic drives and hiking trails. Outside the parks, the region offers historic towns such as Fort Steele, beauty spots like Kananaskis Country, and the soothing waters of Radium Hot Springs.

Best for
Hiking trails and wildlife encounters

Home to
Banff National Park, Yoho National Park, and Jasper National Park

Experience
A luxurious soak in the Miette Hot Springs within Jasper National Park

PAGE 148

THE PRAIRIES

Golden wheat fields and grasslands that reach to the horizon characterize the prairies of central Canada. But this vast area is home to further varied landscapes, from aspen parkland in the west, through the sandy beaches of Lake Winnipeg in the east, to the frozen tundra of northern Manitoba. Bookending the region are the cities of Calgary (best known for its western-themed events) and cosmopolitan Winnipeg. Those keen to glimpse polar bears or the Northern Lights should head northward, where remote Churchill on Hudson Bay remains a popular place to experience both.

Best for
Dinosaur fossils and polar bear spotting

Home to
Calgary, Royal Tyrell Museum, and Prince Albert National Park

Experience
The awe-inspiring spectacle of the Northern Lights in Churchill

$\rightarrow$

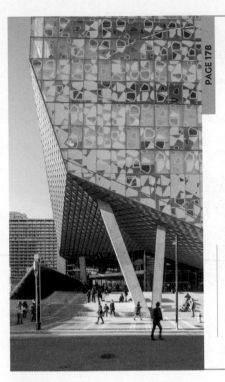

PAGE 178

TORONTO

The iconic CN Tower, which dominates the skyline for miles around, is a suitable focal point of Canada's largest city. Close up, Toronto's dynamic buzz radiates from the lakefront parks of the Harbourfront, through the shiny skyscrapers of downtown, to the tempting sights and smells of Chinatown and other vibrant ethnic neighborhoods. The city's cultural offerings are immense; spend your time exploring Toronto's excellent museums and art galleries, its bustling markets, and its lively historic districts teeming with hip restaurants, bars and boutiques.

Best for
World-class museums and stylish restaurants

Home to
CN Tower, Royal Ontario Museum, and the Art Gallery of Ontario

Experience
A three-course meal in the CN Tower's revolving restaurant, with glorious views of the city below

PAGE 200

ONTARIO

Studded with sparkling lakes and waterways, this enormous province stretches from the Great Lakes to Hudson Bay. Northern Ontario is a land of turbulent rivers, dense forests, and Arctic tundra, accessible only by air and a handful of scenic road and rail routes. The fertile southern and eastern regions have sleepy farming towns, island-dotted bays, and sprawling wilderness areas around Lake Superior and in Algonquin Provincial Park. They are also home to the nation's capital, Ottawa; Toronto, its largest city; and its biggest visitor attraction, Niagara Falls.

Best for
Stunning lakes and thrilling outdoor activities

Home to
Ottawa, Niagara Falls, and the National Gallery of Canada

Experience
A boat ride to the mist-veiled base of Niagara Falls

MONTREAL

Montreal is a mosaic of traditionally French and English neighborhoods, sprinkled with multi-cultural communities. This lively mix makes it one of Canada's most interesting cities. Those fresh to Montreal should head for Plateau Mont-Royal, the best place to catch the unique vibe along with some amazing city views. By the riverfront, the historic buildings and narrow, cobblestone streets of Vieux-Montréal are home to stylish restaurants, bistros and boutiques. The compact city center also offers exquisite churches and outstanding art museums.

Best for
Unbeatable art museums

Home to
Basilique Notre-Dame-de-Montréal and the Musée des Beaux-Arts

Experience
A cable-car ride up the side of Montreal Tower, to take in wonderful vistas from the viewing deck

→

PAGE 260

QUEBEC CITY

The essence of French Canada can be found in this delightful city that sits on the edge of the Saint Lawrence River, with its European architecture and Parisian ambiance. This is a city for wandering: explore the winding cobbled streets, the splendid cathedrals and civic buildings inside the old city walls, the lively market at the Vieux Port, and the Citadelle with its breezy waterside views. Let the relaxed pace continue into the evenings, when you can soak up the atmosphere with leisurely meals in the charming cafés and elegant squares of the Basse-Ville.

Best for
French culture and historic architecture

Home to
La Citadelle, Place Royale, and the Basilique-Cathédrale Notre Dame de Québec

Experience
A rummage through the art and specialty shops of the rue du Petit-Champlain, before lingering over coffee in an old-town café

PAGE 276

QUEBEC PROVINCE

Each fall, fiery red and gold maple forests transform this French-speaking region into one of the most beautiful places in the country. At its heart is the mighty Saint Lawrence River, bordered in the north by the scenic Charlevoix coast and the Laurentian Mountains, which are dotted with charming French villages and churches. To the south, the rocky cliffs and mountains of the Gaspé Peninsula offer superb hiking trails, while caribou herds and polar bears roam the tundra of the remote Nunavik territory in the far north.

Best for
Flaming fall colors

Home to
Gatineau, the Canadian Museum of History, and Sainte-Anne-de-Beaupré

Experience
A trip to Sucrerie de la Montagne to see how maple syrup is made (and sample the results!)

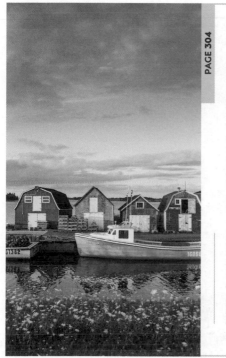

PAGE 304

THE MARITIMES

With rocky coastlines, picturesque fishing villages, and long sandy beaches, the beauty and lure of the sea is always close at hand in the Maritimes, though each province maintains a distinctive flavor. New Brunswick is home to French-speaking Acadian villages, quiet coves and the tide-carved Bay of Fundy, while Prince Edward Island, with its emerald farmland and golf courses, is an ideal destination for cycling and hiking. In Nova Scotia, the sparkling bays and weathered fishing towns embody the romance of the sea.

Best for
Beautiful seascapes and cozy country inns

Home to
Halifax, Prince Edward Island, and the Fortress of Louisbourg

Experience
Breathtaking landscapes on Prince Edward Island, fictional home of Anne of Green Gables

$\rightarrow$

NEWFOUNDLAND AND LABRADOR

PAGE 332

In Newfoundland, the mountains of Gros Morne National Park rise high above sparkling blue fjords. Labrador's landscape is similarly imposing, with coastal vistas that are often set against a backdrop of glittering icebergs. This remotely beautiful Atlantic region is a popular vacation spot due to its friendly, historic towns, wide-open spaces and grand spectacles of nature. It's also a good place for whale-watching excursions or trips to see Labrador's caribou herd.

Best for
Rugged coastal scenery

Home to
St. John's and Gros Morne National Park

Experience
A boat tour into the narrow Western Brook Pond fjord to see wildlife and waterfalls in Gros Morne National Park

YUKON

PAGE 350

The harsh romance of the gold rush days still lingers over this starkly beautiful land, which is characterized by daunting mountains, frozen lakes, and glacial valleys. Beyond the old mining towns of Whitehorse and Dawson City, an adventurer's paradise awaits. Head into this remote region to hike beneath the soaring peaks in Kluane National Park and Reserve, or canoe the icy waters of the Stewart River. In summer, the midnight sun never sets, while the Aurora Borealis illuminates dark winters with ribbons of colored light.

Best for
Adventure travel and the unmatched spectacle of the Northern Lights

Home to
Whitehorse

Experience
An afternoon of Arctic animal watching at the Yukon Wildlife Preserve

NORTHWEST TERRITORIES AND NUNAVUT

Still one of the most remote destinations on earth, the vast, untouched terrain of the Northwest Territories will reward those who venture here with superlative hiking. Much of the landscape is harsh, featuring barren tundra, frozen forests, and stark mountains. Yet an abundance of wildlife flourishes here, from great herds of bison to polar bears. Nunavut is also home to the indigenous Inuit, who still practice their traditional lifestyle.

Best for
Inuit art and culture

Home to
Yellowknife and Baffin Island

Experience
A thrilling plane ride to reach Aulavik National Park, one of the world's most isolated wildlife destinations

←

1 False Creek and the skyline of downtown Vancouver.

2 Cyclists and joggers on the Seawall in Stanley Park.

3 Coffee brewing at Revolver on Cambie Street.

4 Neon sign for Art Deco venue the Commodore.

Canada brims with travel possibilities, from two-day tours around the big cities to grand odysseys across the entire region. These itineraries will help you to chart your own course through this vibrant and varied country.

2 DAYS

in Vancouver

Day 1

Morning After a leisurely latte at Revolver *(325 Cambie St)* and people-watching on Robson Street, head to the lovely Stanley Park *(p80)*. The Seawall here is flat and easily circumnavigated in an hour; you can book an e-bike and a tour guide to cycle it or, if you're feeling less energetic, board the hop on-hop-off bus. Don't miss the totem poles near Brocton Oval or the Vancouver Aquarium, which is worth going to for its mesmerizing jellyfish tank alone. Afterward, head down to False Creek to take an aquabus across to Granville Island *(p82)*, a small peninsula dominated by a huge food market brimming with fresh produce, fishmongers, cheese makers, butchers and bakers.

Afternoon After a hearty lunch at the market, take a 20-minute bus ride from Granville Loop Park to Mount Pleasant, a vibrant neighborhood filled with boutiques, galleries, coffee shops, and craft breweries. Nearby Brassneck Brewery *(2148 Main St)* is a favorite with thirsty locals sporting hipster beards and plaid shirts. When you've had your fill of craft beers, take another short bus ride up to Chinatown and enjoy a stroll around the tranquil Dr Sun Yat-Sen Classical Chinese Garden *(p87)*.

Evening Work up an appetite browsing aromatic apothecary and grocery stores on Keefer and East Pender streets before having dinner at Bao Bei *(p87)*. If you have to join a waiting list for a table, enjoy a cocktail at The Keefer Bar *(135 Keefer St)*.

Day 2

Morning Take the SeaBus across Burrard Inlet to North Vancouver and bus to Grouse Mountain *(p90)* for a panoramic view of the city. Take the same bus to the spectacular Capilano Suspension Bridge *(p90)* and visit the First Nations Cultural Centre, located in the same park, to see demonstrations of weaving, beadwork, and carving. Before jumping back on the SeaBus, check out Lonsdale Quay *(p91)*, a market selling a tempting array of fresh produce and hand-crafted items.

Afternoon Back in the city centre, splurge on a massage at the Fairmont Pacific Rim's Willow Stream Spa *(1038 Canada Place)*, just a short walk from the Waterfront Station. Fully recharged, take a stroll around trendy Gastown *(p78)*, Vancouver's oldest neighborhood, with its indie art galleries and souvenir shops housed in Victorian buildings. The quirky Police Museum was once a morgue, while the Steam Clock is picture-perfect when it toots and puffs every 15 minutes. Wine lovers can head to Salt Tasting Room in Blood Alley for a pre-dinner drink – your server will likely tell you all about the alley's fascinating history.

Evening Gastown's restaurants range from funky to fine dining. Sidle up to the bar at Sardine Can *(26 Powell St)* for Spanish tapas and a sherry. After dinner, catch a show at the nearby Commodore *(868 Granville St)*. This Art Deco venue is known for its sprung dance floor. If you want to party the night away afterward, Granville Street is definitely the place to be.

→

1 Thrillseekers tackling the EdgeWalk at CN Tower.

2 Distillery Historic District.

3 Fossils at the Royal Ontario Museum.

4 Diners enjoying a meal at Bisha Hotel's KOST restaurant.

2 DAYS
in Toronto

Day 1

Morning Rocket up to the top of the CN Tower *(p186)*, where the views on a clear day are outstanding. If you dare, the EdgeWalk is a (safe) 20-minute outdoor walk around the unbounded perimeter of the main viewing pod, but you must book well in advance and arrive early – there can be a long wait for the elevator. Alternatively, if heights are not your thing, hop on the Queen Streetcar to Humber Bay for a terrific view of the skyline. Brunch or lunch at the St. Lawrence Market *(p192)*, which comprises three buildings. Make a beeline for the South Market, packed with over 120 specialty vendors, then explore the North Market, known for its Saturday Farmers' Market.

Afternoon Hip and happening Leslieville is one of Toronto's best kept secrets. Take the Queen Streetcar to charming Queen St East, lined with trendy shops and cafés. Head down Dundas St towards Bayview Ave. On your way, try to grab a patio seat at Rooster Coffee House *(479 Broadview Ave)*, overlooking nearby Riverdale Park – its coffee is cited as among the city's best.

Evening Continue on foot to the Distillery Historic District *(p193)*, where you can relax over a pint at one of the microbreweries. Once the largest distillery in the British Empire, today its buildings are occupied by art galleries, boutiques, and restaurants.

Day 2

Morning Centrally located Kensington spans about 10 city blocks, all pedestrian-friendly. At its heart is Kensington Market *(p190)*, where a cacophony of different cultures collide, providing surprising smells, sounds, and tastes in a wide range of spice shops and eateries. If you want a more structured visit, you can book in advance for some great food tours. Surrounding the market are buskers, street artists, and a range of shops.

Afternoon If you need some more retail therapy, make your way to Yorkville. The shops here could seriously damage your credit card. Once you've shopped 'til you've dropped, check your bags at the Royal Ontario Museum (ROM) *(p184)*, and explore the staggering collection of over six million objects. Alternatively, visit the Bata Shoe Museum *(p191)*, which tells a fascinating story of people through shoes. Refuel at the Hyatt rooftop bar *(4 Avenue Rd)*.

Evening Head over to Second City *(51 Mercer St)*, billed as the world's premier comedy club, for plenty of laughs delivered by top-notch talent. Along with its sister club in Chicago, this improvisational theater troupe has launched the careers of countless comedians. Nearby, at the stylish Bisha Hotel *(80 Blue Jays Way)*, take the elevator to KOST, its rooftop restaurant, for amazing Baja-Mexican cuisine.

7 DAYS
in BC and the Rockies

Day 1

After touring Vancouver (p26) make the long drive east to Kamloops (p122) on the scenic Trans-Canada Highway (Highway 1). The route follows spectacular deep valleys cut by the Fraser and Thompson rivers through the rocky Coast Mountains. At Hope, carry on north through the Fraser Canyon (p122), stopping at Hell's Gate to suspend yourself over the canyon in an air-tram. A suspension bridge crosses back over this part of the thundering river, which has three times the volume of water at Niagara Falls. Manning Park Lodge (7500 BC-3) is a perfect stopping point to stretch your legs and have lunch. End your day in Kamloops, where gold was discovered in 1856 in the North Thompson River, just above the town. There are plenty of options for casual dining before bedding down for the night at your hotel.

Day 2

Back on Highway 1, make the two-and-a-half-hour journey to Revelstoke (p127). Head straight for the gondola, which transports you above the clouds, with panoramic views at 7,700 ft (2347 m)

of the Rocky Mountains, the Columbia River Wetlands, and the charming town of Golden. Continue up to Eagle's Eye Restaurant (1500 Kicking Horse Trail) for lunch with a view. If you're ready for another drive, wind your way 16 miles (26 km) uphill through the Meadows in the Sky Parkway, which takes you through forests of cedar and hemlock, spruce and fir to the subalpine wildflower meadows of Mount Revelstoke National Park (p127).

Day 3

Explore nearby Golden, the gateway to Yoho National Park (p138). Surrounded by marshy wetlands, it's home to some of BC's richest bird habitats. One of the best ways to experience this area is from the seat of a canoe; you can flat-water paddle the Columbia River with a tour led by a skilled naturalist. After an active day, wind down with a delicious dinner at the Cedar House Restaurant (735 Hefti Rd, Golden), set on 10 acres (4 ha) of private land surrounded by mountainside, and serving local, natural meats and BC's best wines. End your meal with a nightcap and s'mores.

1 Air-tram over Hell's Gate.

2 Emerald Lake Lodge.

3 Shops in Banff.

4 Great Bear on cliffs in BC.

5 Red canoes for hire on Lake Louise, Banff National Park.

Day 4

Get back on Highway 1 and head towards Field for lunch. This tiny historical hamlet is studded with B&Bs. Locals know to arrive early for lunch at Truffle Pigs Bistro & Lodge *(100 Center St)* to avoid lines. Drive to Emerald Lake *(p138)* and walk off your meal on the scenic trail around the lake before kicking back for the evening.
At the exceptional Emerald Lake Lodge *(1 Emerald Lake Rd)*, make sure you have a drink at the oak bar – salvaged from a 1890s Yukon saloon – before dinner.

Day 5

Start the day with a leisurely drive to the gorgeous Lake Louise in Banff National Park *(p134)*. There's a good chance you'll see grizzlies from the Lake Louise Gondola, which takes you a breathtaking 6850 ft (2088 m) above the valley floor. Afterwards, head to Banff *(p133)*. The resort town is choc-a-bloc with shops, restaurants and hotels, but the best sleepover (and spa) is at the Fairmont Banff Springs Hotel *(405 Spray Ave)*. After exploring the town, take a guided tour of the hotel and have a cocktail in one of the lounges.

Day 6

The 144-mile (232-km) stretch of road that runs from Banff to Jasper is the Columbia Icefields Parkway *(p143)*, and it's incredible. Start your day early to make the drive, and try to spend at least six hours on the road here, depending on weather and wildlife viewing. Before making the final stretch, take a detour to Miette Hot Springs *(p142)*, 37 miles (60 km) northeast: the relaxing soak is well worth the journey. You can grab a bite to eat overlooking the springs at Fiddle Valley Café before driving on to Jasper for a relaxing Italian meal at ALBA *(610 Patricia St)*.

Day 7

Get up early to enjoy spectacular views on the Jasper Tramway *(p140)*, Canada's longest and highest cable car, linking Jasper with a vantage point 9,465 ft (2,885 m) above sea level. The gorgeous Pyramid Lake *(p141)* is also just a short drive away. Grab a light lunch in town before driving three hours to Edmonton airport, where you can catch a flight to Halifax to continue your journey in the Maritimes *(p32)* or make your way home.

7 DAYS
in the Maritimes

Day 1

Arrive in Halifax *(p312)* and stroll the cobblestone streets in the Historic Properties, the country's oldest-surviving waterfront warehouses, where you can shop and stop for brunch. Afterwards, head to the fascinating Maritime Museum of the Atlantic *(p314)* to explore the collection before discovering courtyards and arched tunnels with Alexander Keith's Brewery Tour *(www.alexanderkeiths brewery.com)*. End the day with dinner at Chives Canadian Bistro *(1537 Barrington St)*. If you're a night owl, carry on to one the bars located along Argyle Street.

Day 2

Pick a picnic lunch at Halifax Seaport Farmers' Market *(p314)* – where over 250 vendors showcase farm-to-table produce and maritime delicacies – before taking a day trip to dreamy Peggy's Cove *(p329)*. Walk along the spectacular granite seashore to Peggy's Point Lighthouse. On your way back, cool down at Dee Dee's *(110 Peggys Point Rd)* for homemade ice cream, but save some room for dinner with a view at Rhubarb *(8650 Peggys Cove Rd)*.

Day 3

Fortify yourself with a hearty breakfast before beginning the three-hour drive to Annapolis Royal *(p325)*. Break up the journey with lunch and a glass of Nova Scotia wine on the patio of one of the many wineries located in Wolfville *(p324)*. After arriving in Annapolis Royal, spend a few hours exploring the Port-Royal National Historic Site *(p325)*. In the evening, set out for St. George Street and dine at one of the many local restaurants there, before hearing some spooky stories on the candlelit graveyard tour at the Fort Anne National Historic Site.

Day 4

Drive to Digby for the three-hour ferry to Saint John *(p322)*. Afterward, drive down the coast to picturesque Saint Andrew-by-the-Sea *(p329)*. Grab some lunch by the beach and book yourself in for a boat tour around the coast. Whale watching here is nothing short of incredible – you might see humpbacks, finbacks, minke whales and the North Atlantic right whale. Also impressive is the Algonquin Hotel *(184 Adolphus St)*, which

1 Lighthouse at Peggy's Cove.

2 Fishing boats in low tide at Alma.

3 North Atlantic Right Whales near St. Andrews by-the-Sea.

4 Walking the ocean floor at Hopewell Rocks.

you must stop into once you're back on dry land. After checking in or grabbing a drink in the Braxton bar here, a spa treatment may be in order. End your day with some freshly caught seafood at the Europa Inn & Restaurant *(48 King St)*.

Day 5

Borrow a bike and grab a trail map from the Algonquin to explore the center of Saint Andrews. Afterward, drive to the little fishing village of Alma for lunch. Time it right to rent a kayak and spend a few hours paddling around Hopewell Rocks *(p331)*. It is best to visit at low tide to get the full effect of the giant rock formations – in some parts you can even leave the kayak and walk across the ocean floor. Afterward, drive to Port Elgin to spend the night.

Day 6

From Port Elgin, drive the Confederation Bridge *(p308)* – the longest bridge in the world – crossing ice-covered water to link New Brunswick with Prince Edward Island. Once across, head straight to Victoria-by-the-Sea *(p308)*, a storybook fishing village, for a lobster roll at the Lobster Barn Pub & Eatery *(p311)*. The coastal drive along Route 19 offers views of red rock cliffs and red sandy beaches. Stop at the National Historic Site of Skmaqn-Port-la-Joye-Fort Amherst *(191 Hache Gallant Dr)*, one of the island's first Acadian settlements. Next up is a pit stop at Cow's Creamery *(12 Milky Way)* for an ice cream before driving about 45 minutes for your final stop in Charlottetown *(p310)*. Grab some dinner before catching *Anne of Green Gables – The Musical* in town.

Day 7

Stroll through the historic downtown core of Charlottetown and tuck into some lobster poutine at the Chip Shack *(2 Great George St)*. *Anne of Green Gables* fans should make a 45-minutes detour to Cavendish to explore the land of Anne at Green Gables Heritage Place *(p309)*. The last ferry from Charlottetown to Pictou leaves at 7:30pm. Enjoy dinner at Pictou Lodge *(172 Lodge Rd)* before heading on to Halifax to continue your trip or begin the journey home.

2 WEEKS

in Canada

Day 1

Start your journey in Toronto. After spending a weekend in the city *(p28)*, wake early to avoid the crowds at Niagara Falls *(p204)*, a 90-minute drive away. The best spot for falls-watching is Table Rock. For another mind-blowing experience, head over to IMAX Niagara and take a virtual plunge over the falls. Nearby is Niagara-on-the-Lake *(p206)*, an impeccably preserved 19th-century town and a great spot for lunch – try and grab a table at the swanky Prince of Wales Hotel *(6 Picton St)*. Afterward, explore the gorgeous Niagara Glen Nature Reserve *(p209)* before returning to downtown Toronto for dinner.

Day 2

Trains depart from Toronto on the five-hour ride to Ottawa about 12 times a day. After making the journey east, grab lunch in the ByWard Market Building *(p212)* before walking over to Parliament Hill *(p210)*. A free, one-hour tour includes the House of Commons and the Senate – as long as politicians aren't in session. There's time back at your hotel for a siesta before getting dolled up for dinner at Play Food & Wine *(1 York St)*.

Day 3

Grab a big breakfast before taking the Au feel de l'eau (Aqua-Taxi) from Rideau Canal locks to cross the river and visit the Canadian Museum of History *(p284)*. Cross the Alexandra Bridge back to Ottawa, and you can't miss the giant spider outside the National Gallery of Canada *(p214)*. After a tour of the gallery, head up to Nepean Point, just behind, for fabulous views of the city. Unwind in the evening with a craft beer and some amazing food at the Manx Pub *(370 Elgin St)*.

Day 4

Take an early two-hour train to Montreal. Once you've arrived in the city, jump on the metro to Place d'Armes near the Notre Dame Basilica *(p242)*. Be sure to

1 Toronto skyline at dusk.
2 The National Gallery of Canada in Ottawa.
3 Notre Dame Basilica in Montreal.
4 Montreal-style bagels.
5 Barn in New Brunswick.

go inside – it's one of Quebec's crown jewels. Art lovers should also visit the Musée des Beaux-Arts (p246), which showcases the best of Canadian art, as well as notable European artists. Afterward, stroll pedestrian-friendly Vieux-Montréal, and walk the waterfront promenade along the Vieux-Port (p258). With its old-world vibe and French culture, this area very much resembles Paris. Rue Prince Arthur Ouest is the street to go to find a great restaurant, many of which endorse bringing your own booze.

Day 5

Arrange to meet a professional guide and foodie in your hotel lobby for a culinary and culture tour, beginning with a "Lumberjack Special" breakfast of cretons (a spicy Quebec pork pate), baguette and strong coffee at Jean Talon Market (p250). Walking through the historic Saint Laurent and Saint Denis neighborhoods and Montréal's Mile End is like stepping back in time. Although the area is packed with the newest, trendiest shops and restaurants, these coexist side by side

with century-old establishments. Many eateries feature poutine, bagels and smoked meat – all mandatory dishes in Montreal. After lunch, head to Spa Scandinave and relax in its thermal bath waters before dinner at Ristorante Da Emma (777 de la Commune St), which was once a woman's prison and now serves up the best Roman cuisine outside of Italy. Round off your day at the Place des Arts (p252), where famous musicians perform most Saturdays and Sundays.

Day 6

It's all about the journey, not the destination, today. Leaving Montreal at 1pm, VIA Rail transports you overnight on its "Océan" trip across Atlantic Canada to Halifax (arriving at 10am). Some of its comfy sleeper cabins in the plush "Renaissance" cars even have en-suite showers. You'll cross the Saint Lawrence River as dinner is served and wake to spectacular forests and rural farms in New Brunswick at breakfast. Closer to Halifax, look out for the giant grain elevators and the spectacular Bedford Basin, a huge enclosed bay.

→

1

2

Day 7

After arriving in Halifax, grab lunch and pick up a hire car before making your way to Cape Breton Island (p316), a four-hour drive away. Enter an 18th-century time-warp at the Fortress of Louisbourg (p319), a partial reconstruction of a French fortress that operates as a living history museum. Later in the afternoon, drive 90 minutes to overnight in the village of Baddeck (p317), once home to Alexander Graham Bell and considered to be the beginning and end of the famous Cabot Trail. Reward yourself after a long day of traveling with a lobster dinner at the Silver Dart Lodge (257 Shore Rd).

Day 8

Get up early for a full day driving the Cabot Trail (p316). Grab a picnic lunch to enjoy at one of many scenic stops along the way and don't forget to pack your binoculars – as you drive through Cape Breton Highlands National Park, there's a good chance you'll spot eagles soaring above. The whole trail takes around eight hours to drive. For a shorter trip, head west along the coastal road to the park,

then detour to Pleasant Bay for a whale-watching tour before retracing the same stretch of road. End your day at the Glenora Inn & Distillery in Mabou (p318).

Day 9

Check in for the five-and-a-half-hour flight from Halifax to Edmonton in Alberta. After touchdown, grab some lunch and head to the city center (p167). Explore the shops at West Edmonton Mall, home to 800 stores, before visiting Fort Edmonton Park, a living history museum recreating a Hudson's Bay Company trading post. Enjoy a top-notch dinner in the evening at Rge RD (10643 123 St NW).

Day 10

Pick up a hire car and drive 37 miles (60km) to the heart of the mountain range in Jasper, stopping to explore some of the extraordinary hiking trails and bike routes around Jasper National Park (p140). Marvel at the lovely scenery around Pyramid Lake (p141) before hopping on the amazing Jasper Tramway cable car (p140), which whisks you almost to the summit of

① The stunning Cabot Trail along
Cape Breton Island.

② Moose in Jasper National Park.

③ Touching the ice cave of
the Athabasca glacier.

④ Downtown Vancouver skyline.

⑤ Peak 2 Peak Gondola, Whistler.

the Whistlers for panoramic views. If you can, arrange to stay at the Fairmont Jasper Park Lodge (1 Old Lodge Rd), where room service comes on a bicycle.

Day 11

Set off early for the drive to Banff and immerse yourself in the grandeur of the Rockies on the the Columbia Icefield Parkway (p143). Stop in at Athabasca Glacier to board an ice explorer and walk on the glacier surface. Take to the road again before stretching your legs and taking in the view at Peyto Lake (p135), then carry on toward beautiful Lake Louise (p134) for lunch. On arrival in Banff (p133), relax after the long drive at the Upper Hot Springs Pool.

Day 12

Get your hiking gear on and spend the day in Yoho National Park (p138). Drive up to the Little Yoho Valley, park the car and walk five minutes to the base of Takakkaw Falls, the second tallest waterfall in Canada. Lunch at the Truffle Pigs Bistro (p33) in the tiny village of Field, before

heading onward to Emerald Lake (p138). Spend the afternoon canoeing or hiking the trails around the brilliant turquoise lake before heading back to your hotel.

Day 13

From Emerald Lake you'll get to Kelowna in five hours without stopping, leaving plenty of time for an Okanagan wine tour (p116). If you can, book into a tour that stays at Burrowing Owl in Oliver (500 Burrowing Owl Pl). The guest houses here are surrounded by a 140-acre (56-ha) vineyard, with ochre hillsides in the distance and a top Tuscan-style restaurant.

Day 14

Drive to Kelowna airport to take the 60-minute flight to Vancouver. If you've time before your flight home, take a day trip to Whistler Blackcomb (p114). There are frequent bus shuttles from the airport, so have your camera ready, sit back and enjoy the famous Sea to Sky Highway. Take the bus back to Vancouver airport or continue on to the city (p26) to conclude your epic tour of Canada.

Horseshoe Falls

Horseshoe Falls thunders over the Canada/US border. One of three separate cascades that make up Niagara Falls, it is the most powerful waterfall in North America and the country's biggest natural attraction. Visit between April and October when the water flow is at its strongest, and take a truly awesome boat trip below the raging torrent *(p204)*.

→

The dramatic spectacle of Horseshoe Falls at sunset

CANADA FOR
NATURAL
WONDERS

Canada's enormous size means it spans many different types of terrains and is home to some of the finest natural spectacles on the planet. From the fall glory of its vast forests to its icy glacial lakes and majestic mountains, there is plenty to take your breath away in every season.

The Great Lakes

With their mighty winds and rolling waves, lakes Superior, Michigan, Huron, Erie, and Ontario often resemble inland seas. Together, they contain enough water to flood the whole of Canada. The largest, Lake Superior *(p234)*, is the biggest freshwater lake in the world. Enjoy exhilarating watersports such as kayaking, or take a relaxing hike along its unspoiled shores.

←

Golden trees in the fall on the forested coast of Lake Superior

TOP
4
NORTHERN LIGHTS LOCATIONS

Churchill
One of the world's very best places to see the Northern Lights *(p177)*.

Yellowknife
You can see the lights for up to 28 weeks of the year in this city *(p364)*.

Muncho Lake
Aurora appearences are beautifully reflected in the still waters of this lake *(p126)*.

Melfort
This Saskatchewan town dubbed itself the "City of Northern Lights" because of how often they were seen there.

Canadian Rockies

Some of the towering peaks in the Canadian Rockies are so high that they never lose their snow. This magnificent range includes 50 mountains over 10,000 ft (3,048 m) in height and encompasses five national parks, four of which comprise a single UNESCO World Heritage Site *(p129)*.

→

Snow-covered peaks at sunrise in Kananaskis Country, Alberta

Rainforests

British Columbia's lush Pacific coast *(p104)* boasts nearly a quarter of the world's temperate rainforest. Whether you're hiking a backwoods trail or driving a scenic road, keep an eye out for the diverse wildlife: bald eagles, cougars, wolves, and bears can all be spotted here.

→

Lush old-growth rainforest in the Cathedral Grove, located in the MacMillan Provincial Park on Vancouver Island

Whale Watching

Churchill *(p176)* offers the best chance to see the striking white beluga whales, known as the White Ghosts of the North. You can also observe them in Tadoussac *(p286)*, along with many other types of whale. Rare narwhals, too, can be spotted in Canada's remote Arctic waters *(p369)*.

←

Humpback whale in Witless Bay Ecological Reserve, near St. John's

CANADA FOR
WILDLIFE ENCOUNTERS

Few things can match the excitement of seeing Canada's awesome animals in the wild. Its rich menagerie ranges from playful sea otters to vast herds of antlered caribou, and includes endangered species such as the mighty killer whale and ferocious wolverine.

Bears Everywhere

Canada is one of the few countries in the world where you can view polar bears in the wild, with Churchill *(p176)* a magnet for bears and tourists alike. In national parks and remote areas, you may see grizzlies, black and brown bears. The Great Bear Rainforest on the Pacific Coast is the place to go to catch a glimpse of the unique spirit bears - black bears with a recessive gene that makes them white.

Bull moose wandering Canada's northern forests in the snow ↑

Mighty Moose

With an estimated one million moose across Canada, you're likely to run into at least one of these solitary creatures, with their massive muzzles and broad antlers. In some rural towns you might even find them wandering the streets. There's a large population in the Algonquin Provincial Park *(p218)*, where you can go on moose safaris in a kayak. Moose are strong swimmers, so you might even find them paddling alongside you at some point.

Bald Eagles

Found all over the country, the white-headed, white-tailed bald eagle is Canada's largest bird of prey. For a particularly good chance of spotting them, head for the archipelago of Haida Gwaii *(p124)*, which is home to a large population. Sightings are also common on Cape Breton Island *(p316)* on the Atlantic coast.

↑ Grizzlies on a BC beach, and polar bears *(inset)* on the snow in Churchill

→
A majestic bald eagle perched on the branch of a tree in Haida Gwaii

Panning for Gold

History comes to life when kids try their luck at panning for gold like the prospectors who once flocked to the Yukon to find their fortunes. Set your course for Dawson City (p358), which was the bustling center of the Klondike Gold Rush; the town of Whitehorse (p354); or the Wild Horse River Historic Site. Each of these locations offers numerous gold-panning attractions. Dawson City even hosts annual gold-panning champion-ships across a wide range of skill levels.

→

One eager visitor panning for gold at Fort Steele Heritage Town, British Columbia

CANADA FOR
FAMILIES

Canada's spectacular landscapes are a never-ending playground and offer a huge variety of family adventures, from tracing the path of Gold Rush pioneers to exploring amusement parks. For rainy days, museums throughout the country hold a treasure trove of discoveries to keep boredom at bay.

Amusement Parks

Step back in time at Calgary's 19th-century amusement park in Heritage Park Historical Village (p155), with vintage rides and paddlewheel boat cruises. For more modern thrills, ride the rollercoasters at LaRonde in Parc Jean-Drapeau (p254) or visit the West Edmonton Mall (p166), which features its own water park, amusement park, ice rink, and aquarium.

←

A vast pirate ship, one of the many play attractions at West Edmonton Mall

↑ Sun rising over the barren Badlands, home to the Dinosaur Provincial Park

TOP 3 CANADIAN ZOOS

Toronto Zoo
There's a good collection of Canadian wildlife at this zoo *(p196)*, a firm favorite with animal lovers. The animals are housed in natural conditions.

Calgary Zoo
Canada's most-visited zoo *(p152)*, this place protects many endangered species, including whooping cranes and the Vancouver Island marmot.

Assiniboine Park Zoo
This zoo is part of a large complex that includes a range of kid-friendly attractions, such as butterfly gardens, hiking trails, and a steam-train ride *(p165)*.

The Dinosaur Trail

Drive or walk through the Valley of the Dinosaurs in Dinosaur Provincial Park *(p168)*, where you can see reconstructed skeletons, ancient fossils, and take guided tours from the Field Station. The latter is part of the Royal Tyrrell Museum *(p156)*. Its Dinosaur Hall is dino-heaven, with a Gorgosaurus, a T-rex, and numerous digging programs for kids.

Family-Friendly Festivals

Most Canadian festivals have some activities for kids, but there are dedicated family-focused events as well. Along with magicians, music, and clowns, Toronto's Canada Kids Festival each September has fashion, talent, and comedy shows. Vancouver also has its own International Children's Festival in May, with acrobatics, puppetry, and art activities on the rich agenda.

→ Girl helping to put up colorful bunting for the Vancouver International Children's Festival

Multicultural Cuisine

Given the diversity of Canada's population, it's no surprise that the food on offer is equally vibrant. From Vietnamese rice paper rolls to hearty German *späetzle* (pasta), you'll find a dazzling array of international dishes served all across the country. Particular highlights include Mexican food, authentic Asian fare, and traditional recipes from Southern and Eastern Europe.

→

A popular floating Mexican Restaurant on Fisherman's Wharf in Victoria

CANADA FOR
FOODIES

Canada's vast landscapes provide an abundance of fresh produce, while the country's rich cultural mosaic has created a varied food scene. French and British influences abound here, but you'll also find First Nations game dishes, exotic Asian fare, and hearty Eastern European cuisine on offer.

Magical Markets

Canada's markets are a delight for the senses. Farmers' markets are piled high with fruit and veg, artisan cheeses, and bottles of maple syrup. Ethnic markets proffer traditional breads and mouth-watering international street-food. Head to St Lawrence Market *(p192)* in Toronto or Montreal's Jean-Talon Market *(p250)* for an unmissable experience.

↑ Jean-Talon Market, and poutine served on a street-food stall *(inset)*

Sumptuous Seafood

Two ocean coastlines plus lakes and rivers galore mean seafood and freshwater fish are in abundance in Canada. Top dishes to try include clam chowder, crab cakes, fresh lobster, and sockeye salmon. Fish and chips, inherited from Britain, are also available everywhere. Excellent seafood spots include Raymonds Restaurant *(95 Water St, St. John's)* and Rodney's Oyster House *(469 King St W, Toronto)*.

↑ Feast of freshly caught lobster and warm potato salad

TOP 5
CANADIAN DISHES YOU NEED TO TRY

Poutine
Having originated in Quebec, this meal of French fries with cheese curds and gravy is now tantamount to Canada's national dish.

Montreal Bagels
These are smaller than the New York variety, and are made in a wood-fired oven.

Pierogles
Eastern European dumplings can be found everywhere, with a range of great fillings.

Bannock
This large flat bread originally came from the First Nations people but is now ubiquitous.

Butter Tarts
Simple and delicious pastries, filled with a mix of butter, sugar and eggs, then baked.

↑ Sliced smoked elk heart served with scrambled egg

Meat and Game Dishes

In northern Canada, First Nations people have always smoked meat to survive harsh winters. Today, humble game such as musk ox, moose, and caribou is sent south to grace the tables of fine dining restaurants, where chefs often serve it with French flare. Try smoked caribou – it's delicious and deservedly popular. For top-notch meat and game eateries, try The Trough *(725 9 St, Canmore)* or Klondike Rib & Salmon *(2116 2nd Ave, Whitehorse)*.

Canadian Wine

Canada produces some excellent wines from hybrid grapes, thanks largely to European winemakers who have emigrated here. Delicious ice wine, a dessert wine made from grapes frozen naturally on the vine, is a specialty of the Niagara Peninsula *(p227)*. Other winemaking regions to visit include Nova Scotia's Annapolis Valley and Okanagan Valley in southern BC *(p116)*.

→

Shiraz grapes, used to produce red wine, on the vine in the Okanagan Valley

CANADA FOR
WINE AND
CRAFT BEER

From acclaimed whiskies to traditional wines, beers, and spirits, you certainly won't go thirsty in Canada. Now, a trending boom in artisan distilleries and a flourishing craft brewing scene is adding an exciting new range of libations to the national drinks list.

CANADIAN CRAFT BREWERS

Unibroue
⌂ 80 Rue des Carrières, Chambly
This brewer's falsely named Terrible beer tastes of caramel and Madeira wine.

Grizzly Paw Brewing
⌂ 622 8 St, Canmore
Order sweet Beavertale Raspberry Ale at the best Rockies brewery.

Yukon Brewing
⌂ 102A Copper Rd, Whitehorse
Try the Midnight Sun espresso stout here.

Craft Breweries

Move over Moosehead and Molson; joining Canada's favorite lagers are hoppy ales, fruity IPAs, sweet stouts, and other innovative brews from hundreds of independent craft brewers popping up across the country. Try premium pilsners from Toronto's Steam Whistle Brewing *(255 Bremner Blvd)* or Iceberg Beer from Quidi Vidi Brewery *(35 Barrows Rd)* in St. John's.

Craft Distilleries

Canada has been making its distinctive rye whisky since the first immigrants arrived. Now a new generation of craft distillers is using Yukon Gold potatoes, Saskatoon berries and other homegrown Canadian ingredients to make artisanal gins, vodkas, and more. Try the Ironworks Distillery in Lunenburg *(p328)* for some samplings.

$\longrightarrow$
Bottle of gin and a glass of gin and tonic at the Ironworks Distillery

Cocktail Bars

In tandem with the distilling boom is a rise in stylish cocktail bars. Try traditional Canadian cocktails like the Bloody Mary-esque Caesar or the heady Caribou, or opt for a creative concoction made from the ever-growing list of artisanal spirits. Vancouver's Gotham Bar *(615 Seymour St)* and the Keefer Bar *(p27)* are perfect watering holes.

$\longleftarrow$
Caesar cocktail on the rocks with lime and celery

Wine Festivals

A great way to sample Canadian wines is to attend one of the country's popular wine festivals. In St. Catharines, over 40 wineries offer wine and food pairings during January's Niagara Icewine Festival, while the Niagara Grape and Wine Festival in September features street parades.

↑ Visitors enjoying a bottle of wine at the Niagara Grape and Wine Festival

↑ The sleek, industrial interior of Quidi Vidi Brewery in St. John's

Festivals Galore

Canada has a long history of staging exceptional music festivals. Once the warm weather arrives, you can dance beneath the stars at dozens of multi-day events throughout the summer, where you'll hear top artists and up-and-coming acts from every genre. Popular events include Winnipeg's Folk Festival in July, Montreal's Osheaga Festival in August, and the renowned Festival International de Jazz de Montréal, held every June and July.

→

Crowds surrounding the stage as Hozier perform at the Way Home festival near Toronto

CANADA FOR
MUSIC LOVERS

Canada boasts a wealth of musical talent and caters for all tastes. Summer festivals abound across the country, where you can soak up sounds in the great outdoors. In winter, attend classical concerts at a splendid venue, head for a steamy jazz joint, or enjoy the heady songs of the French *chansonniers*.

Incredible Venues

There's no better place to hear today's musical stars than in one of Canada's historic concert venues, and there are shows to suit all tastes. The Royal Alexandra Theatre in Toronto, which stages Broadway musicals and hosts world-class concert performers, is the country's oldest continuously operating theater. In Vancouver, you can hear Grammy award-winners at the Art Deco Commodore Ballroom, or spend an evening with the symphony orchestra at the opulent Orpheum Theatre.

←

Enthusiastic crowds at an event in Vancouver's Commodore Ballroom

TOP 5 CANADIAN SINGER-SONGWRITERS

Leonard Cohen
This poet-turned-singer was born in Montreal.

Joni Mitchell
Mitchell is renowned for her folk classics.

Neil Young
Toronto-born Young produced acclaimed folk-rock albums.

k.d. lang
This versatile singer from Edmonton has won several Grammies.

Buffy Sainte-Marie
Of Cree heritage, she is the only First Nations person to have won an Oscar.

Chansonniers

The troubadours of French Canada, *chansonniers* have their roots in the traditional music of the first European settlers. Whether upbeat or melancholy, their simple, haunting songs are almost always romantic. Head to Quebec City's bars to sample an authentic selection of the genre.

→

Legendary *chansonnier* Félix Leclerc performing with his guitar

Razzama-jazz

Canadians love jazz, and aficionados can sample a range of styles at dozens of venues, such as the live bar at Quebec City's historic Hotel Clarendon *(57 Rue Sainte-Anne)* or Toronto's elegant Jazz Bistro *(251 Victoria St)*. There are also more than 20 jazz festivals, many of which are international events.

→

Jazz trombone player entertaining the public in Montreal

Paddle Time

Whether you go solo or join a group tour, the hardest part of canoeing in Canada will be choosing where to plunge your paddle. Top spots include the Thousand Islands *(p220)* – where you can glimpse elusive wildlife against a backdrop of bizarre castles set on miniature islets – and the Fundy National Park *(p330)*, the high tides of which offer spectacular sea-kayaking adventures.

↑ Canoeists paddling gently past the flaming fall colors of Algonquin Park, Ontario

CANADA FOR
ADVENTURERS

From its icy, rushing rivers to its rugged mountain peaks, Canada is a paradise for outdoor enthusiasts. Hit the waves or seek your thrills on dry land; whatever your preference, adventurous souls will find plenty to keep them busy across the country's dramatic landscapes.

Bike the Rockies

In summer, ski slopes turn into splendid mountain biking trails at Whistler *(p114)* and other Rocky Mountain resorts. At Grouse Mountain *(p90)*, just outside Vancouver, you can join a mountain-bike tour or head off on your own to enjoy amazing views over the city, coast, and Columbia Mountains.

←

Mountain bikers tackling breathtaking trails through British Columbia

White-Knuckle Rafts

Canada's fast-flowing rivers offer plenty of opportunities for keen whitewater rafters. Beginners should try the Slave River between Fort Smith and Fort Fitzgerald in the Northwest Territories *(p360)*, where the rapids are relatively gentle. Adrenaline junkies can opt for the rapids of Ottawa River Provincial Park, or the Shubenacadie River in Nova Scotia, where tidal bores create unique rafting conditions.

↑ Whitewater rafters racing through spraying rapids

Surf's Up

You'll find Canada's best surfing conditions along the west coast. Hardcore surfers should head for the Pacific Rim National Park Reserve and the town of Tofino *(p102)*, renowned as Canada's top surfing spot. For Atlantic waves, White Point Beach *(p319)* is one of several popular surfing beaches along the coast of Nova Scotia.

← A surfer balancing amid the waters of a choppy mountain river in Alberta

TOP 4 HIKING TRAILS IN CANADA

Meewasin Valley Trail
A popular riverside trail in Saskatoon.

The West Coast Trail
This Vancouver Island route follows paths used by First Nations ancestors *(p104)*.

The Bruce Trail
From Niagara to Tobermory, this is Canada's oldest and longest marked trail.

The International Appalachian Trail
This route begins at the US border and continues to an island off Labrador.

↑ Kite boarders soaring above the lakes of Squamish, BC

Windy Watersports

The Patricia and Pyramid Lakes *(p141)* provide a scenic mountain backdrop for windsurfing and sailing. Winds gusting across the Great Lakes also make them prime spots for sailing and kitesurfing. When conditions are right, you can even try lake surfing on Lake Huron *(p232)* or Lake Ontario *(p194)*.

TOP 3 OUTDOOR SKATING RINKS

Rideau Canal
Winter's plunging temperatures transform this waterway into the Rideau Canal Skateway, the world's longest skating rink (p220).

Harbourfront Center
From November onwards, Toronto's Harbourfront Center (p198) opens a scenic rink overlooking Lake Ontario.

Grouse Mountain
It's hard to beat the Grouse Mountain (p90) rink for a scenic spin on the ice.

Skating Scenes

Lace up a pair of skates and take a twirl on the ice. There are indoor and outdoor skating rinks, often with music, at parks and plazas across the country, including Toronto City Hall (p188) and Assiniboine Park (p165). Warm up afterwards with a sweet cup of hot chocolate.

↑ Ice skating enthusiasts on the rink in Nathan Phillips Square, Toronto

CANADA FOR
WINTER FUN

Guaranteed snow and dramatic terrain make Canada a mecca for winter sports lovers. Brave the chilly temperatures and dive into this stunning ice-clad landscape, whether that means racing down ski slopes, exploring the woods on snowshoes, or enjoying a swift dogsled ride.

Ski Time

Glorious white-powder slopes, challenging runs, and dramatic scenery make the Canadian Rockies world-renowned for skiing. The biggest resort in the whole of North America is Whistler Blackcomb (p114), where the presence of the Horstman Glacier means year-round skiing and snowboarding. Quebec's Laurentian Mountains (p300) also offers great skiing in Eastern Canada.

←

A skier carving gracefully down the side of a mountain, toward the valley below

↑ A family dashing across the snow behind their team of dogs

Dogsledding

An iconic image of the Great White North, dogsledding is an exhilarating way to explore Canada's snowy outdoors. It's become a popular attraction at ski resorts, towns and national parks, from remote Baffin Island *(p366)* to Montreal's Parc Jean-Drapeau *(p254)*.

Hit the Rink

The speed, skill, and occasional skirmishes of ice hockey – Canada's official national winter sport – make it a thrilling game to watch. Its popularity is huge, with rinks in every town and teams at every school. Book ahead to catch one of the seven big-city teams, such as the Montreal Canadiens.

→

An ice hockey game in Quebec, played in front of a packed arena *(inset)*

Traditional Totems

Totem poles are found only in the Pacific Northwest. Intricately carved from giant red cedar trees, the brightly painted poles depict magical birds and beasts, and are true works of folk art. They may recount a legend, record someone's ancestry or commemorate an event. The Canadian Museum of History (p284) has the world's largest collection of totem poles.

←

Magnificent carved totem poles and brightly colored totem masks

CANADA FOR
INDIGENOUS CULTURE

The Inuit, Métis, and First Nations peoples have given Canada a rich cultural heritage. You can experience it in their art, from towering totem poles to bright contemporary paintings; in the ceremony and regalia of pow wow celebrations; and in the haunting melodies of their unique musical styles.

Ceremonial Splendor

Powwows are energetic celebrations of First Nations culture, with spectacular displays of ceremonial regalia, drumming, dancing, singing, storytelling, and traditional crafts. Held throughout the country, they are attended by tribes across North America. One of the biggest is the Kamloopa Powwow, which takes place each summer in Kamloops, BC (p122).

→

An elaborately costumed dancer at the Kamloopa Powwow

Contemporary Art

While rooted in tradition, contemporary Aboriginal art is bold, exciting, and often political. Look for the vibrant paintings of Daphne Odjig (1919–2016), and the powerful sculptures of Haida artist Bill Reid (1920–98), which can be seen at the Bill Reid Gallery of Northwest Coast Art *(639 Hornby St, Vancouver)*.

TOP 3 CULTURAL COLLECTIONS

The Royal British Columbia Museum
The First Peoples Gallery here has a fine collection of ceremonial masks *(p100)*.

McMichael Canadian Art Collection
Contemporary First Nations and Inuit artworks are the focus of this museum's fascinating indigenous galleries *(p196)*.

Museum of Anthropology at UBC
The huge collection of Northwest coast First Nations art and artifacts here includes outdoor Haida houses and totem poles *(p84)*.

The Spirit of Haida Gwaii, a jade sculpture by Bill Reid, at Vancouver International Airport

Throat singers performing at Manito Ahbee Festival

Indigenous Music

At events such as the Manito Ahbee Festival in Winnipeg and Toronto's Canadian Aboriginal Festival, you may get the chance to hear throat-singing, a fascinating musical form unique to the Inuit, performed in tandem by two women who imitate the sounds of nature. Throat singer Tanya Tagaq is among the young Indigenous artists fusing traditional and mainstream genres to great effect. Another is DJ Shub, who blends drumming and pow wow singing with electronic dance beats.

REPATRIATION OF ARTIFACTS

Museums across Canada are working with First Nations people to return precious tribal artifacts, which have great spiritual and emotional significance. Some have gone to the descendants of the original owners, while others have been designated for use in sacred ceremonies, or to act as inspiration to artists and craftspeople.

Paul Kane

Irish immigrant Paul Kane (1810–71) grew up in what is now Toronto, before embarking upon an epic journey across Canada. He is best known for his extraordinary paintings and sketches of the First Nations people. Famous works include *Mah-Min* (c. 1856) - or "The Feather" – a striking painting of an Assiniboine chief.

$\rightarrow$

Chualpays jouant à l'alcoloh by Paul Kane, in the Musée des Beaux-Arts in Montreal

CANADA FOR
AMAZING ART

Canada's lush forests and majestic mountains have long inspired artists. Many Canadian-born artists went to study abroad and returned to their home country to explore the wilderness armed with a paintbrush, using new styles to capture the unique beauty of its native people and terrain.

Maurice Cullen

Maurice Cullen (1866–1934) left Montreal to study art in Paris. His discovery there of the work of the Impressionists had a profound influence on his style, which can be seen in landscapes such as *A Misty Afternoon, St. John's, Newfoundland* (1910). He was a prominent member of the Canadian Art Club, a collective that encouraged the growth of national art.

A Misty Afternoon, St. John's, Newfoundland (1910), by Maurice Cullen $\uparrow$

Tom Thomson

Avid outdoorsman Tom Thomson (1877-1917) was an esteemed 20th-century Canadian painter. He was the first artist to attempt to express a sense of national identity with his distinctive, brightly colored landscapes of Northern Ontario, and he greatly influenced the country's most celebrated group of painters, the Group of Seven.

← A *Northern Canadian Lake* (c 1915), by Group of Seven painter Tom Thomson

THE GROUP OF SEVEN

From 1920 to 1931, the Group of Seven founded a distinctive Canadian art movement based on a love of their country's natural beauty. These artists, among them J.E.H. MacDonald, Lawren Harris, A.Y. Jackson and Frank Johnston, used luminous colors and visible brushstrokes to depict their favorite places in Nova Scotia, Ontario, and Quebec wildernesses. The Art Gallery of Ontario in Toronto *(p182)* has a permanent and extensive display of their paintings.

TOP 3 ART COLLECTIONS

Musée d'Art Contemporain de Montréal
This contemporary art museum displays works by Canada's top modern artists *(p244)*.

National Gallery of Canada
Home to the country's biggest collection of work by Canadian artists *(p214)*.

Vancouver Art Gallery
This is the largest art gallery in Western Canada, with a fine collection of Emily Carr's best works *(p86)*.

Women studying paintings by Emily Carr, on display at ↓ Vancouver Art Gallery

Emily Carr

Born in Victoria, Emily Carr (1871-1945) was Canada's first prominent female artist and is still considered one of its greatest painters. Her early works depicted the west coast Salish people and their totem poles. She went on to produce many remarkable landscapes featuring Canada's verdant forests.

A Taste of France

French-Canadian cuisine is ubiquitous throughout the country and, though French-influenced, it has often developed into something entirely unique. Hearty meat pies are a specialty, including *cipaille* (sea-pie), which has layers of game meat or fish beneath a flaky crust, and *tourtière*, which has a filling made of ground beef spiced with cloves. La Binerie Mont-Royal *(367 Mont-Royal Ave E)* in Montreal serves *tourtière* by the slice. For traditional French favourites, head to Le Sélect Bistro *(432 Wellington St W)* in downtown Toronto for an authentic *cassoulet* or some exceptionally tasty *bouillabaisse*.

→

A French-Canadian restaurant in the Old Town of Montreal

THE FRENCH CONNECTION

French colonists created the first lasting European settlement in Canada, and their proud cultural legacy lives on. Canadian French is widely spoken in this dual-language nation, and you can also glimpse the French influence in public buildings and taste it in delicious traditional dishes.

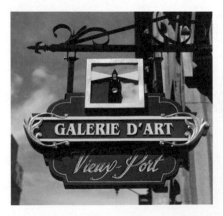

En Français

Over time, Canadian French has developed distinct characteristics from European French. You'll hear different dialects in Quebec *(p276)*, the largest French-speaking territory in the world, and in New Brunswick *(p330)*, where descendants of the Acadians live. In working-class neighborhoods like Montreal's Plateau Mont-Royal, you might catch a street dialect called *joual*, which is informal, slangy, and peppered with anglicisms.

←

Hanging French sign for an art gallery in Vieux-Montréal

FRENCH-CANADIAN CITIES

Quebec City
With its Parisian ambience, this city (p260) is the heart of French Canada.

Montreal
Most residents of this bilingual city (p238) are of French descent.

Ottawa
The citizens of Canada's capital (p210) speak a mix of both languages.

Winnipeg
Home to St. Boniface (p162), this is Canada's second-largest French-speaking community outside Quebec.

→ Costumed girls celebrating the Saint-Jean-Baptiste (John the Baptist) Day in Montreal

Religious Roots
Huge stone churches adorn tiny villages in Quebec province and New Brunswick. A legacy of their Roman Catholic founders, they give towns like Val-Morin a charming French atmosphere. Saint-Jean-Baptiste Day, on June 24, is a public holiday in Quebec, when many French communities celebrate with traditional parades.

French Architecture
Looming over the skyline of Old Quebec, the iconic Fairmont Le Château Frontenac (p270) resembles a turreted French chateau. Montreal's Hôtel de Ville, built in the French Second Empire style, and its magnificent Basilique Notre-Dame-de-Montréal (p242) also bring a European flair to Canada's eastern cities.

→ The copper-roofed Fairmont Le Château Frontenac, lit up at dusk

Beautiful Libraries

Curl up with a good book in one of Canada's architecturally amazing libraries. Vancouver Public Library is an ultra-modern take on the Roman Colosseum, complete with restaurants and a rooftop garden. A former church was stunningly transformed into a luminous literary space at Maison de la Littérature in Quebec City *(p260)*.

←

The light-filled library at Maison de la Littérature

CANADA FOR
BOOKWORMS

Delve deep into Canada's rich literary heritage, which ranges from beloved children's writers to award-winning authors of literature's highest prizes. Visit striking libraries, take part in book festivals and follow in the footsteps of acclaimed novelists, whose works have become favorites on the big screen.

Avonlea Afternoons

The pastoral charms of Prince Edward Island came to life in Lucy Maud Montgomery's (1874-1942) best-selling children's classic, *Anne of Green Gables*. Today you can visit the remains of the simple homestead where she grew up in Cavendish, and the nearby farm at Green Gables Heritage Place that inspired her stories *(p308)*.

TOP 4 FAMOUS CANADIAN WRITERS

Alice Munro (b. 1931)
One of the finest short story writers of all time, Munro won the Nobel Prize in Literature in 2013.

Margaret Atwood (b. 1939)
Best known for her dystopian novel *The Handmaid's Tale* (1985), Atwood won the Booker Prize in 2000 for *The Blind Assassin*.

Michael Ondaatje (b.1943)
His bestselling war drama, *The English Patient* (1992), was turned into an Oscar-winning movie.

Yann Martel (b.1963)
Spanish-born Martel won the 2002 Man Booker Prize for his novel *The Life of Pi*.

The Poet's Corner of Canada

Fredericton *(p322)* was the birthplace and home of Bliss Carman (1861-1929), Sir Charles G.D. Roberts (1860-1943) and Francis Joseph Sherman (1871-1926), and the beauty of New Brunswick was a common theme in their poems. Carmen's birthplace can be visited, as can the University of New Brunswick (from which both Carmen and Roberts graduated) and the Forest Hill Cemetery, where all three authors were laid to rest.

↑ Fall in New Brunswick, a sight that inspired some of Canada's best poets

Top-Notch Festivals

Of Canada's many literary gatherings, the Winnipeg International Writers Festival is one of the best; known as Thin Air, it runs for a week each fall. Writers from around the world appear alongside Canadian literary luminaries for readings and chats, plus there are writing workshops and other events. Other major literary festivals include Calgary's Wordfest and the Vancouver Writers Festival, which are both held in October.

↑ Anne of Green Gables Museum in Kensington, on Prince Edward Island

→ Actress and comedian Lily Singh speaking at Wordfest in Calgary

Brokeback Mountain (2005)

Much of this tragic, cowboy love story was filmed in the Rocky Mountains of south-west Alberta. Moose Mountain and Mount Lougheed stood in for the eponymous mountain, while the much-discussed campsite scenes were shot in Kanananaskis Country *(p144)*. Saddle up with a horseback riding trail company to experience these glorious landscapes for yourself.

←

Jake Gyllenhal set against one of the rugged landscapes that populated Brokeback Mountain

CANADA ON
SCREEN

From rugged outdoor adventures to slick urban dramas, Canada's spectacular landscapes and multicultural cities have made it a favorite location for Hollywood filmmakers. Follow in the footsteps of the stars at these scenic movie and television backdrops.

The Revenant (2015)

The harsh beauty of wilderness locations in Alberta and British Columbia made this brutal survival tale unforgettable. Those keen to echo Leo's journey can immerse themselves in the film's snowy landscape at Fortress Mountain Resort in Kananaskis Country *(p144)* or visit the Badlands of Drumheller, where they'll recognize the rock faces and hoodoo formations along the Dinosaur Trail *(p168)*.

→

One of the bleak, snow-heaped landscapes featured in *The Revenant*

Titanic (1997)
Many Titanic victims are buried in Halifax *(p312)*, which served as the base for the real-life rescue operations. James Cameron filmed a third of his movie here, including the modern expedition scenes. Visit the Titanic exhibition at the town's Maritime Museum of the Atlantic *(p314)*.

↑ Actors Billy Zane and Kate Winslet, within a scene from the 1997 blockbuster *Titanic*

Fifty Shades of Grey (2015)
Vancouver's historic Gastown District *(p78)* stands in for several Seattle and Portland locales in the film version of this erotic bestseller. Fans will also recognize the Fairmont Hotel Vancouver, a city landmark, and buildings at the University of British Columbia.

←

Jamie Dornan and Dakota Johnson performing in *Fifty Shades of Grey*, against a backdrop of Vancouver skyscrapers

Catch Me If You Can (2002)
Another Leonard DiCaprio blockbuster, director Steven Spielberg performed his own cinematic con in this lighthearted crime drama when he substituted locations in Quebec for France. What is allegedly Montrichard Square in the Loire Valley is actually the church of Notre Dame des Victoires in Québec City *(p260)*. Other French scenes were shot in Montréal *(p238)*, including at the Lionel-Groulx Metro Station.

→

Tom Hanks in a *Catch Me If You Can* movie scene being shot in Canada

A YEAR IN
CANADA

JANUARY

△ **Ice Wine Festivals** *(mid–late Jan)*. British Columbia's Okanagan Valley and Ontario's Niagara Peninsula celebrate all things ice wine, with lots of tastings.

FEBRUARY

△ **Winter Carnival** *(Feb 8–17)*. Outdoor events include ice sculptures, a canoe race across the St. Lawrence River, and parties in Quebec City.
Chinese New Year *(Feb, depending on Chinese Zodiac)*. Dancing dragons, fireworks and food in Toronto, Calgary, Ottawa, and Montreal, but Vancouver has the biggest celebration.

MAY

△ **Canadian Tulip Festival** *(mid-May)*. Tiptoe through one million tulips blanketing Ottawa and revel in tulip mania.
Stratford Shakespearean Festival *(May–Nov)*. World-famous performances of the bard's works and other plays in Stratford.

JUNE

Pride Toronto *(Jun)*. A fun, frenzied, and flamboyant celebration of the LGBT community with more than 50 events over 24 days.
△ **National Indigenous Peoples Day** *(Jun 21)*. This day recognizes and celebrates the cultures and contributions of the First Nations, Inuit and Métis and Indigenous peoples throughout Canada.

SEPTEMBER

△ **Toronto International Film Fest** *(mid-Sep)*. Over ten days, movie stars, directors, paparazzi, and the public attend the prestigious TIFF in downtown Toronto.

OCTOBER

△ **Celtic Colors** *(early Oct)*. Communities all over Cape Breton take part in this nine-day festival celebrating their rich Celtic culture.

MARCH

△ **Long John Jamboree** (*late Mar*). Spring's arrival is celebrated with dogsledding, snowmobiling, and lots of eating in Yellowknife.

APRIL

△ **World Ski & Snowboard Fest** (*early Apr*). Specatators, extreme skiers, and ski racers converge in Whistler, BC for six days of high-energy sports and mountain culture.

Toonik Tyme (*mid-Apr*). This week-long festival in Iqaluit includes igloo-building, traditional games, and community feasts.

JULY

△ **Canada Day** (*Jul 1*). People in every province celebrate the nation's birthday with parades, concerts, barbecues, and fireworks.

Calgary Stampede (*mid-Jul*). More than 1.2 million visitors bring out their inner cowboy to celebrate all things western, including a rodeo.

Vancouver Folk Music Festival (*3rd weekend Jul*). This multi-stage music festival at Jericho Beach Park has featured an amazing array of artists since 1978.

AUGUST

Halifax International Busker Festival (*early Aug*). The best street entertainers from around the world perform each year at this fun-packed festival.

Fringe Festival (*mid-Aug*). Theater plays and quality original productions are staged by renowned international performers in Edmonton.

△ **Folklorama** (*mid-Aug*). Multicultural festival of food, performances, and the arts runs for two weeks in Winnipeg.

NOVEMBER

△ **Royal Agricultural Winter Fair** (*early–mid Nov*). The world's largest indoor agricultural fair features the Royal Horse Show and Winter Garden Show at Exhibition Place, Toronto

Santa Claus Parade (*3rd Sunday*). More than 500,000 people watch the longest-running children's parade in the world along this mile-long route in downtown Toronto.

DECEMBER

△ **Winter Festival of Lights** (*early Nov–Jan 31*). Dazzling light displays and a host of events bring holiday cheer to Niagara Falls, Ontario.

A BRIEF
HISTORY

Canada, a country that's been home to the First Nations for thousands of years, stands as a beacon of tolerance and multiculturalism. In the beginning, however, this vast land was a struggle for the Europeans to colonize and was fought over by the English and French for centuries.

Early Survival

Long before the first Europeans crossed the Atlantic, the landscape we now know as Canada was inhabited by various tribes of hunters. These first indigenous settlers developed the skills and culture required to survive the rigors of life in Canada. Despite their disparate lifestyles, the tribes all shared in a common belief: that they were part of nature and not its masters.

The English Invasion

The first successful attempt to colonize Canada was made in 1497, by Italian navigator Giovanni Caboto who landed on the

1 Map of Saint Lawrence River, dated 1632. ↑

2 Painting of Algonquins constructing a wigwam.

3 Jacques Cartier meeting with a First Nations tribe in 1535.

4 Native Americans exchanging furs for goods at Hudson Bay.

Timeline of events

30,000–10,000 BC
Nomadic hunters arrive in North America across a land bridge from Asia

9,000 BC
Aboriginal Peoples are living at least as far south as the Eramosa River near what is now Guelph, Ontario

AD 986
Bjarni Herjolfsson, a Viking sailing from Iceland to Greenland, is the first European to see the coastline of Labrador

1497
The first voyage to North America by Giovanni Caboto

AD 986
Thorfinn Karlsefni starts a trading colony in Labrador, but it is abandoned two years later

shores of Newfoundland on behalf of King Henry VII of England. His crew were welcomed by indigenous tribes. However, the Europeans exposed many natives to devastating diseases, such as smallpox, which they had no resistance to.

The French Arrival

French interest in the New World and its wealth of natural resources began in the 16th century, and explorer Jacques Cartier made his first voyage to the Atlantic provinces in 1534. Soon after, Samuel de Champlain built the first permanent settlement at what is now Quebec City in 1608.

Anglo-French Hostilities

Throughout the 18th century, hostilities between the French and English in Europe spilled over into the New World. Anglo-French tensions were exacerbated by religion: the English were largely Protestant and the French Catholic. This culminated in the colony of Quebec being divided in 1791 into the mainly English-speaking Upper Canada (now Ontario), and majority French-speaking Lower Canada (now Quebec).

THE HUDSON'S BAY COMPANY

In 1610, English voyager Henry Hudson landed at the bay that still bears his name. The bay's access to many key waterways and trading routes ensured the fortunes of the fur trade. Founded in 1670, the Hudson's Bay Company won control of the lands that drained into the bay, gaining a fur-trading monopoly over the area.

1534
Jacques Cartier sails up the St. Lawrence River

1608
Samuel de Champlain founds Quebec City, creating the first permanent European settlement in Canada

1610
Henry Hudson explores Hudson Bay

1676
Population of New France swells to 8,500

1774
The Quebec Act grants French colonists rights to their own language and religion

A British Dominion

In the 1830s, rebellions in Upper and Lower Canada occurred. The response of the British Government was to join together the two colonies into a united Province of Canada in 1840. After a series of conferences from 1864 onward, politicians of the Province of Canada, Nova Scotia, and New Brunswick worked to establish a new country, the Dominion of Canada, on July 1, 1867. British Columbia, a Crown colony since 1858, chose to join the Dominion in 1871, and Prince Edward Island joined in 1873.

The Métis Rebellion

Following confederation, the government purchased from the Hudson's Bay Company the area known as Rupert's Land. The Métis people (descendants of mostly French fur-traders and Aboriginal Peoples) who lived there were alarmed by the expected influx of English-speaking settlers. In 1869, local leader Louis Riel took up their cause and led the first of two uprisings, out of which the new province of Manitoba was created. Riel was ultimately charged with treason and hanged in Regina on November 16, 1885.

↑ Gravestone of Louis Riel, who died campaigning for the rights of the Métis people

Timeline of events

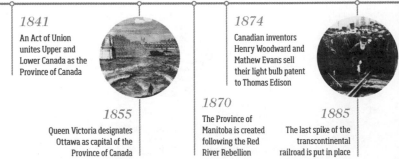

1841
An Act of Union unites Upper and Lower Canada as the Province of Canada

1855
Queen Victoria designates Ottawa as capital of the Province of Canada

1870
The Province of Manitoba is created following the Red River Rebellion

1874
Canadian inventors Henry Woodward and Mathew Evans sell their light bulb patent to Thomas Edison

1885
The last spike of the transcontinental railroad is put in place

Klondike Gold Rush

On August 16, 1896 the most frenzied gold rush in Canadian history started when George Washington Carmack and two Aboriginal friends, Snookum Jim and Tagish Charlie, found a large gold nugget in the Yukon river they later named Bonanza Creek. For the next two years at least 100,000 prospectors set out to find gold in Klondike. In all, the gold rush generated $50 million, but few miners managed to hold onto their fortunes.

Birth of a Nation

The defeat of the Métis and the building of a transcontinental railroad were crucial factors in the settlement of the west. In 1898, the northern territory of the Yukon was established to ensure Canadian jurisdiction over that area during the Klondike Gold Rush. In 1905, the provinces of Saskatchewan and Alberta were created out of Rupert's Land, with the residual area becoming the Northwest Territories. Each province gained its own premier and elected assembly. For the time being, Newfoundland preferred to remain a British colony, but in 1949 it was made Canada's tenth province.

1 The first Parliament session for the Dominion of Canada in 1867. ↑

2 Métis uprising in 1885.

3 Prospectors panning for gold in Klondike in 1899.

Did You Know?

The Klondike Gold Rush inspired novels such as *The Call of the Wild* (1903) by Jack London.

1886
Gold found on the Forty-Mile River

1896
George Carmack, Tagish Charlie and Snookum Jim strike it rich on Bonanza Creek

1897
Steamers from Alaska carry word of the strike to San Francisco and Seattle, setting off a frenzied gold rush

1899
The first Canadians are sent to fight in the Boer War

1900
Quebecois inventor Reginald Aubrey Fessenden sends the first wireless radio transmission

New Arrivals and Prosperity

The impact of the Klondike gold rush led to the expansion of cities such as Vancouver and Edmonton, while the new central Canadian provinces provided a home for many European immigrants eager to farm large tracts of land. By 1911, new immigrants had doubled the populations of the new provinces. Finally Canada began to profit from a prosperous world economy and establish itself as an industrial and agricultural power.

World War I

Canadian troops were the heroes of two major battles in Ypres (1915) and Vimy Ridge (1917). After the war, the country gained recognition as an independent country, winning representation in the League of Nations. This independence was confirmed in 1931 with the passing of the Statute of Westminster, which gave Canada political independence from Britain.

World War II

Canadian allied armies liberated much of the Netherlands and helped force the German surrender of May 8, 1945. When peace

↑ Poster, dating from 1942, designed to boost Canadian morale during World War II

Timeline of events

1917
Munitions ship explodes in Halifax harbor wiping out 2 sq miles (5 sq km) of the town

1918
Canadians break through the German trenches at Amiens, beginning "Canada's Hundred Days"

1931
The Statute of Westminster grants Canada full legislative authority

1944
Canadian troops push farther inland than any other allied units on D-Day

1945
Canada joins the UN after World War II ends

finally came in September 1945, Canada found itself in a strong position. Despite losing 43,000 people in action, the population was growing and the country's efforts to supply the war created durable industries that would power the post-war economy.

An International Voice

Since World War II, Canada's economy has continued to expand. This growth, combined with government social programs such as unemployment insurance and medicare, means Canadians have one of the world's highest standards of living. Canada continues to attract immigrants from around the world, enriching the country's multicultural status.

The English-French Divide

Given all these accomplishments, it seems ironic that the last few decades has also seen Canadians deal with fundamental questions of national identity and unity. The driving force of this debate continues to be the historic English-French rivalry, with several referendums for independence of Quebec. These have so far resulted in a no vote, though the margins have been close.

1 Canadian Pacific Steamships poster, dating from the 1920s.

2 Canadian troops in action during the Battle of the Somme.

3 Painting the Oui logo during the Quebec referendum of 1980.

4 Justin Trudeau at a peace summit.

1965
Canada's new flag is inaugurated after a bitter political debate

1980
Quebec votes against separation in the Quebec Referendum

1999
The Inuit territory of Nunavut established

2005
Same-sex marriage is legalized in Canada

2018
Canada legalizes cannabis for recreational purposes

EXPERIENCE

Exploring the ice cave at Cavell Glacier, Jasper National Park

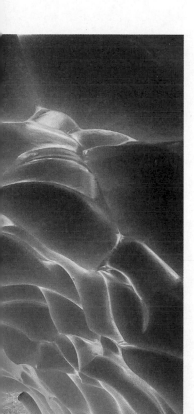

VANCOUVER

Long before the Europeans discovered what is now called Vancouver, the coastal area in which the city stands was inhabited by the Squamish, Tsleil-Waututh, and Xwméthkwyiem First Nations peoples for thousands of years. In 1792, British Captain George Vancouver, the city's eventual namesake, arrived in the Burrard Inlet and found that the Spanish had already claimed the surrounding land. It was the British, however, who persevered in their exploration of this part of the west coast, and eventually kickstarted the lumber industry.

Initially just a sleepy timber town, Vancouver saw its fortunes transformed when, in 1887, the Canadian Pacific Railway decided to move their terminus to what was then called Granville (and quickly renamed Vancouver). The population of the city exploded as new transportation links drew thousands of European and Asian settlers to the area, and by the beginning of the 20th century, Vancouver was becoming a major international port. Today, this city of gleaming glass skyscrapers surrounded by stunning ocean and mountain scenery is a fast-paced multicultural destination. World-class museums, plentiful green spaces, and a renowned food scene continue to draw in visitors from all over the globe.

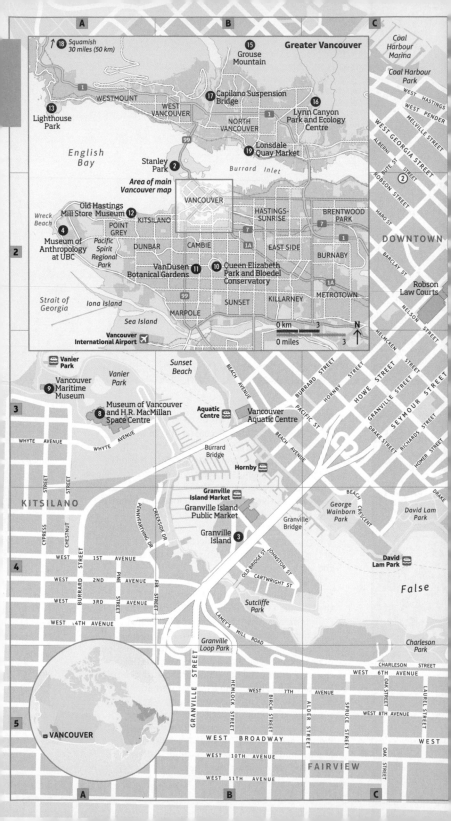

Greater Vancouver

↑ **18** *Squamish 30 miles (50 km)*

15 Grouse Mountain

Coal Harbour Marina

Coal Harbour Park

WEST HASTINGS
WEST PENDER
MELVILLE STREET

WESTMOUNT

WEST VANCOUVER

17 Capilano Suspension Bridge

NORTH VANCOUVER

16 Lynn Canyon Park and Ecology Centre

WEST GEORGIA STREET

ALBERNI STREET

ROBSON STREET

HARO ST

BUTE ST

13 Lighthouse Park

English Bay

2 Stanley Park

19 Lonsdale Quay Market

Burrard Inlet

Area of main Vancouver map

VANCOUVER

HASTINGS-SUNRISE

Old Hastings Mill Store Museum **12**

KITSILANO

POINT GREY

Pacific Spirit Regional Park

DUNBAR

CAMBIE

BRENTWOOD PARK

DOWNTOWN

ROBSON STREET

BARCLAY ST

Wreck Beach

4 Museum of Anthropology at UBC

EAST SIDE

BURNABY

Robson Law Courts

NELSON STREET

Strait of Georgia

11 VanDusen Botanical Gardens

10 Queen Elizabeth Park and Bloedel Conservatory

SUNSET

KILLARNEY

METROTOWN

HELMCKEN STREET

Iona Island

MARPOLE

0 km 3
0 miles 3

N

Sea Island

Vancouver International Airport

Sunset Beach

Vanier Park

Vanier Park

9 Vancouver Maritime Museum

BEACH AVENUE

BURRARD STREET

PACIFIC ST

HORNBY STREET

HOWE STREET

SEYMOUR STREET

GRANVILLE STREET

8 Museum of Vancouver and H.R. MacMillan Space Centre

Aquatic Centre

Vancouver Aquatic Centre

DRAKE STREET

RICHARDS STREET

HOMER STREET

WHYTE AVENUE

WHYTE AVENUE

Burrard Bridge

Hornby

BEACH AVENUE

DRAKE

KITSILANO

Granville Island Market

Granville Island Public Market

BEACH

George Wainborn Park

David Lam Park

CYPRESS STREET

CHESTNUT STREET

PENNYFARTHING DR

CREEKSIDE DR

3 Granville Island

OLD BRIDGE ST

JOHNSTON ST

Granville Bridge

David Lam Park

WEST 1ST AVENUE

BURRARD STREET

PINE STREET

FIR STREET

CARTWRIGHT ST

False

WEST 2ND AVENUE

WEST 3RD AVENUE

Sutcliffe Park

LAMEY'S MILL ROAD

WEST 4TH AVENUE

Granville Loop Park

Charleson Park

CHARLESON STREET

WEST 6TH AVENUE

VANCOUVER

GRANVILLE STREET

HEMLOCK STREET

BIRCH STREET

WEST 7TH

ALDER STREET

AVENUE

SPRUCE STREET

OAK STREET

LAUREL STREET

WEST 8TH AVENUE

WEST BROADWAY

WEST

WEST 10TH AVENUE

FAIRVIEW

OAK STREET

WEST 11TH AVENUE

VANCOUVER

Must Sees

1. Waterfront and Gastown
2. Stanley Park
3. Granville Island
4. Museum of Anthropology at UBC

Experience More

5. Science World
6. Vancouver Art Gallery
7. Chinatown
8. Museum of Vancouver and H.R. MacMillan Space Centre
9. Vancouver Maritime Museum
10. Queen Elizabeth Park and Bloedel Conservatory
11. VanDusen Botanical Garden
12. Old Hastings Mill Store Museum
13. Lighthouse Park
14. BC Place Stadium
15. Grouse Mountain
16. Lynn Canyon Park and Ecology Centre
17. Capilano Suspension Bridge
18. Squamish
19. Lonsdale Quay Market

Eat

1. Bao Bei
2. Kirin Seafood Restaurant
3. New Town Bakery

WATERFRONT AND GASTOWN

📍 E1-E2 🚇 & 🚋 Waterfront ℹ️ Canada Place; www.canadaplace.ca

One of the largest and busiest ports on the continent, the Waterfront is Vancouver's heart. A block away is Gastown, its origin as a tough mill town masked by graceful heritage buildings built in the boom years of the early 1900s.

One of Vancouver's oldest areas, Gastown faces the waters of Burrard Inlet and lies between Columbia Street in the east and Burrard Street in the west. The district grew up around a saloon, opened in 1867 by John "Gassy Jack" Deighton whose statue can be seen on Maple Tree Square. Today, Gastown is a charming mix of cobblestone streets, restored 19th-century buildings, and storefronts. Chic boutiques and galleries line Powell, Carrall, and Cordova streets, and several eateries open onto Blood Alley, named after the city's first slaughterhouses. On the corner of Water and Cambie streets, visitors can hear the musical chimes of the steam clock every 15 minutes.

Canada Place houses a hotel, a convention center, a cruise ship terminal, and a flight simulator attraction.

Stunning views of the harbor can be seen from the SeaBus, a catamaran that ferries passengers across Burrard Inlet.

Waterfront Station occupies the imposing 19th-century former Canadian Pacific Railroad building.

HOWE STREET

SEYMOUR STREET

WEST HASTIN

The Harbour Centre is a modern high-rise building best known for its tower, which rises 581 ft (177 m) above the city.

↑ The graceful red-brick facade of the Neo-Classical Waterfront Station

EXPERIENCE Vancouver

↑ Five sails adorn the roof of Canada Place, echoing Canada's nautical past

↑ Water Street and the steam clock lit up at night

The world's first steam clock is still maintained by the man who built it in the 1970s. It toots every 15 minutes on the corner of Water and Cambie streets.

Water Street boasts gas lamps and cobblestones, as well as shops, cafés, and the famous steam clock.

Reminiscent of New York's Flatiron Building, this triangular structure was built in 1908–9 as a hotel. It is now an apartment block.

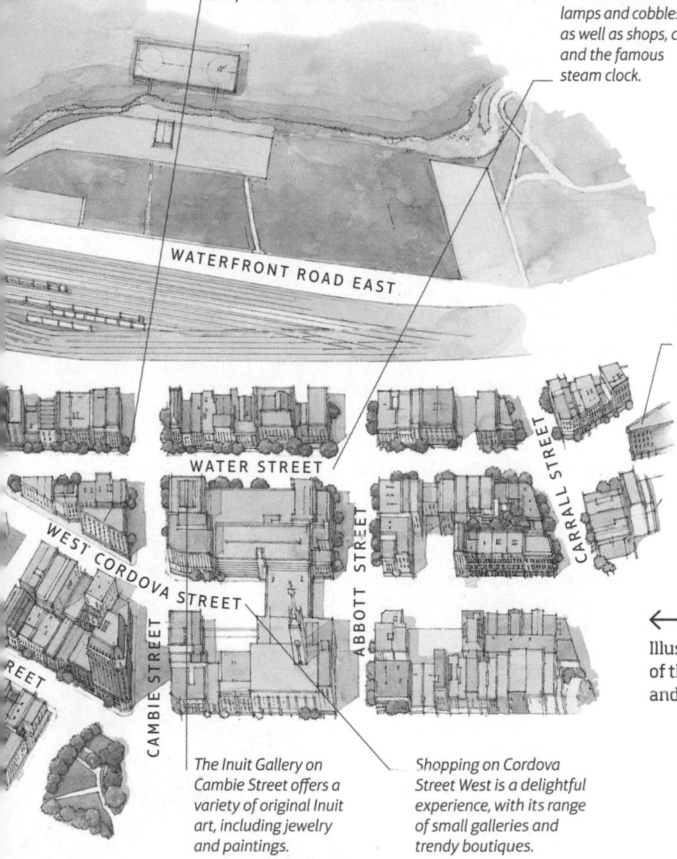

WATERFRONT ROAD EAST

WATER STREET

WEST CORDOVA STREET

CARRALL STREET

ABBOTT STREET

CAMBIE STREET

← Illustrated map of the Waterfront and Gastown

The Inuit Gallery on Cambie Street offers a variety of original Inuit art, including jewelry and paintings.

Shopping on Cordova Street West is a delightful experience, with its range of small galleries and trendy boutiques.

→

The Lost Lagoon, Coal Harbour, and Vancouver's skyline; traveling on the Seawall *(inset)*

STANLEY PARK

◉ B1 🚌 19 ⏱ 24 hours daily Ⓦ vancouver.ca

This beloved green oasis in the middle of the city offers a vast area of natural West Coast rainforest to explore. Discover hiking and biking trails among majestic cedar trees, gaze up at colorful totem poles, and enjoy scenic views of the ocean from the Seawall.

Stanley Park is a magnificent 1,000-acre (405-ha) area of tamed wilderness. The land here was originally home to the Musqueam and Squamish First Nations tribes, but was used by the colonialists as a military reserve because of its strategic position. In 1888 it was established as a city park, dedicated to Governor General Stanley.

Today, the park is filled with natural, cultural, and historical landmarks, sandy beaches, rocky coves, and beautiful picnic areas. Local wildlife, ever-blooming gardens, and the meandering

→

Elek Imredy's *The Girl in a Wetsuit*, on an offshore rock by the Seawall

Seawall – a 5.5-mile (9-km) perimeter trail that can be walked, jogged, or biked – are all part of this amazing urban escape.

The park is also home to the Vancouver Aquarium, where visitors can get up close to various species of marine and jungle life, including sea lions, sharks, penguins, fish, birds, monkeys, and reptiles.

For spectacular views, head to Prospect Point. Set on the northernmost tip of the peninsula, this is the park's highest point, with panoramas stretching across the waters of Burrard Inlet to the Coast Mountains.

💬 INSIDER TIP
Getting Around

Bikes can be rented from shops just outside the southern entrance to the park. Horse-drawn carriage and historic trolley tours are also available, with pick-ups near the Visitor Information booth.

←

View from the Seawall over Coal Harbour and downtown Vancouver in the fall

③

GRANVILLE ISLAND

📍 B4 🚢 Aquabus 🚌 50 🕐 Market: 9am–7pm daily 🌐 granvilleisland.com

This bustling island in False Creek attracts millions of visitors every year. Where once heavy industries belched noxious fumes, there's now artisanal breweries, top comedy clubs, an array of street entertainment and a lively market overflowing with local produce.

Today, this once down-trodden industrial district has a glorious array of boutiques, galleries, and artists' studios in its brightly painted warehouses and tin sheds. There are very few chain stores on the island, and the smaller stores, known for their originality and quality, display a range of local arts and crafts. The island is also a center for the performing arts, and boasts several music, dance, and theater companies.

The Public Market, which is always buzzing with both visitors and locals alike, offers a cornucopia of foods. Choose from locally grown blueberries straight from the Fraser Valley, or cherries and peaches picked ripe from Okanagan orchards. Fresh wild salmon, crab, scallops, and shrimp are piled high, while cheeses, charcuterie, and maple syrup products tempt you at every corner. The food court, too, has a dizzying array of choice, from sushi to pizza, and curry to souvlaki. And if that's not enough to satisfy a hungry appetite, the island is full of other dining options, from waterside cafes to cozy pubs and breweries.

Boats moored in False Creek and the colorful tin roofs of Granville Island ↑

① Granville Island Public Market sells an array of tempting fruit.

② *Giants* by OSGEMEOS, are murals painted on colossal former cement silos.

③ This restaurant terrace overlooks False Creek and downtown Vancouver.

EAT

Dockside

Part of the Granville Island Hotel, this chic restaurant has one of the best patios in the city, located at the edge of False Creek with direct views of downtown Vancouver. Sunday brunch here is legendary, and is best paired with a glass of their homemade microbrew.

🏠 1253 Johnston St
🌐 dockside vancouver.com

$$$

Edible Canada

Even the cocktail ingredients are locally sourced at this casual restaurant, which prides itself on serving sustainable Canadian produce. Sit out on the lovely patio with a view of the bridge above and feast on crispy oysters, duck poutine, elk tartare, and wild mushroom risotto.

🏠 1596 Johnston St
🌐 ediblecanada.com

$$$

Go Fish

A short stroll from the Seawall and Fisherman's Wharf, just west of Granville Island, this take-out shack is a city favorite for fish and chips. Expect long lines during fair weather, and do try the tacones - their take on fish tacos made with fresh-off-the-boat wild salmon.

🏠 1505 1st Ave W
📞 (604) 730-5040 🕑 Mon

$$$

4 (icons)

MUSEUM OF ANTHROPOLOGY AT UBC

A2 ⌂ 6393 NW Marine Dr 🚌 25, 33, 41, 43, 44, 49, 84, 99 B-Line, 480
🕐 10am–5pm Tue–Sun (to 9pm Thu; Jun–Sep: daily) 🌐 moa.ubc.ca

Founded in 1947, the Museum of Anthropology at the University of British Columbia campus is renowned for its displays of Pacific Northwest First Nations craftsmanship.

↑ The imposing glass walls of the museum's Great Hall, lit up at night

The Great Hall

After entering the museum front doors and walking down a short ramp, the space opens up to the light-filled, glass-and-concrete structure of the Great Hall. Glass walls that reach 50 ft (15 m) high are lined with full-size totem poles and carved figures, while traditional canoes and other works flank the surrounding walls.

Multiversity Galleries

Arranged in a labyrinth of glass displays, these spaces house more than 9,000 cultural objects from all around the world. From delicate Inuit bone carvings to West African tribal masks, Chinese opera costumes and Indonesian puppets, there's an almost overwhelming amount of diverse artifacts to admire. Below the display cases are even more pieces to browse through, hidden in drawers just waiting for an eager visitor to open.

ARTHUR ERICKSON

Canadian architect Arthur Erickson (1924–2009) designed the MOA in 1976, inspired by the post-and-beam architecture of the Northwest Coast First Nations. Like much of Erickson's work, which includes the Vancouver Art Gallery, the Provincial Law Courts, and Simon Fraser University (to name just a few), the museum building is made primarily out of concrete and is modernist in style.

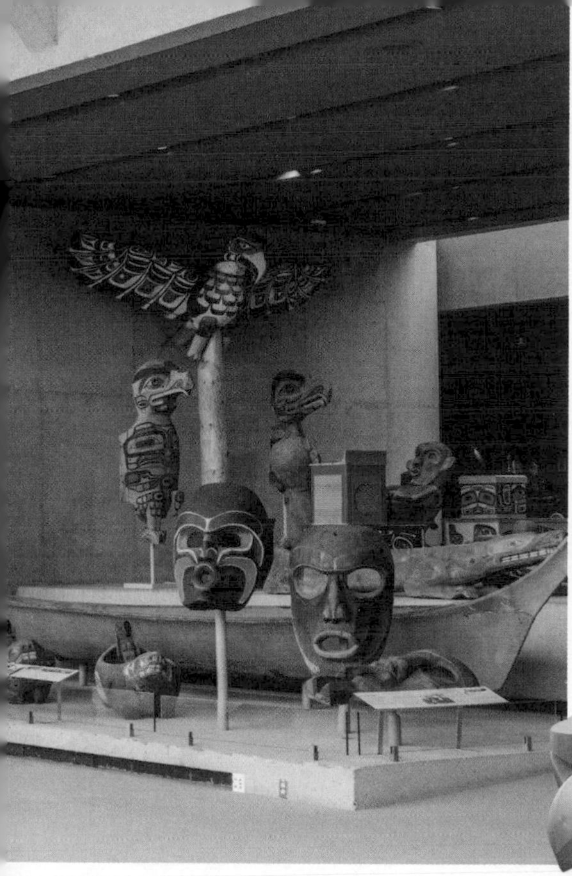

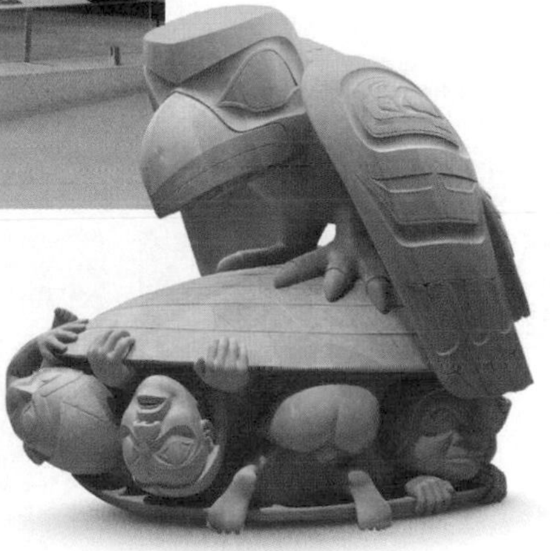

Visitors exploring the museum's exhibits, which include Bill Reid's sumptuous *The Raven and the First Men (right)*

Bill Reid Rotunda

The MOA has the world's largest collection of works by local Haida artist Bill Reid, including his famous sculpture *The Raven and the First Men*. Carved out of yellow cedar in 1980, it is a modern interpretation of a Haida creation myth, depicting the raven trickster trying to coax mankind out into the world from a giant clamshell. This iconic work was featured on the Canadian $20 dollar bill from 2004 to 2012.

Koerner European Ceramic Gallery

Shortly after WWI, fleeing the expansion of Nazi Germany, Walter C. Koerner moved his extraordinary collection of 16th- to 19th-century European ceramics from his native former Czechoslovakia to Canada, where it was eventually donated to the MOA. Now an award-winning gallery displays some 600 pieces of his unique collection, which thankfully survived the arduous journey.

The MOA has the world's largest collection of works by local Haida artist Bill Reid, including his famous sculpture *The Raven and the First Men.*

Outdoor Haida Houses and Totem Poles

Modeled after a 19th-century Haida village are a Haida House and Mortuary House constructed by Bill Reid and 'Namgis artist Doug Cranmer. A reflecting pool, executed in 2010, adds drama to the site and is surrounded by memorial and mortuary poles dating from 1951 to the present.

EXPERIENCE MORE

⑤ Science World

📍 F4 🏠 1455 Quebec St
🚇 & 🚌 Science World
🕐 10am–5pm Mon–Fri,
10am–6pm Sat & Sun
🌐 scienceworld.ca

Overlooking the waters of False Creek is a 154-ft- (47-m-) high steel geodesic dome that houses Vancouver's science center, Science World. The dome was designed for Expo '86 and is now one of the city's most striking landmarks.

In the Eureka! Gallery, visitors can experiment with light, water, sound, and motion. The Search Gallery lets visitors explore nature, while the Puzzles and Illusions Gallery boggles the mind with its optical tricks and hands-on challenges. Children aged 0–5 learn through play as they climb, build, and splash within the Wonder Gallery. The outdoor Ken Spencer Science Park focuses on interactive environmental exhibits.

The museum is renowned for its OMNIMAX® Theatre, which has the world's largest dome screen. Movies that feature space exploration, discovery, and fun animation are shown here.

⑥ Vancouver Art Gallery

📍 D2 🏠 750 Hornby St
🚇 Vancouver City Centre
🕐 10am–5pm daily (to 9pm Tue; admission by donation)
🌐 vanartgallery.bc.ca

What was once British Columbia's imposing provincial courthouse now houses the Vancouver Art Gallery. The building was

> **INSIDER TIP**
> **Park Yourself**
>
> Adjacent to the Dr. Sun Yat-Sen Classical Garden (for which there is a fee), the park by the same name is free to visit. Inside is a pagoda, many ponds, and lush greenery.

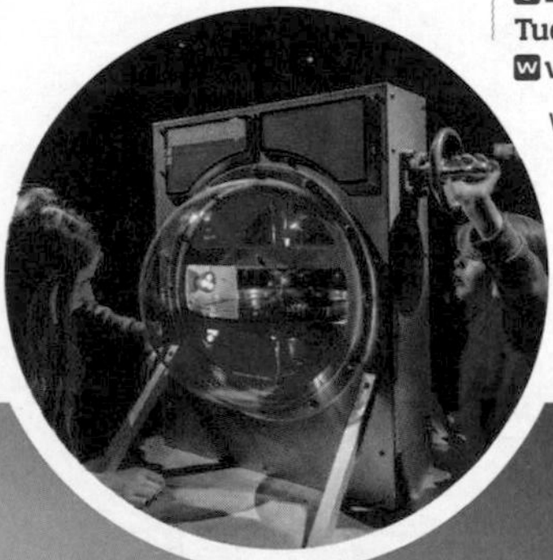

designed in 1906 by Francis Rattenbury, an architect known for the Gothic style of Victoria's Parliament Buildings (p96) and the Empress Hotel (p97). In 1983 the interior was modernized by Arthur Erickson.

The gallery presents a full range of national and international art by ground-breaking contemporary artists and major historical figures, including the most significant body of work by British Columbian artist Emily Carr. The gallery also houses a permanent collection of more than 10,000 works of art. Visitors can take part in talks and tours, or visit interpretive sites and learning centers.

↑ The distinctive dome and an internal exhibit (inset) at Vancouver's Science World

→ A spectacular pagoda in the Dr. Sun Yat-Sen Classical Chinese Garden

 7

Chinatown

F2 **Pender St** **East Hastings & East Pender sts** routes **vancouver-chinatown.com**

Vancouver's Chinatown, the second-largest in North America, is older than the city itself. In 1858 the first wave of Chinese immigrants arrived, drawn to Canada by the promise of gold. Jobs along the Canadian Pacific Railroad attracted even more Chinese workers in the 1880s. Today Chinatown stretches from Carrall to Gore streets and still provides a warm welcome for more recent Asian immigrants.

Declared an historic area in 1970, Chinatown has restored many of its notable houses. The main drag, Pender Street, is the best place to view the architectural details that decorate the upper stories of the buildings, such as highly painted wooden balconies.

Whether buying mouth-watering duck or watching spicy dumplings (won tons) being made at top speed, the main attraction for the visitor is food. There is also a fascinating range of stores, from bakeries to jewelers that specialize in jade. Other highlights include several relaxing tearooms, as well as the nearby Dr. Sun Yat-Sen Classical Chinese Garden, which holds weekly evening concerts of Chinese music under the soft light of lanterns during the summer months.

 8

Museum of Vancouver and H. R. MacMillan Space Centre

A3 **1100 Chestnut St, Vanier Park** **Vanier Park** **22** **Times vary, check websites** **museumofvancouver.ca; spacecentre.ca**

Located in Vanier Park near the Vancouver Maritime Museum (p88), this structure is a distinctive addition to the city's skyline. Built in 1967, the museum's curved, concrete roof is based on a First Nations hat. Outside, a stunning sculpture that looks like a giant steel crab sits in a fountain on the museum's south side.

Displays here include the Orientation Gallery, which re-creates British Columbia's mountainous interior and rocky coastline. Vancouver's history is explored, from the culture of the First Nations to recent everyday life, with exhibits such as the 1950s gallery, with a working jukebox.

At the same location, the H. R. MacMillan Space Centre is popular with both children and adults, who can explore the universe in the Planetarium and in the GroundStation Canada Theatre.

> **Overlooking the waters of False Creek is a 154-ft-(47-m-) high steel geodesic dome that houses Vancouver's science center, Science World.**

EAT

Bao Bei
This modern Chinese brasserie stays open late, offering a range of fancy cocktails, amazing house-made dumplings and an excellent tasting menu.

F3 **163 Keefer St** **bao-bei.ca**

$$$

Kirin Seafood Restaurant
A classic dim sum hotspot with exotic options such as jellyfish and geoduck. There's also a tank from which seafood can be selected. Reservations are recommended.

C2 **1172 Alberni St** **kirinrestaurants.com**

$$$

New Town Bakery
This iconic, no-frills Chinese eatery is renowned for its steamed pork buns and flaky eggs tarts.

F2 **148 E Pender St** **newtownbakery.ca**

$$$

Visitors examining the lush plantlife within the Bloedel Conservatory

9 Vancouver Maritime Museum

⊙ A3 🏠 1905 Ogden Ave, Vanier Park 🚌 Vanier Park ⏱ 10am-5pm daily (to 8pm Thu; adm by donation) 📅 Mid-Sep-mid-May: Mon 🌐 vancouvermaritime museum.com

Located on the waterfront in a spectacular A-frame building, this family-oriented museum celebrates Vancouver's history as a port and trading center. Its star feature is the schooner *St. Roch*, the narrow corridors of which can be wandered on site. Built as a supply ship for the Mounties in 1928, in 1940–42 *St. Roch* became the first ship to navigate the Northwest Passage in both directions.

Other displays include "Map the Coast", which tells the story of British Captain George Vancouver and the crews of the *Chatham* and the *Discovery*, who charted the inlets of the coast of BC in 1792. The Children's Maritime Discovery Centre has a powerful telescope, through which the busy port can be viewed.

10 Queen Elizabeth Park and Bloedel Conservatory

⊙ B2 🏠 4600 Cambie St 🚌 15 ⏱ 10am-5pm daily (Apr & Sep-Oct: to 6pm; May-Aug: to 8pm) 🌐 vandusengarden

Queen Elizabeth Park is located on Little Mountain, Vancouver's highest hill, and offers fine views of the city. Despite being built on the site of two former stone quarries, the park's gardens are continually in bloom from early spring.

The acrylic-domed Bloedel Conservatory is perched on top of the hill, and grows plants from many climatic zones in the world, from rainforest plants and trees to desert cacti. There are also free-flying colorful tropical birds and fishponds filled with Japanese carp.

11 VanDusen Botanical Garden

⊙ B2 🏠 5251 Oak St 🚌 17 ⏱ Daily; times vary, check website 🌐 vandusen garden.org

This 54-acre (22-ha) garden was opened in 1975. In 1960 the land was under threat from its original owners, the Canadian Pacific Railroad, who wanted to use it to build high-rise apartments. It took a campaign by local people and a donation from a wealthy local businessman,

> ### Did You Know?
>
> The Mill museum is owned and run by the Native Daughters of BC, a women's society dating from 1919.

INSIDER TIP
Light Show

In December, the VanDusen Garden hosts an annual Festival of Lights. Highlights include a carousel, food and drink options, and the beautiful grounds illuminated by over a million twinkling lights.

Mr W. J. VanDusen, to save the site. Today, visitors enjoy a spectacular display of over 7,500 families of plants from six continents, set amid lakes and marble sculptures. The Perennial Garden is filled with roses in summer, while September heralds the blazing colors of fall. The Visitor Centre is leading the Garden's green initiatives: the roof uses solar panels and collects rainwater for reuse in the garden.

12 Old Hastings Mill Store Museum

⊙ A2 🏠 1575 Alma St 🚌 4th Ave route ⏱ Jun 15-Sep 15: 1-4pm Tue-Sun; Sep 16-Dec 1 & Feb 14-Jun 14: 1-4pm Sat & Sun 🌐 hastings-mill-museum.ca

The Old Hastings Mill Store was Vancouver's first general store and post office, and one of the few wooden buildings to survive the Great Fire of 1886. Built in 1865, it was moved in 1930 from its original site at Gastown to the shores of Jericho Beach and then to its present home on Alma Street. From the 1940s, local people began contributing a variety of historic artifacts, and today it is an interesting small museum. Behind the pretty clapboard exterior, the

→

The sun dipping below the horizon at the rocky edge of Lighthouse Park

14 (N)(N)(N)

BC Place Stadium

Q E3 **A** 777 Pacific Blvd
B Stadium **C** Varies according to scheduled events
W bcplacestadium.com

Standing out from the city's skyline, the retractable roof of the BC Place Stadium was unveiled in 2011. When the arena opened in 1983, it had a white fabric roof and was the first covered stadium in Canada and the largest air-supported dome in the world. The versatile venue is able to convert in a matter of hours from a football field seating 60,000 people to a more intimate concert bowl seating half that.

Among the famous guests who have visited the dome are Queen Elizabeth II and Pope John Paul II. Visitors keen to catch a glimpse of a celebrity or two can take behind-the-scenes tours (May–Oct: Tue–Fri only) to the locker rooms, playing fields, and media lounges. The stadium also houses the BC Sports Hall of Fame and Museum, which chronicles the history of the region's sporting heroes.

museum's exhibits include a range of Victorian artifacts such as a horse-drawn cab, and an extensive collection of First Nations pieces.

13

Lighthouse Park

Q A1 **A** Off Beacon Lane, West Vancouver **C** 6am–10pm daily **W** lighthousepark.ca

Named for the hexagonal lighthouse built at the mouth of Burrard Inlet in 1910 to guide ships through the foggy channel, Lighthouse Park is an unspoiled area of old growth forest and wild, rocky coast. The trees here have never been logged, and some of the majestic Douglas firs are over 500 years old.

There is a variety of hiking trails in the park, some leading to a viewpoint near the 60-ft (18-m) Point Atkinson Lighthouse. On a clear day you can enjoy stunning vistas across the Strait of Georgia all the way to Vancouver Island. A two-hour hike leads walkers across the fairly rugged terrain of steep rocky outcrops with breathtaking views of the sea and surrounding area. Wear good walking shoes, stay on the trails, and be prepared for inclement weather.

The drive to the park itself is spectacular. Scenic Marine Drive winds along the West Vancouver coastline, clinging to rocky shoreline, and passing some of Canada's priciest real estate. On the way, there are a couple of towns that are worth a stop. Ambleside has a long beach, from where there are great views of Stanley Park and the Lions Gate Bridge. A seawall walkway leads to Dundarave Pier, with panoramic views sweeping across Vancouver to the Strait of Georgia. Dundarave itself is a small village with a pleasing cluster of shops and cafés.

15

Grouse Mountain

📍B1 📍6400 Nancy Greene Way 🚌236 🚢Lonsdale Quay ⏰9am–10pm daily 🌐grousemountain.com

From the summit of Grouse Mountain visitors experience the grandeur of BC's dramatic landscape and stunning views of Vancouver. On a clear day it is possible to see as far as Vancouver Island in the west, the Coastal Mountains to the north and toward the Columbia Mountains in the east.

The famous "Grouse Grind" is a tough 2-mile (3-km) trail to the peak, but most visitors choose to take the Skyride aerial tramway.

In the summer there are many activities, including mountain-bike tours and hang-gliding competitions, plus logger sports such as chain-saw sculpture. In the winter, the summit has all the amenities of a ski resort, including 26 runs, ski schools, and 13 illuminated slopes for night skiing.

At the Refuge for Endangered Wildlife, an enclosed natural habitat that is home to two orphaned grizzly bears and one timber

---

📷 GREAT VIEW
Highview Lookout

For views of the city and Burrard Inlet, head to the Cypress Provincial Park Highview Lookout, under 30 minutes' drive from downtown.

---

wolf, wildlife rangers give daily talks. The Theatre in the Sky presents videos that take viewers on an aerial tour of BC.

16

Lynn Canyon Park and Ecology Centre

📍C1 📍3663 Park Rd 🚌Hastings 🚢Lonsdale Quay, then bus 228 or 229 ⏰Daily; Ecology Centre: Jun–Sep: 10am–5pm daily; Oct–May: 10am–5pm Mon–Fri, noon–4pm Sat & Sun 🌐dnv.org/ecology

Located between Mount Seymour and Grouse Mountain, Lynn Canyon Park is a popular hiking destination, noted for its lush second-growth temperate rainforest. The original 295-ft (90-m) trees were logged in the early 1900s and a few of the huge stumps with circumferences of up to 36 ft (11 m) can still be seen lying on the forest floor.

Several marked trails, some of them steep and rugged, lead through the canyon, with longer hikes heading into surrounding park land. If you venture far enough into the forest, it is possible to see black bears, cougars, and black-tailed deer, but most visitors keep to the main trails where they are more likely to see smaller wildlife. There are wonderful views from the 164-ft (50-m) suspension

---

bridge that crosses the canyon. From here, it's a short walk to 30 Foot Pool, a popular summer spot for sunbathing and swimming, or a 40-minute hike to the beautiful Twin Falls.

The nearby Ecology Centre offers guided walks and interesting displays on the flora, fauna, and ecology of the area. Global environmental concerns are also covered.

17

Capilano Suspension Bridge

📍B1 📍3735 Capilano Rd, North Vancouver 🚌Highlands 236 ⏰Daily; times vary, check website 🌐capbridge.com

The Capilano Suspension Bridge has been popular since it was built in 1889. Pioneering Scotsman George Grant Mackay, drawn by the wild beauty of the place, had already built a small cabin overlooking the Capilano Canyon. Access to the river below was almost impossible from the cabin, and it is said that Mackay built the bridge so that his son, who loved fishing, could easily reach the Capilano River.

The present bridge, which dates from 1956 and is the fourth to be constructed here, hangs 230 ft (70 m) above the canyon and spans 450 ft (137 m), making it one of the

↑ The Capilano Suspension Bridge, stretching above the river

97

The number of elephants the Capilano Suspension Bridge can hold.

longest such bridges in the world. Nature lovers are drawn by the views and the chance to wander through old-growth woods (trees that have never been felled) past a 200-ft (61-m) waterfall. The Treetops Adventure includes seven suspension bridges through evergreens, built 100 ft (30 m) above the forest floor. Not for the faint-hearted, the Cliffwalk has a series of narrow cliffside walkways jutting out above the Capilano River.

18

Squamish

🅟 A1 ⓘ 38551 Loggers Lane; www.explore squamish.com

The town of Squamish is surrounded by vast provincial parks, and lies halfway between Vancouver and

←

A snowboarder navigating the scenic Grouse Mountain Ski Hill at sunset

Whistler, along the scenic Sea to Sky Highway. Once a sleepy logging town, Squamish has grown into a playground for adventurous, outdoorsy types, earning itself the nickname "Canada's Outdoor Recreation Capital."

The town's towering granite landmark, the Stawamus Chief Mountain, is a favorite destination for rock climbers, and hikers can also take one of several trails to reach the top. Next door is the Sea to Sky Gondola, which takes visitors even farther up behind the Chief. From there are several dining options, plus year-round hiking trails and incredible views of the Howe Sound below, crowned by the surrounding Coast Mountains.

The Squamish Spit, on the west side of town, is a top kiteboarding destination, and Squamish's northernmost neighbourhood, Brackendale, is home to North America's largest concentration of wintering bald eagles, which feed on the spawning salmon in the rivers nearby. Just north of town is Alice Lake Provincial Park, and beyond it is the Garibaldi Provincial Park, home to glacier-capped Mount Garibaldi, a dormant volcano and a dream destination for snowmobilers and backcountry skiers during the winter.

19 🍴 ☕ 🛍️

Lonsdale Quay Market

🅟 B1 🏠 123 Carrie Cates Ct, North Vancouver 🚇 Lonsdale ⏰ 9am-7pm daily 🌐 lonsdalequay.com

The striking concrete-and-glass building housing the Lonsdale Quay Market forms part of the North Shore SeaBus terminal. The market has a floor devoted to food – everything from fresh-baked bread to blueberries – as well as an array of cafés and restaurants that serve a variety of ethnic cuisines. On the second floor, visitors will find specialty shops offering a wide choice of hand-crafted products and gift items from local designers, as well as Kid's Alley, a row of child-oriented shops. The complex includes a hotel and spa, and a pub.

💬 INSIDER TIP
Fun on the Quay

Take the SeaBus from Waterfront Station in downtown Vancouver to the quay. On Friday nights during summer, the Shipyards Night Market is on here, with a farmers' market, food trucks, and live shows.

A wooden bridge on the West Coast Trail

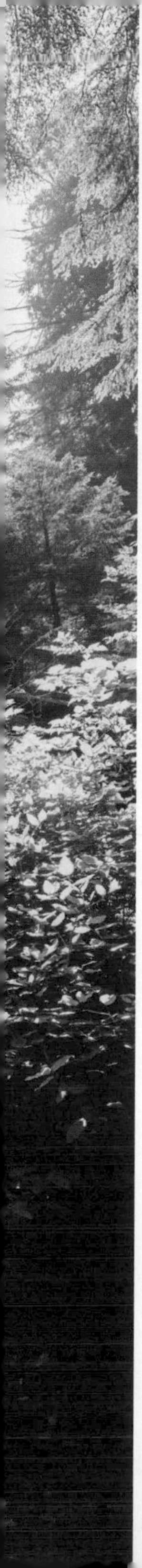

VANCOUVER ISLAND

It was Captain James Cook who claimed Vancouver Island for the British in 1778 when he stepped ashore at Nootka Sound on the west coast of this 290-mile- (460-km-) long island. Until then, the area had been inhabited for more than 10,000 years by the First Nations peoples whose cultural heritage is celebrated in two of Canada's best museums: the Museum of Anthropology at UBC in Vancouver and Victoria's Royal British Columbia Museum.

British Columbia's capital, Victoria, is the arrival point for many on Vancouver Island, and still has a distinctly British atmosphere to it. Visitors here will find a plethora of excellent restaurants to choose from, historic homes to wander through, and miles of uncrowded beaches to stroll along. Farther out on the island, friendly, colorful towns and villages dot the eastern edge, many built up around logging and fishing industries. The wild and rugged west coast is a mecca for surfers and intrepid trail hikers, while the interior offers ancient rainforests and a snowy mountain range to explore.

Cape Caution

Hope Island

Nigei Island

Cape Scott

Hopetown

Kingcome

PORT HARDY 7

Coal Harbour

Winter Harbour

Malcolm Island

Broughton Island

Gilford Island

Port McNeill

Port Alice

TELEGRAPH COVE 8

West Cracroft Island

Nimpkish Lake

Brooks Peninsula Provincial Park

19

Sayward

Cape Cook

Chamiss Bay

Woss

Fair Harbour

Vancouver Island

Tahsis

Nuchatlitz

Nootka Island

Gold River

Bligh Island

28

Strathcona Provincial Park

Yuquot

Pacific Ocean

Hot Springs Cove

Ahousat

Vargas Island

Méares Island

TOFINO 2

4

Ucluelet

VANCOUVER ISLAND

0 kilometers   40

0 miles   40

N

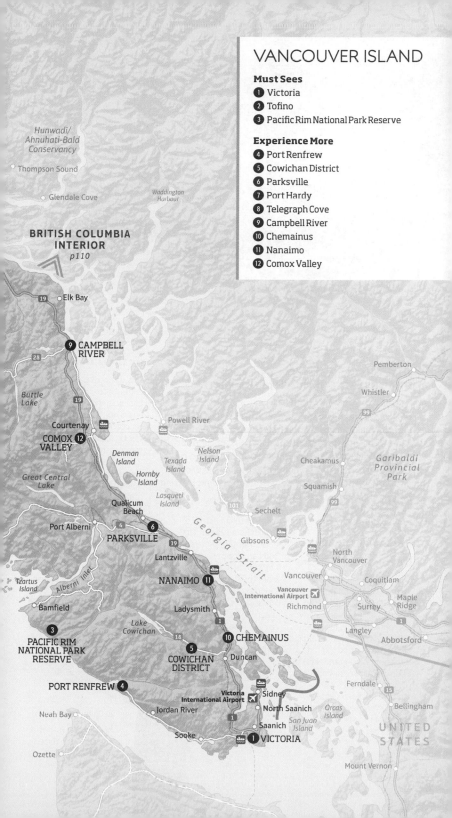

VANCOUVER ISLAND

Must Sees
1 Victoria
2 Tofino
3 Pacific Rim National Park Reserve

Experience More
4 Port Renfrew
5 Cowichan District
6 Parksville
7 Port Hardy
8 Telegraph Cove
9 Campbell River
10 Chemainus
11 Nanaimo
12 Comox Valley

Hunwadi/
Ahnuhati-Bald
Conservancy

Thompson Sound

Glendale Cove

Waddington
Harbour

**BRITISH COLUMBIA
INTERIOR**
p110

Elk Bay

**9 CAMPBELL
RIVER**

Pemberton

Whistler

Buttle
Lake

Powell River

Courtenay

**COMOX 12
VALLEY**

Denman
Island

Nelson
Island

Cheakamus

*Garibaldi
Provincial
Park*

Squamish

Great Central
Lake

Hornby
Island

Texada
Island

Qualicum
Beach

Port Alberni

6

Lasqueti
Island

Sechelt

PARKSVILLE

Lantzville

Georgia Strait

Gibsons

North
Vancouver

Tzartus
Island

NANAIMO 11

Vancouver

Coquitlam

Bamfield

Ladysmith

Vancouver
International Airport

Richmond

Surrey

Maple
Ridge

3

Lake
Cowichan

10 CHEMAINUS

Langley

Abbotsford

**PACIFIC RIM
NATIONAL PARK
RESERVE**

5

**COWICHAN
DISTRICT**

Duncan

PORT RENFREW 4

Jordan River

Neah Bay

Victoria
International Airport

Sidney

North Saanich

Ferndale

*Orcas
Island*

Bellingham

**UNITED
STATES**

Ozette

Sooke

Saanich

*San Juan
Island*

1 VICTORIA

Mount Vernon

↑ The impressive Neo-Classical Parliament Buildings, set among leafy grounds

①

VICTORIA

✈ 16 miles (25 km) N of city 🚗 450 Pandora Ave
🚌 700 Douglas St ⛴ Victoria Clipper/Black Ball Transport
🛈 812 Wharf St; (250) 953 2033

With outstanding historic and cultural sights, pretty Victoria makes a great base for trips around Vancouver Island. The city was established as the capital of British Columbia in 1871. Though it was soon outgrown by Vancouver, it remains the political center of the province, and its leafy parks and gardens, museums, and buzzing harbor area continue to draw in the crowds.

① 🚫 🍴

Parliament Buildings

🚗 501 Belleville St 🕐 9am-5pm Mon-Fri 🌐 leg.bc.ca

Victoria's many-domed Parliament Buildings are an impressive sight, particularly at night, when the facades are illuminated by thousands of lights. Designed by Francis Rattenbury, the grand Neo-Classical buildings were completed in 1897, with a statue of explorer Captain George Vancouver perched on top of the main dome. Visitors can explore the extensive grounds, or take guided and self-guided tours of the interior, where exhibits tell the story of British Columbia and its parliamentary process. You can also observe the Legislative Assembly in action from the Public Galleries, visit the Legislative Library, or make reservations to eat in the Parliamentary Dining Room.

②

Thunderbird Park

🚗 Cnr Belleville & Douglas sts 🕐 8am-11pm daily

This compact park lies at the entrance to the Royal British Columbia Museum (p100) and is home to an imposing collection of plain and painted giant totem poles. During the summer months it is possible to watch artists in the Thunderbird Park Carving Studio working on similar totems. The carved mythical figures tell stories of traditional Coast Salish cultures. Included are Gitxsan memorial poles, a Cumshewa pole, and Kwakwaka'wakw heraldic poles, as well as a a traditional Kwakwaka'wakw "big house".

← Knowledge, one of many giant painted totem poles in Thunderbird Park

③ 🍴
Fairmont Empress Hotel

🏠 721 Government St
🌐 fairmont.com/empress-victoria

Completed in 1908 to a Francis Rattenbury design, the Empress is one of Victoria's best-loved sights. Close to the Parliament Buildings, the hotel overlooks the Inner Harbour and dominates the skyline with its ivy-covered Edwardian splendor.

④
Bastion Square

🌐 bastionsquare.ca

This beautifully restored square faces Victoria's picturesque harbor and contains some of the city's oldest 19th-century buildings. What were once luxury hotels and offices, built during the boom era of the late 1800s, now house several eclectic restaurants. Restoration began in 1963, when it was discovered that the Hudson's Bay Company's fur-trading post Fort Victoria, established in 1843, once stood on this site.

⑤ 🛍️
Market Square

🌐 marketsquare.ca

Two blocks north of Bastion Square on the corner of Johnson Street, Market Square has some of the finest Victorian saloon, hotel, and store facades in Victoria. Most of the buildings were built in the 1880s and 1890s, during the boom period of the Klondike gold rush. After decades of neglect, the area received a face-lift in 1975. The square is now a shoppers' paradise, with a variety of stores selling books, jewelry, musical instruments, and arts and crafts.

⑥ 🏠 🏛️
Helmcken House

🏠 10 Elliot St Square 📞 (250) 356 7226 🕐 10am-5pm Mon-Sat (to 9pm Thu), 1-5pm Sun 🗓️ Sep-May: Mon

Located in Elliot Square in the Inner Harbour area, the home of Hudson's Bay Company employee Dr. John Sebastian Helmcken was built in 1852 and is thought to be one of the oldest houses in British Columbia. The doctor built his house with Douglas fir trees felled in the surrounding forest. The elegantly designed clapboard dwelling contains many of its original furnishings, including the piano, which visitors are permitted to play. Among other exhibits are a collection of antique dolls and the family's clothes, shoes, and toiletries.

> **FRANCIS RATTENBURY**
>
> Born in Britain, Francis Rattenbury (1867-1935) traveled to Canada after working as an architectural apprentice for six years. Shortly after arriving, the 25-year-old won a provincial competition to design the new Parliament Buildings. He went on to design several important structures, including the Fairmont Empress Hotel in Victoria, and the Burns Manor in Calgary. After returning to Britain, he was brutally murdered by his wife's chauffeur and lover.

GREAT VIEWS
Woodland's Trail

This hiking trail in the Government House estate weaves through 22 acres (8.9 ha) of oak forests blanketed with wildflowers. At the Woodland's Viewpoint and towards the edge of the estate, you can take in spectacular views of the Salish Sea.

⑦
Government House

🏠 1401 Rockland Ave
🕐 Gardens: dawn to dusk daily 🌐 ltgov.bc.ca

The present Government House building was completed in 1959 after fire destroyed the 1903 building, which was designed by renowned architect Francis Rattenbury.

As the official residence of the Lieutenant-Governor of British Columbia, the Queen's representative to the province, the house is not open to the public, but visitors can view 14 acres (5.5 ha) of stunning grounds, including beautiful lawns and a lovely Victorian rose garden.

⑧
Beacon Hill Park

🏠 Douglas St 📞 (250) 361 0600 🕐 24 hours daily

In the late 19th century this delightful park was used for stabling horses, but in 1888 John Blair, a Scottish landscape gardener, redesigned the park to include two lakes and initiated extensive tree planting. Once a favorite haunt of artist Emily Carr, this peaceful 184-acre (74.5-ha) park is now renowned for its lofty Garry oak trees (some of which are over 400 years old) and picturesque duck ponds.

⑨
Maritime Museum of British Columbia

🏠 470 Belleville St 🕐 10am–5pm daily 🌐 mmbc.bc.ca

At this fascinating three-story museum in the landmark CPR Steamship Terminal building on Inner Harbour, exhibits tell the story of British Columbia's rich seafaring past. The collection spans from 1775 to the present and includes over 35,000 nautical artifacts, such as ship records, photographs, charts, and models.

⑩
The Bay Centre

🏠 1150 Douglas St 🕐 10am–6pm Mon–Wed & Sat, 10am–9pm Thu–Fri, 11am–6pm Sun 🌐 thebaycentre.ca

The Bay Centre is a shopping mall within walking distance of the Inner Harbour and was constructed behind the elegant facades of several historic buildings on Government Street. The fronts of the famous 1892 Driard Hotel, the 1910 Times Building and the fine, 19th-century Lettice and Sears Building were all, after a campaign by locals, saved from demolition to make way for the mall.

> This peaceful 184-acre (74.5-ha) park is now renowned for its lofty Garry oak trees (some of which are over 400 years old) and picturesque duck ponds.

↑ Dale Doebert's *Moss Lady* sculpture in the foliage of Beacon Hill Park

→
The grand exterior of Craigdarroch Castle lit up at dusk

⑪ 🗺 💳

Emily Carr House

📍 207 Government St
🕐 May-Oct: 11am-4pm Tue-Sat 🌐 emilycarr.com

Emily Carr, one of Canada's best-known artists, was born in 1871 in this charming, yellow clapboard house. It was built in 1864 by prominent architects Wright and Saunders, under instruction from Emily's father, Richard Carr. Located just a few minutes walk, from Inner Harbour, both the house and its English-style garden are open to visitors. All the rooms are appropriately furnished in late 19th-century period style, with some original family pieces. Visitors can see the dining room where Emily taught her first art classes to local children, and Emily's drawing of her father still sits on the mantelpiece in the sitting room, where, as an eight-year-old, she made her first sketches.

⑫ 🗺 💳 🏛

Craigdarroch Castle

📍 1050 Joan Cres 🕐 Jun-Sep: 9am-7pm daily; Oct-May: 10am-4:30pm daily 🚫 Jan 1, Dec 25 & 26 🌐 thecastle.ca.

Completed in 1890, Craigdarroch Castle was the pet project of respected local coal millionaire Robert Dunsmuir. Although it is not a real castle, the design of this manor home was based on that of his ancestral home in Scotland and mixes several architectural styles such as Romanesque and French Gothic.

When the castle was threatened with demolition in 1959, a group of local citizens formed a society that successfully battled for its preservation. Today, the restored interior of the castle is a museum that offers a fascinating insight into the lifestyle of a wealthy Canadian entrepreneur.

The castle is noted for having one of the finest collections of Art Nouveau lead-glass windows in North America, and many of the rooms and hallways retain their patterned-wood parquet floors and intricately carved paneling in white oak, cedar, and mahogany. Every room is filled with opulent Victorian furnishings from the late 19th century and decorated in its original colors, such as deep greens, pinks and rusts. Several layers of the paint have been painstakingly removed from the drawing room ceiling to reveal the original hand-painted and stenciled decorations beneath, including wonderfully detailed butterflies and lions.

> ## Did You Know?
>
> After Dunmuir's wife died, the Craigdarroch estate was subdivided and the castle offered up as a raffle prize.

⑬ 🗺 🏛

Art Gallery of Greater Victoria

📍 1040 Moss St 🕐 10am-5pm Tue-Sat, 10am-9pm Thu, noon-5pm Sun 🌐 aggv.ca

This popular gallery is housed in an 1889 mansion located in the heritage neighborhood of Rockland, a few blocks west of Craigdarroch Castle. Inside, visitors will find a diverse range of works on display, including Canadian contemporary and heritage pieces, an excellent Asian art collection, and temporary exhibitions.

A superb collection of work by British Columbia's premier artist, Emily Carr, is always on display. Highlights include paintings of the British Columbian coastal forests and depictions of the lives of First Nations peoples, as well as photographs and excerpts from her writings.

The gallery is also home to one of Canada's most important collections of Asian art. Look out for the Chinese Bell (cast during the Ming dynasty and presented to the City of Victoria in 1903) and the only original Japanese Shinto shrine in North America (on display amid bamboo and Japanese maple trees in the museum's quaint courtyard garden).

ROYAL BC MUSEUM

EXPERIENCE **Vancouver Island**

📍675 Belleville St, Victoria 🚌3, 4, 28, 30 🕐10am–5pm daily (to 10pm in summer) 🌐royalbcmuseum.bc.ca

Regarded as one of the best museums in Canada, the Royal BC Museum houses a spectacular collection of exhibits tracing the natural and human history of British Columbia. Its superb selection of First Nations artifacts and art is second to none.

Founded in 1886, the Royal BC Museum has an engaging and immersive way of presenting BC history. Stand close to a furry and tusked woolly mammoth and see live crabs scuttling inside a tidal pool in the Natural History Gallery. Stroll through an authentically recreated scene from 19th-century Chinatown in the Modern History Gallery and get a chance to peek inside a 3,000-year-old First Nations pit house. The traveling exhibits too, are remarkable, and cover topics such as the Vikings, Ancient Egypt, and the Mayans. Outside, a dozen replica totem poles carved with colorful mythical figures preside over Thunderbird Park, and you can step inside the 1852 Helmcken House, one of the oldest houses in BC.

Did You Know?

The museum's Carillon (bell tower) was a gift from the Dutch to honor Canada's 100th birthday in 1967.

↑ Totem pole standing outside the exterior of the Royal BC Museum

←
Brightly colored replica totem poles, carved in the Coast Salish tradition, standing tall in Thunderbird Park

Gallery Guide

Natural History Gallery

▽ Located on the second floor, this gallery contains dioramas recreating the sights, sounds, and even smells of areas such as the seashore, the ocean and the coast forest. A Victorian-era mock submarine is also on display.

Becoming BC

▷ On the third floor, walk along wooden sidewalks and cobblestone streets, passing through Victoria as it once was from the 1870s to the 1920s. Displays include storefronts, a replica silent movie theater, a hotel, a dress-maker's studio, a train station, a saloon, and a busy Chinatown street.

First Peoples Gallery

▽ This gallery is dedicated to the First Peoples of BC, with many of the artifacts belonging to the Haida. The central exhibit is the Totem Hall, featuring huge carvings, startling masks, and a ceremonial longhouse belonging to Chief Kwakwabalasami.

Thunderbird Park

▽ This park, established in 1941, surrounds the museum. Exhibits here include some outstanding totem poles, a traditional First Nations big house, the Helmcken House, and St. Ann's Schoolhouse, one of the oldest structures (built in 1844) still standing in Victoria.

↑ Tofino's stunning coastal scenery, seen from above

❷

TOFINO

✈ Tofino/Long Beach Airport 🛈 1426 Pacific Rim Hwy; www.tourismtofino.com

Once an isolated logging outpost, and named for a hydrographer by a Spanish explorer, Tofino is now a busy resort town that attracts surfers, families, and Vancouverites who avoid the long road journey by taking the floatplane. It's home to picturesque sandy beaches, woodland trails, and a celebrated foodie culture.

① 🎨

Tofino Clayoquot Heritage Museum

📍 331 Main St 🕐 May-Aug: 11am-4:30pm Wed-Sun; Sep-Apr: 12:30-4:30pm Sat & Sun 🌐 tofino museum.com

Interesting artifacts, such as whaling harpoons and canoes, are on display at this free museum. It tells the the story of the Nuu-chah-nulth traditional territory and peoples' history, and of the pioneering families and subsequent local timber and fishing industries that developed in the area over the decades. The museum also offers walking tours on a variety of themes, such as the Japanese-Canadian heritage in the area, and the history of Tofino.

───────

②

Roy Henry Vickers Gallery

📍 350 Campbell St 🕐 10am-5pm daily 🌐 royhenryvickers.com

Tsimshian First Nations award-winning artist Roy Vickers welcomes you to his beautiful longhouse-style art gallery, where he exhibits his carvings, original prints, paintings, books, and jewelry. His contemporary, boldly colorful work represents the magnificent natural beauty of the west coast. The longhouse was built by Vickers and his family, along with the late local carver Henry Nolla.

───────

③ 🎨 🎨 🍽

The Whale Centre

📍 411 Campbell St 🕐 8am-8pm daily 🌐 tofino whalecentre.com

Both a hub for organized excursions – including whale watching, bear watching, and hot springs tours – and a free museum, this center showcases artifacts from local shipwrecks and First Nations history. On display are cedar baskets, canoe paddles, traditional whaling equipment used by the First Nations, and marine specimens including a complete gray whale skeleton.

─────────────

🔍 HIDDEN GEM
Natural Spa

For an amazing day trip, try the Hot Springs Cove Sea-to-Sky tour. After a short seaplane flight, walk a trail through old-growth forest to get to seven geothermal rock pools on the edge of the Pacific.

④
Mackenzie Beach

A family favourite, this sheltered beach has calm waters and gentle waves. It's ideal for paddle boarding and skim-boarding, with rental gear available onsite. During low tide small islets are exposed and tidal pools can be seen in the rocky coves.

⑤
Chesterman Beach

Mainly a residential area lined with quaint and quirky homes, this white sandy beach has lovely tidal pools that are home to sea stars, anemones, and tiny crabs. At the north end at low tide, you could almost walk out to the Lennard Island Lighthouse, but the stroll to the privately owned Frank Island is easier. Over at the Wickaninnish Inn, check if the yellow welcome sign is on the Carving Shed door, in which case you can watch wood-carvers busy with their art.

⑥
Cox Bay Beach

Originally named False Bay, the beach here was renamed Cox Bay in 1934 in honour of the British fur trader and explorer John Henry Cox. Driftwood logs are piled high on the beach but there's still plenty of fine, white sand to sink your feet into. Several resorts are based here and professional surfers practice on the big waves in the winter months, getting ready for the competitions that are hosted here in the spring each year.

↑ Surfers tackling the waves on Chesterman Beach

EAT

1909 Kitchen

This gorgeous, marine-inspired restaurant has a large patio perched out over the water. The Pacific Rim-focused menu features such items as cedar-roasted black cod and shrimp-topped pizza, all cooked in a huge Italian wood-fired oven.

🏠 634 Campbell St, Tofino Resort and Marina 🖥 tofino resortandmarina.com

$ $ $

Tacofino

This is the original orange Tacofino food truck that started the popular franchise in 2009. Its bursting burritos and tasty tacos are still the best in all of BC, especially when stuffed with freshly sourced ling cod, chipotle mayo, and crispy cabbage.

🏠 1184 Pacific Rim Hwy 🖥 tacofino.com

$ $ $

Duffin Passage

0 meters 250
0 yards 250
N ↑

Tofino Clayoquot Heritage Museum ①

MAIN STREET

FIRST STREET

MAIN STREET

SECOND STREET

Roy Henry Vickers Gallery ②

CAMPBELL STREET

Village Green

NEILL

③ The Whale Centre

CAMPBELL STREET

NEILL STREET

FIRST STREET

THIRD STREET

FOURTH STREET

STREET

Duffin Cove

GIBSON STREET

Mackenzie Beach 2 miles (3 km) ④
Chesterman Beach 3 miles (4.5 km) ⑤
Cox Bay Beach 4 miles (6 km) ⑥

1909 Kitchen

Tacofino 2 miles (3 km)

③ ⌇ ⌇ ⌇

PACIFIC RIM NATIONAL PARK RESERVE

ℹ **Kwisitis Visitor Centre, 485 Wick Rd, Ucluelet; (250) 726 3500**

Composed of three distinct areas – Long Beach, the Broken Group Islands, and the West Coast Trail – this vast and untamed strip of land is world famous for its whale watching, surfing, kayaking, and hiking adventures.

Long Beach

The rugged, windswept sands of this seemingly endless beach, 15.5 miles (25 km) long, are renowned for their wild beauty. The crashing Pacific waves offer unbeatable year-round opportunities for surfers, both amateur and professional, while beachcombers can explore the beach's numerous rock pools, filled with marine life and scattered with driftwood. Hikers can choose from several scenic trails, including the 1-mile (1.5-km) Schooner Trail, which weaves through lush rainforests bordering the beach.

Broken Group Islands

A mecca for sea kayakers and scuba divers, the Broken Group Islands are an archipelago of some 100 islets clustered close enough for exploring one by one. Discover secret coves for a private picnic, or peer through crystal-clear waters revealing sea stars and other critters scuttling along the ocean floor.

West Coast Trail

Explore 47 miles (7.5 km) of ancient paths and paddling routes used for trade and travel by the First Nations, following the southwestern edge of Vancouver Island. Built up in 1907 to aid in the rescue of shipwrecked survivors

Hiker taking in Pacific views on the West Coast Trail; the suspension bridge over Logan Creek *(inset)* ↑

WHALE WATCHING

More than 20 species of whale are found in British Columbia's coastal waters, and around 22,000 gray whales migrate annually from their feeding grounds in the Arctic Ocean to breed off the coast of Mexico. The whales tend to stay near to the coast and are often close enough to Vancouver Island's west shore to be seen from land. From March to August there are daily whale-watching trips from Tofino, Ucluelet, and Bamfield.

along the coast, this trail is now rated as one of the world's best walking routes. Taking approximately seven days or more, it passes through stunning natural scenery, including moss-draped rainforests, roaring waterfalls rushing down onto the shores of pebble beaches, and deep, rocky gullies hidden by groves of towering cedar trees. Hikers embarking on this once-in-a-lifetime adventure must be experienced and well prepared. The trail is only open between May and September and requires a permit and reservations.

EXPERIENCE MORE

4

Port Renfrew

🚏🚌 *i* **2070 Phillips Rd, Sooke; www.portrenfrew. com**

The last stop at the end of the West Coast Highway, Port Renfrew is a small, friendly fishing village and ex-logging town. A popular day trip from Victoria, the town offers visitors access to Botanical Beach, where a unique sandstone shelf leaves rock pools filled with marine life such as starfish at low tide. It's the perfect place to take a break from nearby city life, with unspoiled scenery in the form of fir-dotted hills and pristine beaches. Recent developments in the area include a cluster of cabins

perched right on the water's edge, and the addition of a pleasant local pub.

Port Renfrew is famed for its hiking along old logging roads: the Sandbar Trail goes through a Douglas fir plantation to a large river sandbar where it is possible to swim at low tide. A more serious hike is the 29-mile (47-km) Juan de Fuca Marine Trail from Port Renfrew to China Beach. This trail offers a range of hikes, from treks lasting several days to short beach walks. The town is also one of two starting points for the West Coast Trail in Pacific Rim National Park Reserve *(p104)*.

> ### Did You Know?
>
> Port Renfrew's Avatar Grove is home to Sitka spruce trees that are almost 1,000 years old.

5

Cowichan District

🚗 & 🚌 **From Duncan** *i* **2896 Drinkwater Rd; www.tourismcowichan. com**

Located on the south central coast of Vancouver Island, about 37 miles (60 km) north of Victoria, the Cowichan District incorporates both the Chemainus and Cowichan valleys. Cowichan means

"warm land" in the language of the Cowichan, one of BC's largest First Nations groups; the area's mild climate means the waters of Cowichan Lake are warm enough to swim in during the summer months. The largest freshwater lake on the island, Lake Cowichan also offers excellent fishing, canoeing, and hiking. Another favorite local activity is tubing down the Cowichan River, the emerald-green waters of which extend 29 miles (47 km) from the lake. Cowichan's magnificent coastline allows ample opportunities to set out to sea, whether in a boat or on a board.

The warm climate here also favors grape-growing. The Cowichan Valley is BC's second-highest wine-producing region, after Okanagan, and is sometimes referred to as "Napa of the North." Self-guided or escorted wine-tasting tours along country back roads are popular.

←

Tubers drifting down a river near Cowichan Lake on a warm summer's day

↑ Fishing trawlers just off the coast of the small harbor town of Port Hardy

Between the town of Duncan and the lake lies the Valley Demonstration Forest, which has scenic lookouts and signs explaining forest management. Duncan is known as the City of Totems, as it displays more than 40 poles in the downtown area. Yellow-painted footprints on the sidewalks guide visitors along the "Totem Trail."

6 Parksville

ℹ 1275 Island Hwy E; www.visitparksville qualicumbeach.com

The relaxed and laid-back town of Parksville swells during the summer months, when both locals and visitors flock to Rathtrevor Beach Provincial Park at the east end of town, which boasts a 1-mile (1.5-km) sandy stretch of natural splendor. At low tide the little tidal pools are of interest for shell and sand-dollar seekers, while bald eagles soar above looking for a tasty meal of crab or fish.

For more wildlife viewing opportunities, visit the nearby North Island Wildlife Recovery Centre, where you can see rescued black bears, owls, turtles, and other animals being rehabilitated.

Foodies shouldn't miss a stop at the Little Qualicum Cheeseworks, making sure to sample their brie, fruit wine, and other delicious goodies produced at the on-site farm. The Coombs Old Country Market is also a great spot for locally produced foods, with freshly baked cinnamon buns and creamy homemade ice cream included among the wares there – just be sure to watch out for the goats on the market rooftop.

7 Port Hardy

ℹ 7250 Market St; www.visitporthardy.com

The quaint harbor town of Port Hardy is the largest community on the northern part of Vancouver Island, and has a good little museum filled with fossils, First Nations artifacts, and relics from early Danish settlers, as well as a gift shop that sells locally crafted wooden carvings. Another worthy stopover is the Quatse River Salmon Stewardship Centre, where visitors can learn all about the life cycle of salmon through fun interactive displays.

Port Hardy makes a convenient gateway to further rural adventures, including kayaking, scuba diving, fishing, and caving. It is also the starting point for the unforgettable BC Ferries Inside Passage route to Prince Rupert and Haida Gwaii, and for thrilling floatplane tours that head to the Great Bear Rainforest.

💬 INSIDER TIP
Sweater Shopping

For an authentic souvenir from the island, seek out the thick, wool Cowichan sweaters traditionally hand-knitted by the Cowichan First Nations of this region.

↑ Telegraph Cove, with the distinctive stilted buildings that dot the village

⑧ Telegraph Cove

🚌 Port McNeill ℹ️ 1594 Beach Dr, Port McNeill; (250) 956 3881

Telegraph Cove is a small, picturesque boardwalk village, with distinctive high wooden houses built on stilts that look over the waters of Johnstone Strait. In summer, the northern resident orcas, drawn by the migrating salmon, come to cavort on the gravel beds in the shallow waters of Robson Bight, an ecological reserve established in 1982. Visitors may view the whales' antics from tour boats or from Port McNeill.

⑨ Campbell River

ℹ️ 1235 Shoppers Row; www.campbellriver tourism.com

Located on the northeast shore of Vancouver Island, Campbell River is renowned as a center for salmon fishing. The waters of Discovery Passage are on the migration route for five major species of salmon, including the giant Chinook. Boat tours are available, which follow the fish up-river. Visitors can rent a fishing boat or try their luck catching fish from the 600-ft (183-m) Discovery Pier in the town.

Just 1 mile (1.5 km) northwest of Campbell River, Elk Falls Provincial Park has large Douglas fir forests and several waterfalls. There are also some terrific views of Elk Falls itself from the suspension bridge.

⑩ Chemainus

🚌🚌🚌 ℹ️ 102-9799 Waterwheel Crescent; www.chemainus.bc.ca

When the local sawmill closed in the late 1970s, picturesque Chemainus transformed itself into a major attraction with the painting of giant murals around the town that depict the history of the region. Local artists continued the project, and today there are more than 40 murals on the outside walls of local buildings, based on real events in the town's past. Larger-than-life images of indigenous Cowichan people, pioneers, and loggers have revitalized the town. Visitors enjoy browsing in the town's various antiques stores and relaxing in the many pleasant sidewalk cafés.

Some 43 miles (70 km) south of Chemainus, Swartz Bay is the departure point on Vancouver Island for ferries to the Southern Gulf Islands and the mainland. Visitors are drawn to the 200 mostly uninhabited islands by their tranquility and natural beauty. It is possible to stroll along

→ Locals splashing in the warm waters of the Comox Valley in summer

TOP 5 VANCOUVER ISLAND'S BEST BEACHES

Chesterman Beach, Tofino
A surfer's paradise for all ability levels.

Sidney Spit Marine Park, Sidney
This fine sandbar is great for family picnics.

Mystic Beach, Sooke
A secluded gem, located along a rainforest trail.

Goose Spit Park, Comox Valley
Head here for evening beach bonfires; firewood is available onsite.

Rathtrevor Beach, Parksville
A sandy stretch, ideal for sandcastle building and beachcombing.

almost empty beaches, where sightings of eagles and turkey vultures are common. There are fishing charters for visitors, and kayaking tours offering stops on isolated shores to view otters, seals, and marine birds.

Salt Spring is the most-populated Gulf island, with about 10,500 inhabitants. In the summer, visitors come to wander around the pretty village of Ganges, where a busy marina surrounds the wooden pier. The village offers stores, cafés, galleries, and colorful markets. At the renowned Saturday Market (Apr–Oct), enjoy listening to live music while browsing the stalls, which offer an array of fresh produce, homemade goods, and arts and crafts.

⑪ Nanaimo

✖🍴🏬🚆 *i* 2450 Northfield Rd; www.tourismnanaimo.com

Originally the site of five villages of the indigenous Coast Salish peoples, Nanaimo was established as a coal-mining town in the 1850s. As the second-largest city on Vancouver Island, Nanaimo has plenty of malls and businesses along the Island Highway, but it is the Old City Quarter on the waterfront, located right in the heart of downtown Nanaimo, that visitors enjoy the most.

The Old City Quarter has many 19th-century buildings, including the Nanaimo Court House, designed by Francis Rattenbury in 1895. The **Nanaimo Museum** includes a re-creation of an old school-room, a First Nations exhibit, and a Sports Hall of Fame, as well as aboriginal artifacts in a village diorama.

Nanaimo Museum
🎨🎟 🏠 100 Museum Way
📞 (250) 753 1821 🕐 10am–5pm Mon–Sat (summer: daily)

⑫ Comox Valley

i 101-3607 Small Rd, Cumberland; www.discovercomoxvalley.com

Overlooked by the Comox Glacier, this valley region comprises the historic city of Courtenay, the seaside town of Comox, and the artsy village of Cumberland, along with other smaller settlements including Denman Island and Hornby Island. Besides the numerous hiking, paddling, and biking trails, the highlight here is Mount Washington Alpine Resort, which offers year-round outdoor activities and one of the deepest snowpacks in North America. Down in the valley there are also colorful festivals, wineries, oyster tastings, and farmers' markets with produce from over 400 local farms, which ensure visitors are kept busy.

Skier jumping off a cliff near Whistler

BRITISH COLUMBIA INTERIOR

One of the most stunning wildernesses in North America, the British Columbia Interior is situated between the Coast Mountains to the west, the Canadian Rockies to the east and the Yukon to the north. When European settlers arrived to trade fur in the region during the 18th century, its rich, fertile landscapes were home to almost 200 distinct First Nation communities. On the remote islands of Haida Gwaii, the Haida people, who have lived in the area for over 13,000 years, still make up around half the population.

Today, the provincal interior is renowned for its natural beauty, ranging from the rolling vineyards of the Okanagan Valley – Canada's top wine-producing region – to the snowy peaks of Whistler Blackcomb, Rossland, and Revelstoke, which draw skiiers from across the globe every winter. BC's beautiful and often uncrowded provincial parks are located throughout, and offer unsurpassed hiking, mountain biking, and wildlife spotting opportunities.

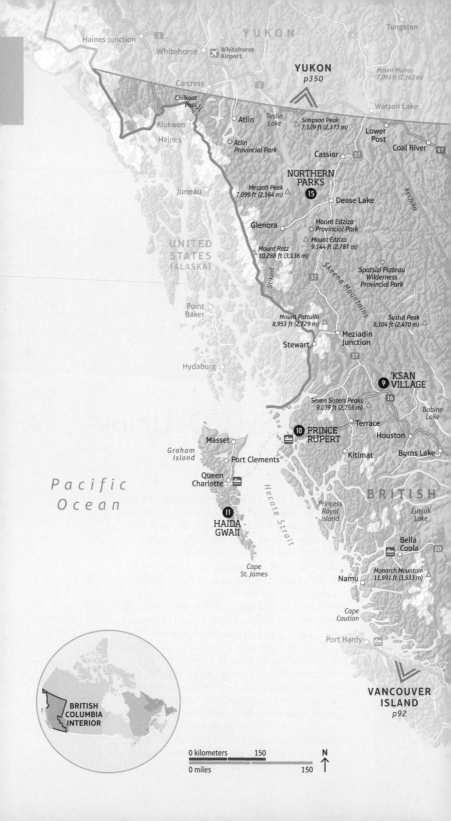

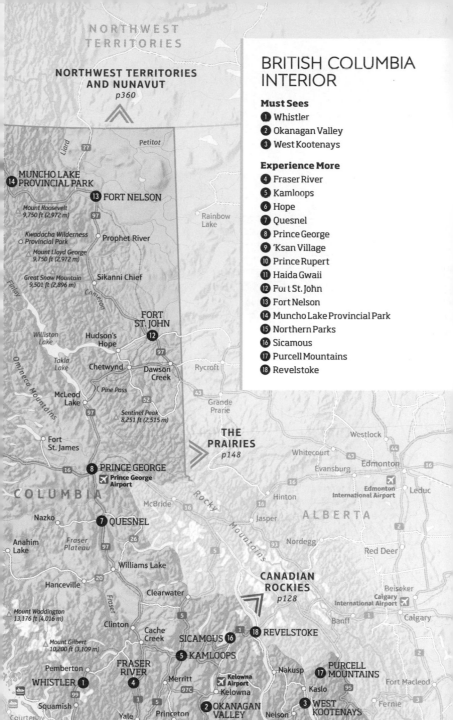

BRITISH COLUMBIA INTERIOR

Must Sees
1 Whistler
2 Okanagan Valley
3 West Kootenays

Experience More
4 Fraser River
5 Kamloops
6 Hope
7 Quesnel
8 Prince George
9 'Ksan Village
10 Prince Rupert
11 Haida Gwaii
12 Fort St. John
13 Fort Nelson
14 Muncho Lake Provincial Park
15 Northern Parks
16 Sicamous
17 Purcell Mountains
18 Revelstoke

❶

WHISTLER

📍 🛈 4230 Gateway Dr; www.whistler.com

Follow the coastal, cliff-hugging Sea-to-Sky Highway from Vancouver and you'll reach the magnificent side-by-side peaks of Whistler and Blackcomb mountains. Set between the mountains, the village of Whistler has hosted both the Olympic and Paralympic Winter Games. It's a year-round destination, where riding powder in winter and biking down the mountain in summer are just a few of the many adventures to be had.

① 🍴 🛍

Whistler Village

Once a stopover along a fur-trading and gold rush route, the village of Whistler became a resort in 1914, when a rural fishing lodge opened its doors at Alta Lake, just west of where the village is today. Now, the cobble-stoned Village Centre is where you'll find a full range of lodges and hotels, shops selling winter gear and souvenirs, fine-dining restaurants, cozy pubs for après-ski, and hopping nightclubs. Dog-sledding and snowmobile-tour outfitters can also be found amongst the shops.

Vestiges of the 2010 Winter Olympics are proudly on display in the Upper Village, notably the Whistler Olympic Plaza. Here you'll find the most luxurious of hotels, top-notch health spas, dimly lit cocktail lounges, and skiers lining up for one of the gondolas and chairlifts heading up Blackcomb Mountain.

② 🛷 🛍

Whistler Museum

🏠 4333 Main St ⏰ 11am–5pm daily (to 9pm Thu) 🌐 whistlermuseum.org

Beginning with the early pioneers, this museum tells the fascinating story of Whistler Blackcomb. Highlights include a section on the 2010 Winter Olympics and a great exhibit on local wildlife. For those wanting to delve more into Whistler's history, several guided walking tours are offered by the museum.

> **🏔 GREAT VIEW**
> **Peak 2 Peak Gondola**
>
> For thrilling views, take a ride on the record-breaking Peak 2 Peak Gondola or dare to walk across the vertiginous Cloudraker Skybridge suspension bridge that sways 6,650 ft (2,000 m) above sea level.

↑ Skiers enjoying the famous powder on Whistler Mountain

Valley during the 20-minute ride to the top. During the summer months, Whistler Mountain becomes a mecca for mountain bikers, with over 155 miles (250 km) of trails suitable for all skill levels.

④
Whistler Olympic Plaza

🏛 Village Stroll

A legacy of the 2010 Winter Olympics, this plaza has a state-of-the-art outdoor performance facility that hosts an array of shows throughout the year, including concerts, sporting events, and cultural festivities. The Olympic Rings are a favourite spot for photos.

⑤
Blackcomb Mountain

With a top elevation of 7,992 ft (2,436 m), this mountain is one mighty playground. A combination of 17 chairlifts and gondolas whisk skiers and snowboarders up to a winter wonderland. Also on offer are zip-trekking opportunities, snowcat tours, and helicopter rides to spot glaciers.

③
Whistler Mountain

Skiers and snowboarders can enjoy over 7 sq miles (19 sq km) of thrilling terrain with more than 100 marked trials, while the Whistler Village Gondola offers superb views of Whistler

EAT

Basalt Wine and Salumeria

The heated patio at this eatery in the heart of Whistler Village is one of the best around and it's always buzzing, especially during happy hour. Try the excellent charcuterie platters or the great value seasonal set menu. The selection of wines and cocktails on offer is superb.

🏛 13, 4154 Village Green 🌐 basalt whistler.com

$$$

Christine's on Blackcomb

Set at 6,102 ft (1,860 m), you'll experience real mountain-top fine dining here, with incredible 360-degree views of the resort below and the surrounding mountain ranges. The food, wine, and service are as sublime as the scenery.

🏛 4545 Blackcomb Way
📞 (604) 938 7437
🕐 For lunch only

$$$

Purebread

This is a true local gem of a bakery, with an amazing, piled-high assortment of sweet and savory croissants, hearty breads, scones stuffed with delicious fillings, picnic-ready sandwiches, pizza tarts, and good strong coffee that never runs out.

🏛 122, 4338 Main St
🌐 purebread.ca

$$$

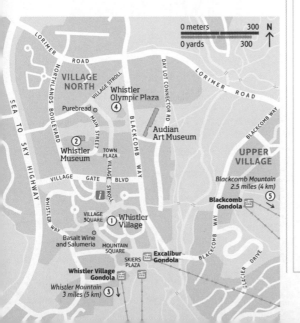

OKANAGAN VALLEY

↑ Sculpture on the shore of Okanagan Lake at Penticton

🛈 238 Queensway, Kelowna; www.tourism kelowna.com

Tucked away behind gently sloping mountains and linked by a string of deep, lengthy lakes, the Okanagan Valley is a five-hour drive east of Vancouver. Dry grasslands, ribbons of grape vines crossing up and down hillsides, and orchards full of peach and cherry trees fill the landscape.

① Vernon

Cattle ranches sprung up here on the flats early on in the 1800s, one of which, the **O'Keefe Ranch**, still exists. Today, Vernon is a popular summer spot for watersports on either Lake Okanagan or the teal-colored Kalamalka Lake. Come winter, ski bunnies flock to the excellent Silver Star Mountain Resort to make fresh tracks in the champagne powder.

O'Keefe Ranch

♿🐾🅿️🍴🏠 🏠 9380 Hwy 97N
🕐 May–Sep: 10am–5pm daily
🌐 okeeferanch.ca

② Kelowna

The biggest city in the Okanagan Valley, Kelowna lies neatly on the shores of Lake Okanagan and is at the center of the wine-and fruit-growing industries. Wine-tastings and fruit-stand-stops aside,

Kelowna's sun-kissed beaches are perfect for families to play and picnic on. Myra Canyon, a short drive away, makes a great day-trip from the city. This thrilling portion of the historic Kettle Valley Rail Trail network is a spectacular spot for hikes and bike rides.

③ Penticton

Laid-back and friendly, this popular destination has two

Did You Know?

The Valley's native Syilx people gave Okanagan its name, which means "place of water."

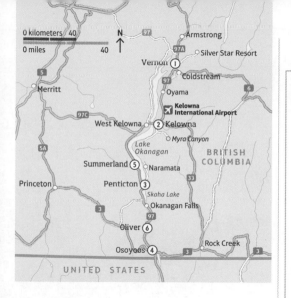

Burrowing Owl Estate Winery
🏠 500 Burrowing Owl Pl, Oliver
Chic, premium winery with a top restaurant and a series of luxurious guest rooms.

Elephant Island Orchard Wines
🏠 2730 Aikens Loop, Naramata
Family-run estate known for its exquisite fruit wines, in particular its Apricot Dessert Wine.

Mission Hill Family Estate
🏠 1730 Mission Hill Rd, West Kelowna
Iconic and ultra-modern, this winery has a sculpture garden within its stunning grounds. Make sure you sample the Pinot Noir.

Nk'Mip Cellars
🏠 1400 Rancher Creek Rd, Osoyoos
Indigenous-owned winery and resort selling top Chardonnays and Rieslings.

See Ya Later Ranch
🏠 2575 Green Lake Rd, Okanagan Falls
Tastings are held inside a beautifully restored early-19th-century hilltop home with spectacular views. Try their Gewürztraminer.

Covert Farms Family Estate
🏠 300 Covert Pl, Oliver
The perfect spot to sample a range of organic wines, tasty charcuterie and delicious pick-your-own produce.

lakefronts – Okanagan Lake and Skaha Lake. Beach life is, understandably, a big focus here. Other activities include gently floating the channel between the two lakes on a comfy tube, hopping from one vineyard to the next on scooters over in neighboring Naramata, or daring to scale the towering Skaha Bluffs, just a short drive south of town.

←
Vineyards in Okanagan Valley, with the Mcintyre Bluff in the distance

④
Osoyoos
Kitschy but thoroughly enjoyable, this resort town experiences some of the driest and hottest summer temperatures in the country, and Osoyoos Lake is the country's warmest freshwater lake; a winning combination that draws many visitors to the beaches along the lakefront every summer for sunbathing and watersports.

⑤
Summerland
This small but charming lakeside town is home to several 19th-century buildings and stunning views from the top of Giant's Head Mountain, an extinct volcano. You can also ride a locomotive here along a preserved section of the Kettle Valley Railway.

⑥
Oliver
Officially labeled as the Wine Capital of Canada, the area around Oliver is home to over 40 wineries, many of which offer excellent dining and accommodation options.

STAY

Halcyon Hot Springs
The luxurious lakeshore chalets and hot-springs spa here offer views of gleaming white peaks.

 Hwy 23, Nakusp
W halcyon-hotsprings.com

$$$

Hume Hotel & Spa
This landmark hotel dating back to 1898 features heritage details and modern rooms.

📍 422 Vernon St, Nelson
W humehotel.com

$$$

→

Flow Peak towering above golden larch forests in Kootenay National Park

3

WEST KOOTENAYS

🚌 ℹ Nelson Visitor Information Centre, 91 Baker St, Nelson; www.nelsonkootenaylake.com

A picturesque region of dense forest and snowy peaks, the West Kootenays is dotted with historic mining towns set on the shores of glacier-fed lakes. Hike, bike, and ski the endless slopes here, explore deep caves, soak in hot springs, or cozy up inside a snug cabin after a long day sightseeing in this remote mountain playground.

Nelson

Nestled into the side of the Selkirk Mountains along the West Arm of Kootenay Lake, Nelson is an attractive former mining and lumber town with an easy-going outdoor-lifestyle vibe. The eateries here are top-notch, as is the locally roasted coffee. The restored downtown core is full of heritage buildings dating back to the 1890s. Take a scenic ride along Nelson's pleasant waterfront and soak up the relaxed atmosphere on Car 23 – a streetcar that operated in the town between 1924 and 1949, before being restored in 1992.

Rossland

This charming mountain resort village really comes alive in the winter months, when the nearby Red Mountain Resort attracts professional skiers and snowboarders for its excellent powder. Old railroad beds, whisky-running routes, and miner's trails crisscross the area and are perfect for mountain biking and hiking in the summer.

Nakusp

Located on the shores of Upper Arrow Lake, this small town is famous for its mineral hot springs, three of which are close to town, and two of which have been developed into comfortable resorts: Nakusp Hot Springs and Halcyon Hot Springs. Up in the nearby Selkirk Mountains are dozens of hiking, mountain biking, and snowmobiling trails. Roughly 25 miles (40 km) south of Nakusp, in the Slocan Valley, are several abandoned silver-mining "ghost" towns – the most fascinating is Sandon, once the unofficial capital of the mining region.

Kaslo

Dominated by the peaks of the Selkirk and Purcell mountains, this fine lakefront village is often referred to as Canada's Little

↑ Historic 19th-century shopfronts on Front Street in Kaslo

Switzerland. A former sawmill and mining boom town, its picturesque streets are lined with frontier-style storefronts and flower-filled gardens. The village's main attraction is the beached SS *Moyie*, a sternwheeler that worked on Kootenay Lake from 1889 until 1957.

HOT SPRINGS

The West Kootenays is peppered with geothermal hot springs, ranging from fully developed spa-like resorts to wilderness backcountry pools. They provide therapeutic bathing in hot waters, rich in sulfates, calcium, sodium, lithium, and magnesium - all said to be good for everyday aches, as well as arthritis.

A DRIVING TOUR
THE WEST KOOTENAYS

Length 340 miles (550 km) **Departure point** Nelson
Stopping-off points Kaslo; Nakusp

Vast, remote, and spectacularly beautiful, the West Kootenays is a region best explored by car. This driving tour should ideally be spread out over several days or more in order to thoroughly enjoy the sights. Keep your eyes peeled for wildlife en route – it's not uncommon to see wild turkeys, deer, and bears crossing the roads in this region. Between October and March, winter tires are required and some high mountain passes may be temporarily closed.

The upscale resort of
Halcyon Hot Springs *is set in some truly spectacular scenery. Visitors can stop here for a relaxing soak in the mineral-rich waters.*

Trout Lake *is a pretty lake renowned for its excellent fishing. Nearby Trout Lake City is a former mining boom town.*

↑ Sunset in the Red Mountain Resort near Rossland

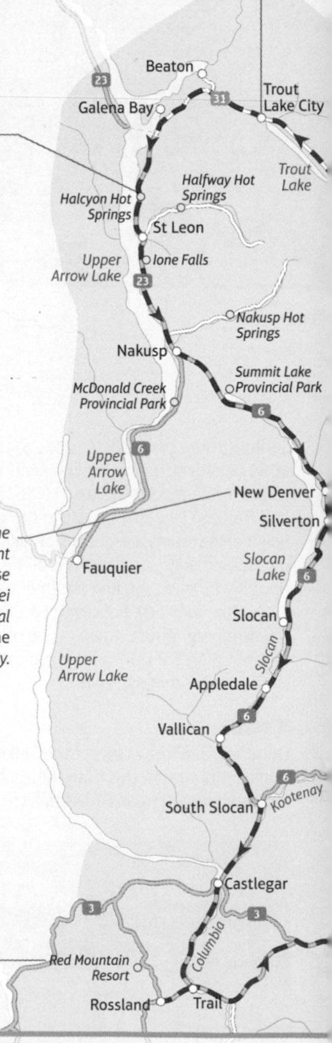

New Denver *was the site of an internment camp for the Japanese during WWII. The Nikkei Internment Memorial Centre (306 Josephine St) tells the full story.*

In winter, day passes are available at the **Red Mountain Resort**, *and the resident snow hosts will be able to direct you to the best ski runs. Non-skiers can take guided tours of the picturesque snow-covered scenery.*

Beaton
Galena Bay
Trout Lake City
Trout Lake
Halcyon Hot Springs
Halfway Hot Springs
St Leon
Ione Falls
Upper Arrow Lake
Nakusp Hot Springs
Nakusp
McDonald Creek Provincial Park
Summit Lake Provincial Park
Upper Arrow Lake
New Denver
Silverton
Slocan Lake
Fauquier
Slocan
Upper Arrow Lake
Appledale
Vallican
South Slocan
Kootenay
Castlegar
Columbia
Red Mountain Resort
Rossland
Trail

↑ Abandoned building and vehicles in the silver-mining ghost town of Sandon

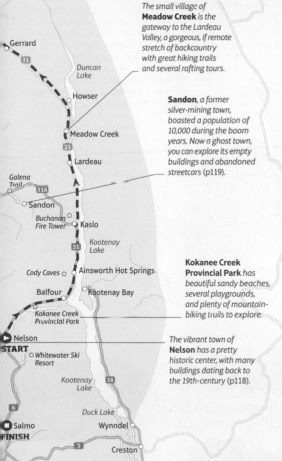

The small village of **Meadow Creek** *is the gateway to the Lardeau Valley, a gorgeous, if remote stretch of backcountry with great hiking trails and several rafting tours.*

Sandon, *a former silver-mining town, boasted a population of 10,000 during the boom years. Now a ghost town, you can explore its empty buildings and abandoned streetcars (p119).*

Kokanee Creek Provincial Park *has beautiful sandy beaches, several playgrounds, and plenty of mountain-biking trails to explore.*

The vibrant town of **Nelson** *has a pretty historic center, with many buildings dating back to the 19th-century (p118).*

🏔 GREAT VIEW
Buchanan Fire Tower

Follow the Blue Ridge Forest Services Road to a retired fire tower on the top of Mount Buchanan. At 6,272 ft (1,912 m), the 360-degree views from the peak here are stunning. Several picnic tables are dotted around near the former lookout.

0 kilometers   25
0 miles   25

N
↑

BRITISH COLUMBIA INTERIOR

The West Kootenays •

Locator Map
For more detail see p112

EXPERIENCE MORE

4

Fraser River

The majestic Fraser River travels 854 miles (1,375 km) through some of BC's most stunning scenery. The river flows from its source in the Yellowhead Lake, near Jasper, to the Strait of Georgia, near Vancouver. Along the way, it heads north through the Rocky Mountain trench before turning south near the town of Prince George. It continues by the Coast Mountains, then west to the town of Hope through the steep walls of the Fraser Canyon, and on toward Yale.

It was Fraser Canyon that legendary explorer Simon Fraser found the most daunting when he followed the river's course in 1808. However, when gold was discovered near the town of Yale 50 years later, thousands of prospectors swarmed up the valley. Today, Yale is a small town, home to the delightful **Yale Museum**, where exhibits focus on the history of the gold rush, as well as telling the epic story of the building of the Canadian Pacific Railroad through the canyon. This section of river is also a popular whitewater rafting area, and trips can be arranged from the town of Boston Bar. At Hell's Gate the river thunders through the Canyon's narrow walls, which are only 34 m (112 ft) apart.

Yale Museum

◈ 🏠 31187 Douglas St, Yale 🕐 May–Sep: daily 🌐 historic yale.ca

---

5

Kamloops

✈ 🚆 🚌 ℹ 1290 West Trans-Canada Hwy; www.tourism kamloops.com

Kamloops means "where the rivers meet" in the language of the Secwepemc First Nations. The largest town by area in BC's southern interior, it lies at the confluence of the north and south Thompson rivers. Three major highways also meet here, as do the Canadian Pacific and Canadian National railroad. European settlement began in 1812, when fur traders started doing business with First Nations peoples. The **Secwepemc Museum and Heritage Park** focuses on the cultural history of the Secwepemc First Nations and has a wide variety of artifacts, including a birch-bark canoe, hunting equipment, traditional clothing, and cooking utensils. Outside, in the Heritage Park, short trails lead visitors through the remains of a 2,000-year-old Shuswap winter village site, which includes four authentically reconstructed winter pit houses. The museum store sells woven baskets, moccasins, and a wide variety of beaded and silver jewelry.

> 💬 **INSIDER TIP**
> ### Great Outdoors
>
> The area surrounding Kamloops is a nature-lover's paradise: the BC Wildlife Park is home to bears, cougars, and wolves, while Sun Peaks ski resort offers outdoor activities all year round.

↑ The serene waters and mountainous backdrop of the Fraser River

In the town center, the Art Gallery has a small but striking collection, including sketches by A. Y. Jackson, one of the renowned Group of Seven *(p54)*.

Secwepemc Museum and Heritage Park
♿ 🕐 🏛 200–330 Chief Alex Thomas Way 📞 (250) 828 9749 🕐 Jun–Aug: daily; Sep–May: 8:30am–4:30pm Mon–Fri

---

❻ Hope
🚌 🛈 919 Water Ave; www. hopebc.ca

Located at the southern end of the Fraser Canyon, Hope is crossed by several highways, including Hwy 1 (the Trans-Canada) and Hwy 3. It is an excellent base for exploring the Fraser Canyon and southern BC, and is within easy reach of several provincial parks. Manning Provincial Park is especially noted for its outdoor activities: swimming, hiking, fishing, plus sailing in summer, and skiing in winter.

> **Did You Know?**
>
> Hope is a major filming location, with credits including *Hope Falls*, *Rambo: First Blood* and *Shoot to Kill*.

❼ Quesnel
🚌 🚗 🛈 703 Carson Ave; www.tourismquesnel.com

Quesnel is a busy logging town that started life as a gold-rush settlement between 1858 and 1861. The town was the last along the Gold Rush Trail, which was lined with mining towns between here and Kamloops. Quesnel occupies an attractive position in a triangle formed by the Fraser and Quesnel rivers. The town's sights include the Riverfront Trail System, a tree-lined path that runs along the banks of both rivers, and the quirky Quesnel Museum. Nearby, Pinnacles Provincial Park features intriguing hoodoos: rocky columns formed over 12 million years ago, when the volcanic surface was eroded by Ice Age meltwaters.

East of Quesnel lies the historic mining town of **Barkerville**, founded by Englishman Billy Barker in 1862. Today, it is a well preserved 19th-century mining town, with over 120 restored or reconstructed buildings and costumed guides. Visitors can see a blacksmith at work in his forge, watch an 1860s-style variety show at the theater, or take a ride on a stagecoach.

Barkerville
♿ 🚻 🏛 87 km E of Quesnel, Hwy 26 🕐 Daily 🌐 bakerville.ca

← A hiker watching the sun set over the stunning Manning Provincial Park, Hope

❽ Prince George
🚌 🚗 🛈 101–1300 First Ave; www.tourism pg.com

The largest town in northern BC, Prince George is a bustling supply-and-transportation center for the region, and is bisected by two major highways. Established in 1807 as Fort George, a fur-trading post at the confluence of the Nechako and Fraser rivers, the town is well placed for exploring the province.

Today, Prince George has all the facilities of a larger city, including a university specializing in First Nations history and culture, as well as its own symphony orchestra, and several art galleries. The Exploration Place Museum and Science Centre lies on the site of the original fort, within the 64-acre (26-ha) Fort George Park, and has a collection of artifacts from Aboriginal cultures, European pioneers, and early settlers.

There are over 1,600 lakes and rivers within an hour's drive of the community, making Prince George a popular summer location for angling enthusiasts.

↑ Exhibits in Prince George's fascinating Exploration Place Museum

← Two elaborately carved totem poles standing within 'Ksan Village

growth of the railroad. The Kwinitsa Railway Museum tells the story of businessman Charles Hay's big plans for the town – which were largely unfulfilled when he went down with the *Titanic* in 1912.

Tsimshian First Nations were the first occupants of the area, and as recently as 150 years ago the harbor was lined with their large cedar houses and carved totems. The **Museum of Northern British Columbia** focuses on northwest coast First Nations culture and history. Tsimshian dance, song, and drama are performed in a traditional longhouse, and there are archeological tours.

Museum of Northern British Columbia
⊘ 🏛 🚪 100 1st Ave W
🕐 Jun-Sep: 9am-5pm daily; Oct-May: 9am-5pm Tue-Sat
🌐 museumofnorthernbc.com

---

9 ♿ 🏛

'Ksan Village

🕐 Grounds: year round; houses: Apr-Sep: 10am-5pm daily 🌐 ksan.org

Located near the ancient village of Gittanmaax, in the community of Hazelton, 'Ksan Village is a re-creation of an 1870 Aboriginal settlement, established in the 1950s to preserve the culture of the Gitxsan First Nations. Gitxsan people have lived in the area for thousands of years, particularly along the beautiful Skeena River valley. Their way of life was threatened by an influx of white settlers, who arrived at Prince Rupert in the 1850s to work their way up-river to mine or farm.

Noted for their skill in carving and painting masks, totems, and canoes, Gitxsan elders are now teaching new generations these skills at 'Ksan Village. Within the complex are seven traditional longhouses, containing a carving school, museum, and gift shop.

> Noted for their skill in carving and painting masks, totems, and canoes, Gitxsan elders are now teaching new generations these skills at 'Ksan Village.

10

Prince Rupert

🚆 🏛 🚍 ⛴ 🏨 ℹ 200-215 Cowbay Rd; www.visit princerupert.com

Prince Rupert is a vibrant port city, and the second-largest on BC's coast. Located on Kaien Island, the city is circled by forests and mountains, and overlooks the beautiful fjord-studded coastline. The busy harbor is the main access point for Haida Gwaii and Alaska.

Like many of BC's major towns, Prince Rupert's development is linked to the

---

11

Haida Gwaii

🚆 ⛴ ℹ 3220 Wharf St, Queen Charlotte; www. gohaidagwaii.ca

Shaped like a bent ice-cream cone, Haida Gwaii (previously called Queen Charlotte Islands) is an archipelago of about 150 islands across from the city of Prince Rupert, separated from the mainland by the often-treacherous waters of the Pacific Ocean.

The islands were left untouched by the last Ice Age, and have an ecosystem unique to Canada. The forests are home to distinctive mammals such as the dusky shrew and short-tailed weasel. There is also a large population of bald eagles, and the spring brings hundreds of migrating gray whales past the shores.

The islands have been the home of the Haida people for thousands of years. Today, the Haida are recognized for their carvings and sculptures from cedar wood and argillite (a black slatelike stone found only on these islands). It was the Haida who led environmental campaigns against logging companies in the 1980s, leading to the founding of the **Gwaii Haanas National Park Reserve and Haida Heritage Site** in 1988. The park is home to centuries-old rainforest, with 1,000-year-old Sitka spruce and red cedar.

Gwaii Haanas National Park Reserve and Haida Heritage Site

 ⏱ Daily (no fee in winter)
🌐 pc.gc.ca

💬 INSIDER TIP
All At Sea

There are two ways to get to Haida Gwaii: by ferry or by air. BC Ferries offers two options, one from Prince Rupert (six hours) and one from Port Hardy via Prince Rupert (15 hours). Advance cabin bookings are recommended.

12

Fort St. John

🚗🚌 ℹ 9324 96th St; www.fortstjohn.ca

Fort St. John is located along the Alaska Highway, which was constructed in 1942 and led to a dramatic increase in the tiny town's population. The highway turned Fort St. John into a busy supply center for the area, and an important link in the region's agricultural growth. The town's greatest boom, however, came when oil was found here in the 1950s, in what proved to be the largest oil field in the province. Today, Fort St. John's pride in its industrial and pioneering heritage is reflected in the local museum, which has an oil derrick at its entrance and a range of exhibits that tell the story of the local oil industry.

13

Fort Nelson

🚗🚌 ℹ 5319 50th Ave S; www.northernrockies.ca

Despite the growth of the oil, gas, and lumber industries in the 1960s and 1970s, Fort Nelson retains the feel of a

northern frontier town. Before the Alaska Highway was built in the 1940s, Fort Nelson was an important stop along the route for the Yukon and Alaska, although until the 1950s it was without running water or electricity. Fur trading was the main activity until the energy boom; even today both Aboriginal and white trappers hunt wolf, beaver, and lynx, for both their fur and their meat.

Today, the town has an air and bus service, a hospital, and good visitor facilities. Local people are famous for their friendliness, and during the busy summer months run a program of free talks describing life in the north to visitors. A small museum displays photographs and artifacts that tell the story of the building of the 1,523-mile (2,451-km) Alaska Highway.

↑ A visitor taking in the vast rainforest of the Gwaii Haanas National Park Reserve

14
Muncho Lake Provincial Park

(250) 776 7000 ⏱Daily

One of three provincial parks that were established after the construction of the Alaska Highway, Muncho Lake occupies the most scenic section of the road. The park encompasses the bare peaks of the northern Rockies, whose craggy limestone slopes are a testament to thousands of years of glacial erosion. The highway skirts the eastern shoreline of Muncho Lake before crossing the Liard River. In early summer, passing motorists are likely to see moose grazing amid meadows filled with colorful wildflowers. The roadside also attracts goats, caribou, and stone sheep, drawn by delicious deposits of sodium, known as mineral licks.

STAY

To stay overnight in the picturesque Muncho Lake Provincial Park, either head for the two main vehicle-accessible campgrounds or opt for the privately owned, more comfortable lodge.

Strawberry Flats Campground
⛺ Mile 438 Alaska Hwy

$$$

MacDonald Campground
⛺ Mile 460 Alaska Hwy

$$$

Northern Rockies Lodge
🏨 Mile 462 Alaska Hwy

$$$

15
Northern Parks

(250) 771 4591

The provincial parks of northern BC comprise Mount Edziza Provincial Park, Spatsizi Plateau Wilderness Provincial Park, and, farther north, Atlin Provincial Park. These offer remote landscapes, with high peaks, ice fields, and tundra.

Established in 1972, Mount Edziza Provincial Park is distinguished by its volcanic landscape, which includes lava rivers, a basalt plateau, and cinder cones. The park can be reached by boat or floatplane. There is no vehicle access in the park land, and only rugged overland trails or chartered floatplanes take visitors through the park's open meadows, arctic birch woods, and over creeks.

Across the highway lies the even harsher country of Spatsizi Plateau Wilderness Provincial Park, which includes the snow-capped peaks of the Skeena Mountains. Gladys Lake, a small lake in the center of the park, is an ecological reserve for the study of sheep and mountain goats. Access to the park is limited to a small road leading from the village of Tatogga along Hwy 37.

Atlin Provincial Park is only accessible from the Yukon on Hwy 7, off the Alaska Highway. About one-third of the spectacular park is covered by large ice fields and glaciers.

16
Sicamous

🚌 🛈 446 Main St; www.sicamouschamber.bc.ca

Sicamous is an appealing waterfront village with charming streets hung with flower-filled planters. Located between Mara and Shuswap lakes, at the junction of the Trans-Canada Highway and Hwy 97A, the town is ideally placed for touring the lakes and the town of Salmon Arm, at the northern end of the Okanagan Valley *(p116)*. Over 200 houseboats are available for renting in the summer, and there are also numerous

← A floatplane docked on the glassy surface of Muncho Lake

marinas and watersport rental companies. The lakes have over 620 miles (1,000 km) of shoreline to explore. From a boat it is possible to view the inlets and forested landscape of Lake Shuswap, where black bears, deer, moose, coyotes, and bobcats have all been spotted along the shore. In summer, visitors and locals flock to the good public beach located on the lake.

17

Purcell Mountains

◫ Kamloops ⓘ 500 10th Ave N/Hwy 95, Golden; (250) 344 7125

The ruggedly beautiful Purcell Mountains face the Rockies across the broad Columbia River Valley. This is one of the most remote regions in the Rockies and attracts hunters and skiers from across the globe. A range of granite spires, called the Bugaboos, also draws mountain climbers. In one of the few accessible areas in the north, the Purcell Wilderness Conservancy covers a vast 8 sq miles (21 sq km).

Carefully regulated hunting expeditions for bear, elk, and mountain goat are permitted here.

From the nearby town of Invermere, one of the most difficult trails in Canada can be accessed; the Earl Grey Pass Trail extends some 39 miles (63 km) over the Purcell Mountains. It is named after Earl Grey, Canada's Governor General from 1904 to 1911, who chose the Purcell range as the place to build a vacation cabin for his family in 1909. The trail he traveled followed an established route used by the Kinbasket peoples of the Shuswap First Nations, but it is notoriously dangerous today; bears, avalanches, and fallen trees are often hazards en route, and the hike should not be attempted by a novice.

18

Revelstoke

ⓘ 301 Victoria Rd West; www.seerevelstoke.com

The mountain community of Revelstoke sits at the entrance to some of BC's most stunning

🔍 HIDDEN GEM
Mt Revelstoke National Park

Open only during the snow-free summer months, the subalpine top of this national park offers incredible panoramic vistas of the Monashee Mountains and the Selkirk range.

provincial parks (starting with Mount Revelstoke, Glacier, and Yoho national parks). Revelstoke capitalizes on such scenery with its own ski resort: Revelstoke Mountain Resort, which has the longest vertical descent of any ski resort in North America, at 5,620 ft (1,713 m). Revelstoke is also home to four heli-skiing and two cat-skiing operations, due to the excellent winter conditions in the area. In summer, rock-climbing, hiking, biking, and watersports take over.

Back in town, the Revelstoke Railway Museum and the Revelstoke Museum and Archives provide information on the town's early Canadian Pacific Railway history.

↑ Sun rising through the mist in the remote Purcell Mountains

Highway through the Canadian Rockies

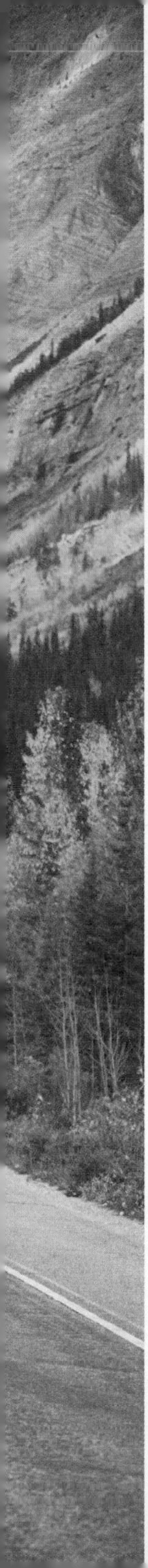

CANADIAN ROCKIES

The Canadian Rockies occupy a band of the provinces of British Columbia and Alberta nearly 500 miles (805 km) wide, and are part of the range that extends from Mexico through the US into Canada. Between 65 and 100 million years ago, a slow but massive upheaval of the Earth's crust caused the rise of the Rocky Mountains and the dramatic, jagged appearance of their peaks, 50 of which are over 10,000 ft (3,048 m) high.

The dramtic scenery and the discovery of natural hot springs at Banff in 1883 inspired the federal government to create Canada's first national park. In 1984, Banff, Jasper, Kootenay, and Yoho national parks were together made a UNESCO World Heritage Site: the superb Canadian Rockies Mountain Parks.

A region of spectacular beauty, the Rockies attract millions of visitors every year, who come to admire its rugged snow-topped peaks, luminous glaciers, and iridescent glacial lakes.

0 kilometers 80

0 miles 80

N

Prince George

Prince George Airport

97

Mount Sir Alexander
10,741 ft (3,274 m)

Grande Cache

40

Dome Creek

Fraser

Rocky

16

Hinton

McBride

Mount Chown
10,879 ft (3,316 m)

40

Quesnel

13 BOWRON LAKE
PROVINCIAL PARK

Mount Robson
12,972 ft (3,954 m)

Barkerville

JASPER
NATIONAL
PARK

16

Tête Jaune
Cache

16

Jasper

3

Likely

Mount Sir Wilfrid Laurier
11,499 ft (3,505 m)

Yellowhead
Pass

Valemount

Mountains

Columbia Mountains

Marguerite

Mount Fraser
10,899 ft (3,322 m)

93

WELLS GRAY
PROVINCIAL PARK

Mount Alberta
11,873 ft (3,619 m)

Williams Lake

12

Blue River

Kinbasket
Lake

Mount Columbia
12,273 ft (3,741 m)

Columbia
Icefield

97

100 Mile
House

Avola

Mica Creek

Columbia

Clearwater

BRITISH
COLUMBIA

Little Fort

BRITISH COLUMBIA
INTERIOR
p110

GLACIER
NATIONAL PARK

5

Clinton

Glacier

Revelstoke

Selkirk Mountains

5

Sicamous

1

Lillooet

Ashcroft

Kamloops

Enderby

23

Pemberton

1

5

Vernon

Coldstream

New Denver

Lytton

Merritt

6

Kelowna

Boston Bar

Westbank

Kelowna
International Airport

Summerland

Castlegar

CANADIAN
ROCKIES

3

Oliver

Rossland

3

Orient

Tonasket

Colville

Winthrop

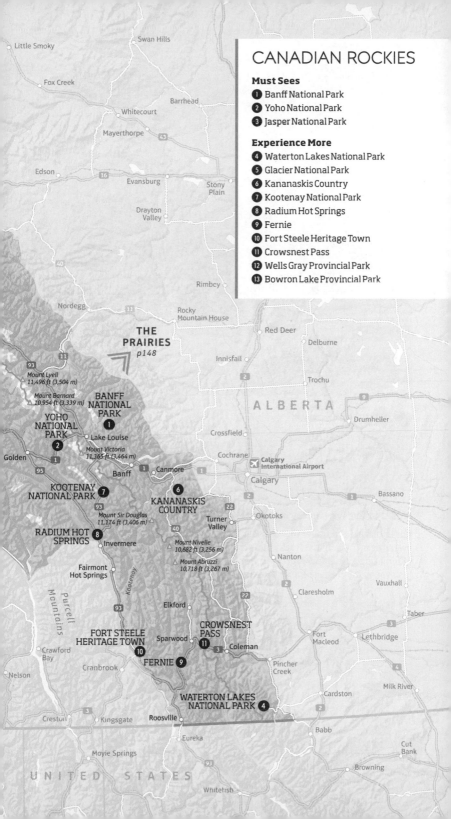

CANADIAN ROCKIES

Must Sees
❶ Banff National Park
❷ Yoho National Park
❸ Jasper National Park

Experience More
❹ Waterton Lakes National Park
❺ Glacier National Park
❻ Kananaskis Country
❼ Kootenay National Park
❽ Radium Hot Springs
❾ Fernie
❿ Fort Steele Heritage Town
⓫ Crowsnest Pass
⓬ Wells Gray Provincial Park
⓭ Bowron Lake Provincial Park

Little Smoky
Fox Creek
Swan Hills
Barrhead
Whitecourt
Mayerthorpe
Edson
Evansburg
Stony Plain
Drayton Valley

THE PRAIRIES
p148

Nordegg
Rocky Mountain House
Red Deer
Delburne
Innisfail
Trochu
Drumheller

Mount Lyell
11,496 ft (3,504 m)
Mount Barnard
10,954 ft (3,339 m)

ALBERTA

BANFF NATIONAL PARK ❶
YOHO NATIONAL PARK ❷
Lake Louise
Mount Victoria
11,365 ft (3,464 m)
Golden
Banff
Canmore
Crossfield
Cochrane
Calgary International Airport
Calgary
Bassano

KOOTENAY NATIONAL PARK ❼
Mount Sir Douglas
11,174 ft (3,406 m)
RADIUM HOT SPRINGS ❽
Invermere
Fairmont Hot Springs

KANANASKIS COUNTRY ❻
Turner Valley
Mount Nivelle
10,682 ft (3,256 m)
Mount Abruzzi
10,718 ft (3,267 m)
Okotoks
Nanton
Claresholm
Vauxhall
Taber

Purcell Mountains
Elkford
Crawford Bay
Nelson
Cranbrook

FORT STEELE HERITAGE TOWN ❿
Sparwood
CROWSNEST PASS ⓫
Coleman
Fort Macleod
Lethbridge

FERNIE ❾
Pincher Creek
Cardston
Milk River

Creston
Kingsgate
Roosville
WATERTON LAKES NATIONAL PARK ❹
Babb
Cut Bank

Moyie Springs
Eureka
Browning

UNITED STATES
Whitefish

BANFF NATIONAL PARK

① ✎ 🍴 🖥 🛍

🚌 ℹ 224 Banff Ave, Banff; www.banfflakelouise.com

It is impossible to travel through Banff National Park and not feel awestruck. The sublime Rocky Mountains soar over a landscape of glimmering glaciers, evergreen forests, swift rivers flowing through lush valleys, and the some of the bluest lakes on earth.

The best known of the Rockies' national parks, Banff was also Canada's first. The park was established in 1885, after the discovery of natural hot springs by three Canadian Pacific Railway workers in 1883. Centuries before the arrival of the railroad, Blackfoot, Stoney and Kootenay peoples lived in the valleys around Banff. Today, Banff National Park covers an area of 2,564 sq miles (6,641 sq km) of some of the most spectacular scenery in the country. Some four million visitors a year come through the town of Banff and the village of Lake Louise to enjoy a range of activities, including caving, rafting, and hiking in summer, and tobogganing, dog-sledding, and ice-climbing in winter.

↑ Downtown Banff during a summer rainstorm

← Mountain climber scaling a large vertical ice wall at Johnston Canyon

↑ Walkway on the peak of Sulphur Mountain, just outside Banff

BANFF

Guarded by sky-high Mount Rundle, the town of Banff grew up around the hot springs that were discovered here in the 1880s. The Canadian Pacific Railway president at that time, Sir William Cornelius Van Horne,

realized the springs would attract visitors, so he built the grand Banff Springs Hotel in 1888. The resort was very popular, and the town quickly expanded to accommodate the influx.

Today, Banff offers visitors a full range of facilities and is an excellent base for exploring the park. The nearby Cave and Basin National Historic Site tells the story of Banff's development and has tunnels to explore, while the Tunnel Mountain summit trail has gorgeous views across the Bow Valley. You can also take a ride in a gondola to the top of Sulphur Mountain, and afterward go for a relaxing soak in the Upper Hot Springs.

INSIDER TIP
Shuttle Buses

To ease congestion along the roads and parking lots, shuttle services are available in Banff and Lake Louise to the various sights. Some shuttle buses are free and some charge a small fee.

STAY

Lake Louise Inn
A range of guest rooms are available, some featuring full kitchens, fireplaces, and Jacuzzi tubs. The inn also has several good dining options, a heated indoor pool and hot tub area, and complimentary bike and snowshoe rentals.

⌂ 210 Village Rd, Lake Louise
ⓦ lakelouiseinn.com

$$$

Storm Mountain Lodge
Former Canadian Pacific Railway cabins have been renovated to provide an authentic experience in the woods with claw-foot tubs and wood-burning fireplaces. There are no kitchen facilities, but gourmet meals are offered by the lodge.

⌂ Hwy 93 S, Banff National Park ⓒ check website for details
ⓦ stormmountain lodge.com

$$$

LAKE LOUISE

EAT

Juniper Bistro

Perched on a hill overlooking the town of Banff, this bistro has a fantastic patio with cozy fireplaces and outstanding views. Try the game duo, which includes succulent bison short ribs, braised rabbit, and truffle mashed potatoes.

📍 1 Juniper Way, Banff
🌐 thejuniper.com

$$$

Lake Agnes Tea House

Supplies are flown in via helicopter to this historic 1905 teahouse at the peak of a popular 2-mile (3-km) trail. You can also continue on to the Plain of Six Glaciers Tea House farther along.

📍 Lake Agnes ⏱ Jun–Oct
🌐 lakeagnestea house.com

$$$

Rocky Mountain Flatbread

If you just want a quick and tasty bite, head to this take-out counter inside the Cascade Mall food court. Organic, locally sourced ingredients are used in their thin-crust pizzas, pastas, and salads.

📍 317 Banff Ave, Banff
🌐 rockymountain flatbread.com

$$$

One of Banff National Park's major draws, the beauty of Lake Louise is an enduring image of the Rockies. Famed for the blueness of its water and the snowy peaks that surround it, Lake Louise also boasts the Victoria Glacier, which stretches almost to the water's edge. Trails around the lake are dotted with information points that explain the lake's formation some 10,000 years ago, at the end of the last Ice Age. The amazing color of the water of this and other lakes in the park comes from deposits of glacial silt, known as rock flour, suspended just beneath the surface.

Dominating the landscape at one end of the lake is the imposing hotel Château Lake Louise, built in 1894. Nearby Lake Louise village makes a great base for exploring the area. During the summer, a gondola carries visitors up to Mount Whitehorn for stunning views of the glacier and the lake. In winter, the area attracts large numbers of skiers and snowboarders.

↑ Canoeists paddling the turquoise waters of Lake Louise

Did you Know?

Peyto Lake is named after Bill Peyto, an early guide and warden in Banff National Park.

→ View over Peyto Lake in winter, from Bow Summit on the Icefields Parkway

BEAR SAFETY

Both grizzly and black bears are found in the Rockies' national parks. Although sightings are rare, visitors should observe the fundamental rules: don't approach the animals, never feed them, don't run, and stay calm. Bears have an excellent sense of smell, so if you are camping be sure to lock food or trash inside a vehicle or in the bear-proof boxes provided. On hikes, make noise, wear bear bells, carry bear spray, and keep dogs on a leash.

SCENIC DRIVES AND TRAILS

Icefields Parkway

The Icefields Parkway (Hwy 93) is a 143-mile (230-km) scenic mountain highway that twists and turns through some of the tallest, most jagged spines of the Rocky Mountains, while offering a chance of seeing grizzly bears and mountain goats along the way. Every turn offers yet another incredible view as the road climbs through high passes from Lake Louise to Jasper.

Bow Summit is the highest point on the highway, at 6,785 ft (2,068 m), and has a side road that leads to the Peyto Lake viewpoint, which looks over snow-topped peaks mirrored in the brilliant blue of the lake.

Moraine Lake

Less well known than Lake Louise, Moraine Lake is every bit as beautiful. A scenic road from Lake Louise winds to the lake, which is ringed by ten peaks each over 10,000 ft (3,000 m) high. A pretty waterside lodge offers accommodations, and several hiking trails start at the lake.

Johnston Canyon

About 12 miles (19 km) west of Banff, one of the best short walks leads from the roadside to Johnston Canyon. Follow wide trails and narrow bridges through the canyon to two impressive waterfalls. On the way, look out for the Ink Pots, a series of pools where vivid blue-green water bubbles up from underground springs.

Lake Minnewanka Drive

This narrow, winding 9-mile (14-km) loop road passes by picnic sites, hiking trails, and three lakes, including Lake Minnewanka, Banff's biggest. Parts of the route are closed in winter, so check before you begin your journey.

Early morning reflection on Cameron Lake, Waterton Lakes National Park

2 ⟨✎⟩ ⟨M⟩ ⟨🍴⟩ ⟨🛍⟩

YOHO NATIONAL PARK

🛈 **Park Visitor Centre: Hwy 1, Field; www.pc.gc.ca**

Set against the stunning backdrop of the snow-draped Rocky Mountains, Yoho National Park is a mecca for outdoor enthusiasts. You can peacefully canoe on jewel-blue lakes; gaze up in awe at veils of pounding waterfalls; or discover remote alpine meadows sweetened with the scent of wildflowers.

Inspired by the beauty of the park's mountains, lakes, waterfalls, and distinctive rock formations, this area was named Yoho, for the Cree word meaning "awe and wonder." Highlights include the Natural Bridge – a rock bridge gradually eroded over the centuries by the icy Kicking Horse River rushing below it – and the Emerald Lake, named for the intense color of its waters.

If the weather allows, don't miss the Takakkaw Falls. Scramble right to the base and feel the mist and thunderous power as glacial meltwater plunges down 1,260 ft (384 m), making it the second tallest waterfall in Canada, after James Bruce Falls. On the way back, watch as trains snake through the Spiral Tunnels in the depths of the aptly named Cathedral Mountain.

Book a visit well in advance to see Lake O'Hara, southeast of Field. Surrounded by hanging valleys and jagged peaks dotted with hiking trails, this picturesque lake is an astounding shade of impossible blue, but it is only accessible by reservation.

←
A rock climber ascends the steep Takakkaw Falls route in Yoho National Park

BURGESS SHALE

This UNESCO World Heritage Site in Yoho National Park was set up to protect an extraordinary group of perfectly preserved marine creatures dating to the Cambrian period, over 500 million years ago. It is one of the few places on earth where both hard body parts and soft tissues have been fossilized, contributing much to the understanding of the origins of life on our planet. Access to the fossil beds is by guided hike.

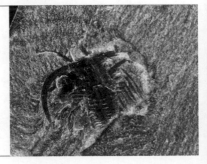

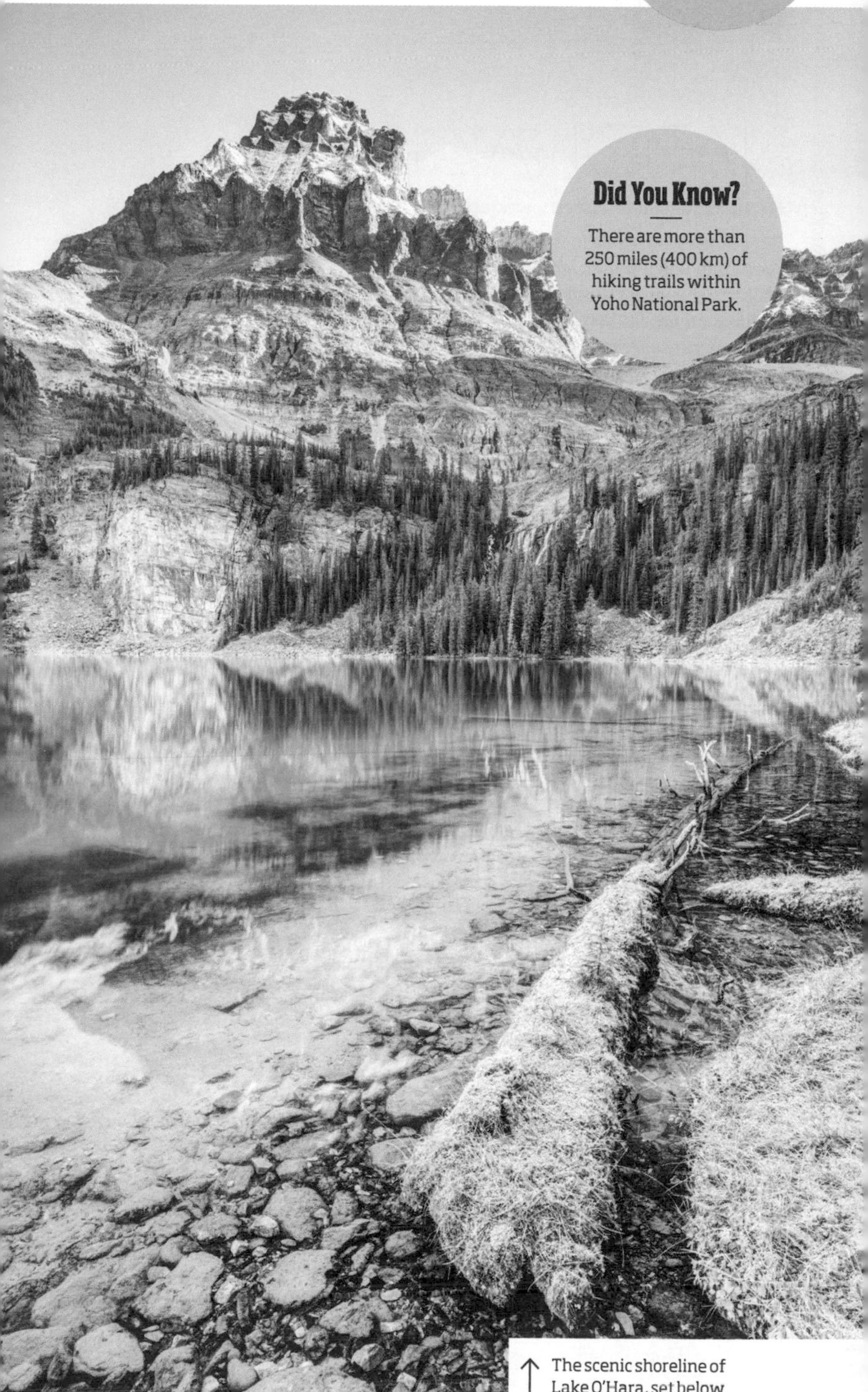

Did You Know?

There are more than 250 miles (400 km) of hiking trails within Yoho National Park.

↑ The scenic shoreline of Lake O'Hara, set below majestic Mount Huber

③ 🏕️ 🚵 🍴 🛍️

JASPER NATIONAL PARK

🛈 500 Connaught Dr, Jasper; www.jasper.travel.com

Big game roam freely in this larger-than-life park, including mountain lions, wolves, and bears. In addition to wildlife spotting, visitors can enjoy breathtaking alpine hikes, awesome paddling, and thrilling mountain-bike rides. The park is also the second-largest dark-sky preserve in the world, so when the sun goes down, look up.

Established in 1907, Jasper National Park is as staggeringly beautiful as anywhere in the Rockies. The most northerly of the four Rocky Mountain national parks, it is also the most rugged and the largest, covering a vast, remote area of 4,200 sq miles (10,878 sq km) of high peaks and valleys dotted with glacial lakes. Most of these areas can be reached only on foot, horseback, or by canoe. Expect to see more wildlife than in any of the other Rockies' parks, and keep in mind that most of the park services are closed between October and April. During this time, visitors who can brave the winter season have an opportunity to cross-country ski on stunning trails that skirt icy lakes. In addition, they can go ice fishing, snowshoeing, or on guided walking tours on frozen rivers. In the summertime, there are a range of day trips that are easily accessible from the park's main town of Jasper.

⛰️ GREAT VIEW
Jasper Tramway

Only a few miles out of Jasper town, this popular tramway takes visitors to a viewing platform near the top of Whistlers Mountain, with panoramic views across the park.

JASPER MOOSE

Moose are the largest member of the deer family and are easy to identify because of their long, gangly legs, palmed antlers, and rather large nose. They're all around the park, even in town, but Maligne Lake is one of the best spots to view them. Note that moose can be aggressive, particularly the males during the mating season from mid-September through November, so take care to observe from a safe distance.

Jasper

Jasper town was established in 1911 as a settlement for Grand Trunk Pacific Railroad workers, who were laying track along the Athabasca River Valley. As with Banff, the coming of the railroad and the development of park resorts went hand-in-hand, and the town expanded. Today, Jasper has a wide range of comfortable lodgings and great eateries.

Patricia and Pyramid Lakes

North of Jasper town, the attractive Patricia and Pyramid lakes nestle beneath the jagged peaks of the 9,065-ft (2,763-m) high Pyramid Mountain. Popular as a day-trip destination from the town, the lakes are noted for their excellent windsurfing and sailing conditions. Equipment rental is available from two lakeside lodges.

↑ Canoeist paddling across Lake Patricia in the fall, and a busy street in the center of Jasper town *(inset)*

Maligne Lake Drive

Scenic Maligne Lake Drive begins 3 miles (5 km) east of Jasper town and leads off Hwy 16, following the valley floor between the Maligne and the Queen Elizabeth ranges. The road travels past many magnificent sights, with viewpoints along the way offering panoramas of Maligne Valley. Among the route's most spectacular sights is the Maligne Canyon, reached by a short hiking trail that explains the special geological features behind the gorge's formation. The road ends at Maligne Lake, the largest natural lake in the Rockies. Boat cruises can take you to Spirit Island in the middle of the waters. There are also several scenic trails surrounding the lake, one of which leads to the Opal Hills and has amazing views of the area. Downstream from Maligne Lake is Medicine Lake, which is famed for its varying water levels, a phenomenon caused by a network of underground caves and channels.

↑ The picturesque snow-capped Mount Edith Cavell

Miette Hot Springs

Situated 38 miles (61 km) north of Jasper, along the attractive Miette Springs Road, these are the hottest springs in the Rockies, reaching temperatures as high as 129°F (54°C). The thermal baths are cooled to a more reasonable 104°F (40°C) for bathers.

Athabasca Falls

Located at the junction of highways 93 and 93A, where the Athabasca River plunges 75 ft (23 m) to the river bed below, these are among the most dramatic waterfalls in the park. Despite being a short drop compared with other falls in the Rockies, the force of the

Did You Know?

The ice in some parts of the Athabasca Glacier is as thick as the Eiffel Tower is high.

Athabasca River being pushed through a very narrow, quartz-rich gorge transforms these waters into a powerful, foaming torrent.

Mount Edith Cavell

Named after a WWI heroine, this mountain is just a short drive south of Jasper town. The scenic road that climbs it is paved but has some rough sections and narrow switchbacks. The road ends at Cavell Lake by the north face of the mountain. From here, a guided trail leads to a small lake beneath the Angel Glacier, while a three-hour walk across the flower-strewn Cavell meadows offers dramatic views of the glacier's icy tongue.

Columbia Icefield

The Columbia Icefield straddles both Banff and Jasper national parks and forms the largest area of ice south of Alaska. The ice field, which covers 125 sq miles (325 sq km), was created during the last Ice Age, though the glaciers have retreated over the last few hundred years – during the early years of the 20th century ice covered the area where the Icefields Parkway now passes. Tours of the Athabasca Glacier, in four-wheel drive Ice Explorers, are available from the center.

The force of the Athabasca River being pushed through a very narrow, quartz-rich gorge transforms these waters into a powerful, foaming torrent.

STAY

Alpine Village

There's a range of cabins facing the Athabasca River at this just-out-of-town resort, with elk often grazing the grass on the pretty, landscaped grounds.

Hwy 93A N, Jasper National Park Oct-Apr alpinevillagejasper.com

$$$

Crimson Jasper

A good value modern hotel close to the train station and within walking distance of downtown. The rooms have mini fridges and microwaves, and there's an indoor pool and fitness room.

200 Connaught Dr, Jasper mpljasper.com

$$$

↑ Northern lights seen from Athabasca Glacier on the Columbia Icefield

EXPERIENCE MORE

4 🗺️ 🍴 ☕ 🛍️

Waterton Lakes National Park

ℹ️ **Park Info Centre (mid-May–Oct); www. watertonpark.com**

Scenery as amazing as any of that found in the Rockies' other national parks typifies the less-known Waterton Lakes National Park. Located in the southwest corner of Alberta along the US border, the park is an International Peace Park and manages a shared ecosystem with Glacier National Park in the US.

🔍 HIDDEN GEM
Crypt Lake Trail

Seek out the 11-mile (17-km) Crypt Lake Trail in Waterton Lakes National Park. You'll hike through lush forest, passing steep cliffs and several waterfalls, before finally reaching a pristine turquoise lake.

↑ Bighorn sheep ram, a resident of Waterton Lakes National Park

The park owes its unique beauty to the geological phenomenon of the Lewis Overthrust, which was forged over a billion years ago (before the formation of the Rockies), when ancient rock was pushed over newer deposits. Thus, the peaks of the mountains rise sharply out of the flat prairies.

Waterton's mix of lowland and alpine habitats means it has the widest variety of wild-life of any of Canada's parks, from bears to bighorn sheep, and from waterfowl to nesting species such as sapsuckers.

5 🗺️

Glacier National Park

ℹ️ **301 Victoria Road W, Revelstoke; (250) 837 7500**

Not to be confused with the park of the same name in the US, Glacier National Park covers 520 sq miles (1,350 sq km) of wilderness in the Selkirk Range of the Columbia Mountains. It was established in 1886, and the park's growth was linked to that of the railroad, which was routed through Rogers Pass in 1885. Today, many of the park's simplest walking trails follow abandoned rail-road lines. Other trails offer visitors stunning views of the park's 150 glaciers, including the vast Illecillewaet Glacier.

The park is known for its very wet weather in summer and almost daily snowfalls in winter, when as much as 75 ft (23 m) of snow may fall in one season. The threat of avalanche is serious here; visitors should stop at the Rogers Pass Center for up-to-date information. The Rogers Pass line was

---

Monument marking the summit of Rogers Pass in Glacier National Park ↓

→ Visitors enjoying the popular swimming pool at Radium Hot Springs

abandoned by the Canadian Pacific Railway due to avalanches, and a tunnel was built underneath it instead. The Trans-Canada Highway (Hwy 1) follows the route of the pass as it bisects the park, en route to the lovely town of Revelstoke *(p127)*.

⑥ Kananaskis Country

🚌 Canmore ℹ️ 907 7th Ave, Canmore; www.kananaskis. com

Kananaskis Country is a verdant park system in the Rocky Mountain foothills, with mountain peaks, lakes, rivers, and alpine meadows. Located southwest of Calgary on the boundary of Banff National Park, this 1,500 sq miles (4,000 sq km) of wilderness is popular for hiking and viewing wildlife such as eagles, wolves, and bears. The town of Canmore serves as the center of this large recreational area, offering plenty of places to stay, as well as information on outdoor activities.

⑦
Kootenay National Park

ℹ️ Kootenay National Park Visitor Center, 7556 Main St E, Radium Hot Springs; (mid-May-Sep); (250) 347 9505

Kootenay National Park covers 543 sq miles (1,406 sq km) and is known for its ecology, climate, and diversity of landscape. The 58-mile (94-km) Kootenay Parkway (Hwy 93S) bisects the park from north to south. It winds through the narrow gorge of Sinclair Canyon, past the renowned Radium Hot Springs pools, along the deep red cliffs of the Redwall Fault, and up over the Sinclair Pass. The road continues into the Kootenay River Valley, past Hector Gorge, and into the Vermilion Valley. Short nature trails introduce you to magical Paint Pots, iron-rich mineral springs with rust-colored clay banks. Visitors will see the Marble Canyon, whose 115-ft (35-m) deep dolomite walls are carved by the glacial waters of Tokumm Creek. The Fireweed Trail at Vermilion Pass take in vibrant regenerating forests growing along the Continental Divide, in the wake of old forest fires.

⑧ Radium Hot Springs

ℹ️ Visitor Center, 7556 Main St E; www.radiumhot springs.com

This small town is famous for its mineral springs and is a good base for exploring the nearby Kootenay National Park. In the summer, flower-filled pots decorate the storefronts of the coffee shops and pubs along the main street, and the town has more motel rooms than residents.

Many of the 1.2 million annual visitors come to bathe in the healing waters of the springs. There are two pools: a hot soaking pool and a cooler swimming pool. Locker rooms, swimsuits, and towels can all be rented, and massages are available.

Visitors can explore the nearby Columbia Valley Wetlands too. Fed by glacial waters from the Purcell and Rocky mountains, the Columbia River meanders through these marsh lands, which provide an important habitat for over 250 migratory waterfowl such as Canada geese and tundra swans.

Did You Know?

Local legend tells of a Bigfoot, or Sasquatch, living in the Rockies. Look out for giant "footprints."

←

A skier tackling perfect powder at the Fernie Alpine Resort

was established in 1864, when gold was discovered at Wild Horse River. Thousands of prospectors and entrepreneurs arrived by the Dewdney Trail, which linked Hope to the gold fields. The town was named after the North West Mounted Police Superintendent Samuel Steele, who arrived in 1887 to restore peace between warring groups of Ktunaxa peoples and European settlers. The town underwent a brief boom with the discovery of lead and silver, but Fort Steele had become a ghost town by the early 1900s, when the mainline railroad was rerouted through Cranbrook instead.

Today, there are more than 60 reconstructed or restored buildings, staffed by guides in period costume, including the general store and Mountie officers' quarters, with personal items such as family photographs, swords, and uniforms. Demonstrations of traditional crafts such as quilt- and ice cream-making are also held

9 Fernie

🚌 ℹ️ 102 Commerce Rd; www.tourismfernie.com

Fernie is an attractive town set amid a circle of pointed peaks on the British Columbia side of Crowsnest Pass. Burned to the ground by a fire in 1904 and again in 1908, the town has since been handsomely reconstructed from brick and stone. Fernie is known for its winter sports, and boasts the best powder snow in the Rockies, with its skiing season running from November to April. The huge nearby Fernie Alpine Resort can take over 13,000 skiers and riders up the mountain every hour. During the summer, the Mount Fernie Provincial Park offers a broad range of magnificent hiking trails , while boat trips and fishing are popular on the many nearby lakes and rivers.

Helicopter trips take visitors close to the mountains to see the formations and granite cliffs particular to this region.

TOP 3 HELI-SKIING COMPANIES

CMH Heli-Skiing, Banff
🅦 cmhheli.com
Guaranteed powder thrills and luxury lodges.

Eagle Pass Heli-Skiing, Revelstoke
🅦 eaglepassheliskiing.com
Explore 530 sq miles (1,372 sq km) of slopes.

Stellar Heli-Skiing, Kaslo
🅦 stellarheliskiing.com
An unbeatable guest-to-guide ratio.

10 🎿🍴🖥️🛍️ Fort Steele Heritage Town

📍 9851 Hwy 95 🕐 Daily
🅦 fortsteele.ca

This living museum is a re-creation of a 19th-century pioneering supply town that

→

Canoeists setting off on their journey around the Bowron Lake Provincial Park circuit

> **Fernie is known for its winter sports, and boasts the best powder snow in the Rockies, with its skiing season running from November to April.**

here. Tours at the nearby Wild Horse River Historic Site include the chance to pan for gold.

---

⑪
Crowsnest Pass

🅭 **Frank Slide Interpretive Centre; www.frankslide.ca**

Crowsnest Pass is located in Alberta 1 mile (1.5 km) off Hwy 3, close to the border with BC. Like most Rocky Mountain passes, it is enclosed by snowcapped mountains. In the early 1900s, this area was dominated by the coal-mining industry and was the site of Canada's worst mine disaster. In 1903, a rockslide on Turtle Mountain fell into the valley below, hitting the town of Frank and killing 70 people. The Frank Slide Interpretive Centre offers two award-winning audio-visual presentations about this tragic event, and a marked

trail through the valley leads hikers to the debris left by the disaster. Visitors can learn more about the mining communities at the Bellevue Mine – which offers tours through its historic mining tunnels – and at Leitch Collieries, a fascinating early mining complex.

---

⑫
Wells Gray Provincial Park

🅿🚂 **Clearwater** 🅘 **416 Eden Rd; (250) 674 3334** Ⓦ **wellsgray.ca**

One of the most beautiful wildernesses in BC, this park offers wonders comparable to the Rockies in the east. The park was opened in 1939 and is distinguished by thundering waterfalls, alpine meadows, and glacier-topped peaks. The Canadian National Railroad and Hwy 5 follow the Thompson River along the park's western

edge, offering stunning views. From the Clearwater Valley Road there are several trails, ranging from easy walks to arduous overnight hikes in remote country. A selection of small trails lead to the spectacular sight of Dawson Falls.

---

⑬
Bowron Lake Provincial Park

🅲 **(250) 320 9305** 🅡 🚌 **Quesnel** 🕐 **May-Sep**

Bowron Lake Provincial Park is located about 76 miles (120 km) east of Quesnel on Highway 26 in the Cariboo Mountains. The park is famed for having a 70-mile (112-km) rectangular waterway composed of nine lakes, three rivers, streams, small lakes, and many portages (trails linking the waterways). The waterway is highly popular as a canoe circuit, and a week-long, ticketed trip is offered regularly, but it is limited to 50 canoeists at a time (some experience is recommended), and must be booked ahead, either by phone or online. The trip is great for wildlife encounters, with frequent sightings of moose and beaver. In late summer, bears come to feed on the spawning sockeye salmon in the Bowron River.

Mule deer bucks in Grasslands National Park, Saskatchewan

THE PRAIRIES

The central Canadian provinces of Alberta, Saskatchewan, and Manitoba are collectively known as the Prairies, and cover a vast region of boreal forest and fertile grasslands. For thousands of years the First Nations thrived here, depending on the herds of bison that roamed the land. They hunted the animals not only for food, but also to produce clothing, shelter, and ceremonial objects. By the end of the 19th century, however, bison were hunted almost to extinction, the likely culprits being the horses and rifles that accompanied the incoming Europeans. These same newcomers built up farming communities on the fertile lands, some taking Aboriginal wives and forming a new cultural grouping, the Métis. By the 20th century, the area's economy had come to rely not only on grain but also on other natural resources such as gas and oil. Today, the Prairies are known for their endless flat fields of golden wheat, punctuated by a series of dynamic towns and cities.

THE PRAIRIES

0 kilometers 200
0 miles 200
N

NORTHWEST
TERRITORIES

Aylmer Lake

Yellowknife   Reliance

Fort Providence

Great Slave Lake

NORTHWEST TERRITORIES
AND NUNAVUT
p360

Hay River

Indian Cabins   Fort Smith

Fort Nelson

Bistcho Lake

Rainbow Lake

High Level   Fort Vermilion

WOOD BUFFALO
NATIONAL PARK **11**

Lake Athabasca   Stony Rapids

Fort Chipewyan

Lake Claire

BRITISH
COLUMBIA

BRITISH
COLUMBIA
INTERIOR
p110

Manning   *Birch Mountains*

Cree Lake

Rycroft   Peace River

Fort MacKay

GRANDE PRAIRIE **9**   Valleyview   Slave Lake   Fort McMurray   La Loche

ALBERTA

Peter Pond Lake   Buffalo Narrows

Wallace Mountain 4,130 ft (1,259 m)   Hondo   Calling Lake   Conklin   Beauval   La Ronge

Fox Creek   Westlock   *Nipin*

McBride   Whitecourt   Boyle

SASKATCHEWAN

Rocky Mountains   Bonnyville   Pierceland **3** **2**

Jasper   EDMONTON **10** **8**   ELK ISLAND
NATIONAL PARK   PRINCE
ALBERT
NATIONAL PARK

Edmonton International Airport   Leduc   **15** VEGREVILLE   Prince Albert

CANADIAN
ROCKIES
p128   Wetaskiwin   Viking

Bashaw   NORTH BATTLEFORD
AND BATTLEFORD **17**   DUCK
LAKE **19**

Kamloops   Revelstoke   RED DEER **7**   BATOCHE NATIONAL HISTORIC SITE **20**

Banff   Saskatoon International Airport **21**

Kelowna   Calgary International Airport   ROYAL TYRRELL
MUSEUM **2**   SASKATOON

1 CALGARY   Rosetown   Elrose   **11**

Davidson

Castlegar   Brooks   DINOSAUR
PROVINCIAL PARK **14**   **4**

MOOSE JAW

LETHBRIDGE   **12** MEDICINE HAT   Swift Current   **1** **23**

FORT MACLEOD **5** **6**   **13** MAPLE CREEK

Okanogan   CYPRESS HILLS
INTERPROVINCIAL PARK **16**   Eastend

Coolin   GRASSLANDS **18**
NATIONAL PARK

UNITED STATES

THE PRAIRIES

Must Sees
1. Calgary
2. Royal Tyrrell Museum
3. Prince Albert National Park
4. Winnipeg

Experience More
5. Fort Macleod
6. Lethbridge
7. Red Deer
8. Elk Island National Park
9. Grande Prairie
10. Edmonton
11. Wood Buffalo National Park
12. Medicine Hat
13. Maple Creek
14. Dinosaur Provincial Park
15. Vegreville
16. Cypress Hills Interprovincial Park
17. North Battleford and Battleford
18. Grasslands National Park
19. Duck Lake
20. Batoche National Historic Site
21. Saskatoon
22. Regina
23. Moose Jaw
24. Yorkton
25. Fort Qu'Appelle
26. The Pas
27. Riding Mountain National Park
28. Gimli
29. Flin Flon
30. Portage la Prairie
31. Dauphin
32. Steinbach
33. Lake Winnipeg
34. Churchill
35. Selkirk

Peace Bridge over the Bow River in Calgary, lit up at dusk ↑

❶
CALGARY

✈ 11 miles (17 km) NE of city 🚌 Greyhound Bus Station, 850 16th St SW ℹ Tourism Calgary 200, 120, 101 9th Ave SW; www.visitcalgary.com

Calgary is a sophisticated place, a culinary hub with skyscrapers, galleries, and theaters, but it is also a base camp to adventure. The city's western atmosphere, still redolent at times of the frontier, is somewhat at odds with its ultra-modern skyline, which has continued to grow since the oil boom of the 1960s.

① 🏷️ 🍴 🛍️
Calgary Tower

🏠 101 9th Ave SW ☎ (403) 266 7171 🕐 9am-9pm daily 🌐 calgarytower.com

The Calgary Tower is one of the city's tallest structures and was once the tallest building of its type in North America. Two elevators hurtle to the top in 62 seconds, and two emergency staircases are composed of 802 steps apiece. From street level to the top, Calgary Tower measures 627 ft (191 m). At the top there is a revolving restaurant, Sky 360, and a glass-floored observation deck, both of which offer incredible panoramic views across to the Rockies.

② 🏷️ Ⓜ️ 🖥️
National Music Centre

🏠 Studio Bell, 9th Ave SE at 4th St SE 🕐 10am-5pm Wed-Sun 🌐 nmc.ca

The NMC (National Music Centre), opened in 2016, is housed in an award-winning building inspired by the Canadian landscape and instrument designs. As the national home for music in Canada, NMC is known for its collection of over 2,000 rare instruments, artefacts, sound equipments and Canadian music memorabilia, including the Rolling Stones Mobile Studio and one of Elton John's pianos. It also hosts a variety of live music events.

③ 🍴 🖥️ 🛍️
Eau Claire Market

🏠 200 Barclay Parade SW ☎ (403) 264 6450 🕐 8am-4:30pm Mon-Fri

Housed in a brightly colored warehouse, this mall is made up of specialty stores selling a fine variety of gourmet foods, contemporary arts and crafts. There are also cinemas, cafés, and restaurants, and walkways connecting to a footbridge that leads to Prince's Island Park.

④
Calgary Chinese Cultural Centre

🏠 197 1st St SW 🕐 9am-9pm daily 🌐 cultural centre.ca

Located in downtown Calgary, the Chinese Cultural Centre was completed in 1992. It is modeled on the 1420 Temple of Heaven in Beijing, which was used exclusively by emperors. The center was built by artisans from China using traditional skills. The Dr. Henry Fok Cultural Hall is the highlight of the building with its 70-ft- (21-m-) high ceiling and an impressive dome adorned with dragons and phoenixes. Each of the dome's four supporting columns is decorated with lavish gold designs, which represent the four seasons.

___

⑤
Prince's Island Park

This picturesque park lies on a tiny island in the Bow River, and is connected to the city via several bridges, including a pedestrian bridge at the end of 4th Street SW. There are many outdoor festivals and events held here during the hot summer months.

Did You Know?

Prince's Island was created by lumbermen, who dug the lagoon to get logs closer to the Calgary sawmill.

⑥ 🍴 🖵
Arts Commons

🏠 205 8th Ave SE 🕐 Times vary, check website
🌐 artscommons.ca

Opened in 1985, this large complex houses four theaters and a concert hall, as well as five rental boardrooms. Located in the heart of the city on Olympic Plaza, the center hosts a diverse range of events, such as jazz and blues concerts, rodeos, festivals, and live theater.

___

⑦ 🎨 🎭 🏛
Glenbow Museum

🏠 130 9th Ave SE 🕐 Times vary, check website
🌐 glenbow.org

In the heart of downtown Calgary, the Glenbow Museum is one of western Canada's largest museums. It houses an excellent collection of Canadian and contemporary art, as well as a wide range of objects that

EAT

River Cafe
This relaxed upscale dining spot is best enjoyed with brunch out on the patio with its views of the river. The menu includes fresh seafood and superior comfort food.

🏠 25 Prince's Island Park
🌐 river-cafe.com

💲💲💲

chronicle the history of the Canadian West through First Nations and pioneer artifacts. An extensive military collection includes medieval armor and Samurai swords. Glenbow's gallery, Niitsitapiisini, traces the story of the Blackfoot people of the northwestern plains of Alberta and Montana.

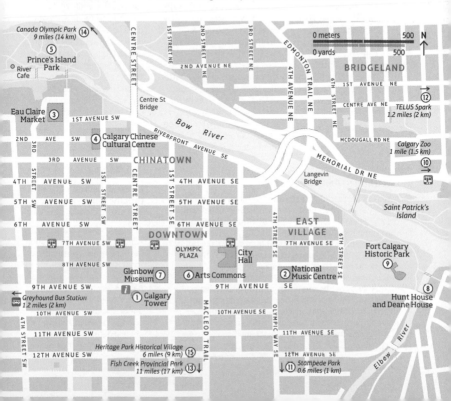

⑧
Hunt House and Deane House

📍 806 9th Ave SE 📞 (403) 269 7747; restaurant: (403) 264 0595 🕐 Deane House: daily

The Hunt House, a small, restored log house, is one of the few buildings left from the original settlement of Calgary in the early 1880s.

Nearby Deane House, also restored, was built for the Superintendent of Fort Calgary, Captain Richard Burton Deane, in 1906. Today, the house is a restaurant, where visitors can enjoy a meal in a delightful period setting.

⑨
Fort Calgary Historic Park

📍 750 9th Ave SE 🕐 Daily 🌐 fortcalgary.com

Fort Calgary was built by the North West Mounted Police in 1875 at the confluence of the Bow and Elbow rivers. The Grand Trunk Pacific Railway arrived in 1883, and the tiny fort town grew to over 400 residents in a year. In 1914, the land was bought by the Grand Trunk Pacific Railway, and the fort was leveled. Pieces of it were discovered during an archeological dig in 1970, and the well-restored site was opened to the public in 1978.

> **CALGARY STAMPEDE**
> An exuberant ten-day festival of all things western, the Calgary Stampede is held every July in Stampede Park. Originally established as an agricultural fair in 1886, the Stampede of 1912 attracted 14,000 people. In the 1920s, one of its still-popular highlights, the risky but exciting covered wagon races, became part of the show.
> Today's festival has an array of spectacular entertainments that dramatize scenes from western history. They can be seen both on site and in Calgary itself. The fair starts with a dazzling parade through the city, and then features the world's largest outdoor rodeo. Other attractions abound, from stage shows and concerts to barbecues and markets.

The reconstructed fort offers an Interpretive Centre, which tells of Calgary's colorful past through exhibits such as a re-created quartermaster's store and carpenter's workshop. There are also delightful walks along the river.

---

⑩
Calgary Zoo

📍 210 St. George's Drive NE & 1300 Zoo Rd NE 🕐 9am–6pm daily (last adm: 5pm) 🌐 calgaryzoo.com

Calgary Zoo prides itself on the presentation of its animals, which can be seen in their appropriate habitats. Canadian Wilds is a series of environments that highlights the diversity of the Canadian landscape and its wildlife, including black bears, elk, golden eagles, snowy owls, and river otters. There are aspen woodlands where it is possible to see the endangered woodland caribou, and visitors can wander the boreal forest environment, maybe spotting the rare whooping crane. Other areas of the zoo are dedicated to Africa and Eurasia, while the Dorothy Harvie Gardens have a vast conservatory showcasing plants and butterflies from around the world.

Also here is the Prehistoric Park, which offers a reconstructed Mesozoic landscape, where visitors can picnic among life-size dinosaurs.

⑪
Stampede Park

📍 1410 Olympic Way SE 🕐 Daily 🌐 calgarystampede.com

Famous as the site of the Calgary Stampede, the park has a horse racetrack, as well as two ice-hockey stadiums, one of which is housed inside the striking Saddledome, named for its saddle-shaped roof. Trade shows, such as antiques and home improvements, and concerts are also held here.

---

⑫
TELUS Spark

📍 220 St. George's Drive NE 🕐 Daily; times vary, check website 🌐 sparkscience.ca

The TELUS Spark is a popular hands-on science center, offering a memorable experience for kids and adults alike. Exhibits include Being Human, Earth & Sky, and the Creative Kids Museum. There is also an interactive outdoor park, an IMAX® theater, and live science demonstrations in the Presentation Theatre.

A tree-lined path in the
Fish Creek Provincial
Park in fall

Did You Know?

Fish Creek Provincial Park's forest is a mix of white spruce, aspen, and balsam poplar.

⑬
Fish Creek Provincial Park

⌂ Bow Bottom Trail SE
🕒 Daily 🌐 albertaparks.ca

Established in 1975, this park covers 5 sq miles (13 sq km) of forest along the Fish Creek valley. Park guides hold slide shows on the region's ecology and history, detailing the park's many archeological sites.

In winter, many of the hiking trails become cross-country ski trails. The Canada goose, the great blue heron, and the bald eagle are among the birds that visit the park during the year.

⑭
Canada Olympic Park

⌂ 88 Canada Olympic Rd SW
📞 (403) 247 5452 🕒 Daily

WinSport's Canada Olympic Park was the site of the 1988 XV Olympic Winter Games.

Visitors can enjoy the facilities all year round, including riding on the bobsleds and luge tracks, mountain biking, and zip-lining. The views toward the Rockies and over Calgary from the 295-ft- (90-m-) high Olympic Ski Jump Tower are stunning. The Park is home to Canada's Sports Hall of Fame, with 12 interactive galleries and some 100,000 artifacts.

⑮
Heritage Park Historical Village

⌂ 1900 Heritage Drive SW
🕒 Village: May–Oct; museum and café: all year
🌐 heritagepark.ca

Heritage Park Historical Village sits on the shore of Glenmore Reservoir and contains more than 70 historic buildings, from outhouses to a two-story hotel, that have been brought here from sites all over western Canada. The buildings have been organized into time periods, which range from an 1880s fur-trading post to the shops and homes of a small town between 1900 and 1914. Most of the 45,000 artifacts that furnish and decorate the village have been donated by residents of Calgary and the surrounding towns, and vary from teacups to steam trains.

Among the most thrilling of the exhibits are three original, operating steam locomotives and a working 19th-century amusement park, which has several rides. Cruise around the Glenmore Reservoir on a replica paddle boat, ride on an electric streetcar to the park's front gates and walk down an urban street from the 1930s. The sense of stepping back in time at the village is enhanced by the clip-clopping of horse-drawn carriages, and by the smells and sounds of shops such as the working bakery and the blacksmith's – all staffed by costumed guides.

> The sense of stepping back in time at the village is enhanced by the clip-clopping of horse-drawn carriages.

2 🎿 🎨 🖥 🛍

ROYAL TYRRELL MUSEUM

📍 1500 N Dinosaur Trail, 4 miles (6 km) NW of Drumheller 🕐 May-Aug: 9am-9pm daily; Sep: 10am-5pm daily; Oct-Apr: 10am-5pm Tue-Sun
🌐 tyrrellmuseum.com

Get up close to the skeletons of dinosaurs that stalked the Alberta Badlands 75 million years ago, and learn about billions of years of life on earth through hands-on displays that the whole family will enjoy.

Ideally situated in the middle of a fossil-rich deposit in the Horsethief Canyon just northwest of the town of Drumheller, the outstanding and one-of-a-kind Royal Tyrrell Museum was opened in 1985. The museum is named after Joseph Burr Tyrrell, a Canadian geologist, who in 1884 accidentally discovered the first significant dinosaur fossil in the Red Deer Valley (p158).

The museum contains more than 160,000 fossils, including the world's largest collection of complete dinosaur skeletons, and numerous fascinating specimens dating from the Ice Age and the start of the Cenozoic Era.

As well as tracing billions of years of natural history through exhibits and inspiring interactive activities, the museum is one of the world's leading palaeontological research centers – a window into the Preparation Lab allows visitors to watch technicians carefully remove fossils from the surrounding rock, preparing them for research and display.

Did You Know?

Tyrrell's first find was named Albertosaurus sarcophagus ("flesh-eating lizard from Alberta").

INTERACTIVE PROGRAMS

The museum offers various programs for kids and adults out in Alberta's Badlands, where it all began. Activities include guided hikes, searching for dinosaur fossils, learning how to excavate a site using professional tools and techniques, and even extended camps. Within the museum itself, you can cast fossils, get involved in indoor digs, see how skeletons are assembled, and attend talks from palaeontologists.

Must See

Museum Highlights

Dinosaur Hall

▽ The main highlight of the museum, this hall has a T-rex hovering over a display of some 40 other complete dinosaur skeletons, including specimens of Stegosaurus and Triceratops.

Cretaceous Alberta Garden

See Alberta as it was 69 million years ago, lush and semi-tropical, and come face to face with a pack of Albertosaurus dinosaurs. Discover what else dared to live in the same neighborhood as these giants, including the Didelphodon, hiding among the ferns.

Mammal Hall

▽ Strange creatures roamed the lands during the beginning of the Cenozoic Era, our current geological time, marking the moment when mammals, initially small, appeared alongside the dinosaurs.

Ice Age Hall

Look up at dramatic displays of woolly mammoth skeletons, sabre-toothed cats, and bison - all of which adapted to a colder climate when their habitat in the Northern Hemisphere was covered in ice - and learn what happened when man appeared in their world.

DINOSAURS IN ALBERTA

It is easier to imagine gunslingers and coyotes in the desertlike badlands of Alberta than it is to envisage the dinosaurs who once lived in this region. Over 75 million years ago the area was a tropical swamp (similar to the Florida Everglades) and the favored habitat of these huge reptiles, which dominated the Earth for some 160 million years. Dramatic changes in the region's climate transformed the area from humid swamp to dry desert, helping preserve an incredible number of dinosaur remains.

FIRST DISCOVERY

Joseph Burr Tyrrell, a 26-year old geologist and mining consultant, found the remains of Canada's first-known meat-eating dinosaur in the Red Deer River Valley of Alberta, in 1884. Tyrrell stumbled across the skull of the 71.5 million year-old dinosaur a few miles from Drumheller while searching for coal deposits. The skull was identified as a new species over a decade later and named Albertosaurus in 1905, honouring the province of Alberta that was newly formed that same year. The Royal Tyrell Museum was subsequently named for Tyrell.

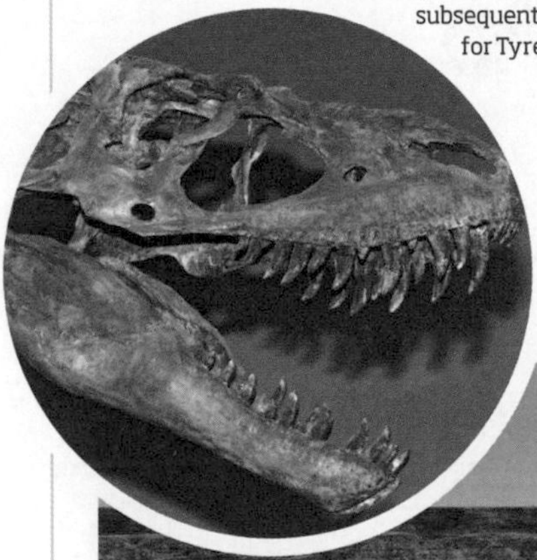

DINOSAURS ACROSS CANADA

Alberta isn't the only province with some of the world's best dinosaur fossil deposits. In 1991, palaeontologists in Saskatchewan found an almost complete skeleton of one of the largest T-rex dinosaurs ever found. In Manitoba, a 43-ft (13-m) Mosasaur skeleton was found in 1974, and in 1984, dinosaur fossils dating back some 200 million years were discovered in the Bay of Fundy.

← Skull of the Albertosaurus now in the Royal Tyrell Museum

↑ Fossils being excavated in Dinosaur Provincial Park

THE GREAT DINOSAUR RUSH

In 1888, Thomas C. Weston, who worked for the Geological Survey of Canada, just as Tyrrell did, found another skull belonging to the Albertosaurus in an area that is now part of the Dinosaur Provincial Park *(p168)*. Subsequently, interest in hunting for dinosaur fossils began to spark, as palaeontologists were eager to claim the finest specimens for their museums. The period from 1910 to 1917 became known as the Great Dinosaur Rush and more than 300 display-worthy dinosaur skeletons of various species were discovered just in Alberta alone during that time. Since then, excavation work and discoveries have continued in the province, with new species of dinosaurs being uncovered even today.

TOP
4 | **DINOSAUR DISCOVERIES**

Albertosaurus Sarcophagus
A close relative of the T-rex, this two-ton, 36-ft (11- m) long dinosaur excelled in speed and agility and may have hunted its prey in packs.

Edmontosaurus
First discovered in 1892 in the Horseshoe Canyon Formation, this duck-billed dinosaur lived about 70 million years ago. It was a herbivore and could move on both two and four legs.

Euoplocephalus
This armoured herbivore was covered in rows of bony plates and high-ridged oval scutes, and it had a heavy club-like tail, all of which helped it defend itself from larger predators.

Parasaurolophus
Known for its large, elaborate cranial crest, the remains of this herbivorous dinosaur were found along the Red Deer River in 1920.

↑ The vast, dry, badlands landscape of Dinosaur Provincial Park

③ 🍴 🛍️

PRINCE ALBERT NATIONAL PARK

🛈 969 Lakeview Dr, Waskesiu; www.pc.gc.ca

Great prairie grasslands give way to a vast boreal forest – home to wandering caribou, moose, and timber wolves – in this jewel of a park. The gently rolling hills and hidden meadows are interspersed by lakes, big and small, making this an ideal destination for a hikers and kayakers.

Established in 1927, Prince Albert National Park covers 1,500 sq miles (3,875 sq km) of wilderness and is one of Canada's most popular parks. The village of Waskesiu is the best place from which to begin exploring the park, offering a variety of year-round accommodation and dining options, and plenty of lakefront beaches and activities. The Mud Creek Trail, one of a dozen shorter hikes, is a 1-mile (1.5-km) loop that skirts the Waskesiu Lake, then follows Mud Creek, where in spring the spawning fish attract black bears. Another highlight is the Lavallee Lake, where the country's second-largest white pelican colony can be seen. For an iconic Canadian experience, Kingsmere and Waskesiu lakes are the best for multi-day canoeing and portaging trips (carrying the canoe overland), with four peaceful campgrounds to choose from along the way.

> 💬 INSIDER TIP
> **Park Activities**
>
> Canoes and kayaks can be rented at the Waskesiu Marina, Heart Lakes Marina, and the Narrows Marina. For a Wild West feel, the Sturgeon River Ranch can take you horseback riding among the free-ranging bison.

Bog in the wild prairie grasslands of Prince Albert National Park ↑

1 Keen hikers should follow the Grey Owl trail, a 12-mile (20-km) route that leads to Beaver Lodge, a log cabin where renowned British conservationist Grey Owl lived alongside beavers from 1931 to 1938 and wrote about the need to protect the wilderness.

2 Hanging Heart Lake, which forms a waterway that leads to Lake Crean, is one of the most popular canoe and kayak trips in the park.

3 Elk are best spotted in aspen on the Elk Trail to the south of the park.

GREY OWL

Legendary British conservationist Grey Owl was born Archibald Stansfeld Belaney. After emigrating to Canada after World War I, Belaney faked a First Nations identity. Inspired by his Mohawk wife, Anahareo, he wrote of wilderness conservation and ran a beaver protection program, becoming the park's first naturalist.

④

WINNIPEG

✈ 6 miles (10 km) NW of city 🚉 Cnr Main St & Broadway
🚌 Greyhound Bus Terminal, 2015 Wellington Ave
ℹ Suite 810, One Lombard Place; www.tourism
winnipeg.com

Winnipeg is a cosmopolitan city located at the geographic heart of Canada. Over half of Manitoba's population lives here, mostly in suburbs that reflect the city's broad mix of cultures. Winnipeg's position, at the confluence of the Red and Assiniboine rivers, made it an important trading center for First Nations people for around 6,000 years. From the 1600s, Europeans settled here to trade fur. During the 1880s, grain became the principal industry of the west, aided by a railroad network routed through Winnipeg. Today, this attractive city makes for an enjoyable and cultural stay.

① 🏛

St. Boniface

ℹ Riel Tourism, 219 Provencher Blvd; www.tourismeriel.com

Canada's second-largest French-speaking community outside of Quebec lives in the historic district of St. Boniface. This quiet suburb faces The Forks across the Red River and was founded by priests in 1818 to care for the Métis and the French living here. In 1844 the Grey Nuns built a convent that now houses the St. Boniface Museum. Priests built the Basilica of St. Boniface in 1818. Although the building was destroyed by fire in 1968, its elegant white facade is one of the city's best-loved landmarks. A video at the Tourism Centre documents the area's history, including Métis leader Louis Riel, who was buried here after his execution in 1885 *(p68)*.

② 🏛 🛍

Children's Museum

🏠 45 Forks Market Rd
🕐 Daily 🅦 childrens
museum.com

Located within The Forks complex, this popular museum provides a series of enticing hands-on exhibits aimed at children from the ages of 3 to 11. Kids can get creative in the Pop m'Art exhibit, or experiment with water in the Splash Lab. In the Engine

> **EXPLORING WINNIPEG**
>
> Most of Winnipeg's sights are within easy walking distance of the downtown area. The Manitoba Museum and Winnipeg Grain Exchange lie east of the Exchange District. At the junction of the Red and Assiniboine rivers is The Forks, a family entertainment center devoted to the city's history. At the junction of Portage and Main streets lie the city's financial and shopping districts with their banks and malls.

↑ Winnipeg's skyline illuminated at night, as seen across the Red River

③ 🍴 💻 🛍️

The Forks National Historic Site

🅰 Forks Market Rd ⏱ Daily 🌐 theforks.com

The historic riverside parkland of The Forks stretches along the west shore of the Red River, from the Esplanade Riel Pedestrian Bridge to the confluence with the Assiniboine River. The riverside walkway offers fine views of the city center and St. Boniface Basilica, and you can access the French Quarter from here via the pedestrian bridge. For more great views, head to the observation tower at The Forks Market and Johnston Terminal. This once bustling railroad terminus is now filled with shoppers searching out crafts, folk art, and specialty food. Kids will enjoy the Variety Heritage Adventure Park, a playground with a pretend fort, located just north of the Children's Museum.

④ 🎡 🎨 🍴 🛍️

Canadian Museum for Human Rights

🅰 85 Israel Asper Way ⏱ 10am–5pm Tue–Sun (to 9pm Wed) 🌐 human rights.ca

In a daring glass and limestone structure designed by Antoine Predock, the Canadian Museum for Human Rights sits at the forks of the Red and Assiniboine rivers, which has been a historic meeting place for over 6,000 years. The museum, which opened in 2014 and is the first national Canadian museum outside Ottawa, dominates the Winnipeg skyline. Its goal is to increase awareness of human rights in Canada and around the world through interactive exhibitions, learning programs, and daily tours. It has ten themed galleries, a wonderful bistro, and a boutique that offers unique fair-trade items.

House, youngsters can play at being train drivers on a reconstructed 1952 diesel engine while learning the history of Canada's railroad. The museum itself is housed within the oldest surviving train repair facility in Western Canada, which dates from 1889.

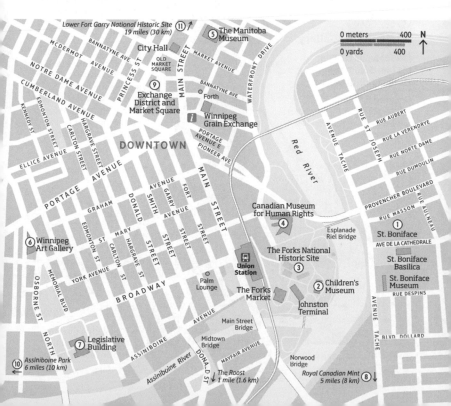

⑤ The Manitoba Museum

⌂ 190 Rupert Ave ▭ 11, 15, 16 ⏰ 10am-4pm Tue-Fri, 11am-5pm Sat & Sun (May-Aug: 10am-5pm daily)
ⓦ manitobamuseum.ca

Outstanding displays of the region's geography and people are imaginatively presented at this excellent museum, which also includes a planetarium and a science gallery. Visitors proceed through chronologically organized galleries with displays that range from prehistory to the present day. Each geographical area also has its own gallery: from the Earth History Gallery, which contains fossils up to 500 million years old, to the re-creation of Winnipeg in the 1920s, including a cinema and a dentist's office. One of the museum's biggest draws is a full-size replica of the *Nonsuch*, a 17th-century ketch.

⑥ Winnipeg Art Gallery

⌂ 300 Memorial Blvd
⏰ 11am-5pm Tue-Sun (to 9pm Fri) ⓦ wag.ca

Designed by local architect Gustavo da Roza, the jagged, modernist design of Winnipeg Art Gallery has made it a

Designed by local architect Gustavo da Roza, the jagged, modernist design of Winnipeg Art Gallery has made it a well-known downtown landmark.

well-known downtown landmark. The WAG was established in 1912, when it became Canada's first civic art gallery. Along with late Gothic and Early Renaissance works, ceramics, and 19th-century Canadian art, the gallery boasts the largest collection of contemporary Inuit art in the world, featuring over 13,000 sculptures, prints, drawings, and textiles. Works by women Inuit artists are particularly well represented, and there are some wonderful monochrome drawings and prints depicting hunting and magical scenes. A new Inuit Art Centre, set to open in 2020, is being constructed next to the existing building of the WAG in order to showcase a much larger portion of this fantastic collection. The gallery's two other significant areas of specialized collecting are the decorative arts and photography, with a sizeable selection of contemporary Canadian pieces.

⑦ Legislative Building

⌂ Cnr Broadway & Osborne
📞 (204) 945 5813 ⏰ Daily

The Legislative Building is built of a rare and valuable limestone, complete with the remains of fossils threaded through its facade. The building is set in 30 acres (12 ha) of beautifully kept gardens dotted with statues of poets such as Robert Burns of Scotland and Ukrainian Taras Shevchenko, which celebrate the province's ethnic diversity. Tours run July–September.

⑧ Royal Canadian Mint

⌂ 520 Lagimodière Blvd
⏰ 9am-5pm Tue-Sat (May-Labour Day: daily)
ⓦ mint.ca

The Royal Canadian Mint is housed in a striking building of rose-colored glass. The mint produces more than four billion coins annually for Canadian circulation, as well as for 75 other countries. Call ahead to book a guided tour.

↑ The distinctive pink-tinted facade of the Royal Canadian Mint

→ A bronze sculpture by Leo Mol, one of many that stand in Assiniboine Park

⑨ Ⓜ Exchange District and Market Square

🏠 492 Main St
🌐 exchangedistrict.org

When the Canadian Pacific Railway built its transcontinental line through Winnipeg in 1881, the city experienced a boom that led to the setting up of several commodity exchanges. Named after the Winnipeg Grain Exchange, this district was soon populated with a solid array of handsome terra-cotta and cut-stone buildings. It is now a National Historic Site and has been restored to its former glory, housing boutiques, craft stores, antique stores, galleries, artists' studios, and residential lofts.

The center of the district is Old Market Square, a popular site for staging local festivals and outdoor concerts.

⑩ Ⓜ Ⓨ Assiniboine Park

🏠 2355 Corydon Ave
🕐 Daily 🌐 assiniboine park.ca

Stretching for 378 acres (153 ha) along the south side of the Assiniboine River, Assiniboine Park is one of the largest urban parks in central Canada. One of its best-loved attractions is the Leo Mol Sculpture Garden, which has some 50 bronze sculptures by the Ukrainian artist, who lived in Winnipeg from 1948 until his death in 2009. The Pavilion Gallery showcases provincial art and also has a permanent exhibition on Winnie-the-Pooh. In summer, the Lyric Theatre hosts live music.

Within the park zoo, Leatherdale International Polar Bear Conservation Centre takes a lead in the polar bear transition program (under which orphaned polar bears from Churchill are relocated). The Interpretive Centre offers visitors insight into the lifestyle of polar bears, the arctic ecosystem, and the damaging effects of climate change.

The park's numerous cycling and walking trails are popular in summer, as is cross-country skiing, skating, and tobogganing in winter.

⑪ ✏ Ⓨ 🛍 Lower Fort Garry National Historic Site

🏠 5925 Hwy 9 ☎ (204) 785 6050 🕐 Mid-May–Jun: 9:30am–5pm Mon–Fri; Jul & Aug: 9:30am–5pm daily

Located 20 miles (32 km) north of Winnipeg on the banks of the Red River, Lower Fort Garry National Historic Site is North America's only restored stone fort from the fur-trading era. Walls and buildings that have stood on the bank of the Red River for over 180 years tell inspiring tales of discovery and struggle. Costumed interpreters bring to life the 17th-century history of the setting through the sounds and smells of tradespeople, such as blacksmiths, fur traders, and cooks.

DRINK

Forth
Pick from the sleek café, subterranean bar, and seasonal rooftop bar at this modern concept space. Cocktail-making workshops and indie movie screenings are also on offer here.

🏠 171 McDermot Ave
🌐 forth.ca

Palm Lounge
Located inside the historic Fort Garry Hotel, this richly decorated cocktail lounge exudes elegance and hosts live jazz in the evenings.

🏠 222 Broadway
🌐 fortgarryhotel.com

The Roost
Sip crafty cocktails and slurp freshly shucked oysters at this rooftop bar, which has an awesome summer patio. Opt for the cozy interior during colder months.

🏠 651 Corydon Ave
🌐 theroostwpg.com

EXPERIENCE MORE

5

Fort Macleod

🚌 *i* 219 Jerry Potts Blvd;
www.fortmacleod.com

Alberta's oldest settlement,
Fort Macleod was established
in 1874 as the first North West
Mounted Police outpost in the
west. Sent to control lawless
whisky traders at the Fort
Whoop-up trading post, the
Mounties *(p171)* set up Fort
Macleod nearby.

Today's town retains many
of its historic buildings, and the
reconstructed fort palisades
house a museum that tells the
story of the Mounties' journey.

The world's oldest and
bestpreserved buffalo jump
lies 11 miles (18 km) northwest of Fort Macleod. **Head-
Smashed-In Buffalo Jump**
is a UNESCO World Heritage
Site. This way of hunting
buffalo, in which aboriginal
people wearing buffalo skins
stampeded herds of the
animals to their deaths over
a cliff, was perfected by the

↑ The reconstructed
fort and museum at
Fort Macleod

Blackfoot tribe. The site
takes its name from a brave
individual whose head was
smashed in when watching
the kill from under the cliff.

Head-Smashed-In Buffalo Jump
⊗ 🏠 Hwy 785, off Hwy 2
📞 (403) 553 2731 🕐 Daily

6

Lethbridge

✈️ 🚌 *i* 2805 Scenic Dr S;
(403) 320 1222 or (1800)
661 1222

Coal, oil, and gas are the
basis of Lethbridge's success.
Alberta's third-largest city
was named after mine-owner
William Lethbridge in 1885,
but First Nations peoples have
inhabited the area since
prehistoric times.

Lethbridge is home to the
notorious Fort Whoop-up,
established in 1869 by whisky
traders John Healy and Alfred
Hamilton. Many First Nations
peoples, drawn by the lure of
the drink, were poisoned or
killed by the illicit brew, which
was made with substances
such as tobacco and red ink.
Today, a reconstruction of Fort
Whoop-up and three galleries
evoke life here in the 1870s.

7

Red Deer

🚌 *i* 101-4200 Hwy 2;
www.visitreddeer.com

Located midway between
Calgary and Edmonton, this
bustling city was founded in
1882 by Scottish settlers as a
stopover point for travelers.
A modern city with good
facilities, Red Deer is the hub
of Alberta's rolling parkland
district. The city's beautiful
reserve of Waskasoo Park is
located along the Red River.

8 ⊗ 🖼️ 🛍️

Elk Island National Park

🏠 Hwy 16 📞 (780) 922 5790
🕐 Daily

Established in 1906 as Canada's
first animal sanctuary, Elk
Island became a national
park in 1913. This 75-sq-miles
(194-sq-km) park provides a
habitat for large mammals
such as elk and moose. It was
also pivotal in Canada's bison
conservation efforts, and is
now home to over 600 bison.

The landscape of transitional
aspen parkland is one of the
most threatened habitats in
North America. Aspen trees
grow mostly on dry ridges,
while balsam, poplar, and white
birch grow near wet areas.
Plants such as willow also
thrive in the wetlands.

Elk Island is both a popular
day trip from Edmonton and
a draw for wildlife photographers. There are 13 hiking trails
of varying lengths, and a range
of other outdoor activities
available all year round.

9

Grande Prairie

✈️ 🚌 *i* 11330 106th St;
www.gptourism.ca

Grande Prairie is a large,
modern city in the northwest
corner of Alberta. Surrounded

← Canoeists paddling in Elk Island National Park at sunset

by fertile farming country, it's a popular stop for travelers heading north toward Dawson Creek and the Alaska Highway. The city is the hub of the Peace River region; it offers extensive shopping opportunities with the added draw of having no provincial sales tax.

The attractive wilderness of Muskoseepi Park also runs through the city center. The **Grande Prairie Museum & Heritage Village** is housed in the park and has 15 buildings containing more than 55,000 historical artifacts. There are several reconstructions, including a 1911 schoolhouse and a church. A renowned display of dinosaur bones from the Peace River Valley is also exhibited at the museum.

Bear Creek, which runs through Muskoseepi Park, has become a magnet for birdwatchers, as sightings of eagles are common. The Grand River wetlands is also home to over 300 bird species.

 INSIDER TIP
Bower Ponds Park

Whatever the weather in Red Deer, Bower Ponds Park will have activities on offer. In summer, enjoy paddleboat, kayak, and canoe rentals. In the winter, there's ice-skating.

Grande Prairie Museum & Heritage Village
🅰 Cnr 102nd St & 102nd Ave
🕐 Daily 🌐 cityofgp.com

⑩
Edmonton

✕⊕🚗🚌 *i* 9797 Jasper Ave; www.explore edmonton.com

Edmonton spans the valley of the North Saskatchewan River and sits in the center of Alberta, of which it is the capital. Its downtown area is centered on Jasper Avenue and Sir Winston Churchill Square, and is an appealing blend of old and new. The West Edmonton Mall contains over 800 hip stores; in contrast, the delightful Alberta Legislature, one of Alberta's oldest buildings, opened in 1913. The **Royal Alberta Museum** (RAM) is the largest museum in western Canada. Located in the Arts District, the striking collection offers a wide range of interactive exhibits, with indigenous stories woven throughout all six human history galleries.

Northwest of downtown is the Telus World of Science, which boasts an IMAX theater.

Royal Alberta Museum
♿ 🅰 9810 103a Ave NW
🕐 10am–5pm daily (to 8pm Thu) 🌐 royalalberta museum.ca

SHOP

Arc'teryx
Outdoorsy types won't want to miss this North Vancouver-based stockist, which carries award-winning outdoor clothing and gear.

🅰 Fl 2, West Edmonton Mall, 8882 170 St, Edmonton 📞 (780) 784 0057

Cacao 70
This tempting franchise, which originated in Montreal, offers chocolate treats in all forms - from chocolate waffles to silky fondue.

🅰 Unit T-123, West Edmonton Mall, 8882 170 St, Edmonton 📞 (514) 523 9000

T & T Supermarket
There's a treasure trove of unusual goodies and trinkets inside this sprawling Canadian-Asian grocery store.

🅰 Fl 2, West Edmonton Mall, 8882 170 St, Edmonton 📞 (780) 483 6638

EXPERIENCE The Prairies

Did You Know?

Wood Buffalo National Park is is about the size of Denmark, with an area of 17,300 sq miles (44,807 sq km).

11
Wood Buffalo National Park

🅰 Fort Smith 📞 (867) 872 7900 🕐 Daily

Canada's largest national park was made a UNESCO World Heritage Site in 1983 because of the range of habitat it offers for rare species such as the wood bison.

There are three different environments here: fire-scarred forest uplands; a large, poorly drained plateau filled with streams and bogs; and the Peace-Athabasca Delta, full of sedge meadows, marshes, and shallow lakes. Sightings of bald eagles and peregrine falcons are common, and the park is the only remaining natural nesting site of the rare whooping crane in the world.

12
Medicine Hat

🅰 📧 ℹ 330 Gehring Rd SW; www.tourismmedicine hat.com

The south Saskatchewan River Valley is the picturesque setting for the town of Medicine Hat, which was founded in 1883 as a center for natural gas extraction. Medicine Hat also became a hub for the manufacture of clay products, due to the natural abundance of clay along the river banks. Today, the **Medalta Potteries National Historic Site** in the 150-acre (60-ha) Historic Clay District is a living, working museum dedicated to telling the stories of the industry.

Medalta Potteries National Historic Site
🅰 713 Medalta Ave SE 🕐 Tue-Sat 🔗 medalta.org

13
Maple Creek

📧 ℹ 114 Jasper St; www. maplecreek.ca

Located on the eastern edge of the Cypress Hills and affectionately known as "Old Cow Town," Maple Creek was established as a ranching center in 1882. The town still has a look of the Old West, with trucks and Stetson-wearing ranchers filling the downtown streets. Its many original 19th-century store-fronts include the elegantly refurbished Commercial Hotel with its marble-floored lobby. The town is also well located to serve as a gateway to the popular Cypress Hills Interprovincial Park.

14
Dinosaur Provincial Park

🅰 Rte 544 📞 (403) 378 4342 🕐 Daily

Two hours' drive southeast of the town of Drumheller, the UNESCO World Heritage Site of Dinosaur Provincial Park, established in 1955, contains some of the world's richest fossil beds. Located along the Red Deer River Valley, the park includes dinosaur skeletons mostly from the late Cretaceous Period, about 75 million years ago (p158). More than 300 mostly intact skeletons have been discovered here, and over 30 institutions worldwide have specimens from this valley on display.

From Drumheller it is possible to drive the 30-mile

A dazzling sunset over the hoodoos in Dinosaur Provincial Park

→ Giant *pysanka* at Vegreville, the largest such sculpture in the world

(48-km) **Dinosaur Trail** through the "Valley of the Dinosaurs." The loop passes the Royal Tyrrell Museum, takes in stunning views of the badlands landscape from highpoints such as Horseshoe Canyon, and leads to intriguing rock hoodoos.

Dinosaur Trail
🛈 Drumheller; www.
traveldrumheller.com

SHOP

Elliot Home and Lifestyle

An attractive gift shop selling locally made ceramics, textiles, and body care products.

🏠 462 4th St SE, Medicine Hat
🕒 Sun & Mon
🌐 shopelliot.com

Inspire Studio, Gallery, and Café

A cozy café, with local art for sale displayed on the shelves and walls.

🏠 675 2nd St SE, Medicine Hat
🕒 Sun 🌐 inspire art.ca

Medalta Potteries National Historic Site

After browsing the museum here, you can buy replica Medalta ware on-site, including the iconic bean pots.

🏠 713 Medalta Ave SE, Medicine Hat
🕒 Sun & Mon
🌐 medalta.org

15

Vegreville

🚍 🛈 Hwy 16A E; www.
vegreville.com

Along the Yellowhead Hwy, east of Edmonton, lies the predominantly Ukrainian town of Vegreville. Its community is famous for producing traditionally Ukrainian, highly decorated Easter eggs (or *pysanky*). Visible from the road is a giant *pysanka* covered with intricate bronze, gold, and silver designs that tells the story of the region's Ukrainian settlers, and celebrates their faith, bountiful harvests, and the protection they received from the RCMP. The egg is 23 ft (7 m) high, and is made of over 3,500 pieces of aluminum.

16

Cypress Hills Interprovincial Park

🏠 Hwy 41 🕒 Daily
🌐 cypresshills.com

Straddling the border between Saskatchewan and Alberta,

the Cypress Hills Interprovincial Park offers fine views of the plains from its 5000-ft- (1500-m-) high peaks. The park's landscape is similar to the foothills of the Rocky Mountains, with its lodgepole pine forests and abundant wildflowers. Walking trails offer visitors the chance to see moose, elk, and white-tailed deer, as well as the many species of bird that stop here during migration, such as the rare trumpeter swan and mountain chickadee.

In the eastern section of the park, in Saskatchewan, **Fort Walsh National Historic Site** houses a reconstruction of Fort Walsh, which was built in 1875 by the Mounties to keep out the illicit whisky traders who were causing trouble among the Aboriginal population. Costumed guides relate the history of the North West Mounted Police.

Fort Walsh National Historic Site
♿ 📞 (306) 662 2645
🕒 Mid-May–Jun & Sep: 9:30am–5pm Tue–Sat; Jul & Aug: 9:30am–5pm daily

Did You Know?

Grasslands National Park has Canada's only remaining black-tailed prairie dog colonies.

17

North Battleford and Battleford

🚍 *i* Jct Hwys 16 & 40; www.battlefords.ca

These two communities, together known as The Battlefords, face each other across the North Saskatchewan River. Named after a ford in the Battle River, the area was the site of age-old conflicts between the Blackfoot and Cree. It was the seat of the North-West Territories government from 1876 to 1882. Today, the communities are thriving industrial centers, although the North Battleford branch of the Western Development Museum focuses on rural life.

The **Allen Sapp Gallery** displays works by one of Canada's best-loved contemporary artists, who died in 2015. Sapp's delicately colored paintings and drawings honor the traditions of the Northern Plains Cree community.

Between the Saskatchewan and Battle rivers is the **Fort Battleford National Historic Site**, containing a well-restored

North West Mounted Police post. The stockade has five original buildings housing a museum, including the lookout point in the commander's residence, officers' quarters, and restored barracks. Costumed guides tell the story of when 500 settlers took refuge in the stockade during the North-West Rebellion.

Allen Sapp Gallery

⌖ 🏛 📍 1 Railway Ave E ⏰ Jun-Sep: 11am-5pm daily; Oct-May: noon-4pm Wed-Sun 🖥 allensapp.com

Fort Battleford National Historic Site

⌖ 📍 Off Hwy 4 📞 (306) 937 2621 ⏰ Mid-May-Jun: 10am-4pm Mon-Fri; Jul-Aug: 10am-4pm daily

18

Grasslands National Park

📍 Jct Hwys 4 & 18 ⏰ Daily (some facilities are open in summer only) *i* Val Marie; (306) 298 2257

Situated in the southwest corner of Saskatchewan, Grasslands National Park was set up in 1988 to preserve one of the last original prairie

grasslands in North America. The park is an area of climatic extremes, where summer temperatures can be as high as 104 °F (40 °C), and winter ones as low as -40 °F (-40 °C). This environment supports a range of rare wildlife, including short-horned lizards and ferruginous hawks. Visitors may hike and camp in the park, but facilities are basic.

East of the park is the striking, glacially formed landscape of the **Big Muddy Badlands**. In the early 1900s, caves of eroded sandstone and deep ravines provided hideouts for cattle thieves such as Butch Cassidy.

Big Muddy Badlands

⌖ 🚶 📍 Off Hwy 34 📞 (306) 267 3312

19

Duck Lake

🚍 🖥 ducklake.ca

Just west of the farming village of Duck Lake lies a plaque commemorating the first shots fired in the North-West Rebellion. On March 26, 1885, a police interpreter and a Cree emissary scuffled during a parley, and the officer was killed. During the ensuing battle, 12 NWMP officers and six Métis died. The Battle of Duck Lake is depicted in a series of vivid murals at the town's interpretive center.

←

A lone bison wandering the landscape of Grasslands National Park

Batoche National Historic Site

🅰 Rte 225 off Hwy 312
📞 (306) 423 6227 🕐 Mid-May–Jun & Sep–mid-Oct: 9am–5pm Mon–Fri; Jul & Aug: 9am–5pm daily

The original village of Batoche was the site of the Métis's last stand against the Canadian Militia, led by Louis Riel and Gabriel Dumont in 1885 *(p68)*.

From the 17th century, white fur traders in the west had married Aboriginal wives and adopted tribal languages and customs. The resulting mixed raced peoples, the Métis, had originally rebeled in 1869 in the Winnipeg area in defense of their land rights. When history began to repeat itself in 1885, Métis rebels recalled Riel from exile in Montana to declare a provisional government at Batoche. Violence erupted into what was to become known as the North-West Rebellion. Riel surrendered, was tried for treason, and hanged in Regina.

Today, the Batoche National Historic Site of Canada occupies the site of the village and

battlefield. The 2.5-sq-miles (6-sq-km) park houses the bullet-ridden St. Antoine de Padoue Church and Rectory, as well as the cemetery where the Métis leaders are buried. An interpretive center features an audio-visual presentation on the history of Batoche through the eyes of the Métis.

Saskatoon

🚆🚌🏨🍴 ℹ 101-202 Fourth Ave N; www.tourism saskatoon.com

Now an agricultural and commercial hub in the middle of prairie country, Saskatoon was founded in 1882 as a temperance colony. The region's history is told in the local branch of the Western Development Museum, which focuses on the town's boom years in the early 1900s, re-creating the main street of

a typical prairie town, including its railroad station. The town also houses the Ukrainian Museum of Canada and the Remai Modern, an art gallery.

The South Saskatchewan River meanders through the city and is bounded by many lush parks, including the outstanding 759-acre (307-ha) **Wanuskewin Heritage Park**. This is devoted to Northern Plains First Nations history, with archaeological sites that confirm the existence of hunter-gatherer communities some 6,000 years ago. Some of the digs are open to the public in the summer. The park's hills and marshy creeks are still held to be sacred lands by the Northern Plains peoples, who act as interpretive guides.

Wanuskewin Heritage Park

🛋🍴🎫🛍 🅰 Off Hwy 11
🕐 9am–4:30pm Mon–Fri, 11am–4pm Sat
🌐 wanuskewin.com

↑ The skyline of Saskatoon, reflected in the South Saskatchewan River

22
Regina

✈ 🚂 🚌 ℹ **1925 Rose St;**
www.tourismregina.com

Regina is a bustling city and the capital of Saskatchewan. Named for Queen Victoria by her daughter Princess Louise, who was married to the Governor General of Canada, Regina was established in 1882 after starting life as a tent settlement called Pile O'Bones. The name was derived from a Cree word describing the buffalo bones left behind after hunting.

Today, Regina is a thriving modern city, whose high-rise skyline contrasts with the 350,000 trees of the man-made Wascana Centre, a 3.5-sq-mile (9-sq-km) park set around a vast lake. The park is a haven for some 60 species of waterfowl, including Canada geese.

The **Royal Saskatchewan Museum** borders the park. Its Earth Sciences Gallery depicts 3.5 billion years of the region's geological history, while the First Nations Gallery traces 10,000 years of local Aboriginal culture in the province.

West of the city center lies the original headquarters for the North West Mounted Police. Today, all Canada's Mounties are trained here, and it is also the site of the **RCMP Heritage Centre**. Here, the story of the Mounties is told from their origin in 1873 (p171). Among the highlights are the ceremonies and drills that are regularly performed by specially trained groups of Mounties, including the Sergeant Major's Parade and Sunset Retreat Ceremonies.

Royal Saskatchewan Museum
⊛ 🏛 🅿 **2445 Albert St**
🕙 **9:30am–5pm daily**
w **royalsaskmuseum.ca**

RCMP Heritage Centre
⊛ ⊛ 🏛 🅿 **5907 Dewdney Ave W** 🕙 **11am–5pm daily**
w **rcmphc.com**

23
Moose Jaw

🚂 🚌 ℹ **Jct Thatcher Drive E & Hwy 1; www.tourism moosejaw.ca**

The quiet town of Moose Jaw was established as a railway terminus by the Canadian Pacific Railroad in 1882. Today, 46 murals celebrate the lives of the early railroad pioneers and homesteaders, decorating buildings around

> 💬 INSIDER TIP
> **Dig Deep**
>
> Head into the tunnels beneath Moose Jaw to brush up on local history; here, entertaining and family-friendly theatrical performances bring the town's Prohibition-era world to life.

← The facade *(inset)* and eye-catching exhibits at the RCMP Heritage Centre in Regina

24 Yorkton

🚌 ℹ️ Jct Hwy 9 & Hwy 16; www.tourismyorkton.com

Founded in 1882 as a farming community, Yorkton is located in central Saskatchewan. The striking architecture of its churches reflects the town's Ukrainian heritage. The local Western Development Museum (one of four in the province) tells the story of immigrants to the region.

25 Fort Qu'Appelle

ℹ️ 160 Company Ave S; www.fortquappelle.com

Named after an 1864 Hudson's Bay Company fur-trading post, the picturesque town of Fort Qu'Appelle is located between Regina and Yorkton on Hwy 10. The **Fort Qu'Appelle Museum** is built on the site of the old fort. It houses Aboriginal artifacts such as antique beadwork and pioneer photographs. The 267-mile (430-km) long Qu'Appelle River widens at the town into a string of eight lakes bordered by several provincial parks. Scenic drives through the region are one of the valley's greatest attractions. East of Fort Qu'Appelle is the **Motherwell Homestead National Historic Site**. This gracious

← "Mac the Moose," an iconic statue that welcomes visitors to the town of Moose Jaw

1st Ave. Nearby, River St has hotels and warehouses that reflect Moose Jaw's time as "sin city" during the 1920s – when Prohibition in the United States meant that illegally produced liquor was smuggled from Canada to Chicago.

The Moose Jaw branch of the Western Development Museum focuses on transportation.

DRINK

Beer Bros
Gastropub offering 27 beers on tap and a pleasant patio, located in the 1906 Prince Edward Building.

🏠 1821 Scarth St, Regina 🌐 beerbros.ca

Bushwakker Brewpub
Housed in a historic warehouse, this friendly pub is known for its delicious blackberry mead and other specialty in-house brews.

🏠 2206 Dewdney Ave, Regina 🌐 bushwakker.ca

Crave Kitchen & Wine Bar
Located in Regina's supposedly most haunted building, this bar-restaurant offers excellent cocktails and a strong wine list.

🏠 1925 Victoria Ave, Regina 🌐 cravekwb.com

house with ornamental gardens was built by politician William R. Motherwell, who so successfully introduced agricultural improvements to the area that he became the province agriculture minister from 1905 to 1918.

Fort Qu'Appelle Museum
◈ 🏠 198 Bay Ave N 📞 (306) 332 5751 🕐 Jun-Aug: 1-5pm daily

Motherwell Homestead National Historic Site
◈ 🏠 Off Hwy 22 📞 (306) 333 2116 🕐 Mid-May-Jun: 10am-4pm Mon-Fri; Jul & Aug: 10am-4pm daily

26
The Pas

 📍 1559 Gordon Ave; www.townofthepas.com

Once a key fur-trading post dating back some 300 years, The Pas is now a major industrial distribution and transportation center for Manitoba's northwest. Nearby Clearwater Lake Provincial Park is named for the lake itself, which is said to be so clear that it is possible to see the bottom at 36 ft (11 m). The park offers a walking trail through "the caves," a geological phenomenon where rock masses split away from cliffs to create huge crevices that provide shelter for various animals, including black bears, moose, wolves, and foxes.

27
Riding Mountain National Park

🅿 Hwys 10 & 19 📞 (204) 848 7275 🕐 Daily

One of Manitoba's most popular natural attractions, Riding Mountain National Park is a vast 1,158 sq miles (3,000 sq km) of wilderness. The best hiking trails and some of Manitoba's most beautiful

scenery are to be found in the center of the park, where the boreal forest meets the rocky Manitoba Escarpment. To the west, a ridge of evergreen prairie and forest is home to moose and elk. A small herd of bison can also be found in the park near Lake Audy. The most developed area is the small town of Wasagaming, where information on the park's network of trails for cycling, hiking, and horseback riding is available. Canoes can also be hired for exploring Clear Lake.

For a unique camping experience, yurts and oTENTiks (a cross between a tent and a cabin) at Wasagaming Campground can be booked through Parks Canada.

28
Gimli

📍 108-94 First Ave; www.gimli.ca

Located on the western shores of Lake Winnipeg, Gimli is the largest Icelandic community outside Iceland. The settlers arrived, having gained the right to land, at nearby Willow Creek in 1875. They soon proclaimed an independent state, which lasted until 1897, when the government insisted that other immigrants be allowed to settle in Gimli. Today, the **New Iceland Heritage Museum** relates the town's unusual history.

Gimli has a distinctly nautical atmosphere, with cobbled sidewalks leading down to a picturesque harbor and a wooden pier. At the Icelandic Festival of Manitoba, held every August, visitors can play at being Vikings, listen to folk music, and feast upon Icelandic specialties.

←
A towering fiberglass Viking statue in Gimli, Manitoba

West of Gimli, Narcisse Snake Dens protect the habitat of thousands of red-sided garter snakes that can be seen here during early spring and early fall on a specially designated short trail.

New Iceland Heritage Museum

 📍108-94 First Ave 🕐 May-Aug: 9am-4pm daily; Sep-Apr: 10am-4pm Mon-Fri, 1-4pm Sat & Sun 🌐 nihm.ca

29
Flin Flon

🅿 📍 Hwy 10A; www.cityofflinflon.ca

Steep hilly streets reflect the fact that Flin Flon lies on Precambrian rock (as old as the Earth's crust itself, formed roughly 3.8 billion years ago), and the area is famous for its distinctive greenstone. The town bears the name of a fictional character of a popular novel, *The Sunless City*

Canoes on the waters of Athapapuskow Lake near Flin Flon ↓

by J. E. P. Muddock. The book was read by a prospector at the time he staked his claim here in 1915. Copper and gold are still mined in Flin Flon, but visitors mostly come to experience the vast wilderness of the nearby Grass River Provincial Park.

The distinctive Grass River, dotted by strings of islands, has been a trade route for centuries, used by Aboriginal peoples and, later, European explorers and fur traders, to travel from northern forests to the prairies. Today, visitors may follow the historic route on guided canoe tours, or simply break for a spot of fishing.

30

Portage la Prairie

🚉🚌 *i* 97 Saskatchewan Ave E; www.city-plap.com

Portage la Prairie lies at the center of a rich agricultural area. The town is named after the French term for an overland detour, as Portage la Prairie lies between Lake Manitoba and the Assiniboine River, which formed a popular waterway for early travelers. Today, this thriving farming community contains the Fort La Reine Museum and Pioneer Village, on the site of the original fort built here in 1738. The museum offers exhibits detailing 19th-century prairie life. The popular railroad display features the cigar-stained car of Sir William Van Horne, founder of the Canadian Pacific Railroad. Pioneer Village re-creates a 19th-century settlement with authentic stores and a church.

31

Dauphin

🚉🚌✈ *i* 100 Main St S; www.tourismdauphin.ca

Tree-lined Dauphin was named after the King of France's eldest son by the French

explorer La Vérendrye. It is a distribution and supply center for the farms of the fertile Vermilion River valley. The town's **Fort Dauphin Museum** is a replica of an 18th-century trading post, with exhibits including a trapper's birch-bark canoe and several early pioneer buildings.

The onion-shaped dome of Dauphin's Church of the Resurrection is a tribute to the town's Ukrainian immigrants, who began to arrive in 1891.

Fort Dauphin Museum
♻️🌀 🏠 140 Jackson St
📞 (204) 638 6630 📅 May-Sep: daily; Oct-Apr: by appt

Did You Know?

Today, over 50 percent of Steinbach's residents still claim a German heritage.

Mennonite Heritage Village

🎨🍴♿ 🚗 Hwy 12 N
🕐 Times vary, check website 🌐 mennonite heritage village.com

33

Lake Winnipeg

🚉🚌 Winnipeg ℹ️ Travel Manitoba; (204) 927 7800 or 800 665 0040

Lake Winnipeg is a huge stretch of water some 270 miles (430 km) long that dominates the province of Manitoba. Today, the resorts that line the lake are popular with locals and visitors alike.

Numerous beaches dot the southeastern coast of the lake, including Winnipeg Beach, one of the province's most popular resort areas. A woodcarving of a head by Hungarian artist Peter "Wolf" Toth stands in the local park. Titled *Whispering Giant*, the sculpture honors the Ojibwa, Cree, and Assiniboine First Nations people of Manitoba.

Grand Beach in the **Grand Beach Provincial Park** has long powdery-white sand beaches and huge grass-topped dunes over 39 ft (12 m) high. Stretching back from the beach, the

32

Steinbach

About an hour's drive southeast of Winnipeg, Steinbach is a closely knit community with impressive businesses in trucking, manufacturing, and especially car dealerships. These are run largely by the Mennonites, members of a Protestant religious sect who are noted for their fair dealing.

The Mennonites came to Steinbach in ox-drawn carts in 1874, having fled from religious persecution in Russia. Despite not having a rail link, the town thrived, as the Mennonites were good farmers and, later, car dealers. The nearby **Mennonite Heritage Village** re-creates a 19th-century Mennonite settlement, with some buildings dating from the 1870s, and a church and school furnished to the period. Its restaurant serves homemade meals such as borscht, a type of creamy cabbage soup. In mid-May, the village hosts Spring on the Farm, featuring a tractor show and traditional food.

TOP 3 BEACHES ON LAKE WINNIPEG

Gimli Beach
📍 Keenora Dr, Gimli
A family-friendly beach set right on the waterfront in Gimli.

Grand Beach
📍 Hwy 59, Grand Beach Provincial Park
There are miles of fine white sand and rolling dunes here.

Patricia Beach
📍 Highway 59, Pembina
Head here for soft sand, a pleasant lagoon, and spots of solitude.

marsh – also known as the lagoon – is one of the park's treasures, and supports many species of bird, such as the rare and endangered piping plover.

Moving west from the lake, Oak Hammock Marsh is composed of tall-grass prairie, meadows, and aspen-oak, which provide an important habitat for over 300 species of bird and animal.

← Antique tractors on display at Steinbach's Mennonite Heritage Village

← Visitors taking in the
spectacular Northern
Lights above Churchill

Today, visitors come to see the
polar bears, beluga whales,
and the splendid tundra flora
in this region. In the spring
the tundra's covering of moss,
lichens, and tiny flowers bursts
into an array of colors. In the
summer beluga whales move
up-river and can be seen
from boat or kayaking trips.
Churchill is also one of the
best places in Canada to see
the Northern Lights (p359).

35

Selkirk

🚌 *i* **Red River North
Tourism, 18 Main St;
www.redrivernorth
tourism.com**

Named after the fifth Earl
of Selkirk, Thomas Douglas,
whose family had an interest
in the Hudson's Bay Company,
Selkirk was established in 1882,
when settlers arrived along
the shores of the Red River.
Today, on Main Street, a 25-ft
(8-m) statue of a catfish pro-
claims Selkirk as the "catfish
capital of North America."
Sport fishing is a year-round
activity, attracting enthusiasts
from across North America.

The city's Marine Museum
of Manitoba on Eveline St
displays six restored historic
ships, including the 1897 S.S.
Keenora, which is Manitoba's
oldest steamship.

**Hecla/Grindstone Provincial
Park** occupies a number of
islands in the lake. A causeway
links the mainland to Hecla
Island, originally inhabited
by the Anishinabe (Ojibwa)
people. The first European
settlers here were Icelanders,
who arrived in 1875. Today,
the lakeside village of Hecla
is a pretty open-air museum
featuring several restored
19th-century buildings.
From Hecla there are hiking
and biking trails that lead
to viewpoints for sightings
of rare waterfowl such as
great blue herons and the
western grebe.

Grand Beach Provincial
Park
🚯 🚗 Hwy 12, nr Grand Marais
📞 (204) 754 5040 🕒 Daily

Hecla/Grindstone
Provincial Park
🚗 Hwy 8, nr Riverton
📞 (204) 378 2261 🕒 Daily

34

Churchill

✈️🚆 *i* **Off Kelsey Blvd;
(204) 675 8863**
ⓦ **churchill.ca**

Located at the mouth of the
Churchill River on Hudson Bay,
this town retains an industrial
feel, with no luxury hotels, few
paved roads, and few trees.
This vast Arctic landscape
is snow-free only from
June through to the end of
September. Churchill has no
road access and can be reached
only by plane or train from
Winnipeg, Thompson, and
The Pas. Despite its remote
situation, Churchill was an
important point of entry into
Canada for early European
explorers and fur traders
arriving by boat in the
18th century. The Hudson's
Bay Company established
an outpost for fur trading
here in 1717.

📷 PICTURE PERFECT
Animal Snaps

Budding wildlife
photographers will
be spoilt for choice in
Churchill. In summer,
beluga whales can be
glimpsed from boat
trips, while polar bear
season is from mid-
October to November.

TORONTO

Located on the northwest shore of Lake Ontario, the area of Toronto was originally settled by the Iroquois during the 17th century, and, after 1720, became a French fur-trading post. Fought over by the US and Britain in the War of 1812, Toronto has since been a peaceful city, growing dramatically after World War II, with the arrival of over 500,000 immigrants.

Today, Toronto has shed its prim, colonial image to become one of North America's most dynamic cities, a cosmopolitan mix of almost three million inhabitants drawn from more than 200 ethnic groups. Reveling in its position as the financial and commercial center of Canada, Toronto also offers fine art museums, suave café-bars, and luxury stores.

TORONTO

Must Sees
1 Art Gallery of Ontario
2 Royal Ontario Museum
3 CN Tower

Experience More
4 Toronto City Hall
5 Fairmont Royal York
6 First Post Office
7 Chinatown
8 University of Toronto
9 Casa Loma
10 Kensington Market
11 Ontario Parliament Building
12 Spadina Museum, Historic House and Gardens
13 Bata Shoe Museum
14 Allan Gardens Conservatory
15 St. Lawrence Market
16 Gardiner Museum
17 Distillery Historic District
18 Hockey Hall of Fame
19 Ripley's Aquarium of Canada
20 TD Gallery of Inuit Art
21 The Beaches and Scarborough Bluffs
22 The Toronto Islands
23 Fort York
24 Toronto Zoo
25 Aga Khan Museum
26 Ontario Science Centre
27 High Park
28 Black Creek Pioneer Village
29 McMichael Canadian Art Collection

Eat
1 Hibiscus Cafe
2 Rasta Pasta
3 Seven Lives Tacos
4 Buster's Sea Cove, Carousel Bakery, Churrasco's

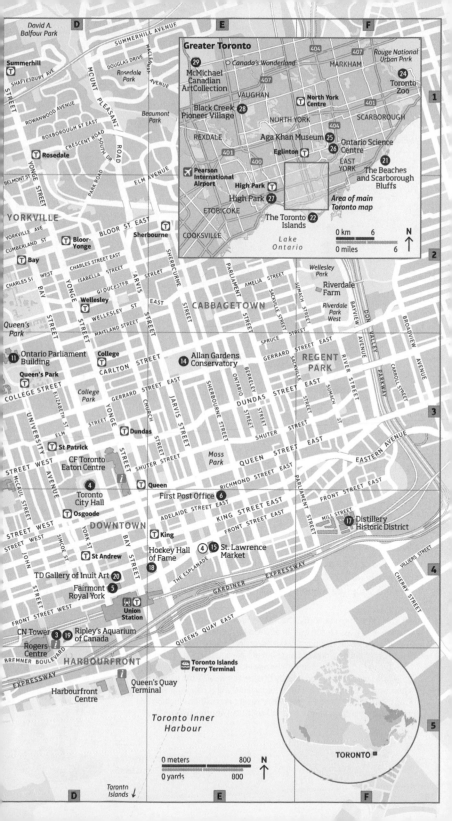

Did You Know?

Every Wednesday, from 6pm to 9pm, admission to the Gallery is free, and special exhibitions are discounted.

① ⊛ Ⓜ Ⓨ ▢ 🏛

ART GALLERY OF ONTARIO

📍 C3 🏠 317 Dundas St W Ⓣ Patrick 🚌 505 & 510 🕐 10:30am-5pm Tue-Sun (to 9pm Wed & Fri, to 5:30pm Sat & Sun) 🌐 ago.ca

Founded in 1900 as the Art Museum of Toronto, the Art Gallery of Ontario (AGO) holds an extensive collection of fine art and modern sculpture spanning the first century to present day.

An iconic structure in the city, the AGO is hard to miss. The billowing titanium and glass facade was an add-on by Canadian-born architect Frank Gehry. Inside, the magnificent art collections are bathed in natural light.

The outstanding works of Canadian art are a national treasure. Along with an extensive collection of superb Henry Moore drawings, maquettes, and sculptures (which were donated by the artist himself), the gallery exhibits significant masterpieces of European art, including paintings by Tintoretto, Frans Hals, Rubens, and Picasso. More recent acquisitions include an impressive collection of African and Australian Aboriginal art.

→

Auguste Rodin's marble sculpture *Eve*, c.1883

← Frank Gehry's iconic wooden spiral staircase inside the AGO

The gallery exhibits significant masterpieces of European art, including paintings by Tintoretto, Frans Hals, Rubens, and Picasso.

↑ Exterior of the glass and titanium extension to the AGO, beautifully lit at night

Gallery Collections

Indigenous and Canadian Art

▽ Works by First Nations, Inuit, and Metis tribes, plus other indigenous art pieces from around the globe, are displayed in this gallery, which reflects on recent and historical practices. The Canadian collection has a premier selection of work by the Group of Seven, and their contemporaries, such as Emily Carr.

Modern and Contemporary Art

▷ Spanning both European and American art from 1900 to the 1960s, the modern collection includes works by Monet, Picasso, and Henry Moore. The contemporary art galleries cover works from 1960 to the present.

European Art

▽ Painting and sculptures made by European artists between the year 1000 and 1900 are shown here, with an emphasis on art from the Middle Ages to the Italian Renaissance. Featured artists include Rubens, Rembrandt, Bernini, Chardin, and Monet.

African Art

▽ Wooden carved figures, traditional tribal masks, weaponry, and royal furnishings are part of this collection, mostly originating from West Africa, from as early as the 1800s. Many of the featured pieces depict themes surrounding birth, survival, death, and regeneration.

② 🔧 Ⓜ 🍴 📷 🛍

ROYAL ONTARIO MUSEUM

📍C2 🏠100 Queen's Park, Toronto Ⓣ Museum or St. George 🚌 5 and 142
🕐 10am–5:30pm daily (to 8:30pm Fri) 🌐 rom.on.ca

Canada's largest museum, the Royal Ontario Museum (ROM) covers the history of human civilization and the natural world in a collection of over six million extraordinary objects.

With an ultra-modern glass, aluminum, and steel addition bursting out of the original Edwardian edifice, the ROM is instantly recognizable. The most visited museum in the country, it houses an extraordinarily wide-ranging collection drawn from the fields of fine and applied art, the natural sciences and archaeology.

↑ Michael Lee-Chin Crystal addition to the original Edwardian ROM building

World Cultures

Items from all around the world, dating back as far as the Stone Age, are on display in various galleries here, including art, weaponry, religious artifacts, and textiles. Don't miss the shrunken head from Peru, or the Canadiana gallery, full of First Nations art. Cultural artifacts from China, Korea, and Japan are also on display, including phenomenal temple art, furnishings, and ceramics.

Natural History

The Natural History galleries contain collections of the natural world, from outer space objects to skeletons of long-extinct creatures. Highlights include sparkling meteorites, towering dinosaur skeletons and even an immersive replica of a bat cave. Many exhibits are hands-on, with visitors allowed to touch and handle natural artifacts and specimens.

↑ Species at Risk display in the Natural History galleries

Timeline

1978–84
▽ The museum undergoes a huge $55 million renovation, which is opened by Queen Elizabeth II.

2002–7
▽ Michael Lee-Chin donates $30 million for the museum to undergo a massive extension project.

1912–14
△ ROM established by the University of Toronto and Ontario government. It opens to the public in 1914.

1989
△ Activists denounce the ROM's *Into the Heart of Africa* exhibit for perpetuating racial stereotypes.

Did You Know?

The ROM contains the world's largest collection of fossils from the Burgess Shale *(p138)*.

Futalognkosaurus

Futalognkosaurus dinosaur skeleton in the main entrance hall of the ROM ↑

Did You Know?

If you buy a meal at the rotating 360 Restaurant, you get free access to the LookOut level.

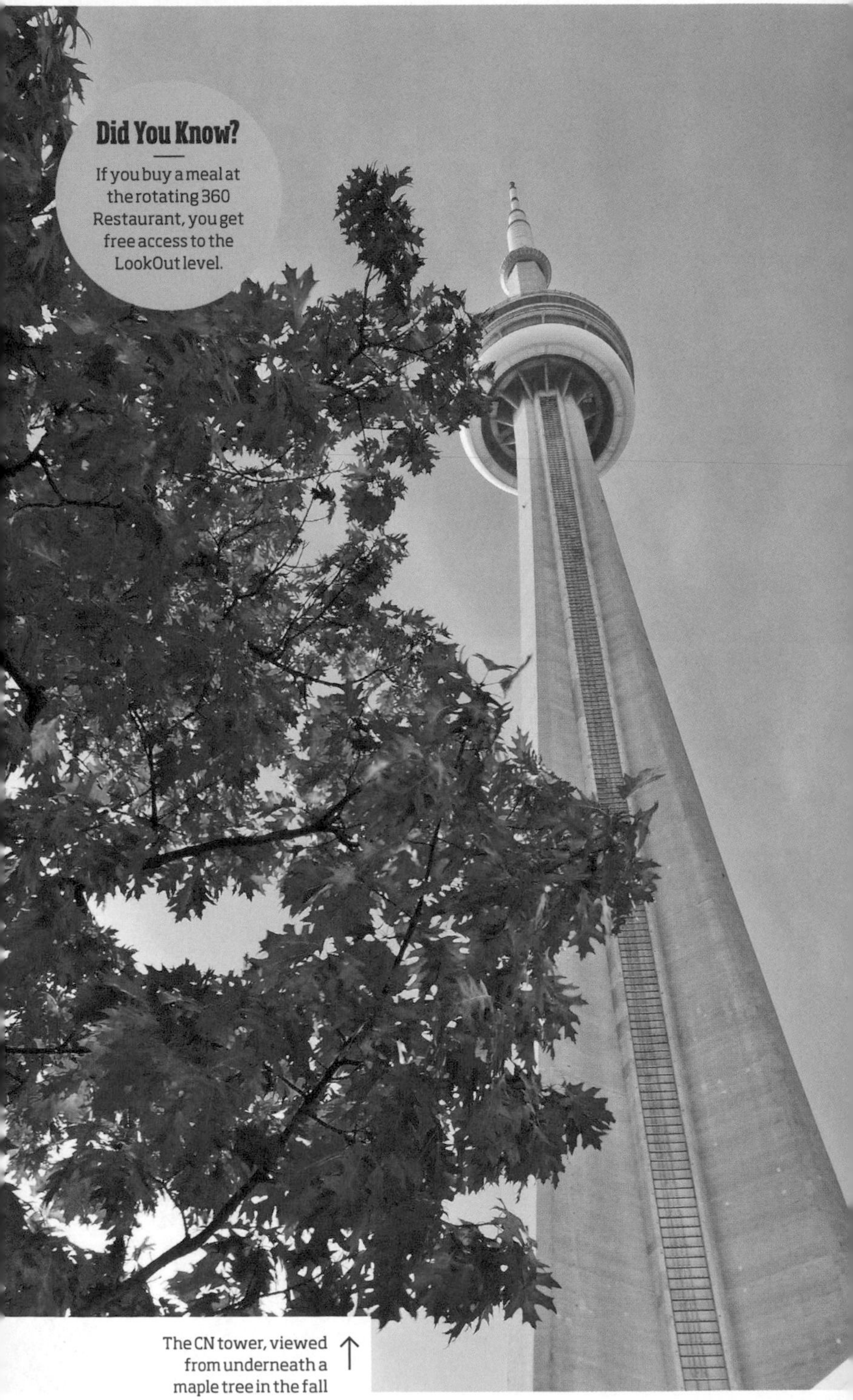

The CN tower, viewed from underneath a maple tree in the fall ↑

3 🏃 Ⓜ 🍴 📷 🛍

CN TOWER

📍 D4 🏢 290 Bremner Blvd, Toronto 🚇 Union 🕐 9am–10:30pm daily
🌐 cntower.ca

Visible from almost anywhere in the city, Toronto's iconic CN Tower is a marvel of 1970s engineering. Originally built as a communications tower, it is now the top tourist attraction in the city. From the viewing levels you can see as far as Niagara Falls on a clear day.

Rocket upwards in under a minute in one of six glass-fronted outside elevators to the LookOut, the most popular level, located at 1,136 ft (346 m). With floor-to-ceiling panoramic windows and a glass floor, it offers visitors the chance to observe the city's main landmarks and Lake Ontario below.

One level down from the LookOut is the Glass Floor, where you can stand, sit, and even jump on reinforced glass and look down at the ground 1,122 ft (342 m) below. Also on this level is the Outdoor SkyTerrace.

Reached by its own elevator, the SkyPod is the highest accessible point on the tower at 1,467 ft (447 m) above the city. For a special experience, get here in time to watch the sun set over the city from above.

EdgeWalk

For thrill-seekers only, this tower attraction is the world's highest full circle hands-free walk. It takes place on a 5-ft- (1.5-m-) wide ledge that encircles the top of the tower's main pod. Be sure to reserve ahead.

> **With floor-to-ceiling panoramic windows and a glass floor, it offers visitors the chance to observe the city's main landmarks.**

↑ Tourists looking at the city below on the Glass Floor level of the CN Tower

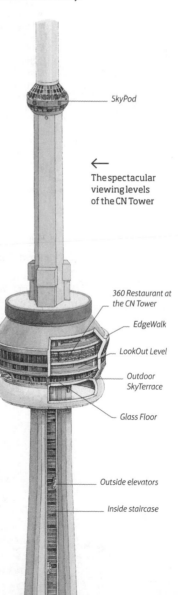

SkyPod

← The spectacular viewing levels of the CN Tower

360 Restaurant at the CN Tower

EdgeWalk

LookOut Level

Outdoor SkyTerrace

Glass Floor

Outside elevators

Inside staircase

Did You Know?

The Toronto Maple Leafs have the largest fan base in the NHL, despite not having won it since 1967.

4 Toronto City Hall

📍D3 🏠100 Queen St W & Bay St 🚇Queen, Osgoode 🚋Queen 501 🕐8:30am-4:30pm Mon-Fri

Completed in 1964, Toronto's City Hall was designed by the award-winning Finnish architect Viljo Revell. At the official opening, Prime Minister Lester Pearson announced "It is an edifice as modern as tomorrow," but for many cityfolk tomorrow had come too soon, and there were howls of protests from several quarters. Even now, after more than 50 years, the building appears uncompromisingly modern. It is the epitome of 1960s' urban planning, with two curved concrete-and-glass towers framing a central circular building where the Toronto councils meet. Nearby, the Old City Hall is a 19th-century Neo-Romanesque edifice, whose towers and columns are carved with intricate curling patterns.

5 Fairmont Royal York

📍D4 🏠100 Front St W 🚇Union 🌐fairmont.com/royal-york-toronto

Dating from 1929, the Fairmont Royal York has long been one of Toronto's most luxurious hotels. It was built opposite the city's main train station for the convenience of visiting dignitaries, but for thousands of immigrants, the hotel was the first they saw of their new city. It was designed by the Montreal architects Ross and Macdonald in contemporary Beaux-Arts style.

Having undergone multi-million-dollar renovations in 2015, the Fairmont remains a firm favorite with high-powered visitors, which have included royalty.

6 First Post Office

📍E4 🏠260 Adelaide St E 🚇King, Queen 🚋501, 504 🕐9am-5:30pm Mon-Fri, 10am-4pm Sat, noon-4pm Sun 🌐townofyork.com

In 1829, the British House of Commons founded their colonial postal service, and five years later established a post office in a far-flung outpost of the newly created town of Toronto. Remarkably, Toronto's First Post Office has survived, weathering many attempts by the city to have it demolished. It's fully functioning, and the world's only remaining example of a post office dating from the British North American postal era still in operation. Visitors make the trip to write a letter with a quill pen and seal it themselves with hot wax. Today's mail, however, is processed by the national service, Canada Post. The First Post Office museum houses a permanent exhibit on the early postal system and a model of the early city of Toronto.

7 Chinatown

📍C4 🚋Queen 501, Dundas 505, College 506, Spadina 510

The Chinese community in Toronto numbers around 531,600, over 12 percent of the city's total population. There have been several waves of Chinese migration to Canada, the first to British Columbia in the

late 1850s during the gold rush. The first Chinese to arrive in Toronto came at the end of the 19th century as workers on the Canadian Pacific Railway, settling in towns along the rail route. The Chinese found work in the Toronto laundries, factories, and on the railways. The last immigration wave saw prosperous Hong Kong Chinese professionals come to live in Toronto in the 1990s.

Chinese Canadians inhabit every part of the city but are concentrated in four Chinatowns, the largest and liveliest of which is focused on Spadina Avenue, between Queen and College streets, and along Dundas Street, west of the Art Gallery of Ontario. These few city blocks are immediately different from their surroundings, with neighborhood sights, sounds, and smells that are reminiscent of Hong Kong. Stores and stalls spill over the sidewalks, offering a bewildering variety of Chinese delicacies, and at night bright neon signs advertise dozens of inviting restaurants.

---

8 Ⓜ

University of Toronto

📍 C3 🏠 25 King's College Circle Ⓣ St George, Queen's Park 🚋 College 506 🌐 utoronto.ca

The University of Toronto grew out of a Royal Charter granted in 1827 by King George IV to Toronto's King's College. Seen by the church as challenging its control of education, the new institution weathered accusations of godlessness and proceeded to swallow its rivals, becoming in the process one of Canada's most prestigious universities.

This unusual history explains the rambling layout of the present campus, a leafy area sprinkled with colleges. The best-looking buildings are near the west end of Wellesley Street. Here, on Hart House Circle, lie the ivy-clad walls and delightful quadrangles of Hart House (1919), built in imitation of some Oxbridge university colleges in Britain. Nearby, King's College Circle contains University College, an imposing Neo-Romanesque edifice dating from 1859; Knox College with its rough gray sandstone masonry; and the fine rotunda of the university's Convocation Hall. UTAC, the University of Toronto Art Centre, has a permanent exhibition of Byzantine icons and other contemporary exhibitions. Round off a visit to the campus with a short stroll along Philosophers' Walk, where the manicured lawns lead behind the Royal Ontario Museum and up to Bloor Street West.

> **Stores and stalls spill over the sidewalks, offering a bewildering variety of Chinese delicacies, and at night bright neon signs advertise dozens of inviting restaurants.**

←

The unusual curved towers of Toronto City Hall, overlooking Nathan Phillips Square

↑ The striking facade and lush surrounding gardens of Casa Loma

⑨

Casa Loma

📍B1 🏠1 Austin Terrace 🚇Dupont ⏰9:30am–5pm daily 🌐casaloma.ca

This unusual Edwardian house was designed by E. J. Lennox, the architect responsible for Toronto's Old City Hall. The unusual structure is a remarkable tribute to its first owner, Sir Henry Pellatt (1859–1939), one of the most influential industrialists of early 20th-century Canada. He made a fortune in hydroelectric power during the early 1900s, harnessing the strength of Niagara Falls for electricity. In 1906, Pellatt decided to build himself a castle. Several years and Can $3.5 million later, construction was halted due to the outbreak of World War I. The 98-room house was finally completed in 1914, but financial ruin forced Pellatt to abandon it less than 10 years later. Today the house and its graceful formal gardens can be toured, or visitors can choose to take part in one of the site's elaborate and immersive escape room games.

⑩

Kensington Market

📍C3 🏠Baldwin St & Augusta Ave 🚋Dundas 505, College 506, Spadina 510 🌐kensington-market.ca

Kensington Market is one of Toronto's most distinctive and ethnically diverse residential areas. It was founded at the turn of the 20th century by East European immigrants, who crowded into the patchwork of modest houses near the junction of Spadina Avenue and Dundas Street, and then spilled out into the narrow streets to sell their wares. The bazaar they established – which houses everything from cheese and patisserie shops to vintage clothing stores – has been the main feature of the area ever since.

⑪

Ontario Parliament Building

📍D3 🏠Queen's Park 📞(416) 325 0061 🚇Queen's Park 🚋College 506 ⏰8am–6pm Mon–Fri (daily from Victoria Day to Labour Day)

There is nothing modest about the Ontario Parliament Building, a vast pink sandstone edifice that opened in 1893 and dominates the end of University Avenue. Ontario's elected representatives had a point to make. The province was a small but exceedingly loyal part of the British Empire,

EAT

Hibiscus Cafe
A family-run vegetarian café known for its buckwheat crepes.

📍C3 🏠238 Augusta Ave 🚫Mon 🌐hibiscuscafe.ca

⑤⑤⑤

Rasta Pasta
This Jamaican take-out counter is a Kensington Market staple.

📍C3 🏠61 Kensington Ave 🚫Mon 🌐eatrastapasta.ca

⑤⑤⑤

Seven Lives Tacos
Head here for some of the best tacos in the city.

📍C3 🏠69 Kensington Ave 🌐7lives.ca

⑤⑤⑤

TORONTO'S NEIGHBORHOODS

The city of Toronto is essentially a jumble of individual neighborhoods, each with its own colorful atmosphere. As well as Chinatown and Kensington Market, seek out Little Italy for its excellent pizzerias and some of the city's best bars; Koreatown for karaoke venues or specialty grocery stores; and Little Portugal for its superb custard tart bakeries.

clamoring to make its mark and possessing the money to do so. Consequently, the Members of Provincial Parliament (MPPs) commissioned this expensive structure in the Romanesque Revival style. Finished in 1892, its main facade is a panoply of towers and arches, set beneath a series of high-pitched roofs.

The interior is equally grand, with gilded Neo-Classical columns and huge stained-glass windows. In 1909, a fire razed the west wing, which was rebuilt in Italian marble. The MPPs were annoyed to find that much of the costly stone was blemished by dinosaur fossils, which can still be seen today in the west hallway. Visitors can sometimes watch the parliament in session.

12

Spadina Museum, Historic House and Gardens

B1 285 Spadina Rd (416) 392 6910 Dupont Jan-Mar: noon-5pm Sat & Sun; Apr-Aug: noon-5pm Tue-Sun; Sep-Dec: noon-4pm Tue-Fri, noon-5pm Sat & Sun Mon; Jan 1, Good Fri, Dec 25 & 26

James Austin, first president of the Toronto Dominion Bank, had this family home built on the bluff overlooking the city in 1866. The last of the Austins moved out in 1982, and the site was acquired by the City of Toronto and the Province of Ontario. Spadina Museum has been restored to reflect how the Austin family lived during the 1920s and 1930s. There are several enjoyable features, notably a trap door in the Palm Room that allowed gardeners to tend to the plants unseen by the family.

13

Bata Shoe Museum

C2 327 Bloor St W St George 10am-5pm Mon-Sat (to 8pm Thu), noon-5pm Sun Good Friday, Dec 25 batashoemuseum.ca

The Bata Shoe Museum was opened in 1995 to display the extraordinary range of footwear collected by Sonja Bata, a member of the eponymous shoe manufacturing family. The building was designed by the prestigious contemporary Canadian architect Raymond Moriyama; it is an angular, contemporary affair complete with unlikely nooks created to look like a chic shoebox.

The collection is spread over several small floors and features three changing exhibitions as well as regularly rotated items selected from the museum's substantial permanent collection. One fixed exhibit is entitled "All About Shoes," which provides the visitor with an overview of the functions and evolution of footwear. It begins with a plaster cast of the earliest-known footprint, discovered four million years after it was made in Tanzania, and has an interesting section on medieval pointed shoes. A second permanent feature is the section on celebrity footwear. This rotating display could include Marilyn Monroe's red stiletto heels, a pair of Elton John's platforms, or Michael Johnson's gold lamé sprinting shoes. There is also a display of unusual and improbable footwear, including unique French chestnut-crushing boots and a pair of US army boots, the soles of which are shaped to imitate the footprint of a Viet Cong irregular.

→ "All About Shoes", one of the permanent exhibitions in the Bata Shoe Museum

↑ The lush foliage of Allan Gardens Conservatory, a haven of greenery in downtown Toronto

⑯ 🎫 🍽 🛍
Gardiner Museum

📍C2 🏛111 Queen's Park
🚇Museum 🕐10am-6pm
Mon-Thu, 10am-9pm Fri,
10am-5pm Sat & Sun
🌐gardinermuseum.on.ca

Opened in 1984, the Gardiner Museum is dedicated solely to ceramic art. It is the only such museum in North America, and is considered one of the world's great specialty

⑭
Allan Gardens Conservatory

📍E3 🏛160 Gerrard St E
📞(416) 392 7288 🕐10am-5pm daily

Originally built in 1858, the Allan Gardens Conservatory is one of the oldest parks in Toronto and makes for a lovely distraction during the cold winter months. Step inside one of several tropical houses and be surrounded by warmth and exotic plant life, where colorful orchids and bromeliads bloom among the green vegetation. Other temperate houses, feeling a little cooler but still wonderfully balmy, are home to citrus trees, sweet flowering jasmine, and camellias set around waterfalls and koi-filled ponds. The lush Palm House is filled with climbing vines, bamboo groves, and of course palms, while by contrast the Arid House is home to all kinds of cacti and succulents. Outside of the conservatory is a charming playground and an off-leash area for dogs.

⑮
St. Lawrence Market

📍E4 🏛92-5 Front St E
🚇King 🕐Times vary, check website 🌐stlawrence market.com

Arrive with an appetite and join the crowds queuing for peameal bacon sandwiches, wood-oven-baked bagels, and the most succulent Portuguese *churrasco* chicken rolls in the city. With over 100 vendors, the main market building, called the South Market, is the city's go-to spot for fine meats, fresh seafood, exotic cheeses, and top-quality fruits and vegetables. The complex's North Market building is being rebuilt, so the weekend farmers' and antiques markets are held in a temporary structure at the Esplanade, just south of the main market building.

← Jun Kaneko's *Untitled,* outside the Gardiner Museum

EAT

Buster's Sea Cove
Expect long lines here for the mouthwatering fish 'n' chips and fresh crab sandwiches.

📍E4 🏛93 Front St E
🕐Sun & Mon 🌐busters-seacove.com

⑤⑤⑤

Carousel Bakery
Tourists and locals alike flock here for the world-renowned Canadian Peameal Bacon Sandwich, 2,000 of which are sold on any given day. Cash only.

📍E4 🏛93 Front St E
📞(416) 363 4247
🕐Sun & Mon

⑤⑤⑤

Churrasco's
Juicy, flavorful, and tender rotisserie chicken with a secret hot sauce - that's what keeps customers returning here year after year. The Portuguese custard tarts are also delicious.

📍E4 🏛93 Front St E
📞(416) 862 2867
🕐Sun & Mon

⑤⑤⑤

museums. The skilfully displayed collection traces the history of ceramics, beginning with Pre-Columbian pottery and a fascinating displays of ancient pieces from Peru and Mexico, which incorporate several grimacing fertility gods.

Examples of brightly colored *maiolica* (glazed, porous pottery) include painted pots made in Italy from the 15th and 16th centuries. Cheerful everyday wares are complemented by later Renaissance pieces relating classical myths and history. English delftware (tin-glazed earthenware) is also well represented in the collection. The 18th-century pieces from France, Austria, Germany, and England are superb – particularly the collection of *commedia dell'arte* figures. Intricately decorated in rainbow colors, these figurines were placed on dinner tables by the aristocracy to delight or even woo their special guests.

The porcelain here is also stunning, with many examples of exquisite Meissen from the 18th century. Packed in its own specially made leather carrying case, one special exhibit is an embellished tea and chocolate service dating from the mid-18th century. Each tiny cup features delicately painted scenes in gold. The porcelain collection also contains over 100 finely decorated scent bottles from all over Europe.

> Opened in 1984, the Gardiner Museum is dedicated solely to ceramic art. It is the only such museum in North America, and is considered one of the world's great specialty museums.

17

Distillery Historic District

📍F4 🚩9 Trinity St 🚌504 to Parliament 🕐10am-7pm Mon-Wed, 10am-8pm Thu-Sat, 11am-6pm Sun 🌐the distillerydistrict.com

The cobbled lanes and preserved Victorian industrial buildings of this pedestrianized shopping and entertainment area, the Distillery District, were once home to the whisky distillery of Gooderham and Worts. The area consists of shops, studios, galleries, bars, and restaurants spread out through 47 redeveloped buildings. Many of the distillery's original features have been retained, such as the pipes and trellises that crisscross above the red-brick alleys.

The area is anchored by the Mill Street Brewery, a fitting landmark, and great place to sample locally made beer. Craft shops and art galleries abound, and packed patios with choice restaurants and cafés seem to be on every corner.

18

Hockey Hall of Fame

📍E4 🚩Brookfield Place, 30 Yonge St 🚇Union, King 🕐Times vary, check website 🗓Induction Day 🌐hhof.com

The Hockey Hall of Fame is a lavish tribute to Canada's national sport: ice hockey. From its simple winter beginnings on frozen lakes and ponds, the game now ignites Canadian passions like no other. The Hall of Fame's ultra-modern exhibition area is inventive, with sections devoted to various aspects of the game. There are displays on everything from the jerseys of the great players to a replica of the Montréal Canadiens' locker room in the old Forum.

Another section traces the development of the goalie's mask, from its humble start to the elaborately painted versions of today. Visitors can try their hand at interactive displays, such as stopping pucks fired by virtual players. Another area displays a collection of trophies, including the Stanley Cup, hockey's premier award.

↑ *Our Game* by Edie Parker, a sculpture standing outside the Hockey Hall of Fame

← A visitor enjoying the spectacular Kelp Forest tank at Ripley's Aquarium

20 TD Gallery of Inuit Art

◉ D4 🏠 79 Wellington St West 📞 (416) 982 4051 🚇 Union, St. Andrew 🕐 8am–6pm Mon–Fri, 10am–4pm Sat & Sun

The TD (Toronto Dominion) Centre consists of five jet-black skyscrapers, a modern tribute to the Toronto Dominion Bank by the architect and designer Mies van der Rohe. The southern tower displays a strong collection of Inuit Art on two levels of its foyer. The exhibits were assembled as a centennial project in the 1960s. Over 100 pieces were bought in a variety of materials, including caribou antler and walrus tusk, but the kernel of the collection is the stone carving. Soapstone sculptures show mythological beasts and spirits, and scenes from everyday life. Some of the finest were carved by Johnny Inukpuk (1911–2007), such as his rawly powerful *Mother Feeding Child* (1962) and *Tattooed Woman* (1958).

19 Ripley's Aquarium of Canada

◉ D4 🏠 288 Bremner Blvd 🚇 Union, St Andrew 🕐 9am–11pm daily (check website for early closures) 🌐 ripley aquariums.com/canada

Located at the base of the CN Tower, this state-of-the-art aquarium opened in 2013 and houses over 16,000 sea creatures. The display of marine life from around the world starts with Ontario's Fishes of the Great Lake Basin, and is followed by the two-story Pacific Kelp Viewing Tank. Deep below the Dangerous Lagoon, a travelator ferries visitors through a tunnel where tooth sawfish and sand tiger sharks swim overhead. To get even closer, visit the tanks filled with bamboo sharks, horseshoe crabs, and stingrays. In Planet Jellies, the fascinating Pacific Sea Nettle jellyfish appear to change color in their back-lit tanks, which makes for a stunning display. The Discovery Centre is an interactive gallery with a touch pool, perfect for children to safely explore.

> 💬 **INSIDER TIP**
> **Down Under**
>
> Many of Toronto's attractions, as well as shops and restaurants, are connected via the PATH, an underground network of walkways. This is a great way to get around in winter while avoiding the harsh weather outside.

21 The Beaches and Scarborough Bluffs

◉ F1 🚋 Queen 501

The Beaches is one of Toronto's most beguiling neighborhoods, with leafy streets running up from the lakeshore. The area lies to the east of downtown, between Woodbine Avenue and Victoria Park Avenue. Queen Street East, the main thoroughfare, is liberally sprinkled with excellent cafés and shops. The Beaches was a originally restrained and quiet neighborhood, but its long, sandy beach and boardwalk have made it extremely desirable. Rollerblading and cycling are popular here; a 2-mile (3-km) boardwalk runs along the beach and is very busy in summer. Many of Toronto's beaches have been approved for swimming; call (416) 392 7161 for water-quality reports.

At its eastern end, the Beaches borders Scarborough, a large suburb whose principal attraction is also along the rocky lakeshore. Here, the striking Scarborough Bluffs, outcrops of rock made from ancient sands and clay, track along Lake Ontario for 10 miles (16 km). A series of parks provides access; Scarborough Bluffs and the Cathedral Bluffs parks offer great views of jagged cliffs, and Bluffers Park is ideal for picnics.

22

The Toronto Islands

F2 **Queen's Quay**
toronto.ca/parks/island

In Lake Ontario, just offshore from the city, the low-lying

Toronto Islands, connected by footbridges, shelter Toronto's harbor and provide easy-going recreation in a car-free environment. Here, amid the cool lake breezes, visitors can escape the extremes of the summer heat, which can reach up to 95°F (35°C). Whatever the weather, there are views of the CN Tower (*p186*).

It takes about an hour to walk from one end of the islands to the other. In the east is Ward's Island, a sleepy residential area; Centre Island, home to the Centreville Amusement Park for children, is in the middle; while westerly Hanlan's Point has one of the country's few public clothing-optional beaches.

23

Fort York

C5 **250 Fort York Blvd**
511, 509 **10am–5pm daily; Sep–mid-May 10am–4pm Mon–Fri**
Good Fri, Dec 25–26, Jan 1 **fortyork.ca**

The British originally established Fort York in

The Toronto Islands, a great place for activities, and for taking in stunning
↓ views of the city (inset)

Did You Know?
———
Baseball legend Babe Ruth hit his first professional home run on the Toronto Islands, in 1914.

1793 to maintain a military and naval presence on Lake Ontario in the turbulent years that followed the American Revolution. The fort was attacked and largely destroyed by US forces during the War of 1812. The British rebuilt the fort after the battle, and their presence helped fuel the growth of the Town of York, now Toronto.

The fort has been restored to its late wartime appearance, with soldiers' barracks, officers' quarters and fortifications. Today, its defensive walls enclose Canada's largest collection of original buildings from the War of 1812.

The fort's visually striking Visitor Centre displays exhibits on varying themes that explore the site's history spanning 200 years. In addition, Fort York attracts thousands of visitors during the festivals and special events held here throughout the year.

HIDDEN GEM
Riverdale Farm

In the Toronto neighborhood of Cabbagetown lies Riverdale Farm. This century-old 7-acre (3-ha) working farm is free and open to the public all year. There are lots of friendly farm animals on site, many of which can be petted and fed.

24

Toronto Zoo

📍 F1 📍 361A Old Finch Ave, Scarborough Ⓣ Kennedy 🚌 86A (weekdays all year plus weekends in summer) 🕐 Times vary, check website 🌐 torontozoo.com

Toronto has one of the world's best zoos, which occupies a large slice of the Rouge River Valley. The animals are grouped according to their natural habitats, both outside, amid the mixed forest and flatlands of the river valley, and inside large, climate-controlled pavilions.

Visitors can tour the zoo by choosing one of the marked trails, or hop aboard the Zoomobile, a 30-minute ride with commentary that gives an excellent overview. It takes about four hours to see a good selection of animals, including such Canadian species as moose, caribou, and grizzly bear. There is also a polar bear enclosure. Splash Island provides a spot for young visitors to cool off in the water, amid walrus and beaver sculptures.

25

Aga Khan Museum

📍 F1 📍 77 Wynford Dr Ⓣ Eglinton 🚌 100 Flemingdon Park east to Wynford Dr 🕐 10am–6pm Tue–Sun (to 8pm Wed) 🌐 agakhanmuseum.org

The first North American museum dedicated to the arts of Muslim civilization, the Aga Khan Museum connects visual and live arts from the Iberian Peninsula to China through exhibitions, education programs, and a full roster of performances in its 350-seat auditorium. The museum's main floor includes a Persian-style salon and rotating displays of the permanent collection, whose exquisite manuscripts, drawings, paintings, decorated ceramics, metalwork, and architectural ornamentation date from the 8th to the 19th centuries. Four temporary exhibitions are displayed on the second floor every year, highlighting the continuum of artistic traditions from early Muslim civilizations to the present day.

Designed by Japanese architect Fumihiko Maki, the museum shares a beautiful site, complete with a landscaped park and formal garden, with the Ismaili Centre, Toronto, designed by Charles Correa. Admission to the Aga Khan Museum is free from 4pm on Wednesdays. Collection and architecture tours are offered from Tuesday to Sunday, and garden tours are usually offered at scheduled times.

26

Ontario Science Centre

📍 F1 📍 770 Don Mills Rd Ⓣ Eglinton or Pape 🚌 Eglinton 100 or Don Mills 25 🕐 10am–4pm Mon–Fri, 10am–7pm Sat, 10am–5pm Sun 🌐 ontarioscience centre.ca

One of Toronto's most popular sights, the Ontario Science Centre attracts children in droves. They come for the center's interactive displays and hands-on exhibits exploring and investigating all manner of phenomena, from the solar system to the

Japanese cherry trees, donated by Toyko, blossom in High Park in spring

and the Laskay Emporium general store, which shows the array of goods that could be bought. Five buildings are credited to Daniel Stong, a 19th-century pioneer: his pig house, smoke house, grain barn, and two contrasting homes (the first a crude log shack, the second a civilized house with a brick fireplace and a garden planted with herbs).

---

29 🏷️ 🍴 🛍️

McMichael Canadian Art Collection

📍 E1 🏠 10365 Islington Ave, Kleinburg 🕐 May-Oct: 10am–5pm daily; Nov–Apr: 10am–4pm Tue–Sun 🌐 mcmichael.com

In Kleinburg, about 30 minutes' drive north of downtown Toronto, Robert and Signe McMichael built themselves a fine log-and-stone dwelling overlooking the Humber River Valley. The McMichaels were also avid collectors of Canadian art, and in 1965 they donated their house and paintings to the province of Ontario. The art collection has greatly increased since then and, with more than 6,000 pieces, is now one of the most extensive collections of Canadian art in the province.

The focus of the McMichael is the work of the Group of Seven (p54), with the permanent galleries dedicated to displaying a selection of their works. The keynote paintings are characteristically raw and forceful landscapes illustrating the wonders of the Canadian wilderness. Both Tom Thomson (a renowned precursor of the Group) and Lawren Harris are well represented. There are also exhibitions of contemporary, aboriginal, and Inuit art.

Did You Know?

Almost a quarter of Canada's population lives within 100 miles (160 km) of Toronto.

human brain. At KidSpark, children up to age eight and under can make music, experiment with tracks, balls, and cogs, or join a construction team to build a house, while older kids will appreciate the AstraZeneca Human Edge gallery.

---

27 🍴 🛍️

High Park

📍 E2 🏠 1873 Bloor St W 🌐 highparktoronto.com

This lakefront, 400-acre (161-ha) park west of Toronto's downtown core is one of the city's largest green spaces and was originally opened in 1876. It is both a recreational and natural park, with various facilities available, including playgrounds, a nature center, a historical museum, and an outdoor pool. The northeastern part of the park is forested and has creeks, ponds, and many walking trails winding through it. For families, the free petting zoo and tractor-train are entertaining, and the Grenadier Pond is good for both fishing and ice-skating.

---

28 🏷️ 🖥️ 🛍️

Black Creek Pioneer Village

📍 E1 🏠 1000 Murray Ross Parkway, Cnr Steeles Ave W & Jane St 🚇 Finch 🚌 60 🕐 Times vary, check website 🗓️ Jan–Apr (except March break) 🌐 blackcreek.ca

Over the years, some 40 19th-century buildings have been moved to historic Black Creek Pioneer Village from other parts of Ontario. Inevitably, the end result is not entirely realistic – no Ontario village ever looked quite like this – but this living history showpiece is still great fun. Staff in period costume demonstrate traditional skills such as baking, candlemaking, and printing. Among the more interesting buildings are the Doctor's House from 1860,

The angular, white granite exterior of the Aga Khan Museum

A SHORT WALK
HARBOURFRONT

Distance 1 mile (1.5 km) **Time** 15 minutes
Nearest subway Toronto Convention Centre

Toronto's Harbourfront has had a varied history.
Lake Ontario once lapped against Front Street,
but the Victorians reclaimed 2 miles (3 km) of land to
accommodate their railroad yards and warehouses.
Ontario's exports and imports were funneled through
this industrial strip until the 1960s, when trade declined.
In the 1980s, the area was given a new lease of life,
and Harbourfront now boasts grassy parks, walkways,
smart apartments, and a cluster of tourist sights in
and around the Harbourfront Centre.

*Once the world's
tallest building, the
CN Tower (p186)
offers views of up to
100 miles (160 km)
over Ontario, and a
glass floor for those
with iron nerves.*

*Ripley's Aquarium of Canada (p194) features
over 16,000 marine creatures, from salmon and
sawfish to sea nettles. Take the tunnel through the
Dangerous Lagoon to be surrounded by 640,000
gallons (2.9 million liters) of shark-infested water.*

START

FRONT ST. W.

*Using enough electricity to light the
province of Prince Edward Island, a
performance at the vast **Rogers Centre**
stadium is an unforgettable experience.*

BREMNER BLVD

*Steam locomotives sit around
the still-operational turntable
at the **Roundhouse**, home to
the Toronto Railway Museum.*

0 meters   150   N ↑
0 yards   150

LAKE SHORE

↑ Train on display outside the
Toronto Railway Museum

*Sailing out onto **Lake
Ontario** and around
the three Toronto
Islands provides fine
views of the city. Small
sailboats, motorboats,
and tours are available.*

Interactive dive show at ↑
Ripley's Aquarium of Canada

Steam Whistle Brewing *at the Roundhouse is a working brewery in a historic former steam train repair facility. Tasting tours are available.*

The **Gardiner Expressway** *divides the city center from the waterfront and leads east to Niagara Falls.*

Did You Know?

Sandbar Sharks and Roughtail Stingrays can be seen in the Dangerous Lagoon at Ripley's Aquarium.

SIMCOE STREET

GARDINER EXPRESSWAY

BLVD. W.

QUEEN'S QUAY

O FINISH

The **Power Plant Contemporary Art Gallery** *hosts changing exhibitions of major international artists.*

Harbourfront *is a lively place for visitors, especially in summer. Private vessels are berthed in the basins at the water's edge and the walkways offer lovely lake views.*

The **Bill Boyle Artport** *is the hub of the Harbourfront Centre, where most of the activity takes place. There is also a performance space.*

Ottawa's Parliament Buildings in the snow

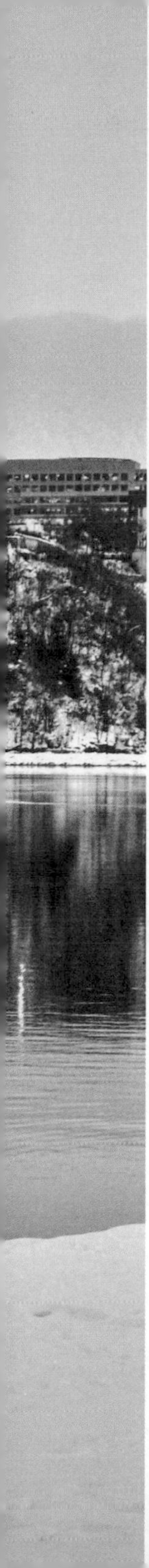

ONTARIO

Ontario is justly famous for its history and natural beauty. The myriad lakes and waterways that dominate the landscape here once served as trade highways through the wilderness for First Nations people and explorers. The Saint Lawrence is one of the world's great waterways and begins near the small, historic city of Kingston.

North of Lake Ontario lies the Canadian Shield, with the ancient lakes, rocks, and forest that epitomize Canada. A favorite with many Canadian vacationers, Algonquin Provincial Park is one of the country's most famous wilderness areas. Also popular is the picturesque Kawartha Lakes region. Rising majestically over the Ottawa River, Canada's capital is a storehouse of national history and stately architecture that attracts over seven million visitors each year.

ONTARIO

Must Sees
1. Niagara Falls
2. Ottawa
3. Algonquin Provincial Park

Experience More
4. Thousand Islands
5. Prescott
6. Rideau Canal
7. Upper Canada Village
8. Kingston
9. Prince Edward County
10. Haliburton Highlands
11. Barry's Bay
12. Combermere
13. Lang Pioneer Village
14. Eganville
15. Kawartha Lakes
16. Hamilton
17. Windsor
18. London
19. North Bay
20. Niagara-on-the-Lake
21. Stratford
22. Brantford
23. St. Jacobs
24. Sainte-Marie among the Hurons
25. Orillia
26. Temagami
27. Lake Erie
28. Sault Ste. Marie
29. Thunder Bay
30. Goderich
31. Muskoka
32. Nottawasaga Bay
33. Sauble Beach
34. Lake Huron
35. Manitoulin Island
36. Lake Superior
37. Point Pelee National Park
38. Georgian Bay Islands National Park
39. Welland Canal
40. Killarney Provincial Park

1

NIAGARA FALLS

🚗🚌 From Toronto 🛈 Table Rock Welcome Centre, 6650 Niagara Pkwy; www.niagarafallstourism.com

Although the majestic rumble of the falls can be heard from miles away, there is no preparation for the sight itself, a great arc of frothing, hissing water crashing over a huge cliff amid dense clouds of spray.

Thousands of sightseers visit Niagara Falls every day, eager to feel the cool mist of the thundering waterfalls on their faces. Created by the Wisconsin glaciation about 10,000 years ago, Niagara Falls actually has three cataracts to gaze at, as the speeding river is divided into twin channels by Goat Island, a tiny spray-soaked parcel of land. On one side of Goat Island is the mighty Canadian Horseshoe Falls, and, on the far side, across the border, is the smaller American Falls, along with the comparatively narrow Bridal Veil Falls. When visiting, take time to stop at some of the other sights in the region, including wildlife preserves, museums, and the town of Niagara Falls. The historic town of Niagara-on-the-Lake (*p226*) is also nearby, and is surrounded by some excellent vineyards and wineries.

↑ Visitors traveling through the mist on the Hornblower Niagara Cruise

Did You Know?

Annie Taylor, a school teacher, was the first to survive going over Horseshoe Falls in a barrel in 1901.

Timeline

1604

▽ French explorer Samuel de Champlain is the first to write about the falls in his journals

1829

▽ Sam Patch becomes the first daredevil to jump into the falls and survive

8,000 BC

△ The features that became Niagara Falls (and the Great Lakes) develop during the Wisconsin glaciation

1804

△ Napoleon Bonaparte's brother Jérôme visits with his bride on their honeymoon

↑ Sunrise over ice fog at the mighty Horseshoe Falls in winter

1918

▽ The Niagara Scow, a barge, is grounded on the rocks where it still remains to this day

2012

▽ Nik Wallenda becomes the first person to walk across the falls in 116 years, using a tightrope

1846

△ Maid of the Mist, a boat tour service *(p206)* operating at the base of the falls, opens for business

1965

△ The Skylon Tower, a 160-m (520-ft) observation tower overlooking Niagara Falls, opens

① Horseshoe Falls

Named for their shape, the 2,600-ft- (790-m-) wide and 188-ft- (57-m-) high Horseshoe Falls are the mightiest of the Niagara waterfalls. Hydroelectric companies have harnessed its raw power, reducing erosion as a positive side effect. At night the falls are illuminated in a rainbow of colors, and firework shows are held nightly in the summer. During the winter months, when crowds are smaller, the ice formations on the falls are quite spectacular.

Stunning close-up views are available from boat trips on the Maid of the Mist or Hornblower Niagara Cruises. Even better is the walk down through a series of rocky tunnels that lead behind Horseshoe Falls, where the noise from the crashing waters is deafening and the wall of water so thick that it blocks out the daylight. This is the Journey Behind the Falls, accessible via the Table Rock Welcome Centre. The center also houses Niagara's Fury, an exciting 4D simulation of the creation of the falls.

② American Falls

New York State, on the US side of the international border, lays claim to this waterfall. Though vast, its 950-ft- (290-m-) wide crest sees a fraction of the volume of the water that is carried over by Horseshoe Falls.

③ Rainbow Bridge

From the elegant span of the Rainbow Bridge there are panoramic views over the falls. The bridge itself crosses the gorge between Canada and the US, and there is a small pedestrian toll to get onto it (cash is required). Here, on sunny days, rainbows rise through the spray, creating amazing photo opportunities.

American Falls

The Rainbow Bridge connects the US and Canadian sides of the town of Niagara Falls.

↓ ⑨ Botanical Gardens and butterfly Conservatory
4.3 miles (7km)

↓ ⑧ Niagara Glen nature Reserve
4 miles (6.5km)

↓ ⑦ Whirlpool Areo Car
2 miles (3.5km)

↙ ⑥ White Water Walk
1.4 miles (2.3km)

Bird Kingdom is Canada's only indoor aviary and features over 400 exotic birds.

Town of Niagara Falls

Clifton Hill is lined with a string of fast-food restaurants and tourist attractions.

Must See

→ Visitors getting up close to Horseshoe Falls on the Journey Behind the Falls

At Horseshoe Falls, 90 percent of the water of the Niagara River roars over a semicircular cliff of the Niagara Escarpment.

The Table Rock Welcome Centre is packed with amenities and offers access to the 4D immersive experience, Niagara's Fury.

①

An elevator behind Horseshoe Falls leads to the Journey Behind the Falls.

Hornblower Niagara Cruises boats gets very close to the foot of the falls. Raincoats are supplied to protect passengers from the spray.

The Skylon Tower gives a bird's-eye view of the falls.

↑ Illustrated map of Niagara Falls and Goat Island, seen from above

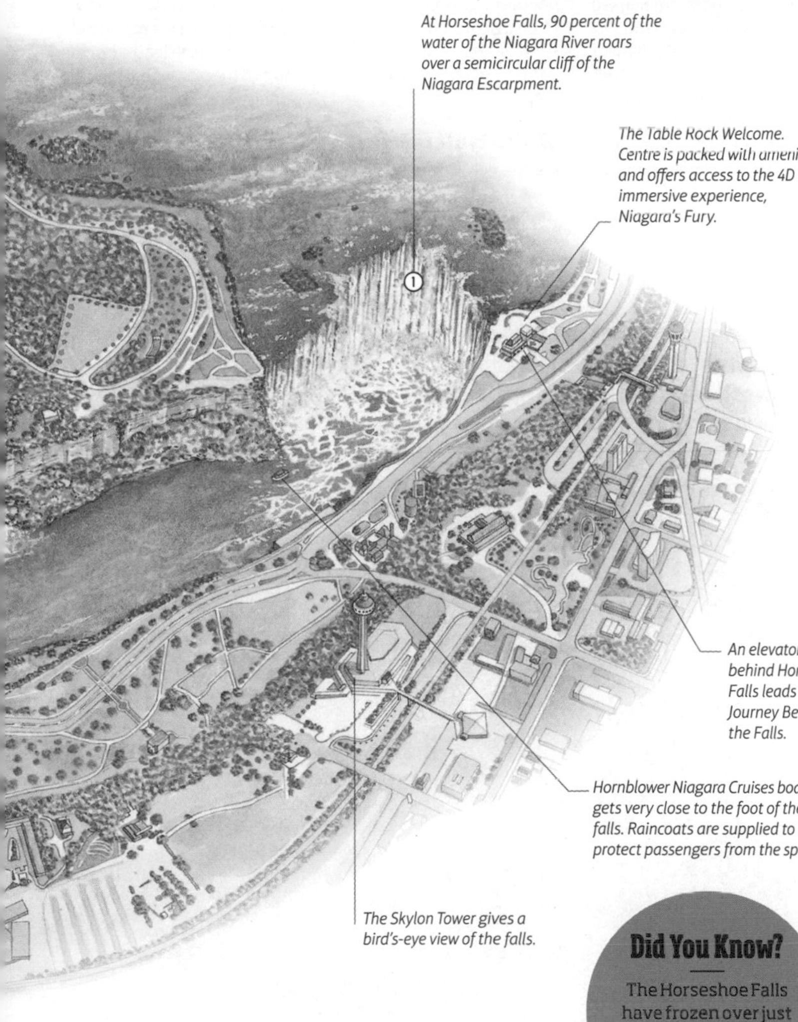

Did You Know?

The Horseshoe Falls have frozen over just once (in 1848). The American Falls have frozen six times.

④
Town of Niagara Falls

Niagara Falls is a welcoming town that stretches along the Niagara River for about 2 miles (3 km). Renowned as a honeymoon destination, the town is well equipped to satisfy the needs of the 14 million people who visit the falls each year. It is divided into three main sections: to the south are the mighty falls themselves; these are flanked by a thin strip of parkland that stretches out along the river bank as far as Clifton Hill, the glitziest street in Ontario, lined with a series of garish amusement park attractions. To the west is the main motel strip, Lundy's Lane. To the north, on Bridge Street, lie the business district and the train and bus stations.

> The Niagara River makes a dramatically sharp turn about 3 miles (4.5 km) downstream from the falls, generating a vicious, raging whirlpool

⑤
Bird Kingdom

Explore a multi-level rainforest filled with exotic creatures and free-flying tropical birds here at the world's largest indoor aviary. Visitors can also get a chance to hold and feed some of these feathered friends. And if you're not afraid of the dark, the Night Jungle is home to owls, bats, and other nocturnal critters, waiting to be discovered.

⑥
White Water Walk

A great way to admire the force of the Niagara River's torrent is from down at the bottom of the canyon. The White Water Walk

GREAT VIEW
Skylon Tower

This huge tower has an observation deck and a revolving restaurant at the top, giving a bird's-eye view of the falls below. It's also open in the evenings, when you can see the falls lit up in a multitude of colors.

provides this close-up view by means of a tunnel and an elevator, which lead from the top of the gorge to a riverside boardwalk. The whirlpools and rapids here are some of the most spectacular, yet treacherous, in the world.

⑦
Whirlpool Aero Car

The Niagara River makes a dramatically sharp turn about 3 miles (4.5 km) downstream from the falls, generating a vicious, raging whirlpool, one of the most lethal stretches of

Tour boat at the base of American Falls in dark, stormy weather ↑

↑ The 1916-designed Whirlpool Aero Car, over the Niagara River

⑧ Niagara Glen Nature Reserve

The small Niagara Glen Nature Reserve lies 4 miles (7 km) downriver from the falls. This segment of the gorge has been preserved in pristine condition, with bushes and low trees tumbling down the rocky cliffside. This is how it may have looked before the coming of the Europeans. Seven different hiking trails lead past boulders, caves, and wildflowers. The walks are easy on the way down but a steep climb on the way up.

⑨ Botanical Gardens and Butterfly Conservatory

The Niagara Parks Botanical Gardens are located 6 miles (9 km) downstream from the falls and comprise 100 acres (40 ha) of beautifully maintained gardens divided into several different zones. One

water in the whole of North America. The effect is created when the river pushes against the northwest side of the canyon, only to be forced to turn around in the opposite direction. The most stunning view of the whirlpool rapids is from the century-old Aero Car, a cable car designed by renowned Spanish engineer Leonardo Torres Quevedo, that crosses the gorge, high above the river.

of the prettiest areas in summer is the rose garden, which displays over 2,400 different varieties. The Butterfly Conservatory, set inside the Gardens, is even more popular. Over 2,000 butterflies are housed in a huge heated dome, where they flit about freely, sometimes landing on delighted visitors. It is one of the largest collections in the world. A series of pathways pass through the dome, leading past the lush tropical flora on which the butterflies make their homes.

EAT

AG
This true farm-to-table fine dining establishment is a welcome respite from all the flashing neon lights in town. Try the juniper-dusted venison loin, and for dessert, the Niagara Maple Rosemary Crème Brûlée.

🏠5195 Magdalen Ave, Niagara Falls ⏰Dinner only ❌Mon 🌐agcuisine.com

$$$

Flour Mill Restaurant
An elegant, cozy restaurant with antique decor inside the Old Stone Inn (which dates from 1904). The locally inspired brunch menu is the best, with delicious eggs benedict, steak and eggs, and other classics.

🏠6080 Fallsview Blvd, Niagara Falls 🌐oldstoneinnhotel.com

$$$

↑ The city's Parliament Buildings overlooking Ottawa River at sunrise

②

OTTAWA

✈ 11 miles (18 km) S of the city 🚆 200 Tremblay Rd, 3347 Fallowfield Rd 🚌 265 Catherine St, 200 Tremblay Rd ℹ Capital Information Centre, 90 Wellington St; www.ottawatourism.ca

Ottawa was a compromise choice for Canada's capital, picked in part because of the rivalry between the English and French, and the cities that grew into today's Toronto and Montreal. Named capital of the Dominion of Canada in 1857, Ottawa has a fine setting on the banks of the Ottawa and Rideau rivers and an identity all its own.

① Ⓜ 🏛

Parliament Buildings

🏛 Parliament Hill, 111 Wellington St 🕐 May & Jun: 9am–7:30pm daily; Jul–Apr: 9am–4:30pm daily 🚫 Jan 1, Jul 1, Dec 25 🌐 parl.gc.ca

Dominating the skyline, the country's government buildings overlook downtown Ottawa in a stately manner. Undaunted by the skyscrapers that have crept up around them in the 150 years since they became Ottawa's center of power, the East and West blocks glow green above the city due to their copper roofing. The Gothic Revival sandstone buildings were completed in 1860. Located on a 164-ft (50-m) hill, the Parliament offers a view of the Ottawa River. Its buildings are distinctly reminiscent of London's Westminster, both in their Neo-Gothic style and in their position. Largely destroyed in a fire in 1916, all the buildings are now restored to their former grandeur and can be toured year round. Visitors can climb the Peace Tower for glorious views of the city, and watch proceedings of the Senate and House of Commons whenever they are in session. Hand-carved sandstone and limestone characterize the interior of the government chambers. In summertime, Mounties patrol the neat, grassy grounds outside the Parliament. On July 1, which is Canada Day, Parliament Hill is the site of a large outdoor concert and celebration.

②

Cathédrale Notre-Dame

🏛 385 Sussex Dr 📞 (613) 241 7496 🕐 11:30am–6pm Mon, 10am–6pm Tue–Fri, 2–6pm Sat, 8am–8:30pm Sun

Built between 1841 and 1865, the twin-spired Cathédrale Notre-Dame is Ottawa's best-known Catholic church. It is situated in the ByWard Market

↑ The stunning arched ceiling of Cathédrale Notre-Dame

area and features a spectacular Gothic-style ceiling. Philippe Parizeau (1852–1938) carved the woodwork in mahogany. In niches around the sanctuary there are wooden etchings of prophets and apostles, crafted by Louis-Philippe Hébert (1850–1917), now painted to look like stone. Joseph-Eugène Guigues, the first bishop of Ottawa, oversaw the completion of Notre-Dame, and his statue is outside the basilica.

___

③ 🗘 Ⓜ 🖵 🏛 Bytown Museum

🏠 1 Canal Lane
🕐 Mid-May-mid-Oct: 10am-5pm daily (to 8pm Thu; mid-Jun-Aug: to 7pm); mid-Oct-mid-Dec & Feb-mid-May: 11am-4pm Thu-Mon
🌐 bytownmuseum.com

Housed in Ottawa's oldest stone building (1827), the Bytown Museum traces the history of Ottawa's early years from the construction of the Rideau Canal through the rough and tumble days of Bytown, to the city's emergence as Canada's capital and beyond. The British Royal Engineer in charge of building the Rideau Canal, Lt. Colonel John By, established his headquarters at this location in 1826. While work was underway, the building was used as a storehouse for military supplies and silver coins. The museum hosts exhibitions, tours, and family events.

___

④ 🗘 🖵 🏛 Canadian War Museum

🏠 1 Vimy Pl 🕐 Times vary, check website
🌐 warmuseum.ca

Canadians may have a reputation as a peaceful people but they have seen their share of the world's battlefields. This museum, housed in a stunning modern building close to Parliament Hill, looks at the country's military history and at how this past has shaped the nation and its people. Exhibits range from the earliest wars fought on Canadian soil between the French and the British to the present day. The LeBreton Gallery houses an extensive collection of military technology including vehicles, artillery, and other artifacts. The Beaverbrook Collection of War Art contains 13,000 works and is one of the largest collections of military art in the world. The Memorial Hall offers a space for quiet reflection. Its concrete walls are reminiscent of the rows of gravestones in Allied war cemeteries, and its sole artifact is the headstone from the grave of Canada's Unknown Soldier. The museum's Regeneration Hall, with its view of the Peace Tower on Parliament Hill, represents hope for a better future. There is no charge for entry to the museum on Canada Day (July 1) and on Remembrance Day (November 11).

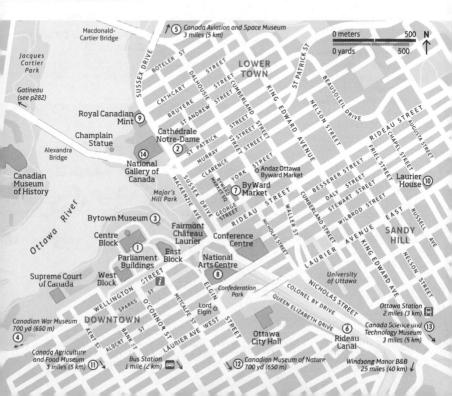

Did You Know?

Ottawa is the world's seventh coldest capital city, ranking below cities such as Moscow and Tallin.

⑤ Ⓜ 🖵 🏛

Canada Aviation and Space Museum

🏠 11 Aviation Parkway
🕒 May–early Sep: 9am–5pm daily; early Sep–Apr: 10am–5pm Wed–Mon 🔲 ingenium canada.org/aviation

This huge building near Rockcliffe Airport houses more than 130 aircraft, which have flown both in war and peace. A replica of the famous 1909 Silver Dart, the first aircraft to fly in Canada, is here, as is the nose cone from the Avro Arrow, the supersonic superfighter that created a political crisis in Canada when the government halted its development in the 1950s. The Spitfire, valiant friend of the Allies in World War II, features alongside historic bush planes such as the Beaver and early passenger carrier jets. Displays detail the exploits of Canadian war heroes, while the Walkway of Time traces the history of world aviation. There is also a full-motion flight simulator that lets visitors take the controls.

⑥

Rideau Canal

Built in the mid-19th century, the Rideau Canal, a UNESCO World Heritage Site, stretches from Ottawa to the city of Kingston (p221). The canal flows through the capital, and is an attractive place to explore with its walking and cycling paths bordering the water. Once used for shipping, the canal is now a recreational area. In summer, visitors stroll along its banks, while through Ottawa's freezing winter an 5-mile (8-km) section of the canal turns into the world's largest skating rink. It is popular with locals during the winter festival, and also as a means of commuting to work.

⑦ 🍽 🖵 🏛

ByWard Market

🏠 Bounded by Cumberland, Sussex, George, and St. Patrick sts 🔲 byward-market.com

This neighborhood bustles all year round: outdoors in the summer, inside in winter. The area is located just east of Parliament Hill, across the Rideau Canal, and offers a colorful collection of craft shops, cafés, and nightclubs. Special attractions include the food market in the ByWard Market Building on George Street, and the cobblestoned Sussex Courtyards.

⑧ 🖉 Ⓜ 🍽

National Arts Centre

🏠 1 Elgin St 🕒 Daily
🔲 nac-cna.ca

Completed in 1969, the National Arts Centre (NAC) has four stages, an elegant canal-side restaurant, and a summer terrace. The original building, designed by noted Canadian architect Fred Lebensold, expanded in 2017 to include a dramatic Elgin Street entrance with stellar views of the capital. The NAC orchestra and many Canadian and international artists perform here regularly. Reserving tickets well in advance is recommended.

⑨ 🖉 Ⓜ 🏛

Royal Canadian Mint

🏠 320 Sussex Dr 🕒 Daily
🔲 mint.ca

Founded in 1908 as a branch of the British Royal Mint, this

↑ Bronze sculpture welcoming visitors to the Royal Canadian Mint

one no longer produces regular Canadian cash currency. Instead, it strikes many special-edition coins and Maple Leaf bullion investment coins. The mint also processes about 70 percent of the country's gold in its refinery, which is among the largest in North America. Tours take place throughout the day; book ahead to ensure you see the process that turns sheets of metal into bags of shiny gold coins. Weekend tours may be less interesting, as the production lines are unlikely to be running.

⑩ 🖉

Laurier House

🏠 335 Laurier Ave E
📞 (613) 992 8142 🕐 Mid-May-Jun & Sep-mid-Oct: 10am-5pm Thu-Mon; Jul & Aug: 10am-5pm daily

A National Historic Site, this Victorian town house was built in 1878 and served as the chief residence of two notable Canadian prime ministers, Sir Wilfrid Laurier and William Lyon Mackenzie King. Beautifully furnished throughout, it houses memorabilia, papers, and personal possessions of both former national leaders.

←

Aircraft on display at the Canada Aviation and Space Museum

⑪ 🖉 🅼

Canada Agriculture and Food Museum

🏠 901 Prince of Wales Dr
🕐 Mar-Oct: 9am-5pm daily; Nov-Feb: 9am-5pm Wed-Sun 🌐 ingeniumcanada. org/cafm

This museum at the Central Experimental Farm, a crop research station and National Historic Site, allows visitors to explore the sights and sounds of farm life through animals, exhibitions, hands-on demonstrations, and delicious foods. The farm's livestock barns and show cattle herds are especially popular with children, and the food cooked in the demo kitchen is always a favorite.

⑫ 🖉 🖥 🛍

Canadian Museum of Nature

🏠 240 McLeod St 🕐 Jun-Aug: 9am-6pm daily (to 8pm Thu); Sep-May: 9am-5pm Tue-Sun (to 8pm Thu) 🌐 nature.ca

Canada's national natural history museum entertains with its well thought-out galleries highlighting birds, mammals, aquatic creatures, fossils, and dinosaurs. The Vale Earth Gallery has beautiful geological specimens, and kids will enjoy the Arctic marine exhibit, where they can captain a research vessel. In the Animalium, visitors get a close-up look at giant snails, tarantulas, and scorpions.

⑬ 🖉 🖥 🛍

Canada Science and Technology Museum

🏠 1867 St. Laurent Blvd
🕐 9am-5pm Tue-Sun
🌐 ingeniumcanada.org/ cstm

Following an extensive, multi-million dollar refurbishment, this museum reopened in 2017 to coincide with Canada's 150th birthday celebrations. There is an emphasis on digital presentation, with exhibits including a wide range of fascinating displays exploring Canada's space history, transportation through the ages, and modern and industrial technology, with an immersive Children's Gallery.

STAY

Andaz Ottawa ByWard Market
This hotel is hung with Canadian art, and features a glassed-in bar that overlooks the Parliament Buildings.

🏠 325 Dalhousie St
🌐 hyatt.com

$$$

Lord Elgin
A historic landmark hotel dating from 1941, with marble bathrooms and a 24-hour gym.

🏠 100 Elgin St
🌐 lordelginhotel.ca

$$$

Windsong Manor Bed & Breakfast
A country home just outside Ottawa, with three spacious bedrooms and an outdoor hot tub.

🏠 1342 Corkery Rd
🌐 windsongmanor.ca

$$$

(14) ⚅ ⚆ ⚇ ⚈

NATIONAL GALLERY OF CANADA

🏠 380 Sussex Dr 🚌 1, 3, 9 🕐 May–Sep: 10am–6pm daily (to 8pm Thu); Oct–Apr: 10am–5pm Tue–Sun (to 8pm Thu) 🌐 gallery.ca

Within a futuristic structure of pink-granite and glass, the National Gallery of Canada houses the country's premier collection of fine art. Here visitors can admire superb national and international masterpieces, from early Aboriginal art to cutting-edge installations by contemporary artists.

A colossal black spider sculpture, created by French-American artist Louise Bourgeois, guards the front entrance to the Gallery. Inside, a light-filled Colonnade takes you to the Great Hall where soaring windows offer views of Parliament Hill and the Ottawa River.

Contemporary Art

The contemporary collection, developed over the last three decades, is on both levels 1 and 2. Featured artists include Chris Ofili, Ai Wei Wei, Mona Hatoum, and Bharti Kher.

Canadian and Indigenous Art

The Gallery's first level houses the world's largest collection of Canadian and indigenous art, mostly dating from the early 18th-century through to modern times. Don't miss the fabulous white sculptures *Shapeshifter* (2000) and *Vienna* (2003), by Brian Jungen. Resembling life-size whale skeletons, they are made out of plastic patio chairs.

European, American, and Asian Art

The second level contains the European, American and Asian galleries, with paintings, sculptures, and decorative arts from the early 14th-century onwards. Paintings in this section are by well-known artists such as Rembrandt, Goya, Van Gogh, and Matisse. American Abstract Expressionism and Minimalism works are also well represented, including pieces by Andy Warhol. The Asian collection includes art from India, dating back to the 2nd century.

Louise Bourgeois's famous *Maman* sculpture, by the entrance to the Gallery ↑

1 This ceremonial Coat is by an unknown Naskapi artist (c. 1840).

2 The European and American galleries feature some 2,000 works.

3 Henry Moore carved this *Reclining Woman* sculpture in Green Horton stone in 1930.

A SHORT WALK
OTTAWA

Distance 1 mile (1.5 km) **Time** 25 minutes
Nearest bus stop Wellington O'Connor

Far more than just the political capital, Ottawa has a vibrant mix of English- and French-speaking residents and a striking combination of historic and modern buildings, with plenty of attractions to keep visitors busy. The core of the capital is relatively contained, and many of the top sights around the Parliament Buildings can be accessed on foot. Running south through the city, the Rideau Canal is Ottawa's recreation ground year round, from boating and strolling during summer months to skating across its icy surface in the freezing Canadian winter.

↑ Canadian Parliament Buildings on a crisp winter's day

The **Parliament Buildings** (p210) are the seat of government. A Changing of the Guards ceremony takes place outside the buildings at 10am daily from late June through late August.

START ▶

The **Centennial Flame** burns continually. It was first lit in 1967 to commemorate a century of Confederation.

WELLINGTON STREET

Built in the mid-19th century, the **Rideau Canal** (p212) is now a playground for visitors, its banks lined with grassy cycling and walking paths.

Annually, on November 11, a memorial service takes place at the **National War Memorial** to honor Canada's war veterans.

Fairmont Château Laurier is a luxury hotel, and arguably Canada's most famous. It has offered sumptuous accommodations to Canada's great and good since it was built in 1912.

0 meters   100
0 yards   100

N →

Did You Know?

Ottawa is one of Canada's youngest cities. Nearly half of all residents are under the age of 35.

A peaceful space in the heart of the busy capital, **Major's Hill Park** *is marked by a statue of an Anishinabe scout, in honor of the First Nations' role in the development of Canada.*

Nepean Point *is a spot from which the whole of central Ottawa can be seen.*

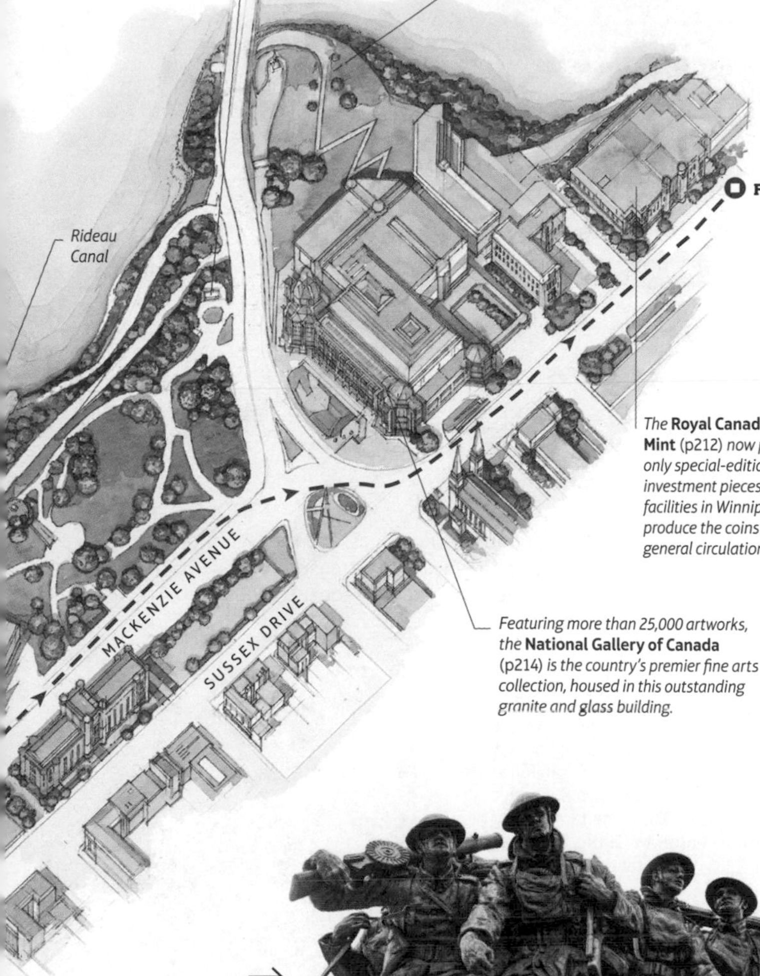
FINISH
Rideau Canal
MACKENZIE AVENUE
SUSSEX DRIVE

The **Royal Canadian Mint** (p212) *now produces only special-edition and investment pieces; newer facilities in Winnipeg produce the coins in general circulation.*

Featuring more than 25,000 artworks, the **National Gallery of Canada** (p214) *is the country's premier fine arts collection, housed in this outstanding granite and glass building.*

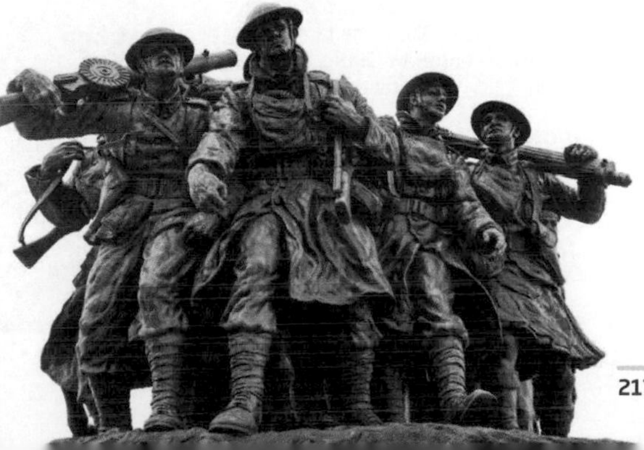

→ Sculpted figures of Canadian soldiers on the National War Memorial

Did You Know?

The park runs public "wolf howls", where staff imitate wolf cries to hear a response.

ALGONQUIN PROVINCIAL PARK

🏠 Hwy 60 🕐 Year-round, but limited services Nov–Mar
🌐 algonquinpark.on.ca

With its dense maple and pine woods, rocky ridges, and thousands of sparkling lakes and rivers, Algonquin is a national treasure. Wildlife abounds here: beavers, moose, and bears are all frequently spotted in their natural habitats, and the park echoes with the hauntingly beautiful call of the loon.

The Parkway Corridor

Hwy 60 is the only road through Algonquin, and it intersects a small portion of the park near its southern edge. Day trippers can follow its 35-mile (56-km) route to catch the park's major sights in a limited timeframe. Along here is the Visitor Centre, Art Centre, and Logging Museum, plus various rental facilities.

Algonquin Logging Museum

This museum brings to life the story of logging in Algonquin. A 1-mile (1.5-km) trail features

→
Paddling a canoe through the calm waters of Herb Lake

↑ Sunrise burning through the early morning fog at the Lake of Two Rivers; Moose wading through lake waters in Algonquin Provincial Park *(inset)*.

a re-created logging camp, a steam-powered amphibious tug called an "alligator", logging equipment, and information panels.

Canoeing in the Park

Over 1,200 miles (1930 km) of canoe trails crisscross the park. They range from beginner and family routes, some as short as 4 miles (6 km), to 43-mile (70-km) advanced treks. Canoe Lake is one of the more popular points for paddling, and mapped routes can be picked up from the Visitor Centre.

Lake Opeongo

The largest lake in the park, Lake Opeongo is famous for its incredible fishing opportunities. Although the lake is popular, it's so vast that there's an array of secluded coves and little islands to discover, making it the perfect spot for a private picnic.

FISHING

Algonquin Provincial Park is renowned for its excellent fishing opportunities, especially trout fishing. Hundreds of lakes in the park are home to native brook trout and lake trout. Spring is the best season for them, particularly the month of May. Bass, perch, and pike are found in the lakes as well. Note that a fishing licence is required to cast your rod and can be bought within the park.

EXPERIENCE MORE

4

The Thousand Islands

🏠 10 King St E, Gananoque; www.1000islands tourism.com

The Saint Lawrence River, one of the world's great waterways, is a gateway for ocean-going vessels traveling through the Great Lakes. Few stretches of the trip compare in charm or beauty to the Thousand Islands, an area that contains a scattering of over a thousand tiny islands, stretching from just below Kingston downriver to the waterside towns and cities of Gananoque, Brockville, and Rockport. Cruises of varying lengths, including some full-day trips to the curious Boldt's Castle, leave from these communities.

Boldt's Castle, on Heart Island across the US border in New York state, was a folly built by millionaire hotelier George Boldt, and abandoned in grief when his wife died in 1904. Oscar, Boldt's head chef at New York's Waldorf Astoria concocted Thousand Island salad dressing here.

Did You Know?

To count as one of the Thousand Islands, land within the river must support at least two living trees.

5

Prescott

🚌 🏠 360 Dibble St W; www.prescott.ca

The major attractions in this 19th-century town are its architecture and access to the Saint Lawrence River. Some visitors come for the excellent scuba diving: there are 22 wrecks that sank during the late 19th- and mid-20th-centuries within an hour's drive.

Fort Wellington National Historic Site, east from the center of town, also attracts many visitors. Originally built during the War of 1812 and rebuilt in 1838, four walls and some buildings remain, one of which now houses a museum.

Fort Wellington National Historic Site

🏠 370 Vankoughnet St, Prescott 📞 (613) 925 2896 🕐 Mid-May-Jun & Sep-mid-Oct: 10am-5pm Thu-Mon; Jul & Aug: 10am-5pm daily

6

Rideau Canal
The Rideau Canal, originally a defensive barrier protecting Canada against the Americans, stretches for 126 miles (202 km) from Ottawa to Lake Ontario. The best way to enjoy this scenic waterway is by boat. A great feat of 19th-century engineering, the system – which is a UNESCO World Heritage Site – allows boaters to float through tranquil farmland and scenic lakes, as well as visit the Rideau Canal Visitor Centre. North of Kingston, the canal also contains a number of provincial parks that offer canoe routes. Also popular is the Rideau Trail, a hiking system linking Kingston and Canada's capital city, Ottawa.

7

Upper Canada Village

🏠 13740 County Rd 2 🕐 Times vary, check website 🌐 uppercanadavillage.com

This re-created 19th-century town is made up of 40 authentic pre-Confederation (1867) buildings, relocated from the surrounding area to save them from flooding during construction of the Saint Lawrence Seaway in the 1950s. Today, it serves as a

←

A cruise boat navigating the Saint Lawrence River around the Thousand Islands

↑ Skaters gliding along the Rideau Canal, which freezes over in winter months

colorful reminder of the province's social history. Costumed villagers work in the forge and the sawmill, while a bakery, cheese factory, and general store are in operation on site. Special events include themed weekends and enthusiastic battle re-enactments.

⑧ Kingston

🚲🏠🍴☕ ℹ 209 Ontario St; www.visitkingston.ca

Once a center for shipbuilding and the fur trade, Kingston was briefly (1841–44) the capital of the United Province of Canada. It is still one of the freshwater sailing capitals of North America and the embarkation point for many local cruises. It is also home to more museums than any other town in Ontario. The restored British bastion Fort Henry National Historic Site of Canada is a military museum brought to life by guards in bright scarlet period uniforms. Canada's top military training university, the Royal Military College of Canada, is also based here, the museum of which tells the story of today's cadets and their forebears (open in summer only).

A short walk away from the Visitor Information Centre and City Hall lies the **Marine Museum of the Great Lakes**. There are displays on the history of the Great Lakes and the ships that sailed on them, including the first ship built for the Lakes here in 1678, and a 3,000-ton icebreaker. The nearby Kingston Mills lock station is a great spot for boat watching and picnicking.

Marine Museum of the Great Lakes
⊛ 🏠 53 Yonge St
🕐 10am–4pm Mon–Fri
ⓦ marmuseum.ca

⑨ Prince Edward County

ℹ 231 Main St W, Picton; www.prince-edward-county.com

Loved by foodies, the once-quiet Prince Edward County is a burgeoning getaway destination. There are now dozens of vineyards squeezed onto the island, which is surrounded by Lake Ontario and the Bay of Quinte. The island is also home to two beaches in Sandbanks Provincial Park. There, mountains of fine sand

reach 82 ft (25 m) and are considered one of the most significant freshwater dune systems in the world.

United Empire Loyalists settled in the county following the American Revolution (1775), founding engaging small towns and a strong farming industry.

TOP 3 WINERIES IN PRINCE EDWARD COUNTY

The Grange of Prince Edward
ⓦ grangewinery.com
Tastings are held in an enormous barn; afterwards enjoy a picnic in the grounds.

Hinterland Wine Company
ⓦ hinterlandwine.com
Known for its sparkling wines, this laid-back winery has a friendly atmosphere.

Waupoos Estates Winery
ⓦ waupooswinery.com
A classic estate overlooking Lake Ontario, with superb ice wines.

Forested islets in Thousand Islands

⑩ Haliburton Highlands

ℹ 12340 Hwy 35, Minden; www.myhaliburton highlands.com

The Haliburton Highlands are one of Ontario's year-round outdoor destinations, famed for their forests, lakes, and spectacular scenery. In the summer, visitors enjoy boating, fishing, and swimming. In fall, busloads of tourists travel to appreciate the celebrated seasonal colors; others come for the deer hunting. Winter brings snowsports enthusiasts to the area's pristine forests and provincial parks.

The arty village of Haliburton is a hotspot for vacationers. Head up Skyline Park Road for stunning views over the area. Scenic Hwy 35 winds north through exceptional landscapes, from Minden to the considerable charms of Dorset.

⑪ Barry's Bay

ℹ Ottawa Valley Tourist Association; www.ottawa valley.travel

Attractive Barry's Bay has a sizeable Polish population, as does its neighbor Wilno, which is the site of the first Polish settlement in Canada. The area is home to many craftspeople, who sell their wares in the local villages. Barry's Bay has a meticulously restored 1890s **railway station**, which now houses a fine collection of railway memorabilia. It also acts as a visitor information and community arts center. Sports facilities can be found at nearby Kamaniskeg Lake and Redcliffe Point, both of which are popular places for renting cottages.

Barry's Bay Railway Station

🏛 19503 Opeongo Line (Hwy 60) 🕐 May-Jun & Sep-mid-Oct: 10am-4pm Thu-Mon; Jul-Aug: 10am-6pm daily; mid-Oct-Dec: 10am-4pm Wed-Sat 🌐 therailway station.ca

⑫ Combermere

ℹ Ottawa Valley Tourist Association; www.ottawa valley.travel

The village of Combermere is a central point for people heading to a number of provincial parks in Eastern Ontario, including Algonquin (p218), Carson Lake, and Opeongo River. Along with Wilno and Barry's Bay, Combermere is one of three Madawaska Valley townships, and is a good tourist center for fuel and refreshments. Just south of the town lies the **Madonna House Pioneer Museum**. This Catholic lay community was founded by Catherine Doherty and has grown to have mission outposts around the world. It is managed by volunteers, who live on its cooperative farm. Since 1963, a recycling program has been raising money for the world's poor.

Madonna House Pioneer Museum

🏛 Hwy 517 🕐 Mid-May-Jul & Sep-Nov: 10am-5pm Thu-Sat; Jul-Sep 10am-5pm Tue-Sat 🌐 madonnahouse.org

---

GREAT VIEW
Dorset Lookout Tower

Head to the top of this lofty tower for some absolutely stunning 360 degree views - especially during fall - of the Lake of Bays and the surrounding area.

← Canoes moored at a dock in the Haliburton Highlands

14 Eganville

i **Ottawa Valley Tourist Association; www.ottawavalley.travel**

This Hwy 60 village is a handy tourist center for visitors to this picturesque region. Local attractions include the **Bonnechere Caves**, which were at the bottom of a tropical sea 500 million years ago. Gradually raised over millennia from the ocean bed, they are covered with fossils of primi-tive life forms. The privately owned site is open for tours in summer.

Bonnechere Caves

⊘ ⊘ ☐ 1247 Fourth Chute Rd
⊙ Mid-May-mid-Oct: daily
ⓦ bonnecherecaves.com

↑ A passage through the deep Bonnechere Caves in Eganville

At the center of the region lies the city of Peterborough, notable for the world's largest hydraulic liftlock. To the north is the Curve Lake Reserve's Whetung Ojibwa Centre, a good place for Aboriginal arts.

North of Peterborough lies **Petroglyphs Provincial Park**, better known to locals as the "teaching rocks" for the 900-plus Aboriginal carvings cut into the park's white marble outcrops. These preserved symbols were made by spiritual leaders to record their dreams and visions. Today the stones are housed in a glass building, built around them in 1984 to protect them from frost.

Petroglyphs Provincial Park

⊘ ☐ 2249 Northey's Bay Rd, Woodview ☎ (705) 877 2552
⊙ Mid-May-mid-Jun & Sep-mid-Oct: Wed-Sun; mid-Jun-Aug: 10am-5pm daily

15 Kawartha Lakes

i **1400 Crawford Dr, Peterborough; www.thekawarthas.ca**

The Kawartha Lakes are part of the 19th-century Trent-Severn Waterway that runs from Lake Ontario to Georgian Bay. Today the area offers many water-based activities, such as cruises and fishing.

13 Lang Pioneer Village

☐ 104 Lang Rd, Keene
⊙ Mid-May-mid-Jun: 10am-3pm Mon-Fri; mid-Jun-mid-May: 10am-4pm daily
ⓦ langpioneervillage.ca

Located on the tiny Indian River 2 miles (3 km) north of Keene, Lang Pioneer Village is a traditional representation of Canada's past, featuring 20 restored 19th-century buildings and heritage gardens. Visitors can watch a restored grist mill in action, and workers in period costumes display ancient skills while telling stories of what life was once like. Villagers also demonstrate traditional methods of work around the home. During the summer season, visitors can enjoy afternoon teas at the Keene Hotel (at an additonal cost). Special events throughout the year focus on how the pioneers celebrated the various harvests and Christmas.

→ The historic grist mill and spillway at Lang Pioneer Village

16

Hamilton

⬦✕🏛🚌 *i* 28 James St N;
www.tourism
hamilton.com

The city of Hamilton sits at the extreme western end of Lake Ontario, some 43 miles (70 km) from Toronto. It was known as a steel town, and the city's mills used to churn out around 60 percent of Canada's total production. Despite the town's industrial roots, Hamilton is a likeable place. One of its most renowned sights is **Dundurn Castle**, an Italian-style villa dating from the 1830s, whose interior holds a fine collection of period furnishings. It was built for the MacNabs, one of the most influential families in Ontario.

Another sight is the Royal Botanical Gardens, comprising forests, marshes, and small lakes over some 2,700 acres (1,093 ha) on the north side of Hamilton harbor. Among the notable gardens here are a fine Rose Garden and the perfumed Lilac Arboretum.

Also in town, the Canadian Warplane Heritage Museum has a display of more than 40 operational aircraft dating from World War II to the jet age.

Dundurn Castle
♿🕑 🏛 610 York Blvd
📞 (905) 546 2872 🕐 Noon–4pm Tue–Sun

17

Windsor

✕⬦🏛🚌 *i* 333 Riverside
Dr W, Suite 103; www.
visitwindsoressex.com

A car-manufacturing town, just like its American neighbor Detroit, Windsor and its factories produce hundreds of US-badged vehicles every day. Windsor has clean, tree-lined streets and a riverside walkway, but its most noted attraction is a riverside casino that draws thousands of visitors. Also of interest is the nearby Art Gallery of Windsor, which is noted for its excellent visiting exhibitions.

The city has many lively bars and cafés, the best of which are along the first three blocks of the main street, Ouellette. During Prohibition, millions of bottles of alcohol were smuggled from Windsor into the US across the Detroit River.

From Windsor, it is an easy 12-mile (20-km) drive south along the Detroit River to the British-built Fort Malden at Amherstburg. Not much is left of the fort, but there is a neatly restored barracks dating from 1819, and the old laundry now holds an interpretation center. This relates the fort's role in the War of 1812, when the English plotted with the Shawnee to invade the US.

STAY

The Barracks Inn
A boutique hotel, housed in a former barracks.

🏠 425 Wilson St E,
Ancaster, Hamilton
🌐 thebarracksinn.com

$$$

Serenity Ranch Bed & Breakfast
A cozy B&B surrounded by miles of lush scenery.

🏠 2171 Wilson St W,
Ancaster, Hamilton
🌐 serenityranchbb.com

$$$

Osler House
A quiet guesthouse with continental breakfasts.

🏠 30 South St W,
Dundas, Hamilton
🌐 oslerhouse.com

$$$

Did You Know?

The Duff Baby House in Windsor was built in 1792 and is considered the oldest building in Ontario.

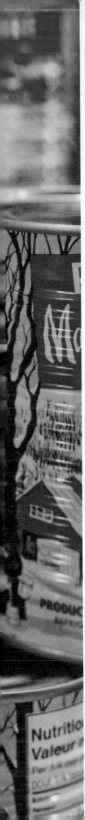

QUEBEC PROVINCE

Quebec is the largest of Canada's provinces and the biggest French-speaking territory in the world, with many of its eight million citizens holding firm to the language and culture inherited from their French ancestors.

In the south, the rich hilly farmland of the Appalachians and scarlet forests of maple trees attract many visitors each year, while the stark beauty of Nunavik's icy northern coniferous forests burst into a profusion of wildflowers in spring, alongside the largest hydroelectric projects in the world. The center of the region is Quebec's natural playground, the Laurentian Mountains, a pristine lake-filled landscape offering fine skiing on ancient mountains. Populated by indigenous peoples until the Europeans arrived in the 16th century, the area was fought over by the French and British until the British gained power in 1759. Today French-speakers dominate.

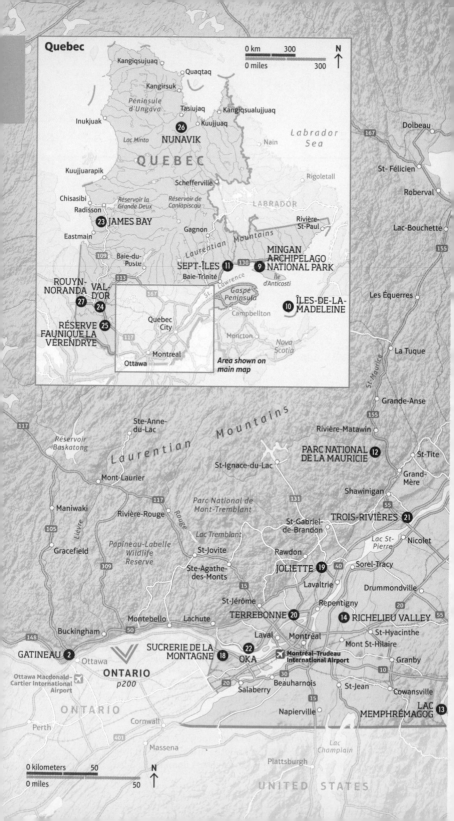

Moored boats reflected in the glasslike water of Hamilton's harbor at sunset

18
London

✕➡🏠🚌 ℹ️ **391 Wellington St; www.londontourism.ca**

London sits in one of the most fertile parts of Ontario and is the area's most important town. It is home to the University of Western Ontario, which has a modern art gallery and a campus with dozens of Victorian mansions. The finest buildings in the town center are the two 19th-century cathedrals: Saint Paul's, a Gothic Revival edifice built for the Anglicans in 1846, and Catholic Saint Peter's Cathedral Basilica, dating from 1885. The city's Museum of Ontario Archaeology focuses on the 1,100-year history of the area. The Lawson Iroquoian Village here is a reconstruction of a 500-year-old site.

19
North Bay

➡🏠🚌 ℹ️ **1375 Seymour St; www.tourismnorthbay.com**

Billing itself as the Gateway to the Near North, North Bay sits at the eastern end of Lake Nippissing, 210 miles (339 km) north of Toronto. The region's most famous residents are the Dionne quintuplets, born in 1934.

Nearby Lake Nippissing is renowned for its fishing and wilderness scenery. Cruises across the lake follow the old French explorer route.

20
Niagara-on-the-Lake

🚌 ℹ️ **26 Queen St; www. niagaraonthelake.com**

Niagara-on-the-Lake is a charming little town of elegant clapboard mansions and leafy streets, set where the mouth of the Niagara River empties into Lake Ontario. Originally known as Newark, the town became the capital of Upper Canada (as Ontario was then known) under this name in 1792. Just four years later, the British decided to move the capital farther away from the US border, and chose York (now Toronto) instead. It was a wise decision. The Americans crossed the Niagara River and destroyed Newark in the War of 1812. The British returned after the war to rebuild their homes, and the Georgian town they

---

> **🔍 HIDDEN GEM**
> ## Wortley Village
>
> Head to this charming neighborhood in London for the city's best independently owned shops, cool cafés, and lively nightlife.

---

constructed has survived pretty much intact.

Today, visitors take pleasure in exploring the town's lovely streets, but the major attraction is **Fort George National Historic Site**, a restored British stockade built in the 1790s just southeast of town. There are ten replica buildings, and guides in old-style British military uniforms describe life in the fort in the 19th century.

Niagara-on-the-Lake is also noted for its excellent wineries, which produce some of the best icewine (a dessert wine produced from grapes frozen on the vine) in Canada.

Fort George National Historic Site

⊘ 🏠 **51 Queen's Parade, Niagara Pkwy** ☎ **(905) 468 6614** ⏰ **Apr & Nov: 10am–5pm Sat & Sun; May–Oct: 10am–5pm daily; Dec–Mar: noon–4pm Sat & Sun**

The facade of Saint Peter's Cathedral Basilica in London ↓

21

Stratford

📍 ℹ 47 Downie St; www.
visitstratford.ca

In 1830, an innkeeper called William Sargint opened the "Shakespeare Inn" beside one of the rough agricultural tracks that then crisscrossed southern Ontario. The farmers who settled nearby called the local river the "Avon" and named the town that grew up here "Stratford," after William Shakespeare's birthplace.

In 1952, local journalist Tom Patterson (1920–2005) organized a Shakespeare Festival. This first event was a humble affair held in a tent, but since then the festival has grown into one of Canada's most important theatrical seasons, lasting from May to early November. The leading plays are still Shakespearean, but works by other playwrights are showcased too, including modern pieces.

Stratford is an attractive town with plenty of riverside parks. The town is geared toward visitors, offering countless guesthouses and several good restaurants. The visitor center organizes heritage walks, which pass by the town's many historic buildings. One architectural highlight is the turreted Victorian town hall. Stratford also has a plethora of art galleries, as well as craft boutiques and other stores.

22

Brantford

📍📍 ℹ 399 Wayne Gretzky Parkway; www.discover brantford.ca

Brantford is an unassuming manufacturing town that

→

An imposing memorial to Alexander Graham Bell in Brantford

🔍 HIDDEN GEM
Brantford Twin Valley Zoo

Located just 15 minutes outside Brantford, this is the perfect spot for kids to wander for an afternoon. The zoo is home to local wildlife as well as some more exotic species.

---

takes its name from Joseph Brant (1742–1807), the leader of a confederacy of tribes called the Six Nations. Himself an Iroquois chief, Brant settled here in 1784. He soon decided that the interests of his people lay with the British, and his braves fought alongside the Redcoats during the American War of Independence (1775–83). Sadly, he had chosen the losing side and, after the war, his band was forced to move north to Canada, where the British ceded the First Nations people a piece of land at Brantford. The Iroquois (Six Nations) still live in this area, and host the Grand River Pow

---

Wow every summer, featuring traditional dances and crafts.

Brantford is also known for its association with the telephone. In 1876, the first ever long-distance call was made from Brantford to the neighboring village of Paris by Alexander Graham Bell (1847–1922), who had emigrated from Britain to Ontario in 1870. Bell's old home, conserved as the **Bell Homestead National Historic Site**, is located on the town's outskirts. The site has two buildings: Bell's homestead, furnished with many original family pieces, and Canada's first telephone business office, moved here from downtown Brantford in 1969.

Bell Homestead National Historic Site

♿ ⏰ 📍 94 Tutela Heights Rd ⏰ 9:30am–4:30pm Tue-Sun 📅 Dec 24-Jan 1 🌐 bell homestead.ca

---

23

St. Jacobs

📍 ℹ 1406 King St N; www.
stjacobs.com

The main street of this charming village is lined with craft shops selling quilts, baked goods, brooms, and furniture. Many of the items are made by the local Mennonite community, who run farms in the countryside. Visit the Mennonite Story Interpretive Centre to gain some insight into the Mennonite and Amish sects' life. Just 2 miles (3 km) down the road, north of Waterloo, is St. Jacobs Farmers' Market. Housed in two cavernous buildings, stalls here sell Bratwurst with sauerkraut, hinting at the German heritage of the area.

24 🚲 🏍️ 🍴 ☕ 🛍️

Sainte-Marie among the Hurons

📍16164, Hwy 12 E, Midland
🕐May–Oct: 10am–5pm daily 🌐hhp.on.ca

Sainte-Marie among the Hurons is one of Ontario's

most compelling attractions. Located 3 miles (5 km) east of the town of Midland, the site is a reconstruction of the settlement founded here among the indigenous Huron peoples by Jesuit priests in 1639. The village is divided into two main sections, one for Europeans (complete with a chapel and workshops), the other for Hurons, with a pair of bark-covered longhouses. Marking the boundary between the two is the small church of Saint Joseph, a simple wooden building (the interior of which has been carefully re-created) where the Jesuits set about trying to convert the Hurons. Their efforts met with a variety of reactions, and the complex relationship between the two cultures is explored here in detail.

↑ Rustic buildings at Sainte-Marie among the Hurons; a kitchen inside *(inset)*

Did You Know?

The Port of Orillia holds an annual "Christmas in June" event, with a turkey buffet.

25

Orillia

🚌 ℹ️ 50 Andrew St S; www.orillia.ca

Orillia is a pleasant country town that was the home of the novelist and humorist Stephen Leacock (1869–1944). Leacock's hugely popular *Sunshine Sketches of a Little Town* poked fun at provincial Ontario life. His old lakeshore home is conserved as the **Stephen Leacock Museum**, containing original furnishings as well as details of the author's life.

Orillia lies along a narrow strip of water linking Lake Couchiching to Lake Simcoe and is a good base from which to cruise both lakes. On the shore, Orillia's Centennial Park has a marina and a long boardwalk that stretches all the way to Couchiching beach.

Stephen Leacock Museum
♿ 📍50 Museum Dr, Old Brewery Bay 📞(705) 329 1908 🕐10am–4pm Mon–Fri

↑ The rocky, tree-lined shores of picturesque Lake Temagami

26
Temagami

🚌 *i* Chamber of Commerce, Lakeshore Rd; www.temagami.ca

The tiny resort of Temagami and its wild surroundings have long attracted fur traders and trappers, painters, and writers, most famously Grey Owl *(p161)*, the remarkable Englishman who posed as an Aboriginal Canadian and achieved celebrity status as a naturalist and conservationist in the 1930s. The resort sits on the distinctively shaped Lake Temagami, which features long fjords and bays as well as 1,400 islands, which are criss-crossed by numerous scenic canoe routes and hiking and mountain-bike trails.

Even more remote is the Lady Evelyn Smoothwater Wilderness Park, farther to the west. The only way in is by canoe or floatplane from Temagami, but the reward is some of Ontario's most stunning scenery. Much more accessible is the 100-ft-(30-m-) high Temagami Fire Tower lookout point, which provides panoramic views of the surrounding pine forests,

and the charming Finlayson Provincial Park, a popular place to picnic and camp; both are located on Temagami's outskirts.

27
Lake Erie

i 660 Garrison Rd, Fort Erie; www.forterie.ca

Lake Erie is named after the First Nations people who once lived along its shores. The Erie were renowned for their skills as fishermen. Some 250 miles (400 km) long and an average of 37 miles (60 km) wide, Lake Erie is the shallowest of the Great Lakes and separates Canada from the US. Its northern shore is one of the most peaceful parts of Ontario, with a string of quiet country towns and small ports set in rolling countryside. Reaching out from the Canadian shoreline are three peninsulas, one of which has been conserved as the Point Pelee National Park *(p234)*, home to a virgin forest and, during spring and summer, thousands of migrating birds.

About 19 miles (30 km) south of Niagara Falls, the small town of Fort Erie lies where the Niagara River meets Lake Erie, facing its sprawling US neighbor, Buffalo. The massive Peace Bridge links the two, and most people cross the border without giving Fort Erie a second look – thus missing one of the more impressive of the reconstructed British forts that dot the Canada-US border. **Old Fort Erie** is a replica

of the stronghold, destroyed by the Americans in the War of 1812. Entry is across a drawbridge, and the interior holds barracks, a powder magazine, and officers' quarters. The fort's battlefield is the site of one of the War of 1812's bloodiest battles, fought here during the siege of the fort in 1814.

Old Fort Erie

♿🅿♿♿🅿 🅰 350 Lakeshore Rd 📞 (905) 871 0540 🕐 Mid-May–Oct: daily

28
Sault Ste. Marie

✈🚌 *i* 99 Foster Dr; www.saulttourism.com

Where the rapids of St. Mary's River link Lake Superior to Lake Huron sits the town of Sault Ste. Marie, one of Ontario's oldest European communities.

The area was originally called "Baawitigong", meaning "place of the rapids," by the Ojibwa people, who used the site as a meeting place. It remains a strong First Nations area today.

The town itself was founded as a Jesuit mission and fur-trading post by the French in 1688. Called the "Sault" (pronounced "Soo"), after the French word for "rapids," the trading station prospered after 1798, when the rapids were bypassed by a canal. Since then, the canal has been upgraded time and again, and today transports the huge container ships to the interior, maintaining a thriving local economy.

→ Point Abino Lighthouse, which stands on the northern edge of Lake Erie

Visitors at a Sault Ste. Marie train station, awaiting the Agawa Canyon Tour Train

Visitors are drawn to Sault Ste. Marie's main tourist attraction, the **Agawa Canyon Tour Train**, which offers day-long rail tours from the city into the surrounding wilderness. The train weaves north through dense forest and over yawning ravines to reach the spectacular scenery of Agawa Canyon, where there is a 90-minute break for lunch.

Agawa Canyon Tour Train

⊗ 🏠129 Bay St ⏰Mid-Jun-mid-Oct: once daily 🌐agawatrain.com

㉙

Thunder Bay

✕➕📧 ℹ️Terry Fox **Information Centre, Hwy 11/17 E; www.visitthunderbay.com**

On the northern shore of Lake Superior, Thunder Bay is Canada's third-largest freshwater port, with its massive grain elevators dominating the city's waterfront. Grain is brought here from the prairies farther west, before being shipped to the rest of the world via the Great Lakes.

The town was originally established as a French trading post in 1679. These early days are celebrated at

Fort William Historical Park, a replica of the old fur-trading post, with costumed traders, French explorers, and First Nations peoples. Fort William was amalgamated with the adjacent town of Port Arthur to form Thunder Bay in 1970.

Fort William Historical Park

⊛⊗⊙⊚⊙ 🏠1350 King Rd ⏰Mid-May-mid-Sep: 10am-5pm daily 🌐fwhp.ca

---

㉚

Goderich

✈️ ℹ️91 Hamilton St; www.goderich.ca

Goderich is a charming town overlooking Lake Huron at the mouth of the Maitland River. It was founded by the British-owned Canada Company in 1825, which had persuaded the Ontario government to part with 2.5 million acres (1 million ha) of fertile land in their province for just 12 cents an acre, a bargain of such proportions that there was talk of corruption. Eager to attract settlers, the company built the Huron Road from Cambridge to Goderich. The town's main streets radiate out from the octagon-shaped center.

Goderich possesses two excellent museums. The first, the **Huron County Museum** houses a large collection of antique farm implements, as well as a military gallery, steam-driven thresher, and a reconstruction of a 19th-century town street. The **Huron Historic Gaol National Historic Site**, built between 1839 and 1842, is a preserved Victorian prison. Fascinating tours are available of its dank cells, the jailers' rooms, and the governor's house.

Huron County Museum

⊗ 🏠110 North St ⏰Times vary, check website 🌐huroncountymuseum.ca

Huron Historic Gaol National Historic Site

⊗ 🏠181 Victoria St N 📞(519) 524 6971 ⏰May-Aug: 10am-4:30pm Mon-Sat, 1-4:30pm Sun; Sep & Oct: 1-4pm Mon-Fri, 10am-4:30pm Sat, 1-4:30pm Sun

---

🔍 HIDDEN GEM
Stone Hunt

There are several open-pit amethyst mines around Thunder Bay that allow you to look for your own purple gems for a fee.

←

The quaint clapboard exterior of Bethune Memorial House, Gravenhurst

31
Muskoka

📧 Gravenhurst, Huntsville ℹ️ 1342 Hwy 11 North RR #2, Kilworthy; www.discovermuskoka.ca

Muskoka comprises an area north of Orillia, between the towns of Huntsville and Gravenhurst. The latter lies at the center of this lake country; a resort at the south end of Lake Muskoka. Here, a national historic site is devoted to the life and work of Doctor Norman Bethune (1890–1939), who pioneered mobile blood transfusion units during the Spanish Civil War. **Bethune Memorial House**, his birthplace, has been restored in late 19th-century style.

Bethune Memorial House

♿ 🏠 235 John St N ☎ (705) 687 4261 🕐 Mid-May–mid-Oct: 10am–4pm daily (late Oct: Thu–Mon)

32
Nottawasaga Bay

🚆 Wasaga Beach or Collingwood ℹ️ 45 St Paul St, Collingwood; (705) 445 7722 or 1 888 227 8667

Part of scenic Georgian Bay, Nottawasaga Bay is one of the region's most popular vacation destinations. Wasaga Beach, with its miles of golden sand, is the longest freshwater beach in the world. As well as swimming and sunbathing, there is the curious Nancy Island Historic Site, behind Beach Area 2. This has been in operation since 1928, and is home to a museum housing the preserved HMS *Nancy*, one of few British boats to survive the War of 1812.

Located on the southern shores of Georgian Bay, Collingwood and the Blue Mountains make an excellent location for hiking, cycling, and paddling in summer. In winter, the resort town of Blue Mountain is one of Ontario's top destinations for downhill skiing and snowboarding.

33
Sauble Beach

🚆 Owen Sound ℹ️ RR1, Sauble Beach; www.saublebeach.com

One of the finest sandy beaches in Ontario, Sauble Beach stretches for 7 miles (11 km) along the shores of Lake Huron – making it the second-longest freshwater beach in the world. The beach takes its name from the moniker given to it by early French explorers: "La Rivière au Sable" (river to the sand). Running behind this beach is a narrow band of campsites, cottages, and cabins. The center of the resort is at the pocket-sized village of Sauble Beach, which has a population of only 500 and has several friendly guesthouses and B&Bs in its quiet backstreets. The most attractive camping is found at Sauble Falls Provincial Park, north of the beach. There is also good birdwatching in the area.

Did You Know?

There have been over 1,000 shipwrecks on Lake Huron, with many ships still lying on the lake floor.

→

A shipwreck in Big Tub Harbour, seen through the clear waters of Lake Huron

34

Lake Huron

ⓘ Sarnia, south shore, (519) 344 7403; Barrie, Georgian Bay, (705) 725 7280; Sault Ste. Marie, north shore, (705) 945 6941
ⓦ ontariotravel.net

Of all the Great Lakes, Lake Huron has the most varied landscapes along its shoreline. To the south, the lake narrows to funnel past the largely industrial towns of Sarnia and Windsor on its way to Lake Erie, while its southeast shore is bounded by a gentle bluff, marking the limit of one of Ontario's most productive agricultural regions. Farther north, the long, thin isthmus of Bruce Peninsula stretches out into Lake Huron, signaling a dramatic change in the character of the lakeshore. This is where the southern flatlands are left behind for the more rugged, glacier-scraped country of the Canadian Shield. This transition can be seen clearly in the area of Georgian Bay. This is an impressive shoreline of lakes, forests, beaches, and villages that attracts large numbers

> Farther north, the long, thin, isthmus of Bruce Peninsula stretches out into Lake Huron, signaling a dramatic change in the character of the lakeshore.

of visitors. The lake's island-sprinkled waters are a popular area for water sports. Outdoor activities here include swimming, hiking, and fishing.

35

Manitoulin Island

ⓘ 70 Meredith St, Little Current; www.manitoulin tourism.com

Hugging the northern shores of Lake Huron, Manitoulin Island is, at 1,100 sq miles (2,800 sq km), the world's largest freshwater island. A quiet place of small villages, farmland, woodland, and lakes, its edges are fringed by deserted beaches. The lake's North Channel separates Manitoulin from the mainland, its waters attracting summer

sailors, while hikers come to explore the island's trails.

The Ojibwa people first occupied the island more than 10,000 years ago, naming it after the Great Spirit – Manitou. First Nations peoples still constitute over a quarter of the island's population. Every August, on Civic Holiday weekend, they celebrate their culture in one of Canada's largest pow wows, the Wikwemikong Cultural Festival (Bay of the Beaver).

On the north shore, Gore Bay houses five tiny museums that focus on the island's early settlers. Nearby, the island's largest settlement is the quiet town of Little Current. From May to October, book a place in advance for the Chi Cheemaun car ferry, which connects Tobermory on the Bruce Peninsula to Manitoulin Island.

36

Lake Superior

i Ontario Travel Information Centre, Sault Ste. Marie; (705) 945 6941

The least polluted and most westerly of the Great Lakes, Lake Superior is the world's largest body of fresh water, with a surface area of 31,700 sq miles (82,000 sq km). It is known for sudden violent storms, long a source of dread to local sailors. The lake's northern coast is a vast weather-swept stretch of wilderness, dominated by granite outcrops and seemingly limitless forest. This challenging area is best experienced in Pukaskwa National Park and Lake Superior Provincial Park, both reached via the Trans-Canada Highway (Hwy 17), as it cuts a dramatic route along the lake's north shore.

37

Point Pelee National Park

⌂ 1118 Point Pelee Dr, Leamington ☎ (519) 322 2365 ⏰ Daily

A long, finger-like isthmus, Point Pelee National Park

> Welland Canal was built to solve the problem of Niagara Falls. The Falls presented an obstacle that prevented boats from passing between lakes Ontario and Erie.

sticks out into Lake Erie for 12 miles (20 km) and forms the southernmost tip of Canada's mainland. The park has a wide variety of habitats, including marsh lands, open fields, and ancient deciduous forest. These woods are a rarity, as they are one of the few places in North America's Carolinian Life Zone, where many of the trees have never been logged. The profusion of species creates a junglelike atmosphere, with red cedar, black walnut, white sassafras, hickory, sycamore, and sumac, all struggling to reach the light.

This varied vegetation attracts thousands of birds, which visit on their spring and fall migrations. Over 370 species have been sighted here, and they can be observed from lookout points and forest trails. Every fall, hosts of orange-and-black monarch butterflies can also be seen here.

A marshland boardwalk trail winds through Point Pelee, with good observation spots along its length. Bikes and canoes can be rented at the start of

the boardwalk, and there is also a concession stand. Farther into the park, the visitor center features displays of local flora and fauna.

38

Georgian Bay Islands National Park

⌂ Beausoleil Island ☎ (705) 527 7200 ⛴ DayTripper: (705) 526 8907 ⏰ Times vary, call ahead

The waters of Georgian Bay are dotted with thousands of little islands, often no more than a chunk of rock guarded by a windblown pine. The bay is large, beautiful, and flows into Lake Huron. Sixty of its islands have been incorporated into the Georgian Bay Islands National Park. The park's center is Beausoleil Island, the hub of the area's wide range of facilities.

Beausoleil is crossed by scenic hiking trails, but it is important to come properly equipped since it is a remote spot. The only way to reach the island is by the DayTripper water taxi from the hamlet of Honey Harbour. The journey takes about 40 minutes. Cruises through the islands aboard the *Miss Midland* depart from the town of Midland from mid-May through mid-October.

In Penetanguishene, east of Nottawasaga Bay, Discovery Harbour is a reconstruction of the British naval base that was established here in 1814. There are replicas of the barracks, a blacksmith's shop, and the

← Canoeists navigating calm waters within Point Pelee National Park

↑ A colorful cabin perched on the shore of a lake in Killarney Provincial Park

original officers' quarters. Two replica schooners, HMS *Tecumseth* and HMS *Bee*, are moored at the King's Wharf. The below-decks area of the former is furnished as per the ship's 1815 log. The remains of its original hull are on display in the HMS *Tecumseth* Centre.

39 Welland Canal

🕐 Daily ℹ️ 1932 Welland Canals Parkway, St. Catharines; www. wellandcanal.com

Welland Canal was built to solve the problem of Niagara Falls. The Falls presented an obstacle that made it impossible for boats to pass between lakes Ontario and Erie. Goods had to be unloaded on one side of the Falls and then carted to the other, a time-consuming and expensive process. To solve the problem, local entrepreneurs dug a canal across the 28-mile (45-km) isthmus separating the lakes early in the 19th century, choosing a route to the west of the Niagara River.

The first Welland Canal was a crude affair, but subsequent improvements have created today's version, which has eight giant locks adjusting the water level by no less than 324 feet (99 m). A remarkable feat of engineering, the canal is capable of accommodating the largest of ships. You can drive alongside the northerly half of the canal, on Government Road from Lake Ontario to Thorold, where seven of the eight locks are situated. The viewing platform at the Welland Canals Centre at Lock No. 3 in St. Catharines provides a great vantage point and has an information center detailing the canal's history. Ships sail the canal from April to December.

40 Killarney Provincial Park

📞 (705) 287 2900
🚉 Sudbury 🕐 Daily

Killarney Provincial Park is a beautiful tract of wilderness with crystal-blue lakes, pine and hardwood forests, boggy lowlands, and the spectacular

La Cloche Mountains, known for their striking white quartzite ridges. This magnificent scenery has inspired many artists, particularly members of the Group of Seven *(p54)*, one of whom – Franklin Carmichael – saw the park as Ontario's most "challenging and gratifying landscape." The park's 60-mile (100-km) La Cloche Silhouette Trail takes between a week and ten days to complete and attracts many serious hikers for its stunning views of the mountains and of Georgian Bay. Canoeists, meanwhile, can paddle on the park's many lakes and rivers by following a network of well-marked canoe routes.

> 💬 INSIDER TIP
> ## Setting Up Camp
>
> For staying overnight in Killarney, there are great yurts at the George Lake Campground *(960 Highway #637)*. For dinner, head into town for excellent fish 'n' chips at Herbert Fisheries *(21 Channel St)*.

A DRIVING TOUR
BRUCE PENINSULA

Distance 62 miles (100 km) **Departure point** The route
follows Route 9 and Hwy 6. It can be reached from Owen
Sound in the south, or Tobermory in the north
Stopping-off point Stokes Bay

The Bruce Peninsula divides the main body of Lake Huron from
Georgian Bay and also contains some of the area's most scenic
terrain. Bruce Peninsula National Park lies along the eastern
shore and boasts craggy headlands and limestone cliffs with
several hiking paths. Beyond the port of Tobermory, at the
peninsula's tip, Fathom Five Marine National Park, comprises
19 uninhabited islands. The park is popular with divers because
of its clear waters and amazing rock formations.

Locator Map
For more detail see p202

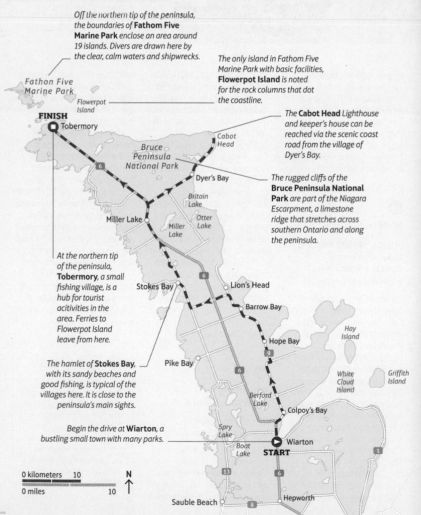

Off the northern tip of the peninsula,
the boundaries of **Fathom Five
Marine Park** enclose an area around
19 islands. Divers are drawn here by
the clear, calm waters and shipwrecks.

The only island in Fathom Five
Marine Park with basic facilities,
Flowerpot Island is noted
for the rock columns that dot
the coastline.

The **Cabot Head** Lighthouse
and keeper's house can be
reached via the scenic coast
road from the village of
Dyer's Bay.

The rugged cliffs of the
**Bruce Peninsula National
Park** are part of the Niagara
Escarpment, a limestone
ridge that stretches across
southern Ontario and along
the peninsula.

At the northern tip
of the peninsula,
Tobermory, a small
fishing village, is a
hub for tourist
acitivities in the
area. Ferries to
Flowerpot Island
leave from here.

The hamlet of **Stokes Bay**,
with its sandy beaches and
good fishing, is typical of the
villages here. It is close to the
peninsula's main sights.

Begin the drive at **Wiarton**, a
bustling small town with many parks.

Visitors relaxing on rock
formations at the Bruce
Peninsula National Park

Interior of the Basilique Notre-Dame-de-Montréal

MONTREAL

Montreal's location at the convergence of the Saint Lawrence and Ottawa rivers made it Canada's first great trading center. It was founded in 1642 by a group of French Catholics as a Christian community and port. Much of its economic power has now moved west to Toronto, and what makes Montreal interesting today is a cultural, rather than a geographical, confluence.

About 70 percent of its 1.75 million residents are of French descent, another 15 percent have British origins, and the rest represent nearly every major ethnic group. Many of its residents speak two or more languages. The communities form a kind of mosaic, with the anglophones in the west, the francophones in the east, and other ethnic communities in pockets all over the city. The most interesting neighborhoods sprawl along the southern slopes of Mont-Royal – the 767-ft (234-m) hill from which the city derives its name. Vieux-Montréal's network of narrow, cobblestone streets huddles near the waterfront, while the main shopping area is farther north along rue Sainte-Catherine.

MONTREAL

Must Sees

1. Basilique Notre-Dame-de-Montréal
2. Musée d'Art Contemporain de Montréal
3. Musée des Beaux Arts

Experience More

4. Oratoire St. Joseph
5. St. Patrick's Basilica
6. Musée Pointe-à-Callière
7. Parc du Mont-Royal
8. Olympic Park
9. Marché Jean-Talon
10. Château Ramezay
11. Centre Canadien d'Architecture
12. Sir George-Etienne Cartier National Historic Site
13. Chinatown
14. Habitat 67
15. McGill University
16. Underground City
17. Place des Arts
18. Rue Sherbrooke
19. Square Dorchester and Place du Canada
20. Parc Jean-Drapeau
21. Jardin Botanique de Montréal
22. Christ Church Cathedral
23. Lachine
24. Cathédrale Marie-Reine-du-Monde
25. Centre d'Histoire de Montréal
26. Musée McCord
27. Centre des Sciences de Montréal
28. Maison Saint-Gabriel

Eat & Drink

1. Dragon Beard Candy
2. Kim Fun
3. Patisserie Harmonie
4. Café Parvis
5. Dominion Square Tavern
6. Escondite

BASILIQUE NOTRE-DAME-DE-MONTRÉAL

⊙ D2 **⌂ 110 rue Notre Dame O** **🚇 Place d'Armes** **🕐 8am–4:30pm Mon–Fri (4pm Sat), 12:30–4pm Sun** **ⓦ basiliquenotredame.ca**

In the center of Place d'Armes the Basilique, Montreal's grandest Catholic church, soars above the cobblestones. The striking building is one of the city's most popular landmarks, with close to a million annual visitors.

The current basilica dates from 1829, when it replaced a smaller 17th-century church that stood on the site. American architect James O'Donnell excelled himself by building a vast vaulted cavern that was Canada's first Neo-Gothic church; it has 3,000 seats in the nave and two tiers of balconies. The church's twin towers rise 226 ft (69 m) above the basilica and are visible across the old city. Inside, the interiors were splendidly redecorated in the 1870s with the intricate woodcarvings of craftsman Victor Bourgeau.

The nave is illuminated by a rose window beneath an azure ceiling.

The main altar is surrounded by delicate pine and walnut woodcarving.

The reredos is the focus of the nave.

The ornate pulpit was sculpted by Philippe Hébert.

← The basilica's impressive stone facade

↑ Spectacular blue and gold interior of the basilica

Lofty twin towers

The Vieux Séminaire, which dates from 1685 and is the second-oldest building in Montreal.

The stained-glass windows, which were imported from Limoges in 1930, each tell a story of Montreal's past.

The pipe organ was built by the renowned organ-maker Casavant in 1891.

↑ Cross-section illustration of the Basilique Notre-Dame-de-Montréal

2 🍴 🎨 🖼 🍽 🏛 🛍

MUSÉE D'ART CONTEMPORAIN DE MONTRÉAL

📍 C2 🏠 185 rue Sainte-Catherine O 🚌 15, 55, 80, 129, 535 Ⓜ Place-des-Arts
🕐 11am–6pm Tue, 11am–9pm Wed–Fri, 10am–6pm Sat & Sun 🔒 Many galleries
closed for renovation until mid-2021, check the website for details 🌐 macm.org

The only museum in Canada dedicated solely to modern and contemporary art, this high-profile institution has an innovative program of exhibitions highlighting the work of both national and international artists.

Opened in 1964, the Montreal Museum of Contemporary Art (MAC) has a permanent collection of approximately 8,000 paintings, drawings, photographs, videos, and installations. Works date from 1939, but the emphasis is on the contemporary. More than 60 percent of the pieces on display are by Quebec artists.

Located in the Place des Arts, a major performing arts complex in the city, the MAC features works by Québécois legends Jean-Paul Riopelle, Paul-Émile Borduas, and Alfred Pellan. At any time, only a small proportion of the 300 artworks in the museum are on display, and pieces are frequently rotated. They occupy the upper floor space, along with visiting items. The museum's temporary exhibitions reflect the latest trends in international art from across the world.

There is also a sculpture garden on site, accessible from the main museum building, which has rotating exhibits and is a good spot for a break during a tour of the galleries. On the exhibition floor, the airy café is perfect for a light lunch, and the gift shop offers an excellent selection of locally made jewelry, home decor, toys, and stationery.

1 These colorful pieces were part of an exhibition by Francine Savard, a respected Québécois artist.

2 DJs play music at the gallery's late-night Nocturne events.

3 Art workshops form part of a range of adult learning programs at the museum.

SPECIAL EVENTS

The museum hosts Family Sundays every Sunday afternoon, with fun arts and crafts workshops designed to get the kids excited about the works on display. And for the grown-ups who need a little encouragement, the MAC occasionally opens its doors for Nocturne nights. During these evenings, visitors can stay until 2am, enjoying interactive tours of the exhibits, creative workshops, DJs playing pop music, a serviced bar, and snacks. Check the website for details.

←

The exterior of the MAC, with banners advertising its 2017–18 Leonard Cohen exhibition

③ 🛍️ 🚫 🍴 📷 🏧

MUSÉE DES BEAUX-ARTS

📍A3 🏠1380 rue Sherbrooke O 🚌24, 356 Ⓜ️Peel, Guy-Concordia
🕐10am–5pm Tue–Sun (to 9pm Wed) 🌐mbam.qc.ca

Five pavilions, each unique and admirable on their own, hold inside an incredible wealth of fine art, spanning many centuries and highlighting some of the top Canadian and international artists of their time. From romantic portraits by Dutch masters to smooth Inuit sculptures, this museum is a must for any art lover.

Archaeology and World Cultures

Reflecting the richness and diversity of ancient art around around the world, the galleries of this 1912 Beaux Arts building display an array of ceremonial masks, ritualistic objects, textiles, and coins. Some date back to the Bronze Age, including Greek, Roman, Middle Eastern, and Egyptian artifacts. The preserved vases, perfume bottles, and funeral urns are particularly striking, as are the Pre-Columbian objects, which mainly come from Mesoamerica. Islamic, Chinese, and Japanese art is also exhibited, and there are several displays of sub-Saharan artifacts.

↑ The grand banner-draped facade of the Musée des Beaux-Arts

Ancient and Modern International Art

This collection features European religious objects from the Middle Ages, masterpieces by Dutch and Flemish artists of the Golden Age, Neo-Classical portraits, and art from Napoleon's personal collection. Modern works are also well represented, with pieces by heavyweight artists such as Cézanne, Dalí, and Picasso.

Quebec and Canadian Art

An exceptional collection of Quebecois and Canadian art by Inuit and First Nations artists are housed in the Claire and Marc Bougie Pavilion. Look out for bone- and stone-carvings from the Arctic, and iconic landscape paintings

GALLERY GUIDE

For Archaeology and World Culture, head to the Michal and Renata Hornstein Pavilion. The Michal and Renata Hornstein Pavilion for Peace houses Ancient and Modern International Art. The Claire and Marc Bourgie Pavilion contains Quebec and Canadian Art; and the Jean-Noël Desmarais Pavilion houses International Contemporary Art. The Decorative Arts and Design collection is in the Liliane and David M. Stewart Pavilion.

← The museum's modern, minimalist interior

Timeline

1860
▲ The Art Association of Montreal (AAM) is founded by Bishop Francis Fulford

1879
The AAM collection moves to its first permanent home at Phillips Square

1912
The AAM is moved to rue Sherbrooke ouest, on the Golden Square Mile

1949
The AAM is renamed, and becomes the Montreal Museum of Fine Arts

1972
The museum is the site of the largest art theft in Canadian history

2011
▽ The Erskine and American Church becomes part of the new Claire and Marc Bourgie Pavilion

by Tom Thomson and the Group of Seven. The works on display date back to the 1960s, with modern pieces by Jean-Paul Riopelle, Claude Tousignant, and Guido Molinari.

International Contemporary Art

Large abstract and figurative paintings, multimedia installations, and modern sculptures are exhibited in the Jean-Noël Desmarais Pavilion. Works are by local and international artists, across a period ranging from the 1980s to the present day. The collection extends out into the Sculpture Garden with pieces by David Altmejd, Jim Dine, Anthony Gormley, and Henry Moore.

Decorative Arts and Design

The Liliane and David M. Stewart Pavilion is home to 4,000 objects from around the globe, and illustrates the impact of early design on later movements, such as Art Nouveau, Art Deco, and Modernism.

Graphic and Photographic Arts

Stunning prints, drawings, and photographs grace the walls of this gallery in the museum's Jean-Noël Desmarais Pavillion. Its vast collection showcases the skill of great masters such as Delacroix, Goya, and Rembrandt.

↑ Works in the Expanding Fields gallery in the Claire and Marc Bourgie Pavilion

EXPERIENCE MORE

4

Oratoire St. Joseph

🗺 A1 🏠 3800 Chemin Queen Mary 🚉 Central Station 🚌 51, 166, 368, 711 Ⓜ Côte-des-Neiges 🕐 Daily 🌐 saint-joseph.org

Every year, two million pilgrims climb the 283 steps (99 of which can be climbed in prayer on the knees) to the entrance of this vast church. Their devotion would no doubt please Brother André (1845–1937), the remarkable man responsible for building this shrine to the husband of the Virgin Mary. It began when Brother André built a hillside chapel to St. Joseph in his spare time. Montreal's sick and disabled joined him at his prayers, and soon there were reports of miraculous cures. Brother André began to draw

pilgrims, and the present oratory was built to receive them. Today, pilgrims can still pray on his tomb. The brother was beatified in 1982 and canonized in 2010.

The church's octagonal copper dome is one of the biggest in the world, stretching 146 ft (44.5 m) high and 125 ft (38 m) wide. The interior is starkly modern; the elongated wooden statues of the apostles in the transepts are the work of Henri Charlier, a French artist and sculptor who was also responsible for the main altar and the huge crucifix. The striking stained-glass windows were made by Marius Plamondon, and feature images from the life of St. Joseph. The main building houses a fascinating museum depicting André's life. Beside the crypt church, a votive chapel is ablaze with flickering candles that have been lit by hopeful pilgrims.

The snow-dusted facade and splendid interior *(inset)* of the Oratoire St. Joseph

5

St. Patrick's Basilica

🗺 C3 🏠 460 René-Lévesque Blvd O Ⓜ Square-Victoria-OACI 🌐 stpatricksmtl.ca

Completed in 1847, this Gothic Revival-style church is the oldest English-speaking Catholic church in Montreal. Known locally as the "Irish Church," it was built to accommodate the large number of Irish immigrants that flocked to the city during the harsh years of Ireland's Great Famine. The interior of the church is decorated with a combination of French fleurs-de-lys and Irish shamrock motifs, marble-encased oak columns, and 150 oil paintings.

---

6 🎟 🍴 🛍

Musée Pointe-à-Callière

🗺 D3 🏠 350 Place Royale 🕐 10am–5pm Tue-Sun 🌐 pacmusee.qc.ca

This archaeology museum has a fascinating collection

In-situ displays beneath the floors of Musée Pointe-a-Calliere

> The steep green bump that rises above the city center is only 767 ft (234 m) high, but Montrealers call it simply "la montagne," or "the mountain."

GREAT VIEW
From the Top

The Montreal Tower's observatory sits some 540 ft (165 m) high, and offers stunning city views. Signs point out sights of interest as far away as 50 miles (80 km).

8 Olympic Park

B1 **3200 Viau St** **Viau, Pie-IX** **Jun-Sep: 1-10pm Mon, 9am-10pm Tue-Sun; Oct-May: 1-6pm Mon, 9am-6pm Tue-Sun** **parcolympique.qc.ca**

Designed for the 1976 Olympic Games, Montreal's Olympic Park showcases a number of stunning modern buildings. French architect Roger Taillibert created the Stadium, now known to many Montrealers as "The Big O," a reference to its round shape. The stadium, which can seat 56,000, is used today for concerts by international stars, as well as for big exhibitions, and as a modern attraction in a historic city. Arching up the side of the stadium is the Montreal Tower, which is the world's tallest inclined tower and offers fine views. A cable car can take visitors to its viewing deck in under two minutes. Nearby, the Biodôme environmental museum (closed for renovation until summer 2019) replicates four world climates, while the Esplanade Financière Sun Life offers free outdoor activities for all the family on weekends.

of First Nations artifacts and exhibits that illustrate the birth of Montreal. The museum consists of six buildings that stand above several archaeo-logically significant sites showcasing major periods in the history of the city, including an old Custom House from 1836, the city's first Catholic cemetery, and the remains of the city's early sewage and river system. The Mariner's House building hosts simulated archaeological digs that kids will enjoy, and the L'Arrivage Bistro, upstairs in the Éperon building, has lovely views of the Vieux-Port.

7 Parc du Mont-Royal

A2 **Central Station** **11, 165, 180** **Mont-Royal** **6am-midnight daily** **lemontroyal.qc.ca**

The steep green bump that rises above the city center is only 767 ft (234 m) high, but Montrealers call it simply "la montagne," or "the mountain." Jacques Cartier gave the peak its name when he visited in 1535, and it, in turn, gave its name to the city. The hill became a park in 1876, when the city bought the land and hired Frederick Law Olmsted, the man responsible for designing New York's Central Park, to landscape it. Olmsted tried to keep it natural, building a few lookouts linked by footpaths. Succeeding generations have added Beaver Lake; a 98-ft- (30-m-) high cross made of steel girders; and the Voie Camillien-Houde, a thoroughfare that cuts through the park from east to west.

The mountain's 250 acres (101 ha) of meadows and hardwood forests still offer Montrealers a precious escape from urban life, as well as spectacular views of the city. The wide terrace in front of the Chalet du Mont-Royal pavilion looks out over the skyscrapers of the downtown core. The northern boundary of the park abuts two huge cemeteries: the Catholic Notre-Dame-des-Neiges and the old and stately Cimetière Mont-Royal (Mount Royal Cemetery), where many of Canada's finest rest. The latter was designated a National Historic Site in 1999, just three years short of its 150th birthday.

Did You Know?

No building in Montreal is allowed to be taller than "the mountain" - hence the city's lack of skyscrapers.

The entrance to Marché Jean-Talon, a bustling market in Montreal's Little Italy

reminiscent of the châteaux back home, with stone walls, dormer windows, and a copper roof. Many of de Ramezay's successors lived here, and the building also housed the West India Company. This is one of the most impressive remnants of the French regime open to the public in Montreal. Of particular interest is the Nantes Salon, with its 18th-century carved paneling by the French architect Germain Boffrand.

Uniforms, documents, and furniture on the main floor reflect the life of New France's ruling classes, while the contents of the cellars reveal the reality for humbler colonists.

EAT

Dragon Beard Candy
Handmade traditional Chinese candy is crafted here from frozen corn syrup and rice flour.

📍C2 🏠52 Rue de la Gauchetière
📞(514) 916 6252

$ⓈⓈ

Kim Fun
Head here for classic Cantonese dim sum, served steaming from a traditional trolley.

📍C2 🏠1111 Rue Saint-Urbain
📞(514) 878 2888

Ⓢ$Ⓢ

Patisserie Harmonie
The shelves of this Hong Kong-style bakery are lined with sweet and savory treats – some decorated with iconic cartoon characters.

📍C2 🏠85 Rue de la Gauchetière
📞(514) 875 1328

$ⓈⓈ

9 🍴 🖥 🏠

Marché Jean-Talon

📍A1 🏠7070 Henri-Julien Ave 🌐marchespublics-mtl.com

Favored by local chefs, this huge covered market in the Little Italy neighborhood has aisles of fresh produce, flowers, baked goods, and meats, interspersed with specialty shops and busy cafés. Opened in 1933, it's one of North America's largest open-air public markets and is an excellent place to spend a couple of hours. You can also stock up on souvenirs here, such as local maple syrup and wines, or sample Montreal's unmatched poutine (p45).

10 🚗 🏍 🖥 🏠

Château Ramezay

📍D2 🏠280 Rue Notre Dame E 🚆VIA Rail 🚌14, 55, 715, Terminus Voyager Ⓜ Champ-de-Mars 🕐Jun-Oct: 9:30am-6pm daily; Nov-May: 10am-4:30pm Tue-Sun 🌐chateau ramezay.qc.ca

When Montreal's 11th governor, Claude de Ramezay, arrived in the city in 1704, he was homesick for Normandy and decided to build a residence that was

11 🚗 🏍 🏠

Centre Canadien d'Architecture

📍A4 🏠1920 Rue Baile 🚌Terminus Voyager Ⓜ Guy Concordia 🕐11am-6pm Wed-Sun (to 9pm Thu) 🌐cca.qc.ca

Inside this large, U-shaped building, well-lit exhibition rooms house a series of regular exhibits in rotation. The primary displays focus on architecture, design, and landscape architecture.

The two arms of the modern building embrace the ornate Shaughnessy House, which faces boulevard René-Lévesque Ouest. Now part of the center, the house was built in 1874 for Sir Thomas Shaughnessy, the president of the Canadian Pacific Railway.

The facility is also a major scholarly institution. Its extensive collection of architectural plans, drawings, models, and photographs is the most important of its kind. The library alone has more than 215,000 volumes on the world's most significant buildings.

> **Chinatown's restaurants specialize in a range of delicious cuisines, fragrantly filling the air with the smell of hot barbecued pork and aromatic noodles.**

Sir George-Etienne Cartier National Historic Site

📍 D2 🏠 458 Rue Notre Dame E 📞 (514) 283 2282 🚇 Central Station 🚌 14, 715, Terminus Voyager Ⓜ Champ-de-Mars ⏰ Mid-Jun-Sep: 10am-5pm Wed-Sun; Oct-late-Dec: 10am-5pm Fri-Sun (26-30 Dec: daily)

George-Etienne Cartier (1814–73) was a Father of Confederation and one of the most important French-Canadian politicians of his day. This national historic site comprises two adjoining graystone houses owned by the Cartiers on the eastern edge of the old town. One is dedicated to Cartier's career, and here you can listen in either French or English to a good summary of the political founding of modern Canada.

The second house focuses on the Cartiers' domestic life as a Victorian upper middle-class family. Visitors can roam the formal rooms and listen to snatches of taped conversation from "servants" talking about their lives.

Chinatown

📍 D1 Ⓜ Champ-de-Mars, Place-d'Armes

The name of this area has become a bit anachronistic, as many of the restaurants and shops in this 18-block district are now owned by Vietnamese and Thai immigrants. Most arrived in Montreal in the wake of 20th-century upheavals in Southeast Asia. The Chinese, however, were here first. They began arriving in large numbers after 1880, along with many European immigrants. The Chinese community stuck together in this corner of the city in an attempt to avoid discrimination from some of the town's residents. As they grew more prosperous, many descendants of the first immigrants moved to the wealthier areas of Montreal, leaving Chinatown to the elderly and to the newer arrivals. Thousands return during the weekends, however, filling the narrow streets with people shopping for silk, souvenirs, and food.

Restaurants specialize in a range of delicious cuisines, fragrantly filling the air with the smell of hot barbecued pork and aromatic noodles.

For those seeking respite from the bustle of the streets, there is a lovely little garden dedicated to the charismatic Chinese leader Sun Yat-sen on rue Clarke.

Habitat 67

📍 E3 🏠 2600 Av Pierre-Dupuy 🌐 habitat67.com

This concrete architectural marvel, built on a land-filled jetty just south of the Old Port section of Montreal, was designed by Israeli-Canadian architect Moshe Safdie in 1967. As part of an Expo 67 pavilion, it was originally intended to deliver the benefits of sub-urban homes, with gardens and private terraces, at an affordable cost. The idealism of this plan was unfortunately lost, but the building remains a symbol of that concept. Today it is a desirable – though expensive – apartment complex, and public guided tours of the building are available.

↑ The unusual cubed structure of Habitat 67, built along the banks of Saint Lawrence River

Interior of the fascinating Redpath Museum, part of McGill University ↑

McGill University

📍 B2 🏛 845 Rue Sherbrooke O 🚇 Central Station 🚌 24, 356 Ⓜ McGill 🕐 9am-6pm Mon-Fri 🌐 mcgill.ca

When it was founded in 1821, Canada's best-known university was set on land left for the purpose by fur trader and land speculator James McGill (1744–1813). The university's main entrance is guarded by the Classical Roddick Gates. Behind them, an avenue leads to the domed Neo-Classical Arts Building, which is the oldest structure on campus.

The rest of the 70 or so buildings that make up the university range from the ornately Victorian to the starkly concrete. One of the loveliest is the **Redpath Museum**, which holds one of the city's most eclectic and eccentric collections. A huge number of fossils, including a dinosaur skeleton, sit alongside African art, Roman coins, and a shrunken head.

Redpath Museum

🏛 859 Rue Sherbrooke W 📞 (514) 398 4861 🕐 9am-5pm Mon-Fri, 11am-5pm Sat & Sun

---

16

Underground City

📍 C2 🚇 Central Station 🚌 Terminus Voyager Ⓜ Peel, McGill, Bonaventure

When Montreal opened its first métro (or subway) lines in 1966, it inadvertently created a whole new layer of urban life: the Underground City.

The first métro stations had underground links to just the two main train stations, a few hotels, and the shopping mall

Did You Know?

Montreal was the third choice for John Lennon and Yoko Ono's "Bed In," after NYC and the Bahamas proved unsuitable.

under the place Ville-Marie office tower. This has turned into a vast network of over 19 miles (30 km) of boutique-lined passages, housing more than 1,600 shops, 200 restaurants, hotels, and film theaters. It is theoretically possible to lead a rich life in Montreal without ever stepping outside.

17

Place des Arts

📍 C2 🏛 260 Blvd de Maisonneuve W 🚌 15, 55, 80, 125, 129 Ⓜ Place des Arts 🌐 placedesarts.com

This complex of halls and theaters sits at the heart of the Quartier des Spectacles entertainment district and is Montreal's prime center for the performing arts. Both the Orchéstre Symphonique de Montréal (Montreal Symphony Orchestra) and the Opéra de Montréal (Montreal Opera) make their home here. The buildings share a spacious plaza with the superb Musée d'art Contemporain (p244).

on the slopes of Mont-Royal in an area that became known as the Golden, or Square, Mile. Rue Sherbrooke between Guy and University was their main street, and its shops, hotels, and churches were the most elegant in the country.

Some of that elegance survived the modernizing bulldozers of the 1960s. Holt Renfrew, Montreal's upscale department store, and the stately Ritz-Carlton Hotel still stand. So do two exquisite churches, the Presbyterian St. Andrew and St. Paul, and the Erskine American United, which boasts stained-glass windows by Tiffany. Boutiques, bookstores, and galleries fill many of the rows of graystone townhouses. Millionaires not quite wealthy enough to make it into the Square Mile built graceful row homes on the nearby rues de la Montagne, Crescent, and Bishop. Many of these now house trendy shops and bistros.

⑱

Rue Sherbrooke

📍C2 🚉Central Station 🚌Terminus Voyager Ⓜ Sherbrooke

In the latter half of the 19th century, Montreal was one of the most important cities in the British Empire. Its traders and industrialists controlled about 70 percent of Canada's wealth, and many built themselves fine homes

⑲

Square Dorchester and Place du Canada

📍B3 🚉Central Station 🚌Terminus Voyager Ⓜ Peel, Bonaventure, Lucien-L'Allier

These two open squares create a green oasis in downtown Montreal.

On the north side of boulevard René-Lévesque, statues including Canada's first French-Canadian prime minister, Sir Wilfrid Laurier, share Square Dorchester with a war memorial. On place du Canada, a statue of the country's first prime minister, Sir John A. Macdonald, looks out over the stately boulevard René-Lévesque.

The buildings surrounding the park are eclectic. The mix includes a Gothic church; a shiny, black bank tower; and the Sun Life Building (1933), a huge stone fortress that housed the British Crown Jewels during World War II.

EAT & DRINK

Café Parvis
This relaxed, bright space is popular for brunch, but also open late for pizza and wine.
📍B2 🏠433 Rue Mayor 🌐cafeparvis.com

$$ⓢ

Dominion Square Tavern
Serving fine cocktails and beer since 1927, this classy hotspot offers a great European menu.
📍B3 🏠1243 Rue Metcalfe 🌐ctaverne dominion.com

$$ⓢ

Escondite
In this dimly lit Mexican bar, you'll find amazing mojitos and a long list of specialty tequilas to go with the tasty tacos.
📍C3 🏠1206 Union Ave 🌐escondite.ca

$$ⓢ

↑ Fall colors brightening the Place des Arts in downtown Montreal

20 Parc Jean-Drapeau

♀F1 🅰1 Circuit Gilles Villeneuve ☎(514)872 6120 Ⓜ Jean Drapeau 🚇Vieux-Port ⏰6am–midnight daily

Encompassing the two islands of Île-Sainte-Hélène and Île-Notre-Dame, Parc Jean-Drapeau is a popular visitor's attraction and a hub for major events, such as Piknic Electronik, an electronic music festival which is held every Sunday during summer.

The forested Île-Sainte-Hélène, sitting in the middle of the Saint Lawrence River, has played a key role in Montreal's emergence as a modern city. Originally named after Samuel de Champlain's wife, it was the site of Expo 67, the world fair that brought millions of visitors to the city that year.

Several reminders of those days remain – most notably La Ronde, the fair's amusement park, and the dome that served as the United States Pavilion. This is now the Biosphère, an interpretive center that examines the Great Lakes and Saint Lawrence River system. Nearby is the Fort de l' Île-Sainte-Hélène, built in 1825

to protect Montreal from a potential American attack. Its red-stone walls enclose a grassy parade square that is used today by re-creations of two 18th-century regimental military formations that fought each other over the future of New France until 1759. The fort also houses the **Musée Stewart**, a small but excellent museum of social and military history, with educational activities for schools and younger visitors.

The Île-Notre-Dame, a 286-acre (116-ha) wedge of land encircled by the Saint Lawrence Seaway, did not exist until 1967, when it was created with rock excavated for the Montreal métro system. It shared Expo 67 with Île-Sainte-Hélène.

Île-Notre-Dame's most popular attraction by far is the monumental Casino de Montréal, a province-owned gambling hall that never closes. Every day, thousands line up at its tables and slot machines.

There are also more refined entertainments – a rowing basin, excavated for the 1976 Olympics, superb floral gardens, and a carefully filtered body of water, which is the site of the city's only

swimming beach. Île-Notre-Dame's Circuit Gilles-Villeneuve plays host to Formula 1 races.

Musée Stewart

🌐 🅰20 Chemin Tour de Lille ⏰10am–5pm Wed–Sun (end Jun–Sep: Tue–Sun) 🌐stewart-museum.org

21 Jardin Botanique de Montréal

♀A1 🅰4101 Rue Sherbrooke E Ⓜ Pie-IX 🚌185, 139 ⏰Times vary, check website 🌐espace pourlavie.ca

Montreal's botanical garden is among the largest in the world, a fine accomplishment for this northern city with a cold winter climate. Its 185 acres (75 ha) enclose 30 outdoor gardens, 10 greenhouses, a "courtyard of the senses," in which blind interpreters help visitors discover exotic flowers, and a bug-shaped Insectarium. Its most peaceful havens are the 6-acre (2.5-ha) Chinese Garden, a delightful replica of a 14th-century Ming garden, and the exquisite Japanese Garden.

㉒
Christ Church Cathedral

📍C3 🏠635 Rue Sainte-Catherine W 🚉Central Station 🚌35, 61, 168, 420 Ⓜ McGill 🕐8am–6pm Mon-Fri & Sun, 10am–6pm Sat 🌐montrealcathedral.ca

Architect Frank Wills finished Christ Church in 1859 as the seat of the Anglican bishop of Montreal. This graceful Gothic building has exterior walls studded with gargoyles and magnificent stained-glass windows, some from the William Morris studio in London. The church was too heavy for the land, and the stone spire was replaced in 1940 with an aluminum steeple. Noon concerts are often held in the cathedral's cool interior.

HIDDEN GEM
Steel Sculpture

Art enthusiasts should seek out Alexander Calder's monumental 65-ft (20-m) *Three Discs* sculpture, also known as "The Man," in Parc Jean-Drapeau.

↑ The Fur Trade at Lachine National Historic Site, one of the suburb's most interesting buildings

㉓
Lachine

📍B2 🏠Blvd St Joseph ☎(514) 873 2015 🚌191 Ⓜ Lionel Groulx

Lachine is a suburb of southwest Montreal and includes a small island of the same name west of the Lachine Rapids, where the Saint Lawrence River widens to form Lac-Saint-Louis. Lachine is now part of Montreal, but has a long history of its own. The old town along blvd Saint-Joseph is charming. Many of its fine old homes have now become restaurants and bistros. One of the oldest houses, built in 1670, is now the Musée de Lachine, a historical museum and art gallery. The Fur Trade at Lachine National Historic Site is a building dedicated to the fur trade, which for years was Montreal's main support.

The Canal de Lachine, built in the 19th century to bypass the rapids, links the town to the Vieux-Port. The canal itself is now blocked to shipping, but the land along its banks has been turned into parkland with a bicycle trail.

← A dazzling light display at sunset in the Jardin Botanique de Montréal

↑ The splendidly ornate interior of the Cathédrale Marie-Reine-du-Monde

24

Cathédrale Marie-Reine-du-Monde

⦿ C3 ⌂ 1085 Rue de la Cathédrale ⓡ Central Station 🚌 150, 178, 350, 355, 747 Ⓜ Bonaventure 🕐 7am-7pm Mon-Fri, 7:30am-7pm Sat & Sun 🌐 cathedralecatholique demontreal.org

When Montreal's first Catholic cathedral burned down in 1852, Bishop Ignace Bourget decided to demonstrate the importance of the Catholic Church in Canada by building a new one in a district domina-ted at the time by the English Protestant commercial elite.

To show his flock's loyalty to the Pope, he modeled the new church on St. Peter's Basilica in Rome.

The cathedral, which was completed in 1894, has dimensions that are a quarter of those of St. Peter's. The statues on the roof represent the patron saints of all the parishes that constituted the Montreal diocese in 1890. The magnificent altar canopy, a replica of the one Bernini made for St. Peter's, was cast in copper and gold leaf. Another reminder of Bourget's loyalty to Rome can be found on the pillar in the northeast corner of the church. Here lies a marble plaque listing the names of all the Montrealers who served in the Papal armies during the Italian wars of independence in the 1850s.

25

Centre d'Histoire de Montréal

⦿ D3 ⌂ 335 Place d'Youville 🚌 35, 61, 75 Ⓜ Square Victoria 🕐 10am-5pm Wed-Sun 🚫 Mid-Dec-mid-Jan 🌐 ville.montreal.qc.ca

The exhibits in this museum trace the history of Montreal from the earliest indigenous settlements to the modern age, with the focus on everyday life. The museum is housed in a handsome,

red-brick fire station with a gracefully gabled roof built in 1903. There are three floors of exhibits. On the first floor, "Traces. Places. Memories," the museum's permanent exhibition, traces five passages in Montreal's history, beginning in 1535 with the meeting of First Nations peoples and European explorers and ending with the cultural boom of the 1960s. The museum's second and third floors are devoted to year-round changing exhibitions showcasing the city's advancements, its people, and their experiences. A third-floor observation deck offers a scenic view of the Vieux-Port and Vieux-Montréal.

26

Musée McCord

⦿ B2 ⌂ 690 Rue Sherbrooke St W ⓡ Central Station 🚌 24 Ⓜ McGill 🕐 10am-6pm Tue, Thu & Fri, 10am-9pm Wed, 10am-5pm Sat & Sun (Jul & Aug: also Mon) 🌐 mccord-museum.qc.ca

Lawyer David Ross McCord (1844–1930) was an avid collector of virtually every-thing that had to do with life in Canada, including books, photographs, jewelry, clothing, furniture, documents, papers, paintings, toys, and porcelain.

In 1919, McCord donated his considerable acquisitions to McGill University with a view to establishing a museum of Canadian social history. That collection, now more than 1,500,000 artifacts, is housed in a stately limestone building that was once a social center for McGill students.

The museum has a good section on early history, an exceptional display of folk art, and a particularly fine collection of Aboriginal and Inuit items, featuring clothing, weapons, jewelry, and pottery. A separate room is devoted to the social history of Montreal. The museum's most celebrated possession is a vast collection of photographs that chronicle every detail of daily life in 19th-century Montreal.

↑ Centre des Sciences de Montréal, with a giant molecular sculpture on its entrance steps

27 🗦 🍴 🖥 🛍
Centre des Sciences de Montréal

📍D2 🚶King Edward Pier
🚇Central Station 🚌715
Ⓜ Place d'Armes 🕐9am–4pm Mon–Fri, 10am–5pm Sat & Sun 🌐montreal sciencecentre.com

Dominating the Vieux-Port's King Edward Pier, this huge, airy building is home to a number of permanent and temporary exhibitions that focus on technology, engineering, and science, as well as other subjects. Among the permanent exhibitions, "Water in the Universe" investigates the science behind water molecules and the quest to find alternative sources of water in space. The experience will appeal to all age groups, and includes a rock from the moon that can be touched.

Attached to the Centre des Sciences de Montréal is the

←

The warm red-brick facade of the Centre d'histoire de Montréal

IMAX Telus Theater that shows educational documentaries in 3D on its immense screen. The price of admission can vary greatly depending on the combination of exhibits and films that you choose to see.

28 🗦 🎭 🍴 🖥 🛍
Maison Saint-Gabriel

📍B2 🚶2146 Place de Dublin
Ⓜ Charlevoix, Square Victoria 🚌57, 61 🕐Mid-Jun–Sep: 1–5pm Mon–Sat; Oct–mid-Jun: 10am–5pm Tue–Sun (closed 11:45am–12:45pm) 🌐maisonsaint-gabriel.qc.ca

This isolated fragment of New France at first appears lost among the apartment buildings of working-class

💬 INSIDER TIP
Get Crafty

Among the many exhibits of the Centre des Sciences de Montréal, try to time your visit to experience Fabrik. This special workshop takes place every afternoon at 2pm (noon on weekends), and visitors can create and experiment with the provided crafts.

Pointe-Saint-Charles. It was a farm when the formidable Marguerite Bourgeoys, Montreal's first schoolteacher and now a canonized saint, bought it in 1668 as a residence for the religious order she had founded in 1655.

The house, rebuilt in 1698 after a fire, is a fine example of 17th-century architecture, with thick stone walls and a steeply pitched roof built on an intricate frame of original heavy wooden timbers.

Marguerite Bourgeoys and her tireless sisters worked the farm and ran a school on the property for Aboriginal and colonial children. They also housed and trained the *filles du roy* (the "king's daughters") – orphaned young girls sent abroad to be the women of his new colony. Now a museum and historic site, Maison Saint-Gabriel was inaugurated in 1966. The building itself is over 300 years old, and inside the house's chapel, kitchen, dormitory, and drawing rooms are artifacts dating from the 17th century, deftly arranged as though they were still in use. These include a writing desk used by Marguerite Bourgeoys herself and a magnificent vestment and cope, embroidered by a wealthy hermit who lived in a hut on the property.

A SHORT WALK
VIEUX-MONTRÉAL

Distance 0.5 miles (1 km) **Time** 15 minutes
Nearest métro Place-d'Armes

Historic churches, cobblestone streets, horse-drawn *calèches*, and a bustling international port characterize Vieux-Montréal. This is the oldest part of the city, where Montreal's founders built the Catholic village that was to become Montreal on the Saint Lawrence River in 1642. As the city expanded in the mid-20th century, Vieux-Montréal fell into decline, but the district underwent a renaissance in the 1980s. The remaining 18th-century buildings were transformed into upscale restaurants, stylish bistros, and chic boutiques. Today, the old quarter epitomizes the romance, culture and *joie de vivre* of the metropolis, while the constant activity of mega-freighters and cruise boats in the Vieux-Port is a reminder that Montreal is the shipping gateway to the Great Lakes.

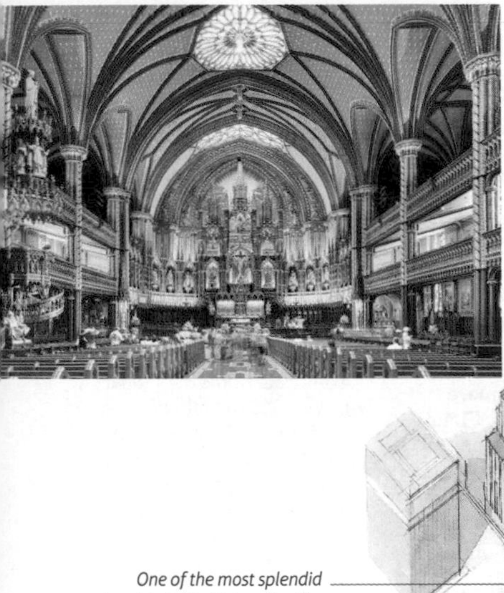

← Stunning interior of the Basilique Notre-Dame de Montréal

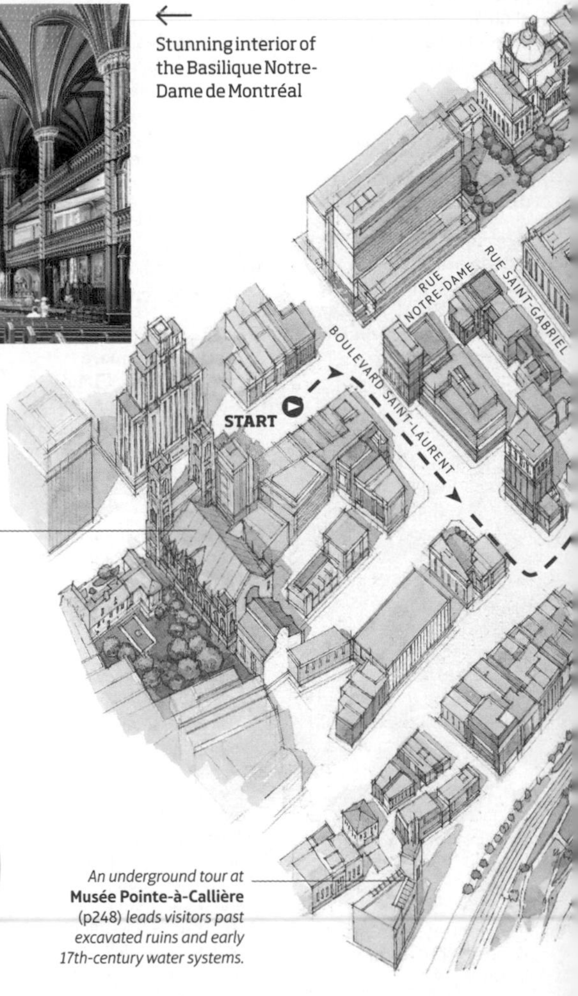

One of the most splendid churches in North America, the *1829* **Basilique Notre-Dame de Montréal** *(p242) is the city's Catholic showpiece, with a spectacularly decorated and colorful interior.*

START ▶

RUE NOTRE-DAME

RUE SAINT-GABRIEL

BOULEVARD SAINT-LAURENT

Did You Know?
———
Early 17th-century settlers called Montreal Ville-Marie, or "City of Mary."

An underground tour at **Musée Pointe-à-Callière** *(p248) leads visitors past excavated ruins and early 17th-century water systems.*

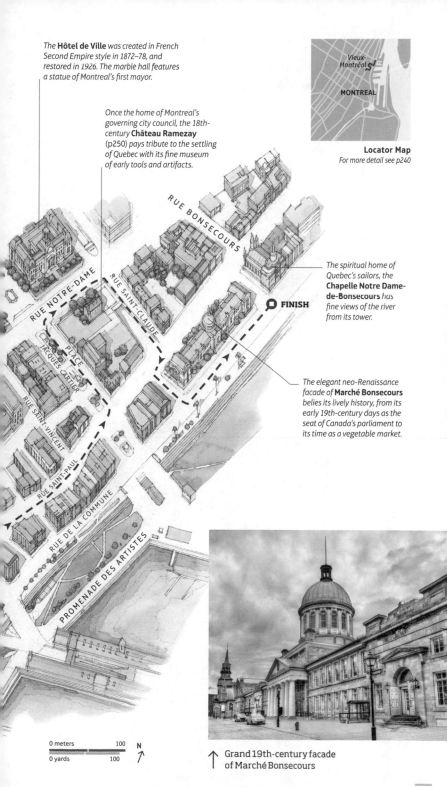

The **Hôtel de Ville** was created in French Second Empire style in 1872–78, and restored in 1926. The marble hall features a statue of Montreal's first mayor.

Once the home of Montreal's governing city council, the 18th-century **Château Ramezay** (p250) pays tribute to the settling of Quebec with its fine museum of early tools and artifacts.

Locator Map
For more detail see p240

Vieux-Montréal

MONTREAL

RUE BONSECOURS

RUE NOTRE-DAME

RUE SAINT-CLAUDE

PLACE JACQUES CARTIER

RUE SAINT-VINCENT

RUE SAINT-PAUL

RUE DE LA COMMUNE

PROMENADE DES ARTISTES

FINISH

The spiritual home of Quebec's sailors, the **Chapelle Notre Dame-de-Bonsecours** has fine views of the river from its tower.

The elegant neo-Renaissance facade of **Marché Bonsecours** belies its lively history, from its early 19th-century days as the seat of Canada's parliament to its time as a vegetable market.

0 meters 100
0 yards 100

N

↑ Grand 19th-century facade of Marché Bonsecours

QUEBEC CITY

The heart and soul of French Canada, Quebec City sits overlooking the Saint Lawrence River on the cliffs of Cap Diamant. One of the oldest communities on the American continent, Quebec City was discovered as an Iroquois village by the French explorer Jacques Cartier and founded as a city in 1608 by explorer Samuel de Champlain.

Today, as provincial capital, the city is the seat of regional government, and is at the center of French-Canadian nationalism. Parisian in atmosphere, with every tiny street worth visiting, Quebec City is almost entirely French-speaking. The European ambiance and architecture, and the city's crucial historical importance, all contributed to the Historic District of Old Quebec being named a UNESCO World Heritage Site in 1985.

QUEBEC CITY

Must Sees

1. La Citadelle
2. Place-Royale
3. Basilique-Cathédrale Notre-Dame de Québec

Experience More

4. Musée National des Beaux-Arts du Québec
5. Fairmont Le Château Frontenac
6. Terrasse Dufferin
7. Musée de la Civilisation
8. Musée du Fort
9. Place d'Armes
10. Monastère des Ursulines
11. Hôtel de Ville
12. Rue du Trésor
13. Rue du Petit-Champlain
14. Séminaire de Québec

Eat

1. Bistro L'Orygine
2. Frites Alors
3. La Galette Libanaise
4. Restaurant MNBAQ

Shop

5. Galerie Art Inuit Brousseau
6. La Boutique de Noël de Québec
7. Roots

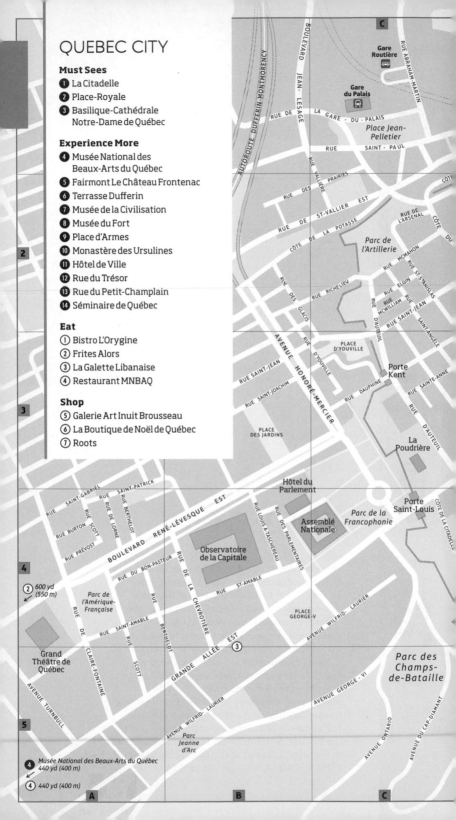

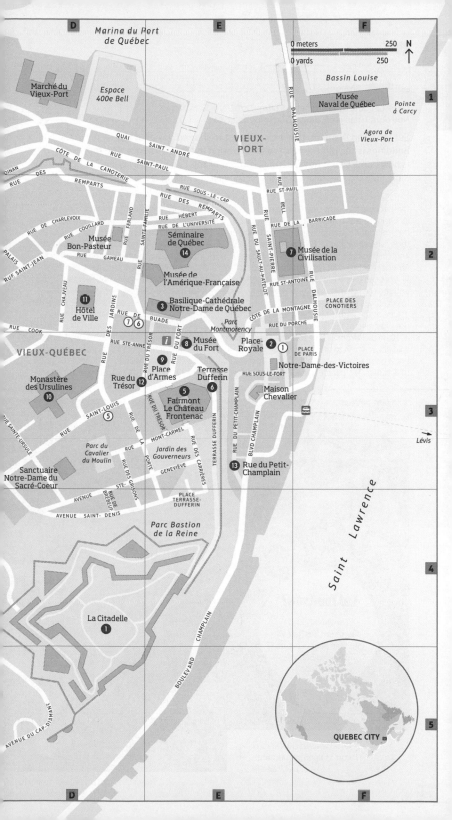

1

LA CITADELLE

D4 1 Côte de la Citadelle May-Oct: 9am-5pm daily; Nov-Apr: 10am-4pm daily lacitadelle.qc.ca

Set atop Cap Diamant, this impressive star-shaped group of ten buildings is the largest military fortification in North America. The fort is now home to the Royal 22nd Regiment of the Canadian Army, and daily military spectacles are staged for visitors during the summer.

Overlooking the Saint Lawrence River, La Citadelle was begun by the French in 1693, but many of the battlements that you can see today were built by the British between 1820 and 1850 to defend Quebec against a feared American attack that never materialised. Visitors can take a tour around the fortress, and see the regiment perform their daily tasks as well as their parade drill.

One of the highlights of any visit is watching the Changing of the Guard, which takes place at 10am daily from 24 June to Labor Day. New soldiers march in to the beat of a regimental brass band to relieve the old soldiers from their duties. The parade is accompanied by the regiment's mascot: a goat called Batisse. At noon daily, and at 9:30pm every day during summer months, visitors can also watch as a cannon is ceremonially fired from the Citadelle.

Other notable sights include the splendid Governor-General's Residence, the official home of Canada's governors-general since the 19th century; the Cape Diamond Redoubt, the fort's oldest structure; a powder-magazine-turned-chapel; and the Neo-Classical Dalhousie Gate, the original gateway to the Citadelle. There are also two fascinating museums tracing the history of the Royal 22nd Regiment, with exhibits including rare military documents and antique armaments.

Did You Know?

The Royal 22nd Regiment has had at least ten goat mascots, all named Batisse, since 1955.

Aerial view of the famous star-shaped battlements of La Citadelle ↑

① The rooftop of the Fairmont Le Château Frontena can be seen from the battlements overlooking Old Quebec.

② A historic cannon is positioned in front of the barracks within La Citadelle complex.

③ A brass band accompanies the Changing of the Guard ceremony, performed by the Royal 22nd Regiment of the Canadian Army.

ROYAL 22ND REGIMENT

Known colloquially as the Van Doos (a British pronunciation of the French for twenty-two, vingt-deux), the Royal 22nd Regiment's 2nd Battalion has been the Guard for La Citadelle since 1969. This prestigious group has been honored for their bravery in the Korean War (1950–53) and for other peace-keeping roles since then. Their ceremonial uniforms were designed by the British, and include bright scarlet tunics, and tall bearskin hats.

2

PLACE-ROYALE

◉ E3 ⌂ Rue Notre Dame 🚌 1, 11

The literal and spiritual heart of Quebec City, Place-Royale is a quaint, cobblestoned square that witnessed the birth of New France. Lined with restored 17th-century stone buildings, it was here that French explorer Samuel de Champlain built the city's first structure in 1608.

Of all the squares in Canada, Place-Royale undoubtedly has the most history. Samuel de Champlain, the founder of Quebec, is thought to have planted his garden on this site, and the French colonial governor Frontenac turned it into a market in 1673. A bust of Louis XIV was installed in 1686, and the square was named Place-Royale. Today it remains much as it did in the 17th century, exuding an air of elegance and delicate grandeur. The steep-roofed houses with pastel-colored shutters were once the homes of wealthy traders, but the square declined during the 19th century. It is now fully restored and a favorite with street performers.

↑ The colorful rooftops and stonework of buildings near the historic Place-Royale

EXPERIENCE Quebec City

Timeline

1608
△ Samuel de Chaplain builds Quebec's first settlement on this site

1759
The British army destroy much of the city, leaving Place-Royale in ruins

1815–60
The square loses its role as a center of commerce in the industrial revolution

1967
▽ The government invests in renovating the square, bringing it back to its former glory

Eglise Notre-Dame-des-Victoires

Although small, this lovely stone Roman Catholic church dominates the square. It is one of the oldest churches in North America, and was constructed in 1688 on the ruins of Samuel de Champlain's first outpost. The building was largely destroyed during the Battle of the Plains of Abraham in 1759 – a brief but significant battle during the Seven Years' War – but was rebuilt soon after. The church is open daily to visitors in the summer, and admission is free. Inside there are a number of lovely 18th- and 19th-century paintings.

← The charming cobblestoned streets of Old Quebec City

EAT

Bistro L'Orygine
Located just behind the Place-Royale in the heart of old Quebec City, this sleekly stylish restaurant features a gorgeous organic menu of modern Canadian cuisine. For a dinner that won't disappoint, start with the fresh oysters, opt for the Guinea fowl for your main, and finish with their daily dessert. There are plenty of vegan-friendly options available, too. During summer months, be sure to ask for a table on their pleasant shaded patio.

⌂ 36 rue Saint-Pierre
🕒 Mon-Tue; 2-5:30pm Wed-Sun
🌐 lorygine.com

$ $ $

3 MB

BASILIQUE-CATHÉDRALE NOTRE-DAME DE QUÉBEC

◉ E2 🏠 16 rue de Buade 🚌 11 ⊙ Daily 🌐 notre-dame-de-quebec.org

This magnificent cathedral is the principal seat of the Roman Catholic archbishop of Quebec, whose diocese once stretched from here to Mexico. Despite restorations after fire- and battle-damage over the centuries, it retains a remarkable unity of style.

The first church built on this site dates back to 1647, and parts of the original structure, including portions of the walls and the bell tower, are still intact. Most of today's exterior is from renovations completed in 1771. The Neo-Baroque interior was also reconstructed after a devastating fire in 1922. Some modern materials have been used, but sensitively, to re-create the light feel; glowing stained-glass windows, richly gilded decoration, and the graceful baldachin over the main altar add to the effect. Ecclesiastical treasures and paintings from the time of the French regime can be seen, including a chancel lamp given by Louis XIV.

As part of the cathedral's 350th anniversary celebration, a holy door was constructed, one of just two outside Europe, and only the eighth in the world. It is sealed until 2025.

The cathedral's large crypt was Quebec City's first cemetery, with more than 900 bodies interred underneath the altar, including 20 bishops and four governors of New France. Rumor has it that the father of New France, Samuel de Champlain, may be buried somewhere near the cathedral. Archaeologists have been searching for his tomb since the 1850s.

↑ The soaring ceiling and gilded altar inside the cathedral

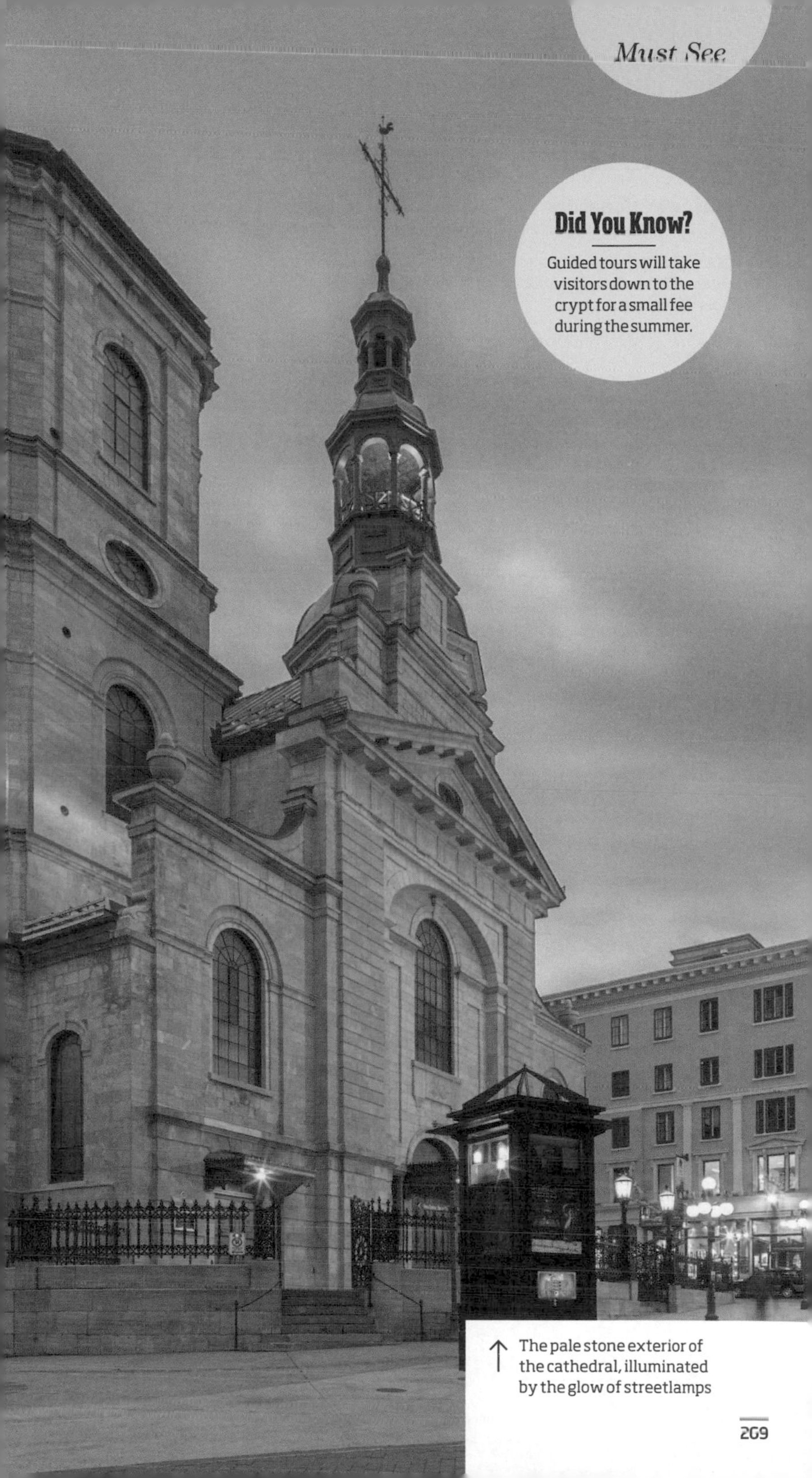

Did You Know?

Guided tours will take visitors down to the crypt for a small fee during the summer.

↑ The pale stone exterior of the cathedral, illuminated by the glow of streetlamps

EXPERIENCE MORE

4

Musée National des Beaux-Arts du Québec

Q A5 **A** 179 Grande Allée Ouest **C** Tue–Sun **C** Public hols **W** mnbaq.org

With over 30,000 pieces of art, the MNBAQ is dedicated to Quebec artists and their work, dating from as early as the 17th century to the modern day. The collection is housed in four pavilions, all connected through underground tunnels. Of particular interest is the Charles-Baillairgé Pavilion, a former prison dating from 1861. Some of the cells have been preserved and reveal the original prison conditions. The Central Pavilion has a gorgeous rooftop garden with views of the city, and the sculpture garden contains 15 pieces to admire.

5

Fairmont Le Château Frontenac

Q E3 **A** 1 Rue des Carrières **W** fairmont.com/frontenac-quebec

The steep, copper-roofed landmark that dominates the skyline of Old Quebec is a luxury hotel, built by the Canadian Pacific Railway on the heights overlooking the Saint Lawrence River. In the 19th century, US architect Bruce Price designed the hotel as a French-style château on a huge scale, with dozens of turrets, towers, and a high roof studded with rows of dormer windows. Building continued for almost a century after the first section of the hotel was opened in 1893, with a final part completed in 1993. Made from brick and stone, the hotel now has 611 guest rooms and two upscale restaurants, as well as elegant public areas.

Interior and exterior *(inset)* of the Pierre Lassonde Pavilion ↓ at the MNBAQ

Did You Know?

Le Château Frontenac was one of the first hotels built by the Canadian Pacific Railway.

6

Terrasse Dufferin

Q E3

Sweeping along the top of Cap Diamant from Fairmont Le Château Frontenac to the edge of the Citadel, the Terrasse Dufferin boardwalk is well equipped with benches and kiosks, and offers an excellent opportunity to take in unmatched views of the Saint Lawrence River, the Laurentian Mountains, and Île d'Orléans. It was built in 1879, and extends for 1394 ft (425 m) alongside the town. During winter, Les Glissades de la Terrasse, a dramatic ice slide for toboggans, is installed on the terrace, while in the summer months you will find street performers along its winding length.

→ The Terrasse Dufferin, with its toboggan ice slide set up in winter

Musée de la Civilisation

☐ E2 ☐ 85 Rue Dalhousie ☐ Late Jun–early Sep: 10am–5pm daily; early Sep–late Jun: 10am–5pm Tue–Sun ☐ mcq.org

Renowned Canadian architect Moshe Safdie designed this contemporary limestone and glass building in Basse-Ville to house Quebec's museum of history and culture. Although highly up to date in feel, the construction of the Musée de la civilisation has won several prizes for blending in well with its historic surroundings. Three heritage buildings are part of the museum's structure including Maison d'Estèbe, an 18th-century merchant's house. Museum exhibits include "This is Our Story," which reflects on the city's First Nation and Inuit history, and the remains of a 250-year-old French flat-bottomed boat. Many exhibits are hands-on, and there are regular workshops for families,

during which participants are encouraged to try on costumes from different eras. Access to all workshops is included in the standard ticket price.

Musée du Fort

☐ E3 ☐ 10 Rue Sainte-Anne ☐ Daily ☐ Public hols ☐ museedufort.com

Military history is brought to life at this museum in impressive sound and light shows re-enacting six Quebec sieges and battles, including the famous battle of the Plains of Abraham and Benedict Arnold's march to Quebec. There is also a collection of war relics and a 400-sq-ft (37-sq-m) model of Quebec City and its outlying regions as it was in 1750, allowing visitors to fully appreciate the strategic importance of this city. Head to the gift shop for a wonderful selection of historical books on Old Quebec, plus interesting souvenirs and collectables.

> Although highly up to date in feel, the construction of the Musée de la Civilisation has won several prizes for blending in well with its historic surroundings.

EAT

Frites Alors
Get your authentic poutine fix at this local fast-food chain, with nearly 20 mouth-watering options.

☐ A4 ☐ 122 Cremazie Ouest ☐ fritealors.com

$$$

La Galette Libanaise
Head here for fresh and fast Lebanese sandwiches. You can eat in or get them to go.

☐ B4 ☐ 641 Grande Allée Est ☐ lagalette libanaise.com

$$$

Restaurant MNBAQ
There are flavorful dishes and a chic patio at this museum eatery, headed by chef Marie-Chantal Lepage.

☐ A5 ☐ 179 Grande Allée Ouest ☐ 11am–5pm daily ☐ signemclepage.com

$$$

9

Place d'Armes

📍E3

French colonial soldiers once used this attractive, grassy square just north of Fairmont Le Château Frontenac as a parade ground, but its uses today are more congenial. Open horse-drawn carriages wait here to offer visitors a journey that reveals Old Quebec in all its charm. In the center, the Monument de la Foi commemorates the 300th anniversary of the 1615 arrival of Catholic Recollet missionaries. On the southwest corner, next to the fine Anglican cathedral, lies the grand early 19th-century former Palais de Justice. The Musée du Fort *(p271)* opposite contains a large scale model of Quebec City in the 19th century.

10

Monastère des Ursulines

📍D3 🏠Rue Donnacona
📞(418) 694 0694 🕐Daily

In 1639, Mère Marie de l'Incarnation brought the Ursuline order of nuns to Quebec and oversaw the construction in 1641 of the nunnery, which later burned

← The Monument de la Foi, which towers above the place d'Armes

down. Today, visitors can see the Saint-Augustin and Sainte-Famille wings, which date from a period of rebuilding between 1686 and 1721. Once surrounded by fruit orchards, the charming complex has gradually evolved over the past four centuries. One of the buildings is North America's oldest girls' school (boys have been admitted since 2010). Nearly a hundred nuns still live and work here, so access is limited. The beautifully decorated chapel and French antiques, including Louis XIII furniture, scientific instruments, paintings, and embroideries, are displayed in the Musée des Ursulines within the monastery. The museum also tells the story of the nuns' educational and missionary achievements; Mère Marie completed the

first Huron, Algonquin, and Iroquois dictionaries, for example. Copies are on display, alongside embroidery and liturgical clothes from the 17th to 19th centuries.

11

Hôtel de Ville

📍D2 🏠2 Rue des Jardins
📞(418) 641 6010 🕐8:30am-4:30pm daily

This imposing building stands in the heart of the city at the western end of the rue de Buade, a popular gathering place for Quebec artists offering their wares. Still the town hall to the city today, it was inaugurated in 1896, and built on the site of College des Jésuites, a major building in New France. Its grounds are the focus for both locals and visitors: the small park here holds theater performances in the summertime, while in winter it is home to a traditional outdoor market.

↑ Rue du Petit-Champlain, lit by festive lights in the weeks before Christmas

14 ♿ 🏛
Séminaire de Québec

📍 E2 🏠 1 Rue des Remparts
📞 (418) 692 3981 🕐 Summer

In 1663, the first bishop of Quebec, François de Laval, built a seminary next to his cathedral to train Catholic priests. Over the centuries it has been added to and now forms a graceful complex of buildings centered on a peaceful courtyard.

Within the seminary, visitors can admire the excellent 18th-century paneling that covers the walls of the chapel. The Musée de l'Amérique franco-phone is part of the complex and has an eclectic collection, including a converted chapel.

12
Rue du Trésor

📍 D3

This tiny alley, just across rue de Buade from Holy Trinity cathedral, is something of a Quebecois institution. Closed to cars, the little street is packed in summer with visitors eager to have their portraits drawn, painted, or caricatured by the dozens of street artists who gather here. The tradition began in the 1960s when two young artists hung their works here to bypass the gallery process, and others flocked to follow their example.

> 💬 **INSIDER TIP**
> **Feeling Festive**
>
> If you're visiting Quebec City during the holiday season, the German Christmas market at the Hôtel de Ville is a great spot for caroling and sampling sweet treats.

13
Rue du Petit-Champlain

📍 E3 🌐 quartierpetit champlain.com

The oldest staircase in the city – the aptly named Escalier Casse-Cou, or Breakneck Stairs – descends from Haute-Ville past several levels of gift shops to end on this narrow little walkway in the oldest part of the town. French artisans built homes here as early as the 1680s, and Irish dockworkers moved to the area in the 19th century. Much of the historic architecture remained, but the area fell into decline early in the 20th century. The workers' homes have been transformed into 50 art and speciality shops and restaurants, and the short pedestrian walkway has become one of the liveliest spots in old Quebec City. While often crowded, some interesting boutiques can be found.

SHOP

Galerie Art Inuit Brousseau

A fine art gallery promoting the works of Inuit artists, with an emphasis on sculpture.

📍 D3 🏠 35 Rue Saint Louis 🌐 artinuit brousseau.ca

___

La Boutique de Noël de Québec

It's a winter wonderland all year round at this Christmas-dedicated shop; head here for an array of decorations and ornaments.

📍 D2 🏠 47 Rue de Buade 🌐 boutiquedenoel.ca

___

Roots

This Canadian leisurewear company offers clothing and accessories for every age, all stamped with their iconic beaver logo.

📍 D2 🏠 49 Rue de Buade 🌐 roots.com

A SHORT WALK
QUEBEC CITY

Distance 1 km (0.5 miles) **Time** 15 minutes
Nearest bus stop Des Jardins

With its beautiful riverside setting, historic sites, and narrow cobblestone streets – all of which earned it World Heritage status in 1985 – the Historic District of Old Quebec (also known as the Basse-Ville or Lower Town) is a pedestrian's dream. Poised on the Cap Diamant escarpment overlooking the St Lawrence River and Les Laurentides, this part of the city is rich in cultural pride and exuberance. Stroll its streets and take in the distinctive winding staircases, beautifully preserved historic buildings and bustling cafés.

*Built in 1647, **Basilique Notre-Dame-de-Québec** provides a rich setting for relics from early French rule in Quebec, and Old Master paintings.*

↑ Elegant interior of the 17th-century Basilique Notre-Dame-de-Québec

*The elegant 1804 stone Neo-Classical façade of **Holy Trinity Anglican Cathedral** conceals an English oak interior.*

START ⊙

DE BUADE

DES JARDINS

SAINTE ANNE

DES JARDINS

SAINT LOUIS

__Musée du Fort__ brings military history to life with sound-and-light shows re-enacting six Quebec sieges and battles, and numerous war relics.

__Fairmont Le Château Frontenac__, one of Quebec City's best-known landmarks, has dominated the skyline since 1893, and has 611 luxurious guest rooms.

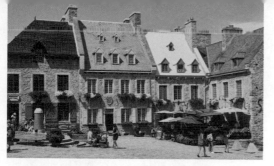

↑ Pretty Place-Royale, the site of Nouvelle-France's first settlement

Historic District
QUEBEC CITY

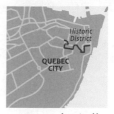

Locator Map

For more detail see p262

PORT DAUPHIN
DU SAULT AU MATELOT
SAINT PIERRE
FINISH
SAINT PIERRE
NOTRE DAME
TERRASSE DUFFERIN
0 meters
100
0 yards
100
N

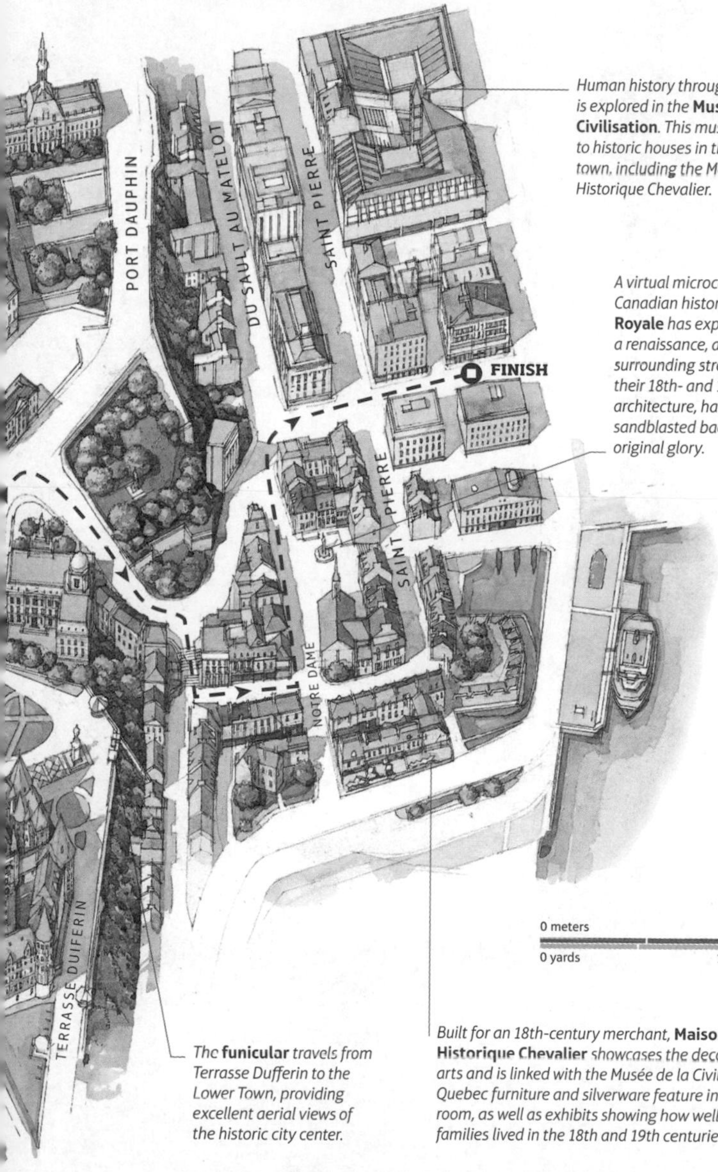

Human history through the ages is explored in the **Musée de la Civilisation***. This museum is linked to historic houses in the rest of the town, including the Maison Historique Chevalier.*

A virtual microcosm of Canadian history, **Place-Royale** *has experienced a renaissance, and the surrounding streets, with their 18th- and 19th-century architecture, have been sandblasted back to their original glory.*

The **funicular** *travels from Terrasse Dufferin to the Lower Town, providing excellent aerial views of the historic city center.*

Built for an 18th-century merchant, **Maison Historique Chevalier** *showcases the decorative arts and is linked with the Musée de la Civilisation. Quebec furniture and silverware feature in every room, as well as exhibits showing how well-to-do families lived in the 18th and 19th centuries.*

QUEBEC PROVINCE

Must Sees
① Sainte-Anne-de-Beaupré
② Gatineau

Experience More
③ Tadoussac
④ Saguenay River
⑤ Parc de la Chute Montmorency and Île d'Orléans
⑥ Baie-Comeau
⑦ Chicoutimi
⑧ South Shore
⑨ Mingan Archipelago National Park
⑩ Îles-de-la-Madeleine
⑪ Sept-Îles
⑫ Parc National de la Mauricie
⑬ Lac Memphrémagog
⑭ Richelieu Valley
⑮ Sainte-Croix
⑯ Sherbrooke
⑰ Charlevoix Coast
⑱ Sucrerie de la Montagne
⑲ Joliette
⑳ Terrebonne
㉑ Trois-Rivières
㉒ Oka
㉓ James Bay
㉔ Val d'Or
㉕ Réserve Faunique La Vérendrye
㉖ Nunavik
㉗ Rouyn Noranda

1 ⓂⒷ

SAINTE-ANNE-DE-BEAUPRÉ

🏠 10018 Ave Royale 🕐 Jun-Sep: 7am-9:30pm daily; Oct-May: 8am-5pm daily 🌐 sanctuairesainteanne.org

The oldest pilgrimage site in North America, Sainte-Anne-de-Beaupré dates back to 1658. Dedicated to the mother of the Virgin Mary and Quebec's patron saint, it is one of Canada's most sacred places.

In the 1650s, a group of sailors who landed here after surviving a shipwreck vowed to build a chapel in honor of St. Anne, who is said to have healing powers. The present Neo-Romanesque basilica was built in 1926–46, and was the fifth church to be built on this site. Over 800,000 visitors now visit every year, and pillars by the entrance are covered with the crutches of worshippers who claim to have been cured by St. Anne. The dome-vaulted ceiling is decorated with gold mosaics portraying the life of the saint. A separate building next to the main shrine features two floors of religious exhibitions on St. Anne and 300 years of pilgramage to this holy site.

The gold statue that sits on top of the facade was saved from the fire that destroyed the 19th-century basilica.

Stained-glass windows show the progress of pilgrims through the shrine, with the rose window as the centerpiece.

BASILICA STATUS

In 1876, St. Anne was proclaimed patron saint of Quebec, and in 1887 the existing church was granted basilica status. The Redemptorist order became the guardians of the shrine in 1878.

Entrance to the basilica's upper floor

Gilded ciborium over the
high altar inside Sainte-
Anne-de-Beaupré ↑

*A richly decorated
statue overlooks the
relics of St. Anne
on the upper floor.*

*A faithful copy of
Michelangelo's Pietà in
St. Peter's sits at the
ambulatory's north end.*

→
Gold statue depicting
Jesus condemned to death,
by Joseph-Émile Brunet

↑ Flaming fall colors surrounding Meech Lake in Parc de la Gatineau

② 🍽 🛍

Casino du Lac-Leamy

⌂ 1 Blvd du Casino
🕑 24 hours daily
🌐 casinos.lotoquebec.com

Three million visitors a year are lured to this glittering casino, which is equipped with 1,800 slot machines and 64 gaming tables. Owned by the Quebec government, the casino opened in 1996 and is set in a park full of flowers and fountains. There's 24-hour entertainment, with first-rate restaurants, a buzzing nightclub, and a full-scale on-site theater.

②

GATINEAU

✈ Ottawa International 7 miles (12 km) S of the city
🚌 200 Tremblay Rd, Ottawa 🛈 103 Rue Laurier; www.tourismeoutaouais.com

Gatineau (known as Hull until 1992) is based just across the river from Ottawa, in the province of Quebec, and is often considered to be a more relaxed and fun-loving counterpart to the national capital. Right from Hull's establishment in 1800, the city's liquor laws were far more lenient than Ottawa's, so this was where Ottawa politicians came to party. Gatineau is also home to Canada's most-visited museum, the Canadian Museum of History, which provides a fascinating tour of the country over the past 1,000 years.

①

Parc de la Gatineau

⌂ 33 Scott Rd 🕑 Daily
🌐 ncc-ccn.gc.ca

This 140-sq-miles (360-sq-km) oasis of lakes and rolling hills between the Gatineau and Ottawa rivers is a weekend playground for city residents. The park contains an estate that belonged to the former Canadian prime minister William Lyon Mackenzie King, within which you will find fragments of Gothic buildings.

↑ Nighttime view across the illuminated Alexandra Bridge, looking toward Gatineau

> Built in 1900, the handsome, steel-framed Alexandra Bridge - also known as the Interprovincial Bridge - spans the Ottawa River and links Ontario to Quebec.

③
Maison du Citoyen

🏠 25 Rue Laurier ☎ (819) 243 2345 🕐 8:30am-4:30pm Mon-Fri

The heart of this complex is a vast atrium, the Agora, meant to serve as an all-weather gathering place for Gatineau's citizens, as well as an airy meditation center for the city's workers. Opening from it is the City Hall, a library, a theater, and an art gallery.

④
Alexandra Bridge

Built in 1900, the handsome, steel-framed Alexandra Bridge – also known as the Interprovincial Bridge – spans the Ottawa River and links Ontario to Quebec. It can be accessed on foot, bicycle, or by car, and approximately 22,000 vehicles cross the bridge every day. Pedestrians can take in fine views of the river, the Canadian Museum of History, and the Parliament Buildings in Ottawa.

⑤ 🍴 🖥
Promenade du Portage

Linked with the two of the city's main bridges across the Ottawa River, this main route downtown is full of lively cafés, restaurants, and even a microbrewery. After dark, the promenade and nearby Place Aubry become the focus of the city's excellent nightlife.

EAT

Les Brasseurs du Temps
A lively brewpub with a lovely outdoor terrace, housed in a renovated stone heritage building. Their house-made brews are paired with delicious tapas. There's an on-site museum, too - craft beer enthusiasts should make sure to ask for a guided tour.

🏠 170 Rue Montcalm
🌐 brasseursdu temps.com

$$$

Edgar
Come for the busy brunch at this rustic local favorite, and enjoy a friendly, intimate atmosphere and hearty portions. Aim for a spot on the sidewalk patio to sample a true slice of Gatineau life.

🏠 60 Rue Bégin 🕐 Mon
🌐 chezedgar.ca

$$$

La Pataterie Hulloise
The search for Gatineau's best poutine is over. This take-out joint fries fresh-cut potatoes just right, before adding a generous serving of squeaky soft cheese curds and a layer of smooth, savory gravy. A one-stop shop for those craving their next fix of Canada's national dish.

🏠 311 Bvld Saint-Joseph
🌐 lapataterie hulloise.com

$$$

(6) 🔨 🎨 🍴 ☕ 🛍️

CANADIAN MUSEUM OF HISTORY

🏛️ **100 Laurier St** 🕐 **Times vary, check website** 🌐 **historymuseum.ca**

The curved shapes of this grand limestone building are reminiscent of glaciers, rivers, and waves; a fitting design for a museum that's all about Canada. The exterior space offers panoramic views of Ottawa on all sides, and the interior is equally impressive, with spectacular exhibits that trace the country's history from prehistoric times to the present.

Located on the banks of the Ottawa River, the Canadian Museum of History was built in the 1980s to be the storehouse of the country's human history. The architect, Douglas Cardinal, wanted the undulating facades of both buildings to reflect the Canadian landscape. The more curved hall is the Canadian Shield Wing, which is home to the museum's offices. The Glacier Wing displays the exhibits. Its entrance is stunning; the dramatic interior of the Grand Hall contains the world's largest collection of totem poles and is the architectural focal point of the museum. The Children's Museum is also a real draw, while the CINÉ+ Theatre offers the ultimate cinema experience.

Elaborately carved totem poles dominating the Grand Hall of the Museum's Glacier Wing ↑

The eye-catching exterior of the museum, with its dramatic curving walls ↑

Did You Know?

The museum offers free admission every Thursday evening from 5pm to 8pm.

Gallery Highlights

Grand Hall

▽ Besides the collection of totem poles, this hall contains six traditional First Nations longhouses. Artifacts of the First Peoples of the Northwest Coast can also be viewed, as well as works by renowned Haida artists.

First Peoples Hall

▷ Located on level 1, this hall highlights the historic, cultural, and artistic achievements of Canada's First Nations, Métis, and Inuit peoples over the last 20,000 years. Everyday objects, such as clothing, tools, stone pots, canoes, and ceremonial artifacts are on display.

Canadian History Hall

▽ Located on levels three and four, this hall is a remarkable journey through Canada's history, from the dawn of human habitation 15,000 years ago to the present day. Don't miss the 3,900-year-old ivory carving of a woman's face.

Canadian Children's Museum

The Canadian Children's Museum on level two is an extremely popular space that contains a "world tour" of hands-on exhibits, allowing kids to travel by exploring other cultures. It's fully interactive, with costumes, toys, games, and even a full-size colorful bus to play with.

EXPERIENCE MORE

❸ Tadoussac

🚌🚍 𝘪 197 Rue des Pionniers; www.tadoussac.com

Lined with boutiques, the old streets of this little town make a gentle start to exploring the local stretch of the Saint Lawrence River. In 1600, French traders picked this site to establish the first fur-trading post in Canada, noticing that for generations First Nations people had held meetings here to trade and parley. In the 19th century, the first Hôtel Tadoussac was built, and steamships began to transport well-heeled tourists to the village for a taste of its wilderness beauty.

Justifying two centuries of tourism, the scenery here is magnificent. Backed by rocky cliffs and towering sand dunes, the waterfront faces over the estuary where the Saint Lawrence and Saguenay rivers meet. In the town itself, the re-creation of the 17th-century fur-trading post and the oldest wooden church in Canada – the Petite Chapelle, built in 1747 – are popular.

The main attraction in Tadoussac, however, can be found offshore. Whale watching tours offer trips into the estuary to see many species in their natural environment. The thriving conditions in the estuary support a permanent colony of white beluga whales, which are joined in summer by minke, fin, humpback, and blue whales.

❹ Saguenay River

🚉 Jonquière 🚌 Chicoutimi 𝘪 412 Blvd Saguenay E, Chicoutimi; www.saguenaylacsaintjean.ca

The Saguenay River flows through North America's southernmost natural fjord. This was formed by a retreating glacier splitting a crack in the Earth's crust during the last Ice Age, 10,000 years ago. Inky waters, 985 ft (300 m) deep in places, run for 95 miles (155 km) beneath towering cliffs. Due to the exceptional depth, ocean liners can travel up to La Baie, a borough of Saguenay.

Running from Lac Saint-Jean to the Saint Lawrence estuary, the Saguenay is best known for its lush river banks and thriving wildlife. Much of the pretty Bas Saguenay, the lower half of the river, is a national marine park with a healthy population of whales.

Beautiful views of the fjord can be had from the western shore at Cap Trinité, a cliff that rises over the channel with a well-known statue of the Virgin Mary surveying the scenery from the lowest ledge.

❺ Parc de la Chute Montmorency and Île d'Orléans

𝘪 Montmorency Falls: www.sepaq.com/montmorencyfalls; Île d'Orléans Tourist Centre: 490 Côté du Pont, Saint Pierre, (418) 828 9411

Located 8 miles (13 km) northeast of Quebec City, Montmorency Falls is Quebec's

TOP 3 WHALE-WATCHING COMPANIES

Croisières
ⓦ croisieresaml.com
Choose from Zodiac-style boats or larger, more stable crafts to watch whales and seals in their natural habitat.

Les Écumeurs du St. Laurent
ⓦ lesecumeurs.com
If you're looking for value for money, the small Zodiac whale-watching tours offered by this company are a good budget option.

Mer et Monde
ⓦ meretmonde.ca
Head here for guided sea-kayaking activities, which allow you to get thrillingly close to the region's whales.

↑ A frost-covered town lines the banks of the wide Saguenay River

The tumbling waters of Montmorency Falls, edged by autumnal woods ↑

most celebrated waterfall. Over 98 ft (30 m) higher than Niagara Falls, the cascade is created as the Montmorency River empties out into the Saint Lawrence River. The park surrounding the falls offers a suspension bridge, an aerial cable car, a 980-ft (300-m) zip-line and a series of trails that climb the surrounding cliffs.

A bridge nearby crosses the river to the Île d'Orléans, the villages of which allow a fascinating glimpse into rural life in Quebec.

6
Baie-Comeau

🚗🚌🚢 *i* 337 La Salle; www.ville.baie-comeau. qc.ca

This midsize town owes its existence to the *Chicago Tribune*

Did You Know?

In 1995, a referendum proposing independence for the province of Quebec was defeated by only 1 percent.

newspaper, which in 1936 built a mill near the mouth of the Manicougan River to supply its printing presses with paper. Declared a historic district in 1985, Baie-Comeau's oldest area is the Quartier Amélie.

Paper production remains a vital industry here, but Baie-Comeau is most important today as a gateway to the huge Manic-Outardes hydroelectric power complex, situated along Hwy 389. The most spectacular example is Manic-5, 132 miles (212 km) north of town. Its arched Daniel-Johnson Dam holds back a vast reservoir that fills a crater geophysicists believe may have been created by a meteorite millennia ago.

7
Chicoutimi

🚉 Jonquière 🚌 Chicoutimi *i* 412 Blvd Saguenay E, Bureau 100; (418) 543 9778

Snug in the crook of mountains on the western shore of the Saguenay, Chicoutimi is one of northern Quebec's most expansive towns, and the cultural and economic center of the region. A stroll along the town's riverside offers good views of the surrounding

mountains and the confluence of the Chicoutimi, Du-Moulin, and Saguenay rivers.

Once a center for paper manufacturing, Chicoutimi still has a large pulp mill, the **Pulperie de Chicoutimi**. Though no longer operational, the plant can be toured, and an adjacent museum shows visitors the intricacies of this faded Quebecois industry.

Pulperie de Chicoutimi

♿ 🏛 300 Dubuc 🕐 Late Jun-Aug: 9am-6pm daily; Sep-late-Jun: 10am-4pm Wed-Sun 🌐 pulperie.com

Stunning fall foliage reflected on a lake in Quebec

8

South Shore

◻️📧🚌 Rivière-du-Loup
ℹ️ 148 Rue Fraser, Rivière-du-Loup; www.bas saintlaurent.ca

Communities here can trace their roots back to the old 18th-century settlers of New France. Dotted along the flat, fertile farmland of the south shore of the Saint Lawrence River west of Gaspe and inland toward Montreal, the villages cover the area between the region's largest towns of Montmagny and Rimouski. Rivière-du-Loup, a seemingly unremarkable town in this stretch, provides for many people a taste of true Quebec. Featuring a historic stone church that rears above the skyline, the old town rambles along hilly streets, and its 18th-century cottages have a French atmosphere.

Farther along the main Route 132, Trois-Pistoles boasts a history that goes back to 1580, when Basque whalers arrived. The offshore Île-aux-Basques was a whaling station in the 16th century, and today is protected as a bird sanctuary. Toward the region's commercial center, Rimouski, lies the Parc National du Bic, a small preserve of 13 sq miles (33 sq km)

↑ An aerial view of the South Shore, which lies along the Saint Lawrence River

dedicated to the two forest zones that it encloses, and its varied coastal wildlife.

9

Mingan Archipelago National Park

📧🚌 Sept-Îles ℹ️ 1401 Blvd l'Aure; (418) 962 1238

Located along the north shore of the Gulf of Saint Lawrence, the Mingan Archipelago National Park protects more than 1,000 islands and islets. This unspoiled northern wilderness is popular with outdoor enthusiasts, who visit the area for its harsh landscape, rich wildlife, and untouched ecosystems. As well as the abundant wildlife, the islands are home to the largest concentration of monoliths in Canada. Eroded over many centuries by the sea, these limestone carvings have surreal shapes. Visitors can book a trip to admire the monoliths by boat.

Until 1974, the Île d'Anticosti, east of the archipelago, was private property. The past owner, French chocolate tycoon Henri Menier, bought the island in 1895 and stocked it with a herd of white-tailed deer for his friends to hunt. Now numbering 150,000, the deer herd is firmly ensconced but can still be hunted. Wildlife abounds; over 150 species of bird live in the relatively unspoiled forest and on the beaches. The island is separate from the Mingan Archipelago National Park, so there is no admittance fee.

10

Îles-de-la-Madeleine

🚻🚐 ℹ️ **128 Chemin Principal, Cap-aux-Meules; www.tourisme ilesdela madeleine.com**

Linked to the mainland by scheduled flights and ferries, many of the 12,000 residents of these remote islands have taken to painting their homes in an assortment of mauves, yellows, and reds. This results in a striking view on approach, whether by sea or air. The islands themselves have much to offer any visitor who makes the effort to see them; they are home to what are reputed to be some of the best beaches in the country, celebrated for their fine sand and sheltered position.

> **Located along the north shore of the Gulf of Saint Lawrence, the Mingan Archipelago National Park protects more than 1,000 islands and islets.**

11

Sept-Îles

🏨🚐🚌 ℹ️ **1401 Blvd Laure W; www.tourismeseptiles.ca**

Until the 1950s, Sept-Îles led a quiet existence as a historic, sleepy fishing village. After World War II, however, the little settlement, located on the shores of a large, circular bay, drew the attention of large companies to use as a base for expanding the iron-mining industry in northern Quebec. Now the largest town along the north shore of the Gulf of Saint Lawrence, Sept-Îles has turned into Canada's second-largest port as part of the Saint Lawrence Seaway. Although boasting the best of modern marine technology, the town also offers a reminder of its long-standing history. Vieux-Poste, near the center

of the town, is a reconstruction of a fur-trading post, and there is a small museum with First Nations art and artifacts.

Despite its industrial importance, Sept-Îles is an area of considerable natural beauty. Miles of sandy beaches rim the nearby coastline, and the salmon-rich Moisie River flows into the Gulf of Saint Lawrence just east of the town. The seven rocky islands that gave the city its name make up the Sept-Îles Archipelago Park.

One of the seven islands, Île Grand-Basque, is a popular local camping spot. Another, Île du Corossol, is now a bird sanctuary that teems with gulls, terns, and puffins, and can be toured with a guide. Cruises are available for guided trips between islands.

Puffins *(inset)* and the strangely shaped monoliths in
↓ Mingan Archipelago National Park

↑ Visitors photographing the burnished fall colors of Parc National de la Mauricie

⑫ 🚴 Ⓜ️ 🖥️ 🏛️

Parc National de la Mauricie

📍 Off Hwy 55 N Shawinigan 🚌 Shawinigan 🕐 Daily 🌐 pc.gc.ca

Campers, hikers, canoeists, and cross-country skiers love this 207-sq-mile (536-sq-km) stretch of forest, lakes, and pink Precambrian granite. The park includes part of the Laurentian Mountains (p300), which are part of the Canadian Shield, and were formed between 950 and 1,400 million years ago. La Mauricie's rugged beauty is also accessible to motorists, who can take the

↑ A sculpture in Lac Memphrémagog of the lake's mythical monster

road between Saint-Mathieu and Saint-Jean-des-Piles. From here, there is also a drive with good views of the narrow Lac Wapizagonke valley. With trout and pike in the lake, the area is an angler's delight.

---

⑬ Lac Memphrémagog

🚌 ⛴️ Magog 🛈 2911 Milletta, Magog; www. tourisme-memphremagog. com

This area belongs to the Eastern Townships, or the "Garden of Quebec" that stretches from the Richelieu River valley to the Maine, New Hampshire, and Vermont borders in the US. Set among rolling hills and farmland, in a landscape that is part of the Appalachians, the Townships are among Canada's top maple-syrup producers.

Lac Memphrémagog itself is long, narrow, and surrounded by mountains. It even boasts its own monster, a creature named Memphré, first spotted in 1798. The lake's southern quarter dips into the state of Vermont, so it is no surprise that the British Loyalists fleeing the American Revolution were this region's first settlers. Their influence can be seen in

the late 19th-century red-brick-and-wood-frame homes of lakeside villages such as Georgeville and North Hatley, and in the resort city of Magog at the northern end of the lake.

Benedictine monks from France bought one of the lake's most beautiful sites in 1912 and established the Abbaye Saint-Benoît-du-Lac. Today the monks produce cider and a celebrated blue cheese called l'Ermite. They are also renowned for Gregorian chant, and visitors can hear them sing mass in the abbey church.

---

⑭ Richelieu Valley

🛈 1080 Chemin des Patriotes Nord, Mont Saint-Hilaire; www.vallee-du-richelieu.ca

This fertile valley follows the Richelieu River from Lake Champlain to the confluence with the Saint Lawrence River. **Fort Chambly**, also known as Fort Saint Louis, in the industrial town of Chambly, is the best preserved of a series of buildings that the French erected to defend this vital waterway from Dutch and British attack. It was built from solid stone in 1711 to replace the original wooden fortifications set up in 1675. A museum in Saint-Denis–sur–Richelieu commemorates Quebecois patriots who fought in the failed 1837 rebellion against British rule.

Today, the river flows past attractive villages surrounded by orchards and vineyards; Mont Saint-Hilaire affords fine views of Montreal, and is famed for its apple plantations.

Fort Chambly

⊗ ☐ 2 Rue de Richelieu, Chambly 📞 1 888 773 8888 or (450) 658 1585 ⏰ Mid-May–Jun & Sep–mid-Oct: 10am–5pm Wed–Sun; Jul–Aug: 10am–6pm daily

15

Sainte-Croix

ℹ️ 6375 Rue Garneau; (418) 926 2620

This town is best known for **Domaine Joly-De Lotbinière**, a stunning estate built in 1851 by the local squire according to the Picturesque style. The estate's charming wooden

---

manor house is surrounded by terraces of walnut trees stretching down to the river, and rare plant finds include 20 red oaks estimated to be over 250 years old.

Domaine Joly-De Lotbinière

⊗ ☐ Rte de Pointe-Platon ⏰ Mid-May–mid-Oct: 10am–5pm daily 🌐 domainejoly.com

---

16

Sherbrooke

🔼🚃🚌 ℹ️ 785 Rue King W; www.destination sherbrooke.com

The self-styled "Queen of the Eastern Townships," Sherbrooke is this region's industrial, commercial, and cultural center. The city lies in a steep-sided valley, with the historic quarter delightfully situated among the rolling farmlands of the Saint-François and Magog rivers. The first settlers were British Loyalists from the New England states. Although their heritage survives in street names, and in the fine old homes and gardens of Sherbrooke's North Ward, today the city is over-whelmingly French-speaking. From the town center runs the promenade du Lac-des-Nations, a lovely waterfront park with 12 miles (20 km) of attractive cycling and walking trails.

17

Charlevoix Coast

ℹ️ 495 Blvd de Comporté, La Malbaie; www.tourisme-charlevoix.com

The Charlevoix Coast runs 124 miles (200 km) along the north shore of the Saint Lawrence River, from Sainte-Anne-de-Beaupré in the west to the mouth of the Saguenay Fjord. A UNESCO Biosphere Reserve because of its fine examples of boreal forest, the area is a slim band of flowery rural beauty on the edge of tundra. Gentle valleys protect old towns reaching to the river, with coastal villages sheltering beneath tall cliffs.

The region's Parc des Grands Jardins is a vast expanse of lakes and black-spruce taiga forest with a herd of caribou. Farther downstream is the tiny and tranquil Isle-aux-Coudres. The lush, green farmland of this island is sprinkled with historic farms and a windmill.

← An attractive row of historic town houses in Sherbrooke

MAPLE SYRUP

There is more to Canada's ancient maple forests – long the pride of Quebec and Ontario – than their annual display of beauty. Every fall, turning leaves splash crimson and orange across the south, but it is in springtime that the trees give up their most famous product: maple syrup. It goes with everything from pancakes to potato chips, so don't pass up an opportunity to try this decadently sweet tree sap while in Canada. You won't be alone – more than Can $100 million is spent on maple products every year.

THE STORY OF MAPLE SYRUP

The first maple-sugar farmers were the indigenous peoples of North America. An Iroquois legend tells the story of a chief in ancient times who, hurling an ax at a tree, found it stuck in the trunk at the end of the next day, dripping sweet fluid. That night the chief's wife boiled the day's hunt in the sap, and maple syrup was born.

MAPLE SYRUP PRODUCTS

Today, maple syrup is most popularly used as a topping for waffles, pancakes, and French toast, but boiled for longer, it hardens into a pale golden sugar that can be used as a sweetener for drinks or eaten like candy. Maple butter, maple-cured ham, and a Quebecois favourite, sugar pie, are just some of the delectable products benefiting from the sweet stuff.

↑ Men tapping for sap in 1907, using age-old methods still employed today

↑ Maple-leaf-shaped bottle of Canadian maple syrup

Did You Know?
—
The maple leaf is the national symbol of Canada, officially established on the flag in 1965.

↑ Sugar shack, a building used for making maple syrup, in Elmira

Collecting the Sap

▽ Cuts are made low in the trunk of the maple trees sometime in the late winter or early spring as the sap rises. The sap is gathered over a period of about two to three weeks in buckets or in tubes and taken directly to the sugar shack, where it is processed.

Boiling the Sap

▷ After the harvesting, the excess water in the sap is boiled down. Boiling maple sap involves 84 pts (40 liters) of sap to create 2.2 pts (1 liter) of syrup. The sap bubbles over a wood fire (maple wood is best) until about 98 percent of its water content evaporates.

Stirring the Syrup

▽ Modern processes use mechanized evaporators to boil the sap and draw off the steam, but even hi-tech methods still require a final hand-stirred simmering. The gold color and maple flavor develop as distillation takes place.

Bottling

▷ Finally, the syrup is graded according to quality; clear golden fluid, produced at the start of the season, is the most prized, and is generally bottled.

↑ Part of the Sucrerie de la Montagne, a traditional sugar shack in a maple forest

18 (icons)

Sucrerie de la Montagne

⌂ 300 Chemin St-Georges, Rigaud ▣ ⊙ Year round; times vary, check website ⍵ sucreriedelamontagne.com

This Quebec Heritage site is set in a 123-acre (50-ha) maple forest on top of Rigaud Mountain near Rang Saint-Georges. It is entirely devoted to the many delights of Quebec's most famous commodity, the maple tree and its produce (p294). The Sucrerie features a reconstructed 19th-century sugar shack, where collected maple sap is distilled and boiled in large kettles to produce the internationally renowned syrup. More than 20 rustic buildings house a fine bakery, a general store, and cozy cabins for overnight guests. The heart of the complex is a huge 500-seat restaurant that serves traditional banquets of ham, pea soup, baked beans, pork rinds, and pickles, as well as dozens of maple-based products. Folk music accompanies the nightly feast. The tour includes an explanation of the maple syrup-making process, which is generally thought to have originated with the Aboriginal peoples. They later imparted their secrets to European settlers, whose traditional methods are still in use today.

19

Joliette

▣ *i* 500 Rue Dollard; (450) 759 5013

Two Catholic priests are responsible for turning this industrial town on L'Assomption River into a cultural center. In the 1920s, Father Wilfrid Corbeil founded the Musée d'Art de Joliette, whose collection ranges from medieval religious art to modern works. In 1978, Father Fernand Lindsay started the Festival International de Lanaudière, a series of summer concerts by some of the world's best-known musicians.

The nearby town of Rawdon, 11 miles (18 km) west, has a deserved reputation as a place of great natural beauty. Trails wind away from the small town along the Ouareau River, leading to the picturesque Dorwin Falls.

20

Terrebonne

▣▣▣ *i* 3645 Queen Street; 1 800 363 2788

In 2001, three communities northwest of Montreal – Lachenaie, La Plaine, and Terrebonne – officially merged to form the city of Terrebonne. Lachenaie and Terrebonne itself are the oldest sectors, both founded in the 1670s, though a fire in 1922 engulfed many of the original buildings.

The real gem here is the **Île-des-Moulins**, a pre-industrial complex of living history with water-powered mills for grinding grain, carding wool, and sawing lumber. One of the biggest buildings is the three-floor factory that was the first large-scale bakery in Canada. Built by the Northwest Company in 1803, it made the ship's biscuits that sustained the *voyageurs* who paddled west every year to trade for furs for the company.

> The Sucrerie features a reconstructed 19th-century sugar shack, where collected maple sap is distilled and boiled in large kettles to produce the internationally renowned syrup.

Terrebonne is also the center of Quebec's horse-riding culture, and rodeo and ranching events take place regularly.

Île-des-Moulins
📍866 Rue St-Pierre
🕐Jun-Sep: 1-9pm daily
🌐iledesmoulins.com

㉑
Trois-Rivières

➕🏛🚌🚆 ℹ1457 Rue Notre Dame; www.tourisme troisrivieres.com

Quebec is one of the major paper producers in North America, and Trois-Rivières is a main center of that industry. This fact often hides the rich historical interest that Trois-Rivières has to offer. The first colonists arrived here from France well before the city was founded in 1634. Although not many colonial dwellings remain, the city's charming old section has a number of 18th- and 19th-century houses and shops, many now cafés and bars.

Ursuline nuns have been working in the city since 1697, and the core of the old city is the **Monastère des Ursulines**, a rambling complex with a museum that traces the history of this teaching order,

the oldest in the province. Tours of the chapel and, in summer, the gardens and old schoolrooms are offered. Also here is an 18th-century manor house, the Manoir Boucher-de-Niverville. This cultural and historical site hosts displays on the rich history of the region.

Monastère des Ursulines
🎨🕐 📍734 Rue des Ursulines 🕐Times vary, check website 🌐musee-ursulines.qc.ca

㉒
Oka

🚌🚆 ℹ183 Rue des Anges; (450) 479 8389

The prettiest way to approach this village is on the small ferry that chugs across the Lake of Two Mountains from Hudson. From the water, the small Neo-Romanesque 1878 church is visible through the trees. Oka's Abbaye Cistercienne was founded by a group of monks who moved to Canada in 1881. The church's decor is somewhat stark, but the Neo-Romanesque architecture is simple. Although the abbey is now closed, a shop in the nearby **Abbaye Val Notre-Dame** sells the Oka cheese that the monks developed. Nearby, the Parc d'Oka covers about 7 sq miles (20 sq km) of ponds and forests. It features the best beach and campground in the Montreal area.

Abbaye Val Notre-Dame
🕐 📍220 Chemin de la Montagne-Coupée
🕐9am-5pm Mon-Sat (store open daily) 🍴Lunch
🌐abbayevalnotredame.ca

←

The ornate interior of the Monastère des Ursulines in Trois-Rivières

㉓

James Bay

ℹ Tourisme Quebec; (877) 266 5687

The thinly populated municipality of James Bay is roughly the size of Germany – about 135,000 sq miles (350,000 sq km) – which makes it much larger than most other municipalities in the region. Its landscape changes from forest to taiga to tundra, becoming gradually more inaccessible in the frozen northern parts.

However, what James Bay lacks in infrastructure it amply makes up for in power capacity. Its six major rivers, which all flow into the bay, can produce enough electricity to light up the whole of North America. So far, the Quebec government has spent over Can $20 billion in building a third of the dams for what is already one of the biggest hydroelectric projects in the world. Five power plants produce nearly 16,000 megawatts of electricity to power much of Quebec and parts of the northeastern US. Le Grand 2 (known as LG-2) is the biggest dam and underground generating station in the world.

The main town in the area is the small tourist center of Radisson, which offers good views of the surrounding country. Not all of the bay's dams and dikes can be seen, but the massive dams and series of reservoirs, especially LG-2, which is just east of town, are visible from above.

㉔

Val d'Or

🚌 ℹ 1070 3rd Ave E; (819) 824 9646 or 1 877 582 5367

Val d'Or is principally a mining town and is a major center in the northwestern part of Quebec. The town sights here are not architectural but vivid living-history attractions of mines and historic villages from the area's heritage of lumber trade and mining. Miners have been digging gold, silver, and copper out of the ground around Val d'Or since the 1920s. A climb to the top of the 60-ft (18-m) Tour Rotary on the edge of town reveals many still-active mineheads.

La Cité de l'Or is built around the abandoned Lamaque gold mine, formerly one of the richest sources of gold in the area. In its heyday of the early 20th century, the mine had its very own small town site with a hospital and accommodations for all workers as well as visiting executives. Much of the Village Minier de Bourlamaque is still intact and was declared a Historic Site in 1979. Visitors can tour the village, the old analysis office and laboratories, and the minehead. For an extra fee, fascinating tours are available down the 295-ft (90-m) mine shaft.

La Cité de l'Or
⊗⊗ 🅿 90 Ave Perrault
🕒 Late Jun–early Sep: 9am–6pm daily 🌐 citedelor.com

㉕

Réserve Faunique La Vérendrye

📞 (819) 736 7431
🚉 Maniwaki 🕒 Summer

This wildlife preserve is situated approximately 292 miles (471 km) to the north-west of Montreal on Highway 117. It is celebrated for long, meandering waterways and, with hundreds of miles of canoe trails, is popular among canoeists. Its rivers are usually gentle, and the 5,020 sq miles (13,000 sq km) of wilderness are home to large numbers of moose, bear, deer, and beaver. The land is almost untouched, but there are several campgrounds here for those who seek a truly peaceful break. Hwy 117 traverses the park, providing access to many of its lakes and rivers, and is the starting point of hiking trails.

> Caribou herds, polar bears, and musk oxen roam the taiga and frozen Arctic tundra that covers this region. Beluga whales and seals can be seen swimming its icy waters.

← An isolated cabin in James Bay, entirely surrounded by snowdrifts and forest

The remotely beautiful landscape and caribou residents *(inset)* of Nunavik ↑

26

Nunavik

↗ *i* Nunavik Tourism Association; www. nunavik-tourism.com

In the far north of Quebec, the pristine Nunavik territory covers an area slightly larger than continental Spain. Its inhabitants number about 12,000, nearly all of them Inuit, who live in 14 communities. This is Quebec's last frontier, a wild and beautiful land that is virtually inaccessible except by airplane. Caribou herds, polar bears, and musk oxen roam the taiga and frozen Arctic tundra that covers this region. Beluga whales and seals can be seen swimming its icy waters.

Kuujjuaq, near Ungava Bay, is Nunavik's largest district, with a population of 2,400. This is a good starting point for expeditions to the valley of Kangiqsujuaq and the rugged mountains around Salluit. Visitors come to this region to appreciate the many varieties of wildlife that roam freely in their natural setting. Summer is the best time for a trip; temperatures rise, though the ground remains frozen all year round. Nunavik territory has no

railroads (and hardly any roads) and should be explored only in the company of a seasoned and reliable guide. Many Inuit groups and communities offer guide services and the opportunity to experience life on the land with Inuit families.

27

Rouyn-Noranda

🚐 *i* 1675 Larivière Ave; www.tourisme-rouyn-noranda.ca

All developed areas in the north of Quebec are based on heavy industry. Rouyn and Noranda sprang up virtually overnight in the 1920s, when prospectors found copper in the region. They merged into one city in 1986. Noranda is a carefully planned company town, built to house the employees of the now-defunct Noranda copper mine. The Glencore Smelter, one of the biggest and most efficient in the world, is based

just outside the center of town and can be visited by only by arrangement.

Rouyn is less structured and more commercial. Noranda residents often go here for recreation, and it is useful as a refreshment and fuel center for those traveling to the northern wilderness. The Maison Dumulon, a reconstruction of Rouyn's first general store, celebrates its pioneer spirit with displays on the first settlers.

> 💬 INSIDER TIP
> **Budget Ready**
>
> Prices in Nunavik, especially foodstuffs, are high compared to the rest of Quebec. This is due to the cost of transporting goods via air and sea into such remote communities.

A DRIVING TOUR
LAURENTIAN MOUNTAINS

Distance 108 miles (175 km) **Departure point** Val-Morin
Stopping-off points Ste-Agathe-des-Monts; St-Jovite

This whole region, from the lively resort of Ste-Adele in the south to north of St-Jovite (also known as Tremblant), is nature's own amusement park, full of lakes, rivers, hiking and cycling trails, and ski runs visited all through the year. The mountains are part of the ancient Laurentian Shield, and are over a billion years old. Dotted with appealing, old French-style towns, this is a superb area to relax in or indulge in some vigorous sports in the national parks.

The tallest of the Laurentian range, with a vertical rise of about 2,116 ft (645 m), **Mont Tremblant** is a popular international year-round resort.

QUEBEC

Laurentian Mountains

Locator Map
For more detail see p278

Lac Tremblant

Pic Johannsen
△ 3,058 ft (932 m)

Pic Pangman
△ 2,949 ft (899 m)

Rivière Rouge

△ Pic White
2,880 ft (878 m)

FINISH
Tremblant

Rivière du Diable

△ Mont St-Bernard
1,312 ft (400 m)

Lac Ouimet

La Conception

Lac Duhamel

117

327

Plenty of tiny hotels and street cafés add to the charm of **La Conception**.

St-Jovite

Full of historic architecture, **Saint-Jovite** village lies in a wooded valley.

323   327

0 kilometers   6

0 miles   6

N
↑

→
The stunning clear blue waters of Lac des Sables, near the town of Sainte-Agathe-Des-Monts

↑ Flowers in bloom and quaint houses around Mont Tremlant lake

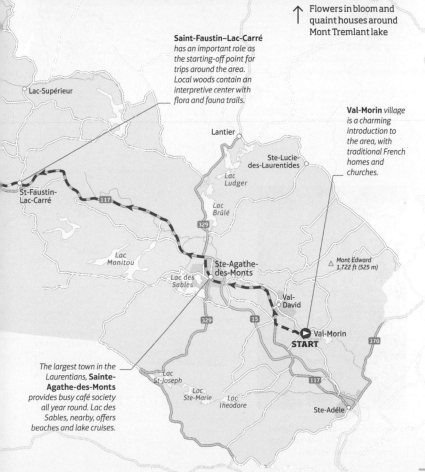

Saint-Faustin–Lac-Carré
has an important role as the starting-off point for trips around the area. Local woods contain an interpretive center with flora and fauna trails.

Val-Morin *village is a charming introduction to the area, with traditional French homes and churches.*

Lac-Supérieur

Lantier

Ste-Lucie-des-Laurentides

Lac Ludger

St-Faustin-Lac-Carré

117

Lac Brûlé

329

Lac Manitou

Ste-Agathe-des-Monts

Mont Edward
1,722 ft (525 m)

Lac des Sables

Val-David

329   15

▶ Val-Morin
START

370

The largest town in the Laurentians, **Sainte-Agathe-des-Monts** *provides busy café society all year round. Lac des Sables, nearby, offers beaches and lake cruises.*

Lac St-Joseph

Lac Ste-Marie

Lac Theodore

117

Ste-Adéle

A DRIVING TOUR
GASPÉ PENINSULA

Distance 639 miles (1,029 km) **Departure point** Grand Métis
Stopping-off points Stay the night in Gaspé or Percé as the
journey is too long to complete in a single day

Known in French as La Gaspésie, the Gaspé Peninsula stretches
out north of New Brunswick to offer Quebec's wildest and most
appealing scenery. As the peninsula spreads east, clumps of trees
become dense pine forests, and the landscape becomes rough
and rocky; cliffs along the northern coast reach 1,500 ft (500 m).
The Chic-Choc mountains reach heights of 4,000 ft (1,300 m)
and provide some of the province's best hiking. Shielded by the
mountains, the southern coast harbors 18th-century fishing
villages, inland fruit farms, exotic gardens, and wilderness
national parks. Trips into the interior on the secondary road
299 are ideal for seeing the rocky wilderness.

*Located at the entrance
to the Parc National de
la Gaspésie and the
wildlife reserves of the
Chic-Chocs,* **Sainte-
Anne-des-Monts** *is a
19th-century village
with fine restaurants
and good salmon
fishing nearby.*

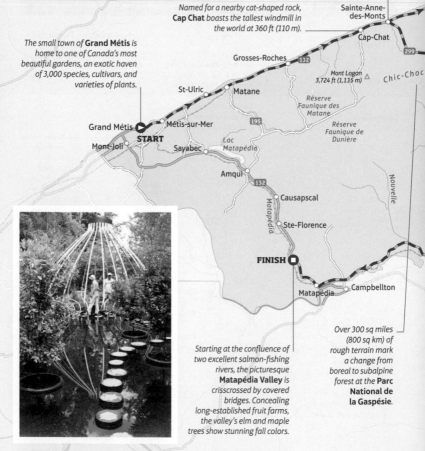

Named for a nearby cat-shaped rock,
Cap Chat *boasts the tallest windmill in
the world at 360 ft (110 m).*

Sainte-Anne-
des-Monts

Cap-Chat

The small town of **Grand Métis** *is
home to one of Canada's most
beautiful gardens, an exotic haven
of 3,000 species, cultivars, and
varieties of plants.*

Grosses-Roches 132

299

*Mont Logan
3,724 ft (1,135 m)* △   Chic-Choc

St-Ulric   Matane

*Réserve
Faunique des
Matane*

Grand Métis   Métis-sur-Mer   195

*Réserve
Faunique de
Dunière*

Mont-Joli   **START**

Sayabec   *Lac
Matapédia*

Nouvelle

Amqui   132

Matapédia

Causapscal

Ste-Florence

FINISH ☐

Campbellton

Matapédia

*Starting at the confluence of
two excellent salmon-fishing
rivers, the picturesque*
Matapédia Valley *is
crisscrossed by covered
bridges. Concealing
long-established fruit farms,
the valley's elm and maple
trees show stunning fall colors.*

*Over 300 sq miles
(800 sq km) of
rough terrain mark
a change from
boreal to subalpine
forest at the* **Parc
National de
la Gaspésie**.

↑ Contemporary garden designed
for the Le Festival International
de Jardins at Grand Métis

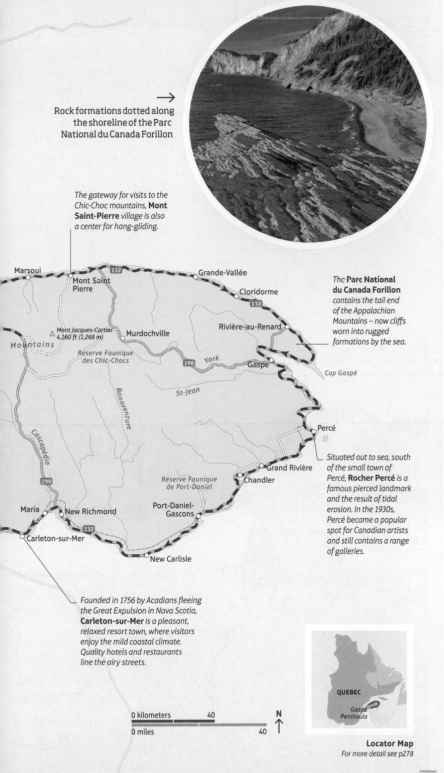

→ Rock formations dotted along the shoreline of the Parc National du Canada Forillon

*The gateway for visits to the Chic-Choc mountains, **Mont Saint-Pierre** village is also a center for hang-gliding.*

*The **Parc National du Canada Forillon** contains the tail end of the Appalachian Mountains – now cliffs worn into rugged formations by the sea.*

Marsoui
Mont Saint Pierre
Grande-Vallée
Cloridorme
132
Rivière-au-Renard
△ Mont Jacques-Cartier 4,160 ft (1,268 m)
Murdochville
Mountains
Réserve Faunique des Chic-Chocs
198
York
Gaspe
Cap Gaspé
Bonaventure
St-Jean
Cascapédia
Percé
299
Réserve Faunique de Port-Daniel
Grand Rivière
Chandler
Maria
New Richmond
Port-Daniel-Gascons
132
Carleton-sur-Mer
New Carlisle

*Situated out to sea, south of the small town of Percé, **Rocher Percé** is a famous pierced landmark and the result of tidal erosion. In the 1930s, Percé became a popular spot for Canadian artists and still contains a range of galleries.*

*Founded in 1756 by Acadians fleeing the Great Expulsion in Nova Scotia, **Carleton-sur-Mer** is a pleasant, relaxed resort town, where visitors enjoy the mild coastal climate. Quality hotels and restaurants line the airy streets.*

0 kilometers   40
0 miles   40

N ↑

QUEBEC
Gaspé Peninsula

Locator Map
For more detail see p278

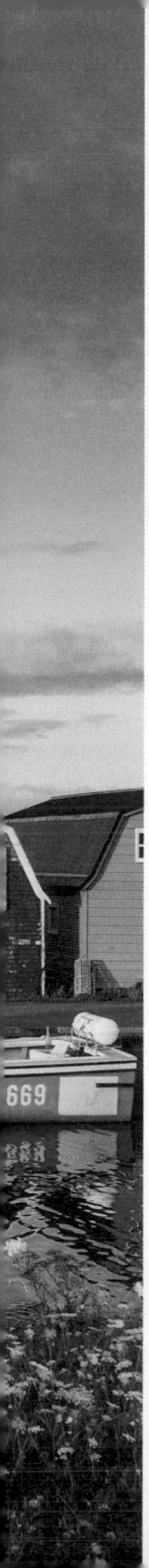

669

THE MARITIMES

The beauty and lure of the sea are always close at hand in the three Maritime Provinces of New Brunswick, Prince Edward Island, and Nova Scotia. Stunning coastal scenery, picturesque centuries-old villages, world-class historic sites, and a wealth of family attractions have made this region one of Canada's top vacation destinations. New Brunswick's ruggedly beautiful Bay of Fundy is matched by the gently rolling landscape of Acadian villages tucked into quiet coves and long sandy beaches. Canada's smallest province, Prince Edward Island, is known for its vibrant green farmlands, red bluffs, and deep blue waters, and is enjoyed by cyclists, anglers, and hikers. Nova Scotia, with its sparkling bays and weathered fishing towns, embodies the romance of the sea. Elegant country inns and historic sites bring the past to life.

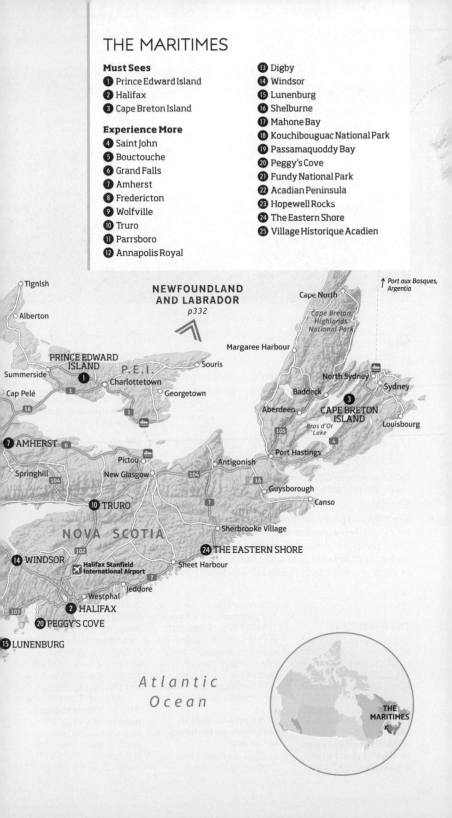

THE MARITIMES

Must Sees
1 Prince Edward Island
2 Halifax
3 Cape Breton Island

Experience More
4 Saint John
5 Bouctouche
6 Grand Falls
7 Amherst
8 Fredericton
9 Wolfville
10 Truro
11 Parrsboro
12 Annapolis Royal
13 Digby
14 Windsor
15 Lunenburg
16 Shelburne
17 Mahone Bay
18 Kouchibouguac National Park
19 Passamaquoddy Bay
20 Peggy's Cove
21 Fundy National Park
22 Acadian Peninsula
23 Hopewell Rocks
24 The Eastern Shore
25 Village Historique Acadien

Tignish
Alberton

NEWFOUNDLAND
AND LABRADOR
p332

↑ Port aux Basques,
Argentia

Cape North

Cape Breton
Highlands
National Park

Margaree Harbour

PRINCE EDWARD
ISLAND 1
P.E.I.
Summerside
Charlottetown
Souris
Cap Pelé
Georgetown
16

North Sydney
Sydney
Baddeck
Aberdeen
CAPE BRETON
ISLAND 3
Bras d'Or
Lake
Louisbourg
105

7 AMHERST 6
Pictou
Springhill
New Glasgow
104
Antigonish
Port Hastings
16
Guysborough
Canso
104

10 TRURO
7

NOVA SCOTIA
Sherbrooke Village

24 THE EASTERN SHORE
102

14 WINDSOR
Halifax Stanfield
International Airport
Sheet Harbour
7
Jeddore
Westphal
103
2 HALIFAX
20 PEGGY'S COVE
15 LUNENBURG

Atlantic
Ocean

THE
MARITIMES

①

PRINCE EDWARD ISLAND

🚇 Charlottetown 🚌🚢 Wood Islands, Borden-Carleton, Souris 🅸 6 Prince St, Charlottetown; www.tourism pei.com

Beautiful and pastoral, Prince Edward Island is famous for its lush landscapes and small historic towns. The island's emerald farmlands, red-clay roads, and sapphire ocean dazzle at every turn, while rounds of golf, picnics at the beach, and freshly caught lobster dinner await.

①
The South Coast

Enchanting vistas are found along the roads of the south shore, between Charlottetown and the Confederation Bridge. Visitors will also find Victoria-by-the-Sea, a small village housing some of the island's most interesting craft shops. En route to Charlottetown is **Fort Amherst-Port-la-Joye National Historic Site of Canada** where the French

built Prince Edward Island's first permanent settlement in 1720. The British captured it in 1758, and built Fort Amherst to protect the entrance to Charlottetown Harbour. While the fort is long gone, the earthworks can still be seen in the parklike surrounds.

Fort Amherst-Port-la-Joye National Historic Site of Canada

⊗ 🅰 Rocky Point 🅲 Jul-Sep 2: daily 🅦 pc.gc.ca

② 🔊🅼🖥

Orwell Corner Historic Village

🅰 Old Uigg Rd, Orwell
🅲 Jun-Oct: 8:30am-4:30pm
Mon-Fri (Jul-Aug: daily)
🅦 peimuseum.ca

Just outside of the small hamlet of Orwell, this historic village re-creates the day-to-day life of a small, rural 19th-century crossroads community. Orwell Corner was thriving well into the 20th century, before changes in transportation and commerce lessened the importance of the settlement. This charming village was then restored and opened as a cultural sight in 1973. Among its buildings are a blacksmith's, church, school-house, and Clarke's store, the social center of the village. At Orwell Corner is the PEI Agricultural Museum, which tells the story of PEI from the mid-1700s to the 1950s.

Just half a mile (1 km) away is the **Sir Andrew Macphail Homestead**. This Victorian house and its surroundings were the much-loved home of Macphail (1864–1938), a local doctor, journalist,

↑ Sand dunes and lapping waves along Cavendish Beach

teacher, and soldier who counted among his friends prime ministers and acclaimed writers, such as author of *The Jungle Book*, Rudyard Kipling. The house features many exhibits dealing with Macphail's life. Outside, trails wind through deep woodlands.

Sir Andrew Macphail Homestead

⊛⊛⊚ ⌂ Off Rte 1, Orwell ⌚Jun–Sep: 9am–5pm daily ⓦmacphailhomestead.ca

③
Cavendish

ℹ 7591 Cawnpore Ln; www.cavendishbeachpei.com

The little town of Cavendish is Prince Edward Island's busiest, particularly during the summer months, when scenic views, beautiful beaches, and the pastoral home of the *Anne of Green Gables* novels all draw the crowds. The best place to get in touch with its charm is at the site of **Lucy Maud Montgomery's Cavendish Home**, where the author lived in a simple homestead for many years. The town is also the location of **Green Gables Heritage Place**, the novels' fictional 19th-century home, set amid lovely gardens. The golden sand of Cavendish Beach is a further draw, particularly with families.

Lucy Maud Montgomery's Cavendish Home

⊛⊛ ⌂Route 6 ⌚Mid-May–mid-Oct: 10am–5pm daily ⓦpeisland.com/lmm

Green Gables Heritage Place

⌂Route 6 ⌚May 21–Oct: 9am–5pm daily ⓦtourismpei.com/green-gables-house

LUCY MAUD MONTGOMERY

The island's most famous author, Lucy Maud Montgomery, was born in Cavendish in 1874. Nearby Green Gables House became the setting of her internationally best-selling novel, *Anne of Green Gables* (1908), set in the late 19th century. The manuscript was accepted only on the sixth attempt. To date, more than 50 million copies of her book have been published in over 36 languages.

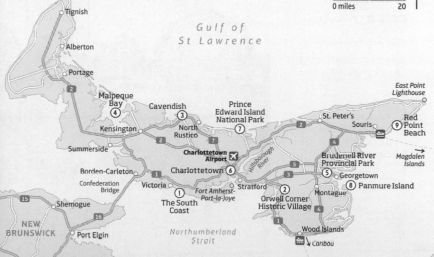

④
Malpeque Bay

This bay is famous for its delicious oysters, with more than ten million caught here every year. On a picturesque harbor, the Malpeque Oyster Barn is a great spot to shuck oysters for yourself. The bay's secluded beaches and gentle rolling waves make this the perfect place for a stroll.

⑤
Brudenell River Provincial Park

⌂Cardigan ⊙Daily (services are seasonal)
ⓦtourismpei.com

Brudenell was an Acadian village before it was burned to the ground by the British in the 18th century. Today, visitors to the provincial park can enjoy a round of golf, join horseback riding tours and travel the river by canoe, kayak, and paddleboard. Families will appreciate the heated pool, playground, and picnic areas. The gorgeous riverfront pathway has lovely walking trails, such as part of the Confederation Trail – a former rail track that extends the length of the island.

⑥
Charlottetown

➕🚌🚍 ℹ️6 Prince St; www.discover charlottetown.com

Known as the birthplace of Canada, Charlottetown is a

↑ The rooftops of Prince Edward Island's leafy Charlottetown

charming, centrally located coastal city. Its charming, tree-lined streets with elegant 19th-century row houses make a gentle start to exploring the outlying lands. Voted a Cultural Capital of Canada, the small city has an abundance of performing arts events, local shopping, and world-class cuisine. The city's national **Confederation Centre of the Arts** hosts an array of live entertainment, including the popular musical *Anne of Green Gables*. **Province House National Historic Site of Canada** is where the 1864 Charlottetown Conference was held, which eventually led to the formation of Canada as a nation. Peake's Quay is perfect for a stroll and offers waterfront shopping, live music, and various dining options. Don't miss trying Cow's ice cream, made to a recipe said to date back to the time of *Anne of Green Gables*.

Confederation Centre of the Arts

⌂145 Richmond St ⊙Daily
ⓦconfederationcentre.com

> **GREAT VIEW**
> **East Point Lighthouse**
>
> Built in 1866, this is the island's easternmost point, where the two tides meet. It is open to the public for a fee and has tremendous views *(404 Lighthouse Rd)*.

Province House National Historic Site of Canada

⌂ 165 Richmond St ⟳ For renovations ⓦ pc.gc.ca

---

⑦ ◈

Prince Edward Island National Park

🚍 Charlottetown 🚍 Wood Islands ⓞ Daily ⓦ pc.gc.ca

Characterized by 25 miles (40 km) of coastline leading onto red cliffs, gorgeous sand beaches, and mild seas, this park offers unbeatable sport and vacationing facilities. There's also an educational Visitors' Centre for those interested in its marine wildlife. With its soft sand and gentle surf, Cavendish Beach is one of the most popular beaches in the park. It has an amusement park that kids will love. Or try North Rustico Beach, which is a favorite with sightseers and affords far-reaching views. At the park's western end, the Homestead Trail leads for 5 miles (8 km) through rustic green woodlands and meadows. The park's quieter eastern side features a long stretch of pristine beach and dunes, and a scenic coastal road. The Reeds and Rushes Trail is a lovely short boardwalk track leading to a freshwater marsh pond, where geese and ducks nest and feed.

---

⑧

Panmure Island

The natural beauty of the island's eastern area is easy to experience on Panmure Island, especially by cyclists who can savor the view thanks to its level roads. In summer, the wooden **Panmure Island Lighthouse** is open, and the view from the top takes in a long vista of the island's white sand beaches, dunes, salt-marshes, and woodlands. The 1853 lighthouse is the island's oldest and is still in use today.

Panmure Island Lighthouse

◈ ⌂ Panmure Island
☎ (902) 838 3568
ⓞ Jul–Aug: 10am–6pm daily

⑨

Red Point Beach

⌂ Red Point Park, Elmira

Characteristic red rocks lead down to this wide beach where the sand squeaks underfoot, much to the delight of children. Nearby is the ferry terminal for the Magdalen Islands, part of Quebec. A five-hour ferry trip takes visitors to a dozen low-lying islands topped with quaint fishing villages and miles of cliff-fronted beaches.

EAT

Blue Mussel Cafe
Rustic and relaxed, this is where the locals come for fresh local mussels, oysters, halibut, and lobster.

⌂ 312 Harbourview Dr, North Rustico Harbour ⟳ Nov–Apr
ⓦ bluemusselcafe.com

$$ⓢⓢⓢ$$

Lobster Barn Pub & Eatery
Lobster rolls are the specialty here, best enjoyed with a refreshing pint.

⌂ 19 Wharf Rd, Victoria
☎ (902) 658 2722
⟳ Nov–Apr

$$ⓢⓢⓢ$$

Water Prince Corner Shop and Lobster Pound
This teal-colored, friendly eatery is known for its scallop burgers. Reservations are recommended.

⌂ 141 Water St, Charlottetown
ⓦ waterprincelobster.ca

$$ⓢⓢⓢ$$

↑ Fishing boats set along the quay in Malpeque Bay

2

HALIFAX

🛫 22 miles (35 km) N of the city 🚆🚌 1161 Hollis St
ℹ 1595 Barrington St; www.discover halifaxns.com

With its bustling waterfront, pretty parks, and unique blend of modern and historic architecture, Halifax is a fascinating city. Its cultured flavor belies its 250-year history as a brawling military town. Founded in 1749, Halifax was planned as Britain's military center north of Boston, and has a long history of adventure as the town where legalized pirates, or privateers, brought captured ships to be shared with the crown. Today, Halifax is one of Canada's foremost centers of higher learning, and has many colleges and four universities.

① 🍴 🛍

Historic Properties

🏠 1869 Upper Water St
🕐 Daily 🌐 historic
properties.ca

The Historic Properties are a wharfside collection of old stone and timber-frame structures, which were originally built in the 19th century to hold the booty captured by privateers. Today, they house an intriguing collection of specialty and gift shops, pubs, and fine restaurants. This is one of the city's favorite gathering spots on warm summer nights, with crowds of leisurely strollers enjoying the lights of the harbor and music drifting from nearby pubs.

②

Old Town Clock

🏠 Citadel Hill

This large timepiece stands at the base of Citadel Hill, and is the city's most recognized landmark. The Old Town Clock was a gift in 1803 from Edward, British Duke of Kent and then military commander, who had a passion for punctuality. He designed the clock with four faces, so that both soldiers and citizens would arrive at their appointed destinations on time. The original clockworks are still intact and in use.

⛰ GREAT VIEW
Hill Hike

After seeing the Old Town Clock, make the short trek up Citadel Hill itself. Considered one of Canada's most visited National Historic Sites, it offers excellent views of the city, the harbor, and Dartmouth.

Historic Properties, also known as Privateers' Wharf, on the waterfront in Halifax

③ Ⓜ
Government House

🏛 1451 Barrington St
📞 (902) 424 7001 🕐 Jul-Aug: Mon, Fri-Sun

The current home of Nova Scotia's Lieutenant Governor, this building has a Georgian facade that lends an urban grandeur. Completed in 1807, it cost over £30,000 (Can $59,200), a huge sum at the time for a humble fishing village. Tours (which are compulsory) last 30 minutes and cover several rooms.

④ Ⓜ
Province House

🏛 1726 Hollis St 📞 (902) 424 4661 🕐 Jul-Aug: 9am-5pm Mon-Fri, 10am-4pm Sat & Sun; Sep-Jun: 9am-4pm Mon-Fri

Built in 1811–19, Province House is the oldest seat of government in Canada, and occupies an entire city block. In 1864, the Fathers of Confederation held two days of meetings here on the formation of Canada. The house is open throughout the year for tours only, and visitors can view the rooms where these plans were laid.

The Old Town Clock was a gift in 1803 from Edward, British Duke of Kent and then military commander, who had a passion for punctuality.

↑ The imposing stone facade of Province House lit up at night

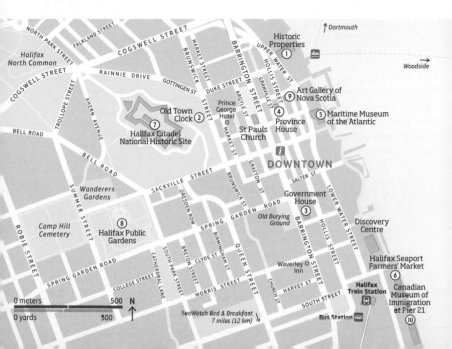

STAY

Prince George Hotel

A contemporary, welcoming hotel with sophisticated, airy rooms that are full of luxury amenities. In the evenings, head to Gio, the excellent on-site restaurant, or relax on the comfortable patio with a few tapas and cocktails.

⌂ 1725 Market St
ⓦ princegeorge hotel.com

$$$

SeaWatch Bed & Breakfast

This seaside home, 7.5 miles (12 km) from downtown Halifax, has two nautically themed suites that include kitchenettes, harbor-view decks, and private entrances. The on-site dock has a Tiki Hut, which is a great place to enjoy sunsets and gourmet meals.

⌂ 139 Fergusons Cove Rd
ⓦ seawatch.ca

$$$

Waverley Inn

A city landmark since 1876, the lovingly restored Waverley is within walking distance of downtown Haliax. It offers period-furnished rooms that Oscar Wilde and P. T. Barnum once stayed in. Breakfast, snacks, and other extras are included in the rate.

⌂ 1266 Barrington St
ⓦ waverleyinn.com

$$$

↑ The original Sambro Lighthouse lens in the Maritime Museum of the Atlantic

---

⑤ ⊗ Ⓜ 🏛

Maritime Museum of the Atlantic

⌂ 1675 Lower Water St
⊙ May–Oct: daily; Nov–Apr: Tue–Sun ⓦ maritime museum.novascotia.ca

This harborfront museum offers extensive displays on Nova Scotia's seafaring history, including small craft, a restored chandlery, and, at the dock outside, the elegantly refitted 1913 research vessel *Acadia*. The museum's most popular exhibit is the *Titanic* display, which offers artifacts recovered from the ship. There are fragments of the vessel's grand staircase, as well as a mural-sized photo showing the staircase in its original state.

---

⑥

Halifax Seaport Farmers' Market

⌂ 1209 Marginal Rd
⊙ 10am–5pm Tue–Fri, 7am–3pm Sat, 9am–3pm Sun ⓦ halifaxfarmers market.com

Established in 1750, this is North America's longest continuously operating market and, since 2010, it has been at its current location in Halifax Seaport, a vibrant area full of shops and bars. From the Maritime Museum it is a pleasant 20-minute walk along Harbourwalk to reach the market. Over 250 vendors are hosted here, selling a variety of handmade arts and crafts, from jewelry and souvenirs to knitwear and beautifully carved wooden items, as well as fresh local produce and a large range of foodstuffs.

EXPLORING HALIFAX

This is an easy town to explore on foot, as many of the better museums, historic sites, shops, and restaurants are located within the fairly contained historic core. Downtown, leading west from Brunswick Street, is hilly and green, ideal for a leisurely walk to appreciate the old-style architecture. Citadel Hill offers excellent views of the city, the harbor, and Dartmouth.

⑦ 🗺️ Ⓜ 🖥️ 🏛️

Halifax Citadel National Historic Site

📍 5425 Sackville St/Citadel Hill ⏰ May-Oct: daily; grounds: all year 🌐 pc.gc.ca

Overlooking the city, this huge star-shaped fortress has a commanding view of the world's second-largest natural harbor. Built between 1828 and 1856, the citadel and its fortifications provided a formidable defense. Visitors can stroll parade grounds where the kilted regiment of the 78th Highlanders perform with twice-daily musket drills. A cannon is fired daily at noon.

⑧

Halifax Public Gardens

📍 Spring Garden Rd ⏰ Mid-Apr-late Nov: 8am-dusk daily 🌐 halifaxpublic gardens.ca

Created in 1836, the Public Gardens are a beautiful oasis of Victorian greenery and color in a bustling city. Tranquil

> **The Public Gardens are a beautiful oasis of Victorian greenery and color in a bustling city. Tranquil paths wind past duck ponds, fountains, and an array of vivid flower beds.**

paths wind past duck ponds, fountains, and an array of vivid flower beds. The garden's ornate bandstand is the site of Sunday concerts.

⑨ 🗺️ Ⓜ 🏛️

Art Gallery of Nova Scotia

📍 1723 Hollis St ⏰ From 10am daily 🌐 artgalleryof novascotia.ca

This gallery is housed in two adjacent buildings: Gallery South, dedicated to the Nova Scotian artist Maud Lewis; and Gallery North, which contains a collection of Canadian historical paintings.

↓ Exterior of the Canadian Museum of Immigration, and items on display *(inset)*

⑩ 🗺️ 🏛️

Canadian Museum of Immigration at Pier 21

📍 1055 Marginal Rd ⏰ May-Oct: daily; Nov-Apr: times vary, check website 🌐 pier21.ca

Canada's entry point for more than a million immigrants and refugees, Pier 21 is now a National Historic Site. It offers powerful and emotional displays featuring fascinating images and firsthand testimonies and artifacts.

The Cabot Trail weaving through the highlands, seen from the Skyline Trail ↑

③

CAPE BRETON ISLAND

🚉 Sydney ✈ from Halifax 🚌 ℹ 96 Hwy 4, Port Hastings; www.cbisland.com

The largest island in Nova Scotia, Cape Breton has a wild beauty that makes for some of the most impressive scenery in Canada. Eagles soar over windswept coastal villages, while inviting pubs are alive with the sounds of Celtic music and fine single-malt whisky, evidence of the islanders' close ties to the Scottish Highlands.

①

Cabot Trail

ⓦ pc.gc.ca

From the rolling highlands, sprinkled with sparkling streams, to fine sandy beaches, the island's 185-mile (298-km) Cabot Trail provides one of the most memorable drives in Canada. Entering the Cape Breton Highlands National Park from the west, the trail ascends along the flanks of the coastal mountains. The 24 lookout points along the trail offer far-reaching views of the highlands rising from the sea. Continuing inland, the trail travels across the highland plateau.

Just past French Lake, the short Bog Walk is a boardwalk trail through a highland fen, with educational panels describing the ecosystem, home to rare orchids. Visitors may even catch a glimpse of the park's many moose grazing here in a wetland marsh.

Crossing the French and Mackenzie mountains, the trail descends dramatically to the charming old community of Pleasant Bay. It then re-enters the highlands, crossing North

→
The Big Ceilidh Fiddle (2005) by Cyril Hearn, port of Sydney

Mountain, which, at 1,500 ft (457 m), is the highest point in the park.

The trail's final descent is into the Aspy River Valley, where a gravel road leads to the base of the 100-ft (30-m) high Beulach Ban Falls.

②

Sydney

ⓦ cbisland.com

The only city on Cape Breton Island, Sydney is the second-largest town in Nova Scotia. With a long history as a mining center and once the location of the biggest steel

hands-on exhibits, including games, kite-flying, and science experiments. For an additional fee, visitors can take the more in-depth, behind-the-scenes "White Gloves Tour" of the estate.

④ Baddeck

ⓦ visitbaddeck.com

Across the lake from the estate of Alexander Graham Bell, who loved this little town, Baddeck lies in rich farmland and is very much the island's premier resort destination. Set on the northwest side of Bras d'Or Lake, the town's amenities are all within easy walking distance: the picturesque main street follows the waterfront and is lined with shops and cafés, while boat cruises around the lake are available from several places on Water Street. A Celtic music festival is held here every October.

ALEXANDER GRAHAM BELL

Alexander Graham Bell was born in 1847 in Scotland. Bell's mother was deaf, and, as a child, he became fascinated by speech and communication. In 1870, Bell and his family moved to Ontario, and later to Cape Breton, whose landscape was reminiscent of the family's Scottish homeland. Bell's work involved transmitting the voice electronically, and he began experimenting with the technology used by the telegraph. In 1876, he transmitted the world's first telephone message, "Watson, come here, I want to see you." Bell resided on Cape Breton until his death in 1922.

plant in North America, the town's main industries are now customer-support centers and tourism. It has a small, attractive historic district around the Esplanade, with several restored buildings, such as Cossit House and Jost House, both dating from the 1870s. Downtown, boutiques, stores, and restaurants can be found along the town's main drag, Charlotte Street.

③ Alexander Graham Bell National Historic Site

🏠 559 Chebucto St, Baddeck 🕐 May–Oct: 9am–5pm daily ⓦ pc.gc.ca

This 25-acre (10-ha) site sits on the shores of Bras d'Or Lake, and was Bell's summer home for 30 years. The museum contains the world's largest collection of photographs, artifacts, and documents about the life and work of this famous humanitarian and inventor. There are early telephones, medical devices, kites, and seaplane models on display, plus a copy of his HD-4 hydrofoil boat, which set a world speed record in 1919. Kids will love the various

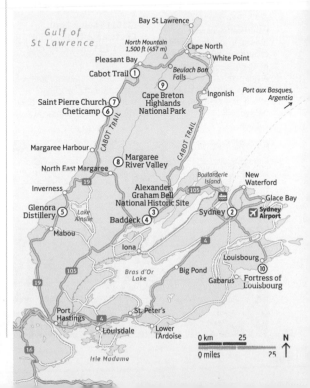

Did You Know?

Gaelic, Acadian French, and Mi'kmaq are still spoken in several communities on Cape Breton.

⑤ Glenora Distillery

🏠 13727 Route 19, Glenville
🕐 Jun–Oct: 9am–5pm daily
🌐 glenoradistillery.com

In the early 1800s, Scottish immigrants flocked to Cape Breton Island, and, finding the land resembled their Highland homeland, they settled and made the island their permanent home. Traditions traveled with them, including the making of a spirited whisky. Glenora Distillery, located on the scenic Ceilidh Trail, maintains these traditions and is Canada's first single-malt distillery. It's renowned for its Glen Breton Rare, a ten-year-old whisky that's made using Cape Breton ingredients, brewed in authentic Scottish copper pot stills, and aged in American oak casks. All guided tours include tastings, and there's a pub, an inn, and a gift shop here too.

⑥ Cheticamp

ℹ️ 15584 Cabot Trail, Cheticamp; www.cheticamp.ca

This vibrant town is the largest Acadian community in Nova Scotia. Its beautiful Saint Pierre Church is visible from miles out at sea. The Acadians of Cape Breton are skilled craftspeople, and the town's seven cooperatives produce pottery and hooked rugs. Cheticamp's best-known rug hooker was Elizabeth LeFort, whose large and intricate works depicting prominent moments in history have hung in the Vatican and in the White House. Several of her finest rugs are on display at the Dr. Elizabeth LeFort Museum at Les Trois Pignons. Cheticamp is also a popular whale-watching destination; tours are available for seeing many varieties.

⑦ Saint Pierre Church

🏠 15114 Cabot Trail, Cheticamp 📞 (902) 224 2064 🕐 Times vary, call to check

Overlooking the harbor at the center of town, Saint Pierre Church was built in 1893. The French Neo-Classical

↑ Low-lying mist over Margaree River Valley at sunrise

exterior is made out of sandstone that was quarried from Cheticamp Island, across the harbor, and transported during the winter across the frozen water by horse. The interior is decorated in Baroque style and features a Quebec-made Casavant organ dating from 1904 – it's one of the first ever built. The church is open to the public; it has a small museum and lovely views from the second floor.

🏔 GREAT VIEW
White Point Hiking Trail

Located at White Point, this relatively easy 1-mile (1.5-km), one-hour hike takes you along a dramatic rocky coastline high up on the cliffs, past an old sailors' graveyard, and with incredible views all around.

← The stunning interior of the Saint Pierre Church in Cheticamp

> **Cape Breton Highlands National Park, with its mountains, green wilderness, and rugged coastal beauty, contains some of Canada's most famous scenery.**

⑧
Margaree River Valley

🅦 cbisland.com

Small and emerald green, the Margaree River Valley is a favorite with hikers, antique hunters, and sightseers. The river has attracted salmon and trout anglers in large numbers since the mid-19th century, and its shores and steep glacial valleys are home to bald eagles and osprey. Paddlers looking for a kayaking challenge will be thrilled with the white rapids and chutes they find here. For a calmer canoe ride, Lake Ainslie, further south, makes for a scenic day trip.
In the little town of North East Margaree, the tiny but elegant Margaree Salmon Museum should fascinate even non-anglers with its beautiful historic rods and reels. Paved and gravel roads follow the Margaree River

upstream to the scenic spot of Big Intervale, where the headwaters come tumbling out of the highlands.

For a taste of Gaelic culture, drive the Ceilidh Trail, a scenic coastal route across a region with a strong Scottish heritage, from the mouth of the Margaree River all the way to the Glenora Distillery (p317).

⑨ 🈯 🖥 🏛
Cape Breton Highlands National Park
🕐 Year-round; Visitor Centre: May–Oct: 9am–5pm 📞 (902) 224 2306

In 1936 the Canadian Government set aside the 367 sq miles (950 sq km) of magnificent highlands at the northern tip of Cape Breton Island to form Cape Breton Highlands National Park.

The park, with its mountains, green wilderness, and rugged coastal beauty, contains some of Canada's most famous scenery. Its best-known feature of is the spectacular 66-mile (106-km) section of the Cabot Trail highway, which traces much of the park's boundary in a loop from Cheticamp to Ingonish. It is the only route through the park, and most attractions are found along it.

At Cape North, a side road leads to the scenic whale-watching destination of Bay St. Lawrence, which is located just outside the park. Farther on, the Scenic Loop breaks away from the Cabot Trail and follows the coast, offering awesome views as it descends to White Point. This road rejoins the Cabot Trail to the east, where it reaches the resort town of Ingonish. The **Cape Breton Highlands Golf Course** here is ranked among the top public golf courses in Canada.

Cape Breton Highlands Golf Course
🈯 🛈 📍 247 Keltic Inn, Ingonish Beach
🅦 kelticlodge.ca/golf

⑩ 🖊 🖼 🍴 🖥 🏛

FORTRESS OF LOUISBOURG

🅰 Rte 22 SW of Louisbourg, Cape Breton Island 🕒 Victoria Day–Thanksgiving: 9:30am–5pm daily; check website for other times of the year 🌐 fortressoflouisbourg.ca

Built between 1713 and 1758, the magnificent Fortress of Louisbourg was France's bastion of military strength in the New World. Today, it is the largest military reconstruction in North America.

Inside the fortress, scores of historically costumed guides bring the excitement of an 18th-century French trading town to life. The streets and buildings are peopled with merchants, soldiers, fishmongers, and washerwomen, all going about the daily business of the 1700s. From the lowliest fisherman's cottage to the elegant home of the Chief Military Engineer, the attention to detail is superb. The costumed interpreters offer information about the fortress, its history, and the lives of people they portray. Although the scale of the reconstruction is immense, much of the fortress remains in ruins, and visitors can walk through the damaged sections out towards the Atlantic coast.

A cluster of reconstructed houses within the Fortress of Louisbourg ↑

1 An antique cart lies empty
    beside one of the fortress's
    brightly colored gates.

2 Gilded details and intricate
    chandeliers decorate the
    interior of the chapel at the
    Fortress of Louisbourg.

3 Attention to detail is paramount
    at the site, as evidenced in the
    period costumes worn during
    a musical procession.

Did You Know?

Locally produced rum
and freshly baked
traditional bread can be
bought on site - be sure
to sample some.

EXPERIENCE MORE

EAT

Billy's Seafood Company

This upscale spot serves some of the best crab dishes in town. There's an on-site fish market, so you can grab some seafood to go, and a bar if you fancy a drink.

◩51 Charlotte St, Saint John
🕒Jan-Mar: Sun
🌐billysseafood.com

$$$

Lily's

Head here for a stunning lakeside location, live entertainment, and excellent local catch of the day. All profits from this friendly restaurant go to the local community.

◩55 Lake Dr S, Saint John 🌐lilylake.ca

$$$

Steamers Lobster Co.

Locals flock to this sea-shack-inspired eatery for their famed lobster rolls - essentially just chunks of fresh lobster meat in a hot-dog bun, but it's unbeatable.

◩110 Water St, Saint John 🕒Mid-Nov-May
🌐steamerslobster company.com

$$$

→

Heaped fruit stalls lining the aisles of the Saint John City Market

④
Saint John

🚌🚆🚢 ℹCity Hall, King St; www.discoversaint john.com

In 1785, 14,000 loyalists fleeing the turmoil of the American Revolution built Saint John in under a year, and it still retains the charm of a small town.

Restoration has made the historic center a delightful place to explore. The Saint John City Market is Canada's oldest continuing farmers' market in Canada, with colorful produce stacked high, fresh seafood vendors, and cafés. In nearby Market Square, an airy atrium links buildings that were once the city's center of commerce. It is now the home of the lively **New Brunswick Museum**. Three floors offer entertaining exhibits on New Brunswick's geological, cultural, and natural history. Children will particularly enjoy the three-level Tidal Tower, where water rises and falls in real time.

Nearby, the Loyalist House Museum is located in an impressive Georgian home, built by Loyalist David Merritt in around 1810.

New Brunswick Museum

⊗🕒 ◩Market Square 🕒Daily 🕒Nov-mid-May: Mon 🌐nbm-mnb.ca

---

⑤
Bouctouche

📧 ℹJun-Sep: 14 Acadia St, (506) 743 8811; Oct-May: Bouctouche Chamber of Commerce, www.ville debouctouche.ca

A seaside town with a strong Acadian heritage, Bouctouche is home to **Le Pays de la Sagouine**. This theme village is named for a washerwoman created by author Antonine Maillet (b. 1929). Theatrical shows here act out her tales. Nearby, the Irving Eco-Centre studies and protects the area's beautiful 8-mile (12-km) network of dunes.

An early stage of Grand Falls, which eventually plunges over 82ft (25m)

Le Pays de la Sagouine

 ⓐ 57 Acadia St
🕐 10am–5:30pm daily
📅 Sep 4 🌐 sagouine.com

6

Grand Falls

📧 ℹ️ Malabeam Reception Centre

The Saint John River flows through a pastoral valley of rolling hills and farmland. The town of Grand Falls consists of one main street, Boulevard Broadway, which is a useful refreshment stop. The town was named for the mighty deluge the Saint John River creates as it tumbles through Grand Falls Gorge. Over time the surge of water has carved a steep 1-mile (1.5-km) gorge.

Upriver, the town of Edmundston offers the New Brunswick Botanical Garden, which has eight themed gardens and two arboretums.

7

Amherst

📧 ℹ️ Rte 104; www.amherst.ca

The bustling town of Amherst overlooks the world's largest marsh, the Tantramar. The Cumberland County Museum is at the home of Senator R. B. Dickey, one of the Fathers of Confederation. Nearby are Fort Beauséjour and its museum, plus the archaeological digs at the Acadian village of Beaubassin.

→
Jonathan Kenworthy's *The Leopard* at Beaverbrook Art Gallery in Fredericton

---

8

Fredericton

✈️ 📧 ℹ️ Fredericton Tourism Division; www.tourismfredericton.ca

Straddling the Saint John River, Fredericton is New Brunswick's provincial capital. Its Victorian homes and waterfront church make it one of the prettiest small cities in Atlantic Canada, while several historic buildings reflect its early role as a British military post. The Beaverbrook Art Gallery contains many fine 19th- and 20th-century paintings, including a Salvador Dali masterpiece. King's Landing, west of Fredericton, is a living history museum that re-creates daily life in a rural 19th-century New Brunswick village.

TOP 3 MARITIMES BEACHES

Aboiteau Beach, Cap-Pelé
Head here for Canada's warmest saltwater swimming area and 3 miles (5 km) of beach ideal for beachcombing.

Killarney Lake Beach, Fredericton
A local favorite, this clear, freshwater lake has a lovely sandy beach and plenty of trails to explore.

New River Beach Provincial Park
Wade in New River's tidal pools, kayak the Bay of Fundy, and build sand sculptures.

↑ The stately white facade of Acadia University in Wolfville, which was founded in 1838

country churches was built on the site of the old village of Grand Pré as a memorial to the Great Expulsion, when the British marched into Acadian territory and forced thousands from Nova Scotia. Visitors can also stroll around the gardens, or take in the site's information center, which features exhibits on the Acadians and their history. After the Great Expulsion, many families hid locally, while some returned in later years.

Grand Pré National Historic Site

♿ 🏛 Hwy 101 🕐 May–Oct: daily 🌐 experiencegrand pre.ca

9

Wolfville

ℹ Willow Park; www. wolfville.ca

The home of the acclaimed Acadia University, Wolfville and the surrounding country-side radiate a gracious charm. Here the green and fertile Annapolis Valley meets the shore of the Minas Basin, and visitors can follow country roads past lush farmlands and sun-warmed orchards.

Much of the valley's rich farmland was created by dikes built by the Acadians in the 1600s. After the Great Expulsion of 1755, the British offered the land to struggling New England villagers on the condition that the entire village would relocate. These hard-working settlers, known as Planters, proved so prosperous that the towns of the Annapolis Valley flourished.

Wolfville and its surrounding area has rapidly gained a reputation as Nova Scotia's wine region. There are over a dozen vineyards in the vicinity, many with tasting rooms open to the public. Wolfville is also home to the Magic Winery Bus, the only hop-on, hop-off winery tour bus in North America.

At the end of a 3 mile (5-km) trail along the Acadian dikes is the graceful church at the **Grand Pré National Historic Site**, part of a UNESCO World Heritage Site. In 1921, a stone church modeled after French

---

STAY

Cliffside Bed & Breakfast

A modern B&B with luxurious suites and exceptional views of Culloden Cove and the Bay of Fundy.

🏠 1820 Culloden Rd, Digby 🌐 cliffside.ca

$$$

Irwin Lake Chalets

Head here for peaceful cedar log cabins – some with private hot tubs – located all along the water.

🏠 680 Loch Haven Ln, Truro 🌐 irwin lakechalets.com

$$$

10

Truro

🏛🚌 ℹ Victoria Square; (902) 893 2922

Located at the hub of Nova Scotia's main transportation routes, Truro is the site of a unique geographical phenomenon, the tidal bore. As the great Fundy tides return landward, they generate a wave, or "bore," that is driven for several miles up the rivers that empty into the basin. Off Hwy 102 is the Tidal Bore Park, where interpretive panels explain the process and people can watch the tide come in. On the nearby Shubenacadie River, visitors can ride the bore in rafts; the waves generated can reach up to 7 ft (2 m) in height.

11

Parrsboro

ℹ Main St; www.town. parrsboro.ns.ca

Located on the north shore of the Minas Basin, Parrsboro is famed as the home of the world's highest tides, which reach over 49 ft (15 m) in height. Rockhounds are drawn to the Minas Basin, whose beaches are scattered with semiprecious gems and fossils. The town's Fundy Geological Museum features fine examples of local amethysts. There are also dinosaur footprints and bones.

⑫
Annapolis Royal

🚌 ℹ Prince Albert Rd; www.annapolisroyal.com

The historic town of Annapolis Royal was the first capital of the colony of Nova Scotia. The British-built Fort Anne National Historic Site witnessed many battles between the English and the French for control of the area. The nearby fur-trading post of Port Royal, the first European settlement in the New World north of Florida, was built in 1605 by Samuel de Champlain. The **Port-Royal National Historic Site** is an exact replica of the original colony, based on French farms of the period, from plans drawn by Champlain. An hour's drive inland from Annapolis Royal lies Kejimkujik National Park and National Historic Site, which covers 147 sq miles (381 sq km) of inland wilderness laced with lakes and rivers.

Port-Royal National Historic Site

🏛 🅰 9 miles (15 km) W of Annapolis Royal 📞 (902) 532 2898 🕐 May-Oct: 9am-5:30pm Tue-Sat

⑬
Digby

🚌🚗🚢 ℹ Shore Rd; www.digby.ca

This town is renowned for the plump scallops that are the prime quarry of its fishing fleet. The area around Digby offers splendid scenery, with the rocky coastal landscape of Long and Brier islands nearby.

The waters off these islands brim with finback, minke, and humpback whales, and whale-watching tours are popular. Some visitors may even spot the rare right whale, as about 200 of the 350 left in the world pass their summers in the area.

⑭
Windsor

🚌 ℹ Hwy 101, exit 6; www.town.windsor.ns.ca

A quiet town whose elegant Victorian homes overlook the Avon River, Windsor was the

home of Judge Thomas Chandler Haliburton, lawyer, historian, and the author of the Canadian "Sam Slick" stories, which achieved enormous popularity in the mid-1800s. His clever, fast-talking character Sam Slick coined idiomatic terms such as "the early bird gets the worm," and "raining cats and dogs." His elegant home is now the **Haliburton House Provincial Museum**, which contains many of his personal possessions, including his writing desk. Windsor is also renowned as the birthplace of hockey, the nation's favorite sport, and home to the Pumpkin Regatta, held every October.

Haliburton House Provincial Museum

🏛 🅰 414 Clifton Ave 🕐 Jun-mid-Oct: daily 🌐 haliburtonhouse.novascotia.ca

↑ The small fishing village of Digby, lit by street lamps as dusk falls

Waves crashing against the rocks at Peggy's Cove

Tourists strolling along the rustic, colorful waterfront of Lunenburg ↑

⑮

Lunenburg

☎ 🄲 May-Sep: (902) 634 8100; Oct-Apr: (902) 634 3170 🅆 explore lunenburg.ca

No town captures the seafaring romance of Nova Scotia as much as Lunenburg, declared a UNESCO World Heritage Site in 1996. In the mid-1700s, the British, eager for another loyal settlement, laid out a plan for Lunenburg. They then offered the land to Protestant settlers from mainland Europe. Although these were mostly farmers, they soon turned to shipbuilding and the town became a center for the trade. Lunenburg is the home port of *Bluenose II*, a replica of Canada's renowned schooner.

The **Fisheries Museum of the Atlantic** fills several buildings along the waterfront. It features retired schooners, touch tanks, and scallop-shucking sessions.

Fisheries Museum of the Atlantic
🄰🄰🄰🄰 🄰 Bluenose Dr 🄾 Mid-May-mid-Oct: daily; mid-Oct-May: Mon-Fri 🅆 fisheriesmuseum.nova scotia.ca

⑯

Shelburne

☎ 🄸 Dock St; www.town. shelburne.ns.ca

A quiet historic town nestled on the shore of a deep harbor, Shelburne was founded by 3,000 United Empire Loyalists fleeing persecution during the American Revolution of 1775. More loyalists followed, and Shelburne's population swelled, making it at the time the third-largest town in British North America. Over time, many of those settlers relocated to Halifax or returned to England, leaving behind the fine 18th-century homes they had built.

A walk along Water Street leads to the **Dory Shop Museum**. This has been a commercial dory (flat-bottomed boat) building shop since its founding in 1880. The museum features displays on the industry and the salt-cod fishery. Upstairs, skilled shipwrights demonstrate the techniques of dory building.

The 1995 film *The Scarlet Letter* was shot in Shelburne, with the whole main street becoming a movie set.

Dory Shop Museum
🄰 🄰 Dock St 🄾 Jun-mid-Oct: daily 🅆 doryshop.nova scotia.ca

⑰

Mahone Bay

☎ 🄸 Destination Southwest Nova Association; www.mahonebay.com

The small town of Mahone Bay has been called the "prettiest town in Canada." Tucked into the bay, the waterfront is lined with homes dating to the 1700s, and at the back of the harbor three stately churches cast their reflection into the still waters.

> According to local legend, the large angel in the sculpture is the original Peggy, sole survivor of a terrible 19th-century shipwreck, for whom Peggy's Cove was named.

The tiny **Mahone Bay Museum** displays exhibits and artifacts relating to the town's settlement by foreign Protestants in 1754, and its prominence as a boat-building center. There is also a collection of 18th- and 19th-century ceramics and antiques.

Mahone Bay Museum

🏠 578 Main St 🕐 Jun-Sep: Tue-Sun 🌐 mahonebay museum.com

18 🔶 🖥️ 🏛️

Kouchibouguac National Park

🏠🚌&🏊 Miramichi 🕐 Daily 🌐 pc.gc.ca

The name of this park comes from the local Mi'kmaq word for "River of Long Tides." The park's 92 sq miles (238 sq km) encompass a salt-spray world of wind-sculpted dunes, salt-marshes packed with wildlife, and miles of fine sand beaches, as well as excellent terrain for cyclists. The Voyageur Canoe Adventure – a three-hour paddle to offshore sandbanks where gray seals bask – is very popular.

19

Passamaquoddy Bay

🚌 Saint Stephen 🚢 Black's Harbour & L'Etete 🛈 Saint Andrews Tourism Bureau; (506) 529 3556

There is a historic charm to the villages surrounding the waters of Passamaquoddy Bay, and none is more intriguing than the resort town of Saint Andrews by-the-Sea. In town, Water Street is lined with boutiques, craft shops, and fine restaurants. At the dock, tour companies offer sailing, whale watching, and kayaking trips. Nearby, the Georgian home built for Loyalist Harris Hatch in 1824 now houses the Ross Memorial Museum, which contains an extensive collection of antiques and art.

Ferries depart regularly for nearby islands. The Roosevelt Campobello International Park is a 4-sq-mile (11-sq-km) preserve built around the elegant summer home of US President Franklin D. Roosevelt. The 34-room Roosevelt Cottage has been restored, and includes artifacts belonging to the family. For Campobello Island, 12 miles (20 km) south of Saint Andrews, a ferry departs from L'Etete to Deer Island, from where another boat goes to Campobello.

Ruggedly beautiful Grand Manan Island is popular with birdwatchers, as it attracts large flocks of seabirds.

20

Peggy's Cove

🛈 Sou'wester Restaurant; www.peggyscove region.com

The still-operational Peggy's Point Lighthouse stands atop granite rocks in Peggy's Cove and is one of the most photographed sights in Canada. The village, with its colorful houses clinging to the rocks, has certainly earned its reputation as one of the area's most picturesque fishing villages, and is a delightful place to stroll through.

⚠️ GREAT VIEW
To the Lighthouse
Nova Scotia has the largest number of lighthouses in Canada, with over 160 that can be visited, all with astonishing views. Many are located along the Lighthouse Route, a scenic roadway that follows the province's southern shore from Halifax to Yarmouth.

The village was the home of well-known marine artist and sculptor, William E. deGarthe (1907–83). Just above the harbor, the deGarthe Gallery hosts a permanent exhibition of many of his works. Right outside the gallery, the *Fishermen's Monument* is a 100 ft (30-m) sculpture by deGarthe, created as a memorial to Nova Scotian fishermen. According to local legend, the large angel in the sculpture is the original Peggy, sole survivor of a terrible 19th-century shipwreck, for whom Peggy's Cove was named.

Just outside the village, at the Whaleback promontory, is a memorial to the victims of the tragic Swissair 111 crash of 1998.

↑ Pretty fishermen's cottage dotted along the shore in Peggy's Cove

↑ Breathtaking natural scenery in Fundy National Park

21 🚶 🚵

Fundy National Park

🏛 Moncton 🚌 Sussex 🚆 Saint John 🕐 May-Oct: daily 🌐 pc.gc.ca

Along New Brunswick's southern shore, the tremendous tides of the Bay of Fundy are a powerful feature of local life. Twice a day, over 100 billion tons of water swirl into and out of the bay, creating a tidal shift of up to 49 ft (15 m) and carving out a stunning wild and rocky shoreline.

One of the best places to experience these renowned tidal wonders is at Fundy National Park, which is filled with wildlife and scenic hiking trails. Here, at low tide, visitors can walk out into the bay for nearly a mile. This area is a favorite with naturalists, who study the fascinating

Did You Know?

The highest tide in the world was recorded in the Bay of Fundy in 1869, and reached 70.9 ft (21.6 m).

creatures that spend half their lives underwater and the other half above.

22
Acadian Peninsula

🏛 & 🚌 Bathurst 🚆 Dalhousie 🚌 56 Salmon Blvd, Campbellton; 1 800 561 0123

The quiet coastal villages, beaches, and gentle surf of the Acadian peninsula have made it a favorite vacation destination. Established here since the 1600s, the Acadians have long enjoyed a reputation for fruitful farming, pretty villages, and a strong folk music tradition (p48).

In Shippagan, a small fishing town, the **Marine Centre and Aquarium** holds tanks with over 3,000 specimens of Atlantic sealife and displays on local fishing industries.

Nearby, the Lamèque and Miscou islands are connected by causeways to the mainland. Visit the Église Ste-Cécile on Lamèque Island, a church with unique painted interiors. It is home to the annual International Baroque

Festival, which takes place every June. Discover the Acadian Peninsula's fascinating flora and fauna at the **Ecological Park**, and learn about the region's five largest ecosystems.

On Miscou Island, a half-mile (1-km) boardwalk leads through a peat bog with signs about this unique ecosystem. The 85-ft- (35-m-) high Miscou Lighthouse is the oldest operating wooden lighthouse in Canada and also a National Historic Site.

Home to many Acadian artists, Caraquet is the busy cultural center of the peninsula. Like the rest of the region, its natural setting is beautiful, and on the waterfront, adventure centers offer guided kayak trips on the Baie des Chaleurs.

Marine Centre and Aquarium
🌐 🚻 ♿ 🏛 100 Aquarium St, Shippagan 🕐 Jun-Sep: 10am-6pm daily 🌐 aquariumnb.ca

Ecological Park
🌐 🚵 🏛 65 Du Ruisseau St, Lamèque 📞 (506) 344 3223 🕐 Late Jun-Aug: daily

23 🚶 🖥️ ℹ️

Hopewell Rocks

📍 **131 Discovery Rd,
Hopewell Cape** 🕐 May–Oct
🌐 **thehopewellrocks.ca**

South of the village of
Hopewell Cape is this phenomenal geological formation
consisting of a series of large
rocks, some as high as 70 ft
(20 m) high, that have taken
on odd shapes from continual
tidal erosion. Due to the Bay
of Fundy's extreme tidal
ranges, these formations are
covered in water twice a day
but they can be completely
viewed at low tide. When the
park is closed for the season
you can still park outside of
the gate and walk down to
the beach along the trails.

24

The Eastern Shore

📍 **Halifax** 🚌 **Antigonish**
🚢 **Pictou** ℹ️ **Canso; (902)
366 2170**

A tour along the Eastern
Shore is a trip through old-
world Nova Scotia, through
towns and villages where life

↑ Strangely shaped
Hopewell Rocks, also
called "Flowerpot Rocks"

↑ A horse-drawn wagon at Sherbrooke
Village on the Eastern Shore

has changed little since the
turn of the 20th century. The
tiny house and farm that
comprise the Fisherman's Life
Museum in Jeddore, Oyster
Ponds (on the access road 37
miles/60 km east of Halifax)
was the home of an inshore
fisherman, his wife, and their
13 daughters around 1900.
Today, the homestead is a
living-history museum, where
guides in period costume re-
enact the simple life of an
inshore fishing family, still the
heart of Nova Scotia culture.
Visitors who arrive at midday
may be invited to share lunch
cooked over a woodburning
stove. There are also daily
demonstrations that include
rug-hooking and quilting,
and visitors can tour the
fishing stage, where salted
fish were stored.

Sherbrooke Village is the
largest living-history museum
in Nova Scotia. Between 1860
and 1890, this was a gold and
lumber boomtown. As the
gold ran out, Sherbrooke once
again became a sleepy rural
village. In the early 1970s,
some 25 of Sherbrooke's
most historic buildings were
restored. Within the village,
scores of costumed guides
bring 19th-century Nova Scotia
to life. A ride on a horse-drawn
wagon offers an overview of
the town; the drivers share
snippets of local history as the
horses trot along the village
roads. At the apothecary,
visitors can watch the careful
mixing of patent medicines,
and those interested in the

Ambrotype Studio can dress
in period costumes then sit
very still while the vintage
camera records their image
on glass. Just outside town a
massive waterwheel turns,
powering the Lumber Mill.

Sherbrooke Village
🚶 😊 🖼️ 📍 **Off Hwy 7** 🕐 **Jun-
Oct: daily** 🌐 **sherbrooke
village.novascotia.ca**

---

25 🚶 🤸 🍴 ℹ️

Village Historique
Acadien

📍 **Route 11, 6 miles (10 km)
W of Caraquet** 🚌 **From
Bathurst** 🕐 **10am–6pm
daily** 🕐 **Aug 15** 🌐 **village
historique acadien.com**

After the tragic deportation
of 1755–63, Acadians slowly
returned to the Maritimes,
clearing new farmlands and
rebuilding their way of life.
The Village Historique Acadien
portrays a rural Acadian community between 1770 and
1949. The village's 60 restored
historic buildings, including
several working farms, cover
900 acres (364 ha).

Throughout the village,
period-costumed bilingual
guides recreate the daily
activities of the 19th century.
Visitors can ride in a horse-
drawn wagon, watch the work
of the blacksmith, print shop,
or gristmill, and also tour
working farms and homes
where women are busy cooking, weaving, and spinning.

Boathouses on a dock in the Change Islands

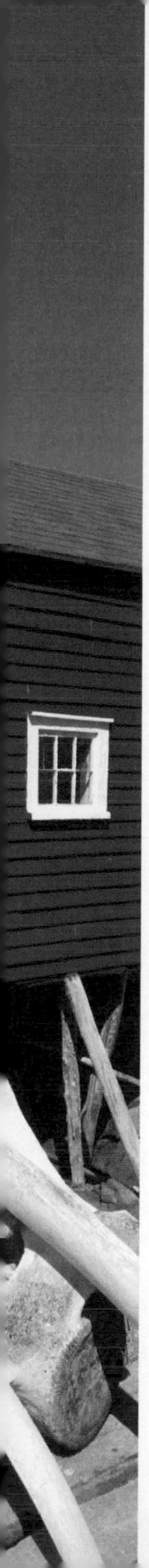

NEWFOUNDLAND AND LABRADOR

With towering peaks, vast landscapes, and 10,500 miles (17,000 km) of rugged coastline, both Newfoundland and Labrador display wild, open spaces and grand spectacles of nature. In this captivating landscape, massive icebergs drift lazily along the coast, whales swim in sparkling bays, and moose graze placidly in flat open marshes.

Newfoundland's west coast offers some of the most dramatic scenery east of the Rockies. The granite mountains of Gros Morne National Park shelter deep fjords, while the eastern part of the island has a more rounded terrain, featuring the bays and inlets of Terra Nova National Park. Part of the area's appeal is retracing the history of past cultures that have settled here, including Maritime Archaic Aboriginal Peoples at Port au Choix, Vikings at L'Anse-Aux-Meadows, and Basque whalers at Red Bay in the Labrador Straits.

NEWFOUNDLAND AND LABRADOR

Must Sees
1 St. John's
2 Gros Morne National Park

Experience More
3 Trinity
4 Labrador City
5 Happy Valley-Goose Bay
6 Nain
7 Gander
8 Avalon Peninsula
9 Saint-Pierre and Miquelon Islands
10 Terra Nova National Park
11 Burin Peninsula
12 Bonavista Peninsula
13 Notre Dame Bay
14 Labrador Straits
15 Battle Harbour
16 The Southwest Coast
17 Churchill Falls

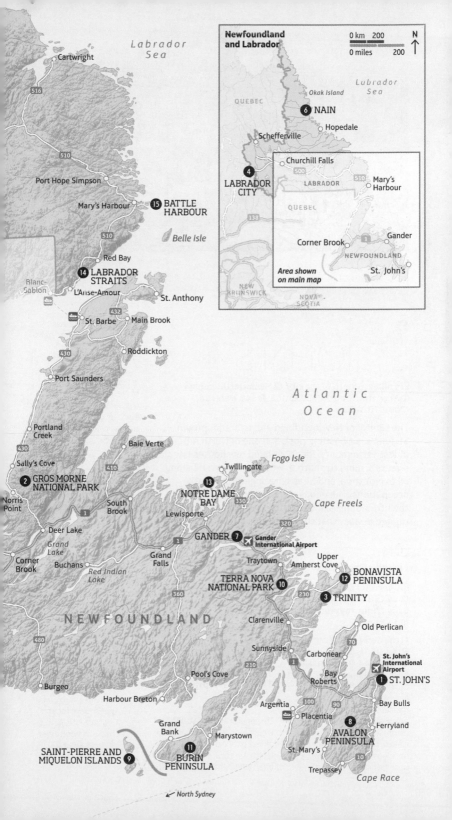

Labrador Sea

Cartwright

516

510

Port Hope Simpson

Mary's Harbour

510

Red Bay

14 LABRADOR STRAITS

Blanc-Sablon

L'Anse-Amour

St. Barbe

15 BATTLE HARBOUR

Belle Isle

St. Anthony

432

Main Brook

430

Roddickton

Port Saunders

430

Portland Creek

Sally's Cove

Baie Verte

410

Twillingate

Fogo Isle

2 GROS MORNE NATIONAL PARK

Norris Point

Atlantic Ocean

13 NOTRE DAME BAY

Lewisporte

330

Cape Freels

1

South Brook

Deer Lake

Grand Lake

1

Grand Falls

GANDER 7 ✈ Gander International Airport

320

Corner Brook

Buchans

Red Indian Lake

360

Traytown

Upper Amherst Cove

TERRA NOVA NATIONAL PARK 10

12 BONAVISTA PENINSULA

3 TRINITY

230

N E W F O U N D L A N D

Clarenville

Old Perlican

480

Sunnyside

70

Carbonear

St. John's International Airport ✈

Bay Roberts

1

210

Pool's Cove

Burgeo

Harbour Breton

Bay Bulls

Argentia

100

90

1 ST. JOHN'S

Grand Bank

Marystown

Placentia

AVALON PENINSULA 8

Ferryland

11 BURIN PENINSULA

St. Mary's

10

SAINT-PIERRE AND MIQUELON ISLANDS **9**

Trepassey

Cape Race

← North Sydney

Labrador Sea

QUEBEC

Okak Island

6 NAIN

Schefferville

Hopedale

Churchill Falls

500

LABRADOR CITY

LABRADOR

510

Mary's Harbour

QUEBEC

138

Corner Brook

1

Gander

Area shown on main map

NEWFOUNDLAND

St. John's

NEW BRUNSWICK

NOVA SCOTIA

❶

ST. JOHN'S

✈ 4 miles (6 km) N of the city 🚌 Memorial University
🚢 Argentia 80 miles (130 km) SE 🛈 348 Water St;
(709) 576 8106

The capital of Newfoundland and Labrador province, St. John's is a bustling port, and one of North America's oldest settlements. Rainbow-hued row houses line the streets around the harbor, where commercial fishing, oil exploration, and boat servicing are still viable occupations. The people of St. John's are known for their friendliness, a delightful counterpoint to the rugged beauty that surrounds this historic town.

①
Murray Premises

🏠 Cnr Water St & Beck's Cove ⏰ 8am–10:30pm daily 🌐 murraypremises hotel.com

At the west end of Water Street stands Murray Premises. Built in 1846, these rambling brick and timber-frame buildings are the last remaining examples of the large mercantile and fish-processing premises that used to be common on the St. John's waterfront. Murray Premises once bustled with the work of shipping cod to world markets. The buildings only just survived a huge fire that engulfed the city in 1892; they mark the western boundary of the fire's devastation. Now a Provincial Historic Site, the restored buildings are home to a boutique hotel and offices.

② 🍴 🛍
The Waterfront

🏠 Water St

Tracing the edge of St. John's waterfront, Water Street is the oldest public thoroughfare in North America, dating to the late 1500s, when trading first started. Once a brawling wharfside lane of gin mills and brothels, Water Street and the parallel Duckworth Street now offer gift shops, art galleries, and some of Newfoundland's top restaurants. Harbour Drive, also along the waterfront, is a great place to stroll, while George Street is the hub of the city's nightlife.

③
Commissariat House

🏠 King's Bridge Rd
📞 (709) 729 6730

Commissariat House, now a Provincial Historic Site, was built between 1818 and 1820 and was once the home of 19th-century British officials. The Georgian building contains a multimedia

Did You Know?

There are more pubs per square foot on George St, St. John's, than anywhere else in Canada.

←
Colorful houses making up the cliffside community of the Battery

experience that depicts early 19th-century life in St. John's. Nearby Government House, which dates from the 1820s, is the official residence of the province's Lieutenant Governor.

___

④

The Battery

🏠 Battery Rd

The colorful houses clinging to sheer cliffs at the entrance to the harbor are known as the Battery. With the look and feel of a 19th-century fishing village, this is one of St. John's most photographed sites. Once considered a challenging place to live, it has now developed into a sought-after location. The community is named for the military fortifications built here over centuries to defend the harbor. Local residents used the battery's guns in 1763 to fight off Dutch pirate ships.

⑤ 🏷️ 🖥️ 🛍️

The Rooms

🏠 9 Bonaventure Ave
🕐 Times vary, check website 🚫 Mon 🌐 the rooms.ca

A major landmark in downtown St. John's, The Rooms is a modern facility housing three provincial institutions: the Provincial Archives; the Museum of Newfoundland, which charts the province's history over the past 9,000 years; and the Art Gallery of Newfoundland and Labrador, which showcases the work of local, national, and international artists. Together these establishments are housed in a unique building that was designed to mimic "fishing rooms," where families would process their catch. There are excellent views over the city from the distinctive granite and glass building. On site, there is a superb café and a well-stocked gift shop. Admission to the museum is free between 6 and 9pm on the first Wednesday evening of every month.

↑ "Connections" exhibit at the Museum of Newfoundland, part of The Rooms complex

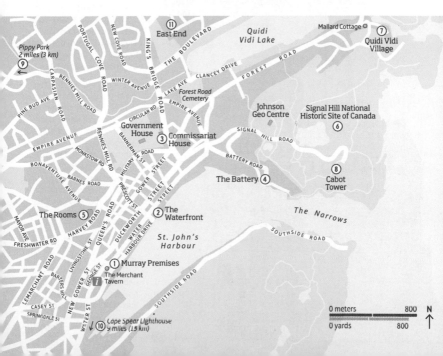

EAT & DRINK

Mallard Cottage

Tuck into delicious and hearty breakfasts, wild game, and local seafood inside this cozy historical home in the Quidi Vidi Village.

🏠 8 Barrows Rd 🕐 Mon
🌐 mallardcottage.ca

$$$

The Merchant Tavern

Bright and airy with an industrial vibe, this restaurant serves up amazing and creative Canadian cuisine and cocktails.

🏠 291 Water St
🕐 Mon 🌐 themerchant
tavern.ca

$$$

⑥

Signal Hill National Historic Site of Canada

🏠 Signal Hill Rd 📞 (709) 772 5367 🕐 Visitor Centre: mid-end May: 10am-6pm Wed-Sun; Jun-Labour Day weekend: 10am-6pm daily; Labour Day weekend-mid-Oct: 10am-6pm Sat-Wed

This lofty rise of land presents spectacular views of the open Atlantic, the harbor entrance, and the historic splendor of the city of St. John's.

---

⑦

Quidi Vidi Village

🏠 Quidi Vidi Village Rd
🕐 Daily

On one side of Signal Hill, the weathered buildings of ancient Quidi Vidi Village nestle around a small harbor. Above the village, the Quidi Vidi Battery was a fortified gun emplacement built in 1762 to defend the harbor entrance. The province's most popular microbrewery, Quidi Vidi Brewery, is also located on the harbor. Tasting tours are offered daily at 11am, and more frequently at weekends.

⑧

Cabot Tower

🏠 Signal Hill Rd 📞 (709) 772 5367 🕐 Visitor Centre: mid-end May: 10am-6pm Wed-Sun; Jun-Labour Day weekend: 10am-6pm daily; Labour Day weekend-mid-Oct: 10am-6pm Sat-Wed

The building of Cabot Tower at the top of Signal Hill began in 1897 to celebrate the 400th anniversary of John Cabot's arrival – an Italian explorer who originally went by the name of Giovanni Caboto. On summer weekends, soldiers in period dress perform 19th-century marching drills. It was here that another Italian, Guglielmo Marconi, received the first transatlantic wireless signal in 1901.

←

Cabot Tower, a stark brick building that sits atop Signal Hill in St. John's

↑ Signal Hill rising rockily above the harbor, with the city of St. John's illuminated below

⑨ Pippy Park

🅐 Nagles Place 🕐 Daily
🅦 pippypark.com

Visitors are sometimes startled to see moose roaming free in St. John's, but it happens regularly in this 3,460-acre (1,400-ha) nature park, located just 2 miles (3 km) from the town center. It is the largest provincially managed park in Canada, stretching more than three times the size of Vancouver's Stanley Park. Pippy Park is also home to the local Botanical Gardens and the only Fluvarium in North America, an environmental educational center with nine underwater windows that look into a rushing freshwater trout stream. Other attractions at the site include camping, a wealth of walking trails, plus a popular golf course and driving range.

⑩ Cape Spear Lighthouse National Historic Site of Canada

🅐 Blackhead Road 🅒 (709) 772 5367 🕐 Visitor Centre: mid-end May: 10am-6pm Wed-Sun; Jun-Labour Day weekend: 10am-6pm daily; Labour Day weekend-mid-Oct: 10am-6pm Sat-Wed

Lying 6 miles (10 km) southeast of town, Cape Spear marks the most easterly point in North America. Set atop seaside cliffs, the majestic Cape Spear Lighthouse has long been a symbol of Newfoundland's independence and marine history. Two lighthouses now stand here: the original, built in 1836, is the oldest in Newfoundland, while beside it stands the graceful, modern, automated lighthouse, added in 1955. The original lighthouse has been restored to show how a 19th-century keeper and his family would have lived.

⑪ East End

🅐 King's Bridge Rd 🅯 (709) 570 2038

East End is one of St. John's most architecturally rich neighborhoods, its streets lined with elegant homes.

> **EXPLORING ST. JOHN'S**
>
> Newfoundland's capital is easily explored on foot. Most of the sights are within a short distance of each other moving east along Water Street. Approaching by sea offers the best view of the harbor, particularly the steep cliff-lined passage on the east side, where the pastel-colored old houses of the Battery *(p337)* cling precariously to the rocks.

② ⊘ 🖵 🛍

GROS MORNE NATIONAL PARK

🚌🚐 St Barbe 🏠 Rte 430, Rocky Harbour; www.pc.gc.ca

Hike along barren earth or climb alpine summits where Arctic foxes dash over the tundra. Navigate narrow fjords cradled between soaring cliffs, where waterfalls vaporize as they tumble. The ancient and moody landscape of Gros Morne is like no other place on earth.

A UNESCO World Heritage Site, Gros Morne is Newfoundland's most scenic landscape masterpiece. Here, the Long Range Mountains rise 2,670 ft (814 m) above a blue fjord that cuts into the coastal range. Some of the world's oldest mountains, these are pre-Cambrian and several million years older than the Rockies. Gros Morne Mountain is one of these and it's a popular, if grueling hike to the top.

Barren and rust-colored, the unique Tablelands area was created during a collision of two continental landmasses over half a billion years ago, when deep ocean crust and rocks of the earth's mantle were thrust upward, instead of forced underneath, which is usually the case. Erosion and glaciation followed and now these ancient parts of our planet lie exposed. Due to the magnesium-rich soil in the exposed peridotite rock, very few plant species can survive here, and so the landscape resembles a desert.

Most of the tourist services are found in the seaside village of Rocky Harbour in the northern section of the park. Hiking along coastal pathways, beach combing around sea stacks, and cruising the fjords are some of the main activities in this area. Those with a keen eye will spot moose and caribou in the forests, and seals and whales around St. Paul's Bay.

↑ Visitors on a boat tour on Western Brook Pond, near Rocky Harbour

💬 INSIDER TIP
Western Brook Pond Boat Tours

A boat tour of Western Brook Pond is the best way to explore the park's steep, glacier-carved fjords, full of waterfalls and wildlife. Tours are generally offered from June to October and require a long walk to the docks in Rocky Harbour.

← Hikers crossing the arid, rocky Tablelands on a clear day

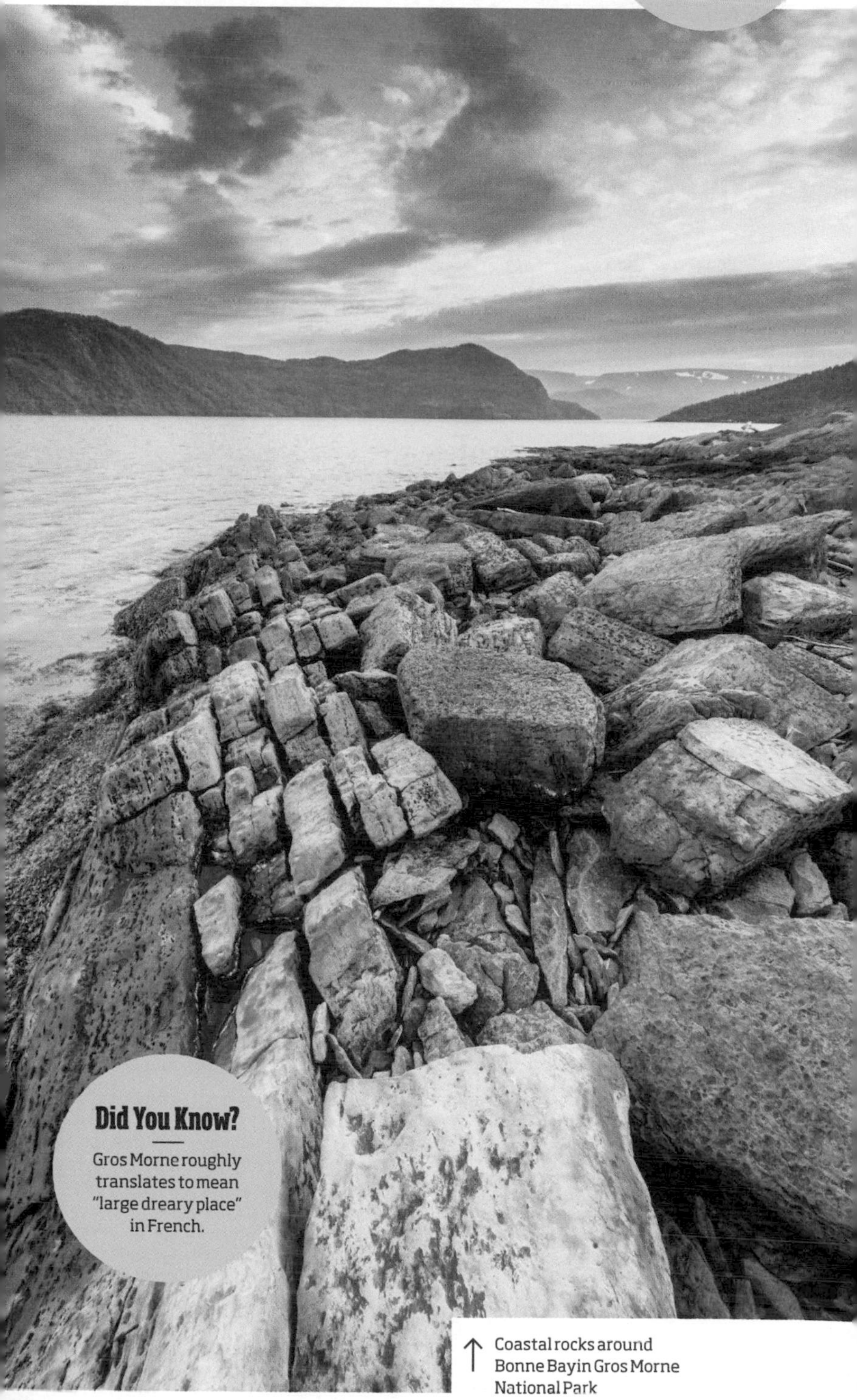

Did You Know?

Gros Morne roughly translates to mean "large dreary place" in French.

↑ Coastal rocks around Bonne Bay in Gros Morne National Park

EXPERIENCE MORE

❸ Trinity

❶ Trinity Visitor Centre, West St; www.town oftrinity.com

The charming village of Trinity, with its colorful 19th-century buildings overlooking the blue waters of Trinity Bay, is easily one of the most beautiful Newfoundland communities. Best explored on foot, it has a range of craft shops and rest-aurants. The Trinity Museum contains over 2,000 artifacts illustrating the town's past.

Also here is Hiscock House, a home restored to the style of 1910, where merchant Emma Hiscock ran the village store, forge, and post office, while raising her six children.

❹ Labrador City

➕▣ ❶ (709) 944 7631

Labrador City is a mining town that shows the industrial modern face of Canada. It is home to the world's largest open-pit iron mine, and the community has largely grown up around this since the late 1950s.

The vast open wilderness surrounding the city is famed as a sportsman's paradise that attracts hunters and anglers from all over the world.

The city's **Gateway Labrador Visitor Center** has an exhibit of artifacts representing the best of Labrador West and its history, culture, and people.

Gateway Labrador Visitor Center

▣ 1365, Route 500
☎ (709) 944 5399
🕘 9am–6pm Mon–Fri

❺ Happy Valley-Goose Bay

➕▣ ❶ Labrador; (709) 896 8787

The largest town in Central Labrador, Happy Valley-Goose Bay was a strategically important stopover for transatlantic flights during World War II. German, Italian, and British pilots now train at the NATO base here.

The nearby community of North West River is home to the Labrador Heritage Museum, where exhibitions depict its fascinating history, paying particular attention to the life of trappers.

❻ Nain

➕▣ ❶ Town Council, Nain; www.tourism nunatsiavut.com

Nain is Newfoundland and Labrador's most northern community. A large part of the small population is Inuit, and the town is rich with traditional art, much of which can be bought at Torngat Arts & Crafts in the center of town.

→

Hopedale Mission National Historic Site, Hopedale near Nain

Picturesque Trinity village, with its colorful 19th-century buildings lining the water

Nain is also home to world-famous carvers such as John Terriak and Gilbert Hay.

The best way to explore Nain and the Nunatsiavut region is by taking the Northern Ranger ferry from Happy Valley-Goose Bay and visiting the small fishing communities along the way. These include Rigolet, the most southern Inuit community in the world; Makkovik, a good place to buy traditional Labrador art; and Postville, once a trading post for Inuit families. Nearby Hopedale boasts some of Canada's oldest wooden-framed constructions, including the **Hopedale Mission National Historic Site**, where stories and artifacts are displayed.

Hopedale Mission National Historic Site

Agvituk Historical Society, Hopedale ☎ (709) 933 3881 ⏰ Daily

---

⑦
Gander

🚫➕ ℹ️ 109 Trans-Canada Hwy; www.gandercanada.com

This small town is a useful tourist center for fuel and food, but is probably best known for its illustrious aviation history. Gander's airport opened in 1938, and was once the largest in the world. In the aftermath of September 11, 2001, 38 jets were rerouted here, nearly doubling the tiny town's population. Gander's hospitality during this time later became the subject of a Broadway musical, *Come From Away*.

In Grand Falls-Windsor, 62 miles (100 km) west of Gander, the Mary March Provincial Museum, named after the last survivor of the now-extinct Beothuk people, traces central Newfoundland's history from the Aboriginal cultures of 9,000 years ago to the industrial age.

EAT

Bistro On Roe
A cozy restaurant with French-inspired dishes. Try the crème brûlée or flourless chocolate cake.

🏠 110 Roe Ave, Gander
🌐 bistroonroe.com

$$$

Bonavista Social Club
Tuck into juicy burgers and wood-fired pizzas, washed down with rhubarb lemonade out on the sunny waterfront patio.

🏠 2 Longshore Rd, Upper Amherst Cove, Bonavista Peninsula
🚫 Mon & Tue; Nov-Apr
🌐 bonavistasocialclub.com

$$$

Lighthouse Picnics
Pick up a freshly prepared feast at the Ferryland Lighthouse and savor it outside with breathtaking views of the Atlantic. Be sure to book ahead.

🏠 Ferryland ⏰ May-Oct: Wed-Sun, lunch only
🌐 lighthousepicnics.ca

$$$

8

Avalon Peninsula

🚉 St. John's 🚢 Argentia
🛈 Dept of Tourism, St.
John's; www.colony
ofavalon.ca

The picturesque community of Ferryland on the Avalon Peninsula is the site of a large-scale archeological excavation of the Colony of Avalon, a settlement founded by English explorer Lord Baltimore and 11 settlers in 1621. This was Baltimore's first New World venture, intended to be a self-sufficient colony with firm principles of religious tolerance.

By the end of the following year there were 32 settlers. The population continued to grow, and for many years it was the only successful colony in the area. Although excavations to date have unearthed only 5 percent of the colony, it has proved to be one of the richest sources of artifacts from any early European settlement in North America. A vast array of pieces have been recovered, such as pottery and household implements. An interpretive center tells the colony's story, and a tour includes the chance to see archaeologists at work.

At the southern end of Avalon Peninsula, **Cape St. Mary's Ecological Reserve** is a nesting seabird colony that can be approached on foot. A short trail leads along seacliffs to a site where over 8,000 northern gannets nest. On the southwest side of the peninsula, overlooking the entrance to the historic French town of

> At the southern end of Avalon Peninsula, Cape St. Mary's Ecological Reserve is a nesting seabird colony that can be approached on foot.

Placentia, visitors can stroll up to the **Castle Hill National Historic Site**. These are the remains of French fortifications dating back to 1662; from here there are fine coastal views.

Cape St. Mary's Ecological Reserve

◈ 🅿 Off Route 100 📞 (709) 277 1666 🕐 Year round; Interpretive Centre: May–Oct

Castle Hill National Historic Site

◈ ◈ 🅿 Jerseyside, Placentia Bay 📞 (709) 227 2401 🕐 Jun–Labour Day: 10am–6pm daily

---

🔍 HIDDEN GEM
Petty Harbour Mini Aquarium

This small, seasonal catch-and-release aquarium on the Avalon Peninsula offers more than 30 educational displays and seven touch tanks filled with local marine life.

The rocky coast and seabird colony *(inset)* of the Avalon Peninsula

→ The attractive French islands of Saint-Pierre and Miquelon, lit up at night

9 Saint-Pierre and Miquelon Islands

✈ 🚌 🚢 ⓦ spmtourisme.fr

These two small islands are not Canadian but French, and have been under French rule since the 17th century. Saint-Pierre, the only town on the island of the same name, is a charming French seaside village. Its **Musée Heritage** details the islands' history, including their lively role as a bootlegger's haven during Prohibition in the 1920s, when over three million cases of liquor passed through this port annually. Many of the harborfront warehouses originally built for this trade are still standing.

Miquelon Island is made up of two smaller islands, Grand Miquelon and Langlade, joined by a narrow, 7-mile- (12-km-) long strand. The road across this sandy isthmus crosses grassy dunes, where wild horses graze and surf pounds sandy beaches. A ferry leaves Saint-Pierre for the village of Miquelon three times a week, usually on Tuesday, Wednesday, and Sunday. Another ferry goes to Langlade every day except Tuesday.

Musée Heritage
Ⓢ 🏠 Rue Maître Georges Lefèvre 97500 🕐 Jun-Oct: Tue-Sun ⓦ musee-heritage.fr

---

10 Terra Nova National Park

🏠 Trans-Canada Hwy 🚌 From St. John's 🕐 May-mid-Oct: daily 🛈 Glovertown ⓦ pc.gc.ca

The gently rolling forested hills and deep fjords of north-eastern Newfoundland are the setting for Terra Nova National Park. The park's Marine Interpretation Centre offers excellent displays on the local marine flora and fauna, including an underwater video monitor that broadcasts the busy life of the bay's seafloor. There are also whale-watching tours on offer.

---

11 Burin Peninsula

🚌 St. John's 🚌 Argentia 🛈 Columbia Dr, Marystown; Jun-Nov: (709) 279 1211; Dec-May: (709) 279 1887

The Burin Peninsula presents some of the most dramatic and impressive scenery in Newfoundland. Short, craggy peaks rise above a patchwork green carpet of heather, dotted by scores of glittering lakes. **The Provincial Seamen's Museum**, in the fishing town of Grand Bank, preserves artifacts collected from the daily life of local seamen. The nearby town of Fortune offers a ferry to the French-ruled islands of Saint-Pierre and Miquelon.

The Provincial Seamen's Museum
Ⓢ 🏠 Marine Dr 📞 (709) 832 1484 🕐 Late-Apr-Sep: 9am-4:30pm Mon-Sat; noon-4:30pm Sun

Sun setting over the rocky shoreline of the Bonavista Peninsula ↑

⑫

Bonavista Peninsula

🚌 St. John's 🚌 Argentia
i Discovery Trail Tourism
Association; (709) 466
3845

Bonavista Peninsula juts out into the Atlantic ocean, a rugged coastal landscape of seacliffs, harbor inlets, and enchanting small villages such as Birchy Cove and Trouty.

The town of Bonavista is believed to be where Italian explorer Giovanni Caboto (*p66*) first stepped ashore in the New World. His monument stands on a high, rocky promontory, near the Cape Bonavista Lighthouse, built in 1843.

Along the waterfront of Bonavista, the huge 19th-century buildings of Ryan Premises, once a busy fish merchants' processing facility, are now restored as a National Historic Site. Inside the three large buildings, there are displays on the history of the fisheries in North America.

---

⑬

Notre Dame Bay

🚌 Gander 🚌 Port-aux-Basques; Argentia (seasonal) *i* Notre Dame Junction, Route 1

On the east side, traditional Newfoundland outports maintain a way of life that echoes their history. The Twillingate Museum, located in an Edwardian rectory, has several rooms furnished with period antiques. Twillingate is often described as the "Iceberg Capital" since the bulk of the huge icebergs floating down through Iceberg Alley are found here. For a close-up look, and whale watching, take a spring or early-summer boat tour.

The rugged Fogo Island is a ferry ride away. Located here is the Fogo Island Inn, now a world-famous luxury hotel. Visitors also go to Change Islands, two tiny islands home to the critically endangered Newfoundland pony.

---

⑭

Labrador Straits

🚌 Blanc Sablon *i* L'Anse au Clair; www.labrador coastaldrive.com

Hauntingly beautiful coastal landscapes explain why this is a popular place to visit. A year-round ferry service crosses the strait from St. Barbe, Newfoundland, to Blanc Sablon, Quebec, just a few miles from the Labrador border. From there, take Route 510, which leads east along the Labrador Coastal

↑ The interior and unusual exhibits of Twillingate Museum, on Notre Dame Bay

Drive through a wild countryside of high, barren hills. The route takes in small outport fishing villages, where fishing is still the economic mainstay for some. Atlantic Canada's tallest lighthouse was built here in 1854, near L'Anse-Amour. Known as the Point Amour Lighthouse, it is now a Provincial Historic Site. Another significant spot to stop is the Maritime Archaic Burial Mound National Historic Site, North America's oldest burial mound.

The highway passes through the town of Red Bay, home to the **Red Bay National Historic Site**, now a UNESCO World Heritage Site. Visitors can learn about the Basque mariners' presence during the 16th century, view the Right Whale Exhibit Museum, and visit the Interpretation Centre. You can also take a short boat ride to Saddle Island, where a tour leads past the foundations of the shanties and shipworks.

Red Bay National Historic Site

⊛ 🏠 Route 510 ☎ (709) 920 2142 🕐 Jun–early Oct: daily

15
Battle Harbour

🚢 Mary's Harbour 🛈 Mary's Harbour, Newfoundland; www.battleharbour.com

Once considered the unofficial capital of Labrador (from the 1870s to the 1930s), Battle Harbour, a small settlement on an island just off the southern coast of Labrador, was once a thriving fishing community. In 1965, the dwindling population was relocated to St. Mary's on the mainland, but all of the town's buildings, many of which date back 200 years, were left standing, and in the 1990s the town was restored. Today, it is a National Historic District.

16
The Southwest Coast

⛴ Ferry dock terminal
🚌 Port-aux-Basques
🛈 Port-aux-Basques; (709) 695 2262

In southern Newfoundland, the Granite Coastal Drive along Route 470 from Channel Port-aux-Basques to Rose

> **GREAT VIEW**
> **Cape Bonavista Lighthouse**
>
> Climb the stone tower of this historic lighthouse (*505 Cape Shore Rd*) to catch a glimpse of giant icebergs floating in the water below.

Blanche leads through a landscape of jagged green mountains and along a rocky, surf-carved shoreline. Near Rose Blanche, a boardwalk trail winds through wildflower-strewn heath to the impressive Barachois Falls. The area is noted for its many shipwrecks, and so the 1873 Rose Blanche Lighthouse stands in defiant splendor atop the headland.

17
Churchill Falls

🛈 Churchill Falls Development Corporation; (709) 925 3335

The town of Churchill Falls is ideally placed for visitors to stock up on supplies and fill up with gas, as there are no service stations between Happy Valley-Goose Bay and Labrador City. Churchill Falls is famed as the site of one of the largest hydroelectric power stations in the world. Built in the early 1970s, the plant is an extraordinary feat of engineering, diverting the Churchill River and its huge volume of water to propel the underground turbines to produce 5,225 megawatts of power – enough power to supply the needs of a small country.

→

Rose Blanche Lighthouse standing proudly on the Southwest Coast

A DRIVING TOUR
NORTHERN PENINSULA

Distance 267 miles (430 km) along Hwy 430 **Departure point** Deer Lake, at junction of Hwy 1 **Stopping-off points** Gros Morne's Wiltondale Visitors' Centre and Tablelands; Port au Choix National Historic Site; Grenfell Museum in St. Anthony

A land of legends and mystery, the Northern Peninsula of Newfoundland offers adventurous travelers the chance to experience over 40 centuries of human history, from early Aboriginal people through colonization to today's modern fishing life. The road north travels along a harsh and rocky coast. Along the way, important historic sites, such as L'Anse-aux-Meadows, tell the story of the earlier cultures who chose this wild land as their home.

Locator Map
For more detail see p334

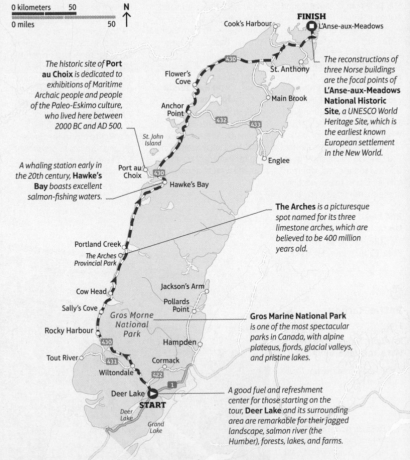

The historic site of **Port au Choix** is dedicated to exhibitions of Maritime Archaic people and people of the Paleo-Eskimo culture, who lived here between 2000 BC and AD 500.

A whaling station early in the 20th century, **Hawke's Bay** boasts excellent salmon-fishing waters.

The reconstructions of three Norse buildings are the focal points of **L'Anse-aux-Meadows National Historic Site**, a UNESCO World Heritage Site, which is the earliest known European settlement in the New World.

The Arches is a picturesque spot named for its three limestone arches, which are believed to be 400 million years old.

Gros Marine National Park is one of the most spectacular parks in Canada, with alpine plateaus, fjords, glacial valleys, and pristine lakes.

A good fuel and refreshment center for those starting on the tour, **Deer Lake** and its surrounding area are remarkable for their jagged landscape, salmon river (the Humber), forests, lakes, and farms.

The sun setting over the
serene Gros Morne
National Park

Northern Lights dance across the night sky, Yukon

YUKON

"Larger than life" is the Yukon's official motto, and
it's justly fitting for one of Canada's last frontiers.
The Yukon's sparsely populated land makes room
for Canada's five highest mountains, a host of
untamed rivers, and several legendary parks.
Though much of this harsh mountainous territory
lies barren, treeless, and frozen for most of the year,
an abundance of wildlife flourishes. Wolves, moose,
bears, and caribou have all adapted to the subarctic
climate, just as the First Nations have done since
the end of the last Ice Age. Even the early fur
traders of the late 1700s, and later, the Klondike
gold rush prospectors of 1896, managed to
persevere through the bleak winter months,
knowing that the midnight sun was waiting for
them come summertime. The Yukon's latitude
may bring on icy days, but they can easily be filled
with thrilling canoe, dog-sledding, and ice-climbing
trips. And at night, the enchanting aurora borealis
dances in colorful ribbons of light against the dark
skies for all to see, a once-in-a-lifetime-sight not
to be missed.

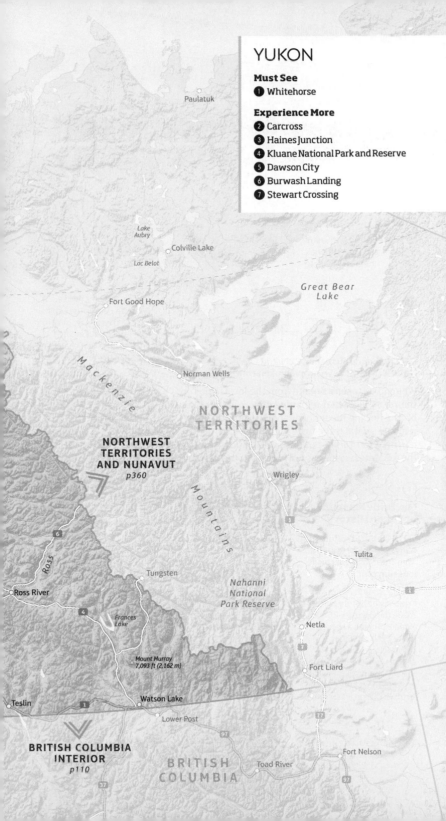

YUKON

Must See
❶ Whitehorse

Experience More
❷ Carcross
❸ Haines Junction
❹ Kluane National Park and Reserve
❺ Dawson City
❻ Burwash Landing
❼ Stewart Crossing

Paulatuk

Lake
Aubry

Colville Lake

Lac Belot

Great Bear Lake

Fort Good Hope

Mackenzie

Norman Wells

NORTHWEST TERRITORIES

NORTHWEST TERRITORIES AND NUNAVUT
p360

Wrigley

Ross

Mountains

Tulita

Ross River

Tungsten

Nahanni National Park Reserve

Frances Lake

Netla

Mount Murray
7,093 ft (2,162 m)

Fort Liard

Teslin

Watson Lake

Lower Post

Fort Nelson

BRITISH COLUMBIA INTERIOR
p110

BRITISH COLUMBIA

Toad River

Forest reflected on the still surface of Lake Laberge, near Whitehorse ↑

WHITEHORSE

✈️🚌 Greyhound bus depot, 2191 2nd Ave
ℹ️ 100 Hanson St; www.travelyukon.com

Whitehorse takes its name from the local rapids on the Yukon River that reminded miners in the gold rush of "the flowing manes of albino Appaloosas." This regional capital is the fastest growing town in the northern territories, but despite all modern amenities, the wilderness is always only a few moments away.

① MacBride Museum of Yukon History

📍 1124 Front St 🕐 Jun-Aug: daily; Sep-mid-May: 10am-4pm Tue-Sat 🌐 macbride museum.com

The MacBride Museum explores the history of the Yukon through over 25,000 exhibits. There's a Natural History gallery, with re-constructions of extinct animals, fossils and minerals; a First Nations gallery, which explores the culture of the 14 tribes that originally settled in Whitehorse; and a gallery on modern history, covering the frenzied Klondike gold rush among other subjects.

② Log Skyscrapers

📍 208 & 210 Lambert St

Several decades old, these log cabins have two or three floors, and are still lived in. Worth a detour, the cabins offer a pleasing respite from the rather functional architecture that characterizes much of the rest of town.

③ Old Log Church Museum

📍 303 Elliott St 🕐 May-Aug: daily; Sep-Apr: by appointment 🌐 oldlog churchmuseum.ca

In August 1900, Anglican missionary Rev. R. J. Bowen was sent to Whitehorse to build a church. He held services in one tent as the log building took shape. The church opened on October 17 and the log rectory was built that winter. These buildings are among the few remaining here from the gold rush period. In 1953, the log church became the Diocese

→ Natural history exhibits in the MacBride Museum of Yukon History

Did You Know?

The world's largest weathervane is in Whitehorse. It sits atop a swivel stand at the airport.

of Yukon cathedral and is said to be the only log cathedral in the world. Now, exhibits and interactive programs feature Inuit and First Nations cultures, and the development of the Anglican church in the north.

④ 🚲 Ⓜ 🏛

S.S. Klondike National Historic Site

🏠 End Second Ave 🕐 Mid-May–mid-Sep: 9:30am–5pm daily 🌐 pc.gc.ca

The Klondike paddle-steamer made ten supply trips each season to Dawson City. In the early 1950s, bridges along the road to Dawson were built too low, blocking passage on the river, so all journeys stopped. The Klondike ceased operating in 1955 and was beached forever in Whitehorse. It is now restored to its heyday in every detail, right down to the 1937 Life magazines on the tables and authentic staff uniforms. The boat is a National Historic Site, with regular guided tours of the interior on offer.

⑤

Lake Laberge

🏠 Klondike Hwy

The largest of the lakes in the area, Lake Laberge is frozen for half of the year, but comes to life in the annual thaw in the summer as a popular destination for swimming, fishing, and boating. The lake is famous among locals as the site of the fictional funeral pyre of Yukon poet Robert Service's *Cremation of Sam McGee*, which relates the story of the demise of a prospector in the gold rush. Trout fishing on the lake is excellent; fish were barged here by the ton during the Klondike gold rush to feed the hordes of hopeful miners.

⑥ 🚲 Ⓜ

Yukon Wildlife Preserve

🏠 Takhini Hot Springs Rd 🕐 Times vary according to the season, check website 🌐 yukonwildlife.ca

This sanctuary was set up in 1965 for research and breeding purposes. A beautiful reserve of forest, grassland, meadows, and water areas, it has 11 species of northern mammal in large enclosures. Moose, bison, elk, caribou, Arctic foxes, lynx, and other animals can all be spotted here, protected in the 740 acre (300 ha) parkland of their natural roaming habitat.

EAT

Alpine Bakery
Wafts of freshly baked bread and pastries drift from this cozy café. The garden patio is a pleasant spot to enjoy the tasty vegetarian pizzas on the menu.

🏠 411 Alexander St 🕐 Sun 🌐 alpinebakery.ca

$$$

Antoinette's
Caribbean-inspired twists like pineapple salsa and jerk-spiced aioli are added to seafood and meat dishes. For dessert, the chocolate rum truffle cake is a must.

🏠 4121 4th Ave 🕐 Sun 🌐 antoinettes restaurant.com

$$$

↑ A mountain bike rider tackling a trail in the region around Carcross

EXPERIENCE MORE

② Carcross

🏨🚍 *i* (867) 821 4431; mid-May–Sep daily

Carcross is a small village that lies at the picturesque confluence of Bennett and Tagish lakes, an hour's drive south of the Yukon's regional capital, Whitehorse. Early miners crossing the arduous Chilkoot Pass on their journey to the bounty of the gold mines in the north named the site "Caribou Crossing" after herds of caribou stormed their way through the pass between Bennett and Nares lakes on their biannual migration. The town was established in 1899 in the height of the gold rush with the arrival of the White Pass and Yukon railroad. "Caribou Crossing" was abbreviated officially to Carcross to avoid duplication of names in Alaska, British Colombia, and a town in the Klondike. Carcross has a strong Aboriginal tradition, and was once an important caribou hunting ground for the Tagish tribe. Tagish guides worked for US Army surveyors during the building of the Alaska Highway in 1942. Just 1 mile (2 km) north is the "smallest desert in the world," Carcross Desert. Blasted by strong winds that allow little vegetation to grow, the sandy plain is barren, but memorable nevertheless.

> "Caribou Crossing" was abbreviated officially to Carcross to avoid duplication of names in Alaska, British Columbia, and a town in the Klondike.

③ Haines Junction

🚍 *i* Kluane National Park and Reserve Visitor Centre, 280 Alaska Hwy; www. hainesjunctionyukon.com

Haines Junction is a handy stop for visitors on the way to the impressive Kluane National Park and Reserve.

The town has a post office, restaurants, several shops, and a few motels. Trips into the park for rafting, canoeing, and hiking excursions can be organized from the town, at the park's administrative headquarters. For rafting, book well ahead. Haines Junction was once a base camp for the US Army engineers, who in

1942 built much of the Alcan Highway (now the Alaska Highway) that links Fairbanks in Alaska to the south of Canada. The St. Elias Mountains tower above the town, and air trips can be taken from here to admire the views of the frozen scenery, glaciers, and icy peaks of this wilderness.

Kluane National Park and Reserve

🚍 Haines Junction ⏰ Year round 🌐 pc.gc.ca

This superb wilderness area is a UNESCO World Heritage Site. Covering 8,487 sq miles (21,980 sq km) of southwest Yukon, the park shares the St. Elias mountain range, Canada's highest, with Alaska. The whole park comprises one of the largest non-polar icefields in the world.

Two-thirds of the park is glacial, filled with valleys and lakes that are frozen year-round, broken up by alpine forests, meadows, and tundra. The landscape is one of the last surviving examples of an Ice Age environment, which disappeared in the rest of the world around 5,000–10,000 BC.

Mount Logan, at 19,551 ft (5,959 m), is Canada's tallest peak. There is excellent hiking here to suit all abilities; many trails are well marked and established, but there are also some less-defined routes that follow the old mining paths. Trecks can range from a two-hour stroll to a ten-day hike.

Kluane's combination of striking scenery and an abundance of wildlife, including moose, Dall sheep, and grizzly bears, make it the Yukon's most attractive wilderness destination. Trips into the park are organized from nearby Haines Junction. Due to the hazardous weather, untamed wildlife, and isolated conditions, safety measures are mandatory here.

Mountain scenery and Dall sheep *(inset)* in Kluane National Park and Reserve ↓

EAT

The Bistro on Bennett

Head to this friendly, rustic eatery for Canadian comfort food with a twist - think bison burgers, elk smokies, and cold beer. There are regular live music nights, too.

📍 Carcross Commons, Carcross 📞 (867) 821 3002

$$⑤

The Drunken Goat Taverna

This long-standing, lively Greek restaurant serves up hearty portions of pizzas, souvlaki and more. In summer, take your meal on the pleasant terrace out back.

📍 950 Second Ave, Dawson City 📞 (867) 993 6989

$$⑤

⑤ Dawson City

 🚗🚌 ℹ️ Cnr Front & King Sts; www.dawsoncity.ca

The town of Dawson City, in the Yukon, came into prominence during the Klondike gold rush of 1898, when the population boomed and the city grew from a moose pasture into a bustling metropolis of some 30,000 people, all seeking their fortune in the new "Paris of the North." The town continues to mine gold, but tourism is now one of Dawson City's key sources of income.

Dawson City Museum has fascinating displays on the gold rush and artifacts from that period. Another popular attraction is **Diamond Tooth Gerties**, the gambling hall complete with a honky-tonk piano and music shows during the tourist season.

Dawson City Museum

⊘ 🏠 595 5th Ave ⏰ Mid-May-late-Sep: 10am-6pm daily; late Sep-mid-May: by appointment 🌐 dawson museum.ca

Diamond Tooth Gerties

⊘ 🏠 Cnr 4th Ave & Queen St 📞 (867) 993 5525 ⏰ May-mid-Sep: daily; variable in winter

⑥ Burwash Landing

ℹ️ Whitehorse; (867) 667 3084

Northwest of Haines Junction, this little village at the western end of Kluane Lake lies just outside Kluane National Park on the Alaska Highway. A community was established in 1905 after a gold strike, and Burwash Landing is now a service center. Visitors can also enjoy panoramas of Kluane Lake to the south.

The village is noted for the **Kluane Museum of Natural History**, with many animal-related exhibits and numerous displays on local natural history. Focus is also given to the traditional lifestyle of the region's tribe of Southern Tutchone people.

Kluane Museum of Natural History

⊘ 🏠 Burwash Landing 📞 (867) 841 5561 ⏰ Mid-May-mid-Sep: 9am-6:30pm daily

⑦ Stewart Crossing

 ℹ️ Whitehorse; (867) 667 3084

East of Dawson City, Stewart Crossing is a small community at the junction of the Klondike Highway and the Silver Trail. During the gold rush in the late 19th century, the area was referred to as the "grubstake," because enough gold could be panned here during the summer to buy the following year's stake. Stewart Crossing also operates as the starting point for canoe trails on the Stewart River, which can be organized in Whitehorse or Dawson City.

About an hour's drive north is the Tintina Trench Rest Area. Providing visible proof of the geological theory of plate tectonics, the trench itself stretches across the Yukon, with layers of millennia-old rock gaping open. "Tintina" means "chief" in the local language, and this is one of the largest geological faults in the Yukon system. This is an ideal place to view the trench, which runs up along the route of the Klondike Highway.

STAY

Bombay Peggy's Victorian Inn & Pub

A cozy hotel with period furnishings and an adjoining pub. The latter gets crowded on weekends, with live music and good cocktails.

🏠 896 Second Ave, Dawson City 🌐 bombaypeggys.com

$$$

Klondike Kate's Cabins

These well-appointed cabins are conveniently located right in the heart of the city.

🏠 Third and King St, Dawson City 🌐 klondikekates.ca

$$$

↑ A family taking in the spectacular landscapes from Burwash Landing

NORTHERN LIGHTS

Witnessing the ethereal dance of the Northern Lights is nothing less than spectacular. And with the Arctic landscape as a backdrop, this natural phenomenon is certainly one of the highlights of the Yukon.

The Northern Lights, or *aurora borealis*, are believed to be the result of solar winds entering the Earth's ionosphere some 100 miles (160 km) above the surface of the planet. Emanating from the sun, these winds collide with the gases present in the Earth's upper atmosphere, releasing energy that becomes visible in the night sky. Vibrant greens, reds, purples, blues, and yellows shimmer in unusual patterns, and are best seen between the months of August and April, when the night skies are at their darkest. The further away you are from the city lights the better the show, as you'll likely have an undisturbed view. Southern Lights exist as well, close to the south pole. Interestingly, Earth isn't the only planet to have auroras – Jupiter, Saturn, Uranus, and Neptune have them as well.

↑ Photographer setting up to capture the Northern Lights over Yukon

MYTHS AND LEGENDS

Numerous stories about the Northern Lights have sprung up over the centuries. The Greeks and Romans named the lights after Aurora, the goddess of dawn, and Boreas, the god of wind. The Vikings believed that the lights were a reflection of the shields and armour of the Valkyrie – immortal female warriors. Early Chinese legends tell of a celestial battle between good and evil dragons breathing fire across the skies. Some Aboriginal groups see the flashes as spirits of dead hunters, while the 19th-century gold prospectors mistook the lights for vapors of gold ore deposits.

↑ Ethereal green lights of the *aurora borealis* reflected in a lake

NORTHWEST TERRITORIES AND NUNAVUT

Still one of the most remote destinations on Earth, this part of Northern Canada – renowned for its Arctic beauty – is now accessible to adventurous travelers in search of untouched terrain. Many of the settlements at this brink of the world were established only in the 20th century. Some of the first towns grew up around Mountie outposts, established to monitor trappers, explorers, and whalers; more recently, defense outposts have developed settlements. Local Inuit communities have gradually given up their nomadic life, and many are now settled around these outposts. These small towns are bases for exploring the stunning surrounds. In the winter, the north descends to -58°F (-50°C), yet in summer warm air sweeps in and the tundra bursts into bloom. The thaw acts in defiance of eight long months of winter, when everything is draped in a blanket of white. This is a startlingly beautiful region, with deserted plains, icy trails, and rare wildlife ripe for discovery.

NORTHWEST TERRITORIES AND NUNAVUT

Must Sees
1. Yellowknife
2. Baffin Island

Experience More
3. Nahanni National Park Reserve
4. Inuvik
5. Fort Providence
6. Norman Wells
7. Hay River
8. Rankin Inlet
9. Banks Island and Victoria Island
10. Baker Lake

Ellesmere Island

Sverdrup Islands

DENMARK (Greenland)

Queen Elizabeth Islands

Baffin Bay

Devon Island

Resolute (Qausuittuq)

Lancaster Sound

Somerset Island

Bylot Island

Pond Inlet

Prince of Wales Island

Borden Peninsula

Brodeur Peninsula

2 BAFFIN ISLAND

Qikiqtarjuak

Cumberland Peninsula

Igloolik

Committee Bay

Prince Charles Island

Nettilling Lake

Pangnirtung

King William Island

Kugaaruk (Pelly Bay)

Melville Peninsula

Arctic Circle

Amadjuak Lake

Hall Peninsula

Gjoa Haven (Uqsuqtuuq)

Repulse Bay

Foxe Basin

Foxe Peninsula

Iqaluit

Iqaluit Airport

NUNAVUT

Southampton Island

Cape Dorset

Kimmirut

10 BAKER LAKE

Coral Harbour (Salliq)

Ivujivik

Kangiqsujuaq

8 RANKIN INLET

Coats Island

Kangirsuk

Whale Cove (Tikirarjuaq)

Tasiujaq

Arviat

QUEBEC PROVINCE
p276

Hudson Bay

Inukjuak

Churchill

QUEBEC

MANITOBA

Kuujjuarapik

York Factory

ONTARIO

0 kilometers 300
0 miles 300

N

↑ Yellowknife's Old Town blanketed in snow on a winter's evening

❶ YELLOWKNIFE

✈ 𝒊 **Northern Frontier Visitors Association, 4-4807 49th St** ⓦ **visityellowknife.com**

Originally an Aboriginal Dene settlement, Yellowknife is named after the yellow-bladed copper hunting knives used by its first residents. The Hudson's Bay Company closed its outpost here in 1823 due to failing profits, but the Old Town thrived again with gold mining in the 1930s, and again after 1945. With improved road communications, the city became the regional capital of the Northwest Territories in 1967. Growing bureaucratic needs and three diamond mines 186 miles (300 km) north of Yellowknife have helped it continue to flourish.

① Ⓜ Legislative Assembly

🏛 **Frame Lake** ⏰ **For tours when council is not in session** ⓦ **assembly.gov. nt.ca**

Built in 1993, this headquarters of local government has a tall domed roof. Signifying equal rights for all ethnic groups, the government chamber is the only one of its kind in the country, with a large oval table to give all delegates equal responsibility, in the manner practiced by Aboriginals. Decorated with paintings and Inuit art, the chamber also features a large polar bear rug. The official public government rooms can viewed on free guided tours when the council is not in session.

The architects of the building were careful not to disrupt the surrounding natural landscape, and the Capital Site includes an expansive peat bog populated with native wildflowers, grasses, birds and waterfowl.

② Ⓜ 🖥 Prince of Wales Northern Heritage Centre

🏛 **4750 48th St** ⏰ **10:30am-5pm daily** ⓦ **pwnhc.ca**

This local museum tells the story of the land, people and history of the Northwest Territories. Displays feature typically northern artifacts, such as mooseskin boats, mammoth tusks, and items illustrating the history of flying in the north. Changing exhibits explain life in the subarctic and Beaufort Delta regions.

③ Old Town

Just half a mile (1 km) north of downtown, the Old Town is situated on an island and a rocky peninsula on Great Slave Lake. By 1947, Yellowknife had outgrown itself, and the New Town rose from the sandy plain southward. An unusual community thrives in the Old Town, many living in older clapboard buildings, log cabins and makeshift shacks and houseboats. A good vantage point from which to survey the area is the Bush Pilots Monument at the north end of Franklin Avenue.

___

(4) 🍴

Wildcat Café

🏠 3904 Wiley Rd ⏰ May-Sep: 11:30am-10pm Mon-Fri, 10:30am-9pm Sat & Sun 🌐 wildcatcafe.ca

The oldest restaurant in the city, this is the most-photographed building in Yellowknife. A true frontier stop, and one of Yellowknife's earliest permanent buildings, the log cabin is set under the

hill of the Old Town and has been refurbished in 1930s style. Its atmospheric interior is reminiscent of the pioneer days even after renovations.

___

(5)

Cameron Falls Trail

🏠 Hidden Lake Territorial Park 🌐 nwtparks.ca

Located about 30 miles (50 km) from Yellowknife, this short but picturesque walking route takes you along the Cameron River to the spectacular Cameron Falls (note that the waterfall is often frozen over in winter).

↑ Locals dragging canoes across the ice to open water near the Old Town

STAY

Bayside B&B

Located in the Old Town on the edge of Great Slave Lake, this B&B has several comfortable rooms and a rustic cabin available. Breakfast is at the terrific on-site Dancing Moose Café.

🏠 3505 McDonald Dr 🌐 baysidenorth.com

💲💲💲

___

Yellow Dog Lodge

Just a 20-minute floatplane flight north-east of Yellowknife lies this well-established wilderness lodge. Choose from rooms in the lodge, private cabins or adventurous floating tents.

🏠 Duncan Lake, Northwest Territories 🌐 yellowdoglodge.ca

💲💲💲

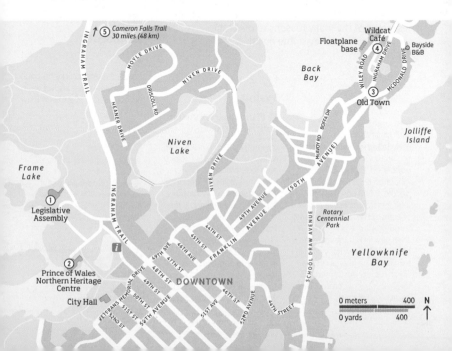

↑ (5) Cameron Falls Trail
30 miles (48 km)

Wildcat Café (4)

Floatplane base

Bayside B&B

Back Bay

Old Town (3)

Jolliffe Island

MOYLE DRIVE

NIVEN DRIVE

INGRAHAM TRAIL

DRISCOLL RD

HEANER DRIVE

WILEY ROAD

INGRAHAM DRIVE

McDONALD DR

BOFFA DR

McAVOY RD

Niven Lake

Niven Lake

Frame Lake

(1) Legislative Assembly

INGRAHAM TRAIL

AVENUE (50TH

49TH AVENUE

49TH AVENUE

FRANKLIN AVENUE

44TH ST

45TH ST

46TH AVE

47TH ST

47TH AVE

48TH ST

49TH ST

50TH ST

51ST ST

52ND ST

VETERANS MEMORIAL DRIVE

50TH AVENUE

51ST AVE

46TH ST

52ND AVENUE

44TH STREET

SCHOOL DRAW AVENUE

Rotary Centennial Park

Yellowknife Bay

(2) Prince of Wales Northern Heritage Centre

City Hall

DOWNTOWN

0 meters 400
0 yards 400

N ↑

②

BAFFIN ISLAND

w nunavuttourism.com

The harsh and isolated, yet compelling and beautiful environment of Baffin Island makes it an excellent destination for travelers looking for an unusual, intrepid experience. Spectacular fjords and knife-edged mountains sparkling with glaciers, wonderful Inuit artworks, and a chance to see the mighty polar bear in its natural but vulnerable habitat: these are just some of the many reasons to make this unforgettable journey to the north.

Part of Nunavut, Baffin Island is one of the most remote places in North America. The island is the fifth largest on the planet, with more than 60 percent of its landmass lying above the Arctic Circle. Sparsely populated, Baffin Island is inhabited by just 11,000 people, 9,000 of whom are Inuit. Most people live in one of eight settlements scattered throughout the island, the chief of which is Iqaluit, the capital of the territory of Nunavut. The only access to these remote settlements is by air, but every community has its own airport.

①

Iqaluit

⊡ 𝒊 Unikkaarvik Visitor Centre, 220 Sinaa St

Meaning "place of many fish" in Inuktitut, Iqaluit is the gateway to exploring Baffin Island. This diminutive capital city has a number of attractions. Perhaps the highlight is the Nunatta Sunakkutaangit Museum, housed in a former Hudson's Bay Company building. A fine collection of Arctic arts and crafts are on display, plus an exhibit on traditional Inuit artifacts such as tools, clothing, and sealskin kayaks. Another major sight is the Legislative Assembly which has beautiful Inuit tapestries and carvings, including an intricately carved narwhal tusk, embedded with gemstones.

Nearby St. Jude's Cathedral is often referred to as the Igloo Cathedral. It's a unique building that was constructed in 1972 but was rebuilt in 2012 after an arson fire.

---

②

Kimmirut

⊡

Located along a rocky harbour, this hamlet is well known as an art colony, particularly for its

↑ Aerial view of Iqaluit, Baffin Island's tiny capital city

←
Photographers taking pictures of walruses on floating sea ice

Inuit carvers who work with ivory, serpentine, soapstone, and marble. It is slightly warmer here than the rest of the island, and the meadows burst into flower during the short summer. Local guides can show visitors how to harvest plants from the area or can take them to the edge of the ice floe to view beluga whales and other marine life.

The Katannilik Park Visitor Centre is located here and can arrange demonstrations of traditional seal-skin sewing, drum-dancing, throat-singing, and bannock-making. Several historic buildings are dotted about, including the first Mountie outpost from 1915.

INSIDER TIP
Getting Around

Traveling around Baffin Island can be difficult, with expensive flights, and limited dining and accommodation options. Taking an expedition cruise on a small boat may be more affordable, and itineraries typically include daily landings for exploring, so you won't miss a thing.

③

Katannilik Territorial Park

Katannilik Park Visitor Centre, Kimmirut; 867 939 2416 Daily

"The place of waterfalls", this surprisingly fertile park has three distinct landscapes dating back to the formation of Earth, leaving a rich variety of exposed rock formations. One of these landscapes is the Meta Incognita Peninsula, which has a glacial-scarred plateau and a series of deep gorges and valleys, home to plenty of Arctic wildlife. The Itijjagiaq Trail begins here, a 75-mile (120-km) overland trail from Iqaluit to Kimmirut.

The park is also the access point to the lush Soper River Valley. The Soper River is a well-known spot for canoeing and kayaking. In summer, caribou come to graze in the lush valley here.

④

Cape Dorset

Mallikjuaq Park Visitor Centre; 867 897 8996

Surrounded by a rolling tundra, the hamlet of Cape Dorset is known for its Inuit artists, namely printmakers. The famous Cape Dorset Print Collection is created and sold here. These prints are characterized by their abstract, brightly coloured depictions of Inuit culture, Arctic land scapes, and Arctic wildlife.

Cape Dorset is also of great interest archaeologically because predecessors of the modern Inuit, the Thule and Dorset peoples, lived in this area. Several sites discovered here date back to 1000 BC, some of which can be seen at Mallikjuak Territorial Park.

Did You Know?

James Bond base-jumped Auyuittuq's Mount Asgard in the 1974 film *The Spy Who Loved Me.*

⑤
Pond Inlet

🔼 ⓦ pondinlet.ca

A jewel in Nunavut's twinkling crown, Pond Inlet is brimming with stunning scenery of mountains, glaciers, and icebergs, and is surrounded by abundant Arctic marine life. It overlooks Eclipse Sound and Bylot Island, which is a migratory bird sanctuary and the location of the Sirmilik National Park. Activities around Pond Inlet include snowmobiling, cross-country skiing and dogsledding to the floe edge, plus exploring ice caves and igloo camping.

⑥ 🚶 🏔
Sirmilik National Park

🅰 Bylot Island, Pond Inlet
📞 867 899 8092 ⓒ Daily

A vast landscape of glaciers, valleys, and hoodoo spires, this park is perfect for skiing, snowmobiling, and paddling expeditions. You can spot snowy owls, narwhal, walruses, and polar bears along the way. For bird-enthusiasts, Bylot Island, on which the park is located on, is a nesting area for over 40 species of migratory birds, including kittiwakes, murres, fulmars, and snow geese. Several Inuit, Thule, and European cultural sites are in the park as well.

→

Rooftops of Pangnirtung, with the peaks of Auyuittuq National Park in the distance

⑦ 🚶 🏔
Auyuittuq National Park

ⓒ Daily ⓦ parkscanada.gc.ca/auyuittuq

Auyuittuq, meaning "the land that never melts" in Inuktitut, is the third-largest national park in Canada at 7,370 sq miles (19,090 sq km). It is one of the few national parks with land above the Arctic Circle. A spectacular destination, the park displays a pristine wilderness of mountains, valleys, and fjords. In spring, the meadows thaw out from under a snowy blanket, and wildflowers burst into bloom. Within the park, wildlife abounds, with animals ranging from Arctic foxes to polar bears sharing the vast territory.

Keen hikers can take on Ulu Peak or the Akshayuk Pass in summer, when it's relatively snow-free. Experienced climbers and base jumpers may want to attempt Mount Thor, the earth's highest cliff face at 5,495 ft (1,675 m).

⑧
Pangnirtung

🅰 Angmarlik Visitor Centre; 867 473-8737
🔼 ⓦ pangnirtung.ca

Called "Pang" by the locals, this little town of 1,550 residents sits at the southern end of the Pangnirtung Fjord, around which is a 62-mile (100-km) hiking trail that is the most popular route on Baffin Island. Some of the cliff faces here are more than 4,900 ft (1,500 m) high.

Pang is situated close to several parks, including the Auyuittuq National Park. The Angmarlik Interpretive Centre is worth a look, with its displays on local Inuit history and culture.

The town is also a hotspot for Inuit artists, and you'll find many traditional prints, carvings, and tapestries on sale at the popular Uqqurmiut Centre for Arts and Crafts. Visitors should also pick up a Pang Hat while they're here – a cozy, wool, crocheted hat in bright colours and patterns.

WILDLIFE ON BAFFIN ISLAND

Despite, and likely because of, the severe climatic conditions they face, some of the planet's most robust and unusual wildlife exists on Baffin Island. Polar bears, Arctic foxes, and caribou are found wandering along its barren lands, while walruses, narwhals, and beluga whales swim in its icy seas. Guided excursions will ensure you'll see and learn more about these unique northern creatures.

Polar Bears

As the largest carnivore on land, the great white bear of the north can be spotted throughout the year. Called *nanuq* in Inuktitut, polar bears are avid swimmers with a keen sense of smell, and spend much of their time prowling the sea-ice for seals.

Arctic Foxes

Lurking around wherever polar bears are hunting, the Arctic fox is a scavenger but also preys on lemmings, birds, and fish. These fierce mammals are active year-round and can survive in icy temperatures of up to -58°F (-50°C) thanks to their incredibly dense and multilayered fur.

Caribou

A North American cousin of the reindeer, caribou migrate across Baffin Island in herds of up to 10,000, covering as many as 1,600 miles (2,575 km) every year. They head north for the tundra in the spring, and south into the forest during winter.

Walrus

Typically found basking on rocks, these huge mammals will dive to the sea bottom to find their favorite food - bivalve mollusks, and can eat up to 4,000 of them in one go. Large walrus herds can be seen in the Foxe Basin, on the western side of Baffin Island.

Narwhals

Known as the unicorns of the sea, these spiral-tusked creatures are unforgettable. The floe edge of Lancaster Sound, on the northern end of Baffin Island, is one of the best places to spot these elusive creatures.

① Polar bear family searching for food on Baffin Island.

② An arctic fox in the summer.

③ A male Caribou.

④ Walrus riding the waves near Foxe Basin.

⑤ Aerial view of Narwhals in the sea off Lancaster Sound.

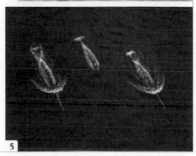

Muskoxen herd on Victoria Island

EXPERIENCE MORE

3

Nahanni National Park Reserve

📍 10002-100 St, Fort Simpson 🚗 Fort Simpson 🕐 Year round 🌐 pc.gc.ca

Nahanni National Park Reserve sits astride the South Nahanni River between the border with the Yukon and the small settlement of Fort Simpson. In 1978, it was one of the first places in the world to be designated a UNESCO World Heritage Site to protect its geological history. The park

is a great wilderness, with four vast river canyons, hot springs, and a spectacular undeveloped waterfall, Virginia Falls. The falls are twice the height of Niagara but have less volume. They boast excellent flora and fauna; at least 16 species of fish enjoy the cascades, and more than 180 varieties of bird live overhead. Wolves, grizzly bears, and woodland caribou also move freely in the park.

The park's main activities are whitewater rafting and canoeing. In summer, water-sports take precedence over walking tours as the rivers thaw and the landscape bursts into bloom. The park is usually reached by floatplane.

↓ The sheer cliffs and glassy lakes of Nahanni National Park Reserve

Did You Know?

In summer, northerly Inuvik experiences 56 straight days of 24-hour sunlight.

4

Inuvik

🚗 ℹ️ 2 Firth St; www. inuvik.ca

About 480 miles (770 km) north of Dawson City, Inuvik lies at the tip of the Dempster Highway, the most northerly road in Canada. The town has only a very recent history. Founded in the 1950s as a supply center for military projects in the NWT, Inuvik prospered in the oil boom of

↑ Our Lady of Victory Church, often called the Igloo Church, on Mackenzie Road in Inuvik

the 1970s. Full of functional contemporary architecture, it has a charm that lies mainly in its location as a good visitors' center for the region – there are a few hotels and several shops, which is no mean feat for a town that boasts just a single traffic light. It is, nonetheless, the most-visited town in the northern Arctic, and popular as a craft center and as a starting point for a tour of the far north.

The settlement of Paulatuk lies 250 miles (400 km) east of Inuvik and is one of the smallest communities in the NWT. It is well placed for hunting and fishing; these activities remain its staple support after many centuries. Its location is also useful as a stepping-stone to the wilderness, as tourism in the region becomes increasingly popular.

⑤ Fort Providence

📧 🚹 Northern Frontier Visitors Association, 4-4807 49th St, Yellowknife; (867) 873 4262

The Dene people call this village "zhahti koe," which means mission house in their language. Fort Providence began life as a Catholic mission. It was later enlarged by Hudson's Bay Company, which set up an outpost here in the late 19th century. The prospect of employment attracted the local Dene First Nations people to settle here permanently. Today, the town is a Dene handicrafts center.

Just north of the village lies the Mackenzie Bison Sanctuary, home to the world's largest herd of rare pure wood bison. The park stretches north along the banks of Great Slave Lake, and bison can be seen along the road.

⑥ Norman Wells

🚹 🕐 Daily 🚹 23 MacKenzie Dr; www.normanwells.com

In 1920 crude oil discoveries were made here near a small Dene settlement. Oil production surged in World War II, when the US established a pipeline to supply oil to the Alaska Highway while it was being built, and the town grew.

Today, Norman Wells is the starting point for the Canol Heritage Trail, a long-distance wilderness trail through to the Canol Road above the Ross River in the Yukon Territory, which links up with the Yukon Highway system. There are few facilities along the trail, making it one of the toughest trekking paths in the world. Despite this, it is a popular destination with experienced hikers.

STAY

The Arctic Chalet Resort
This hotel features comfortable rooms with kitchenettes and ski-to-door access. Other on-site activities include dog-sledding tours, canoeing, and kayaking.

🏠 25 Carn St, Inuvik
🌐 arcticchalet.com

⑤⑤⑤

Nova Inn Inuvik
A modern, simply furnished hotel with cozy fireplaces to warm yourself at after bracing the cold. Continental breakfasts are included.

🏠 300 Mackenzie Rd, Inuvik 🌐 novahotels.ca

⑤⑤⑤

EAT

Big Racks Barbecue
Head to this local favorite for a tasty and varied menu. Expect pizzas, burgers, ribs, and other warming comfort foods - the perfect response to the chill winds of the far north.

🏠 810 Aviq St, Iqaluit
📞 (867) 979 5555

$$$

The Kuugaq Café
This contemporary cafe is known for its hearty fare, with dishes such as char chowder, muskox shepherd's pie, and flavorful stews. Gluten-free options are also available.

🏠 16 Koihok Mahagak Crescent, Cambridge Bay 📞 (867) 983 2662

$$$

❼ Hay River

�"🚌 ℹ️ Hay River Hwy; (867) 874 3180; Jun-Sep

Set on the banks of Great Slave Lake, the small community of Hay River is the major port in the Northwest Territories. A lifeline, the town supplies the High Arctic settlements and the northernmost towns in the country, particularly Inuvik, with essentials. When the river thaws in spring, it supplies freight. The town looks designed for the purpose it serves: the wharves are lined with barges and tugs, as well as the local fishing fleet.

Unusually for this area, Hay River's history stretches back over a millennium. The Dene moved here centuries ago, lured by the town's strategic position at the southern shore of the Great Slave Lake, which offered excellent hunting and fishing. Attractions here are based on local industry; as a shipping center, the harbor is a bustling place to spot barges. The original Dene settlement, now a village of 300 people, sits across the river north from the Old Town and welcomes visitors.

❽ Rankin Inlet

🚗 ℹ️ Kivalliq Regional Visitor Centre, 131 Sivulliq Ave; www.rankininlet.ca

Founded in 1955, when the North Rankin Nickel Mine opened, Nunavut's Rankin Inlet is the largest community on the plateau of Kivalliq, which stretches east of the Canadian Shield to Hudson Bay. This small town is the government center for the Kivalliq region, whose population, now 85 percent Aboriginal, has settled mainly on the coast.

This region is characterized by its rural way of life, stunning scenery, and wildlife, boasting one of the world's largest populations of peregrine falcons. The **Iqalugaarjuup Nunanga Territorial Park**, which lies to the northwest of the town center, contains a traditional *Thule* (ancestor of the Inuit) restored site with stone tent rings, meat stores, and semi-subterranean winter houses.

Iqalugaarjuup Nunanga Territorial Park

🏠 Keewatin, 6 miles (10 km) NW of Rankin Inlet 📞 (867) 975 7700 🕐 Daily, weather permitting

←

A modern version of the stone cairns built by the Inuit, in Rankin Inlet

northern tip of the island. This ranks among the world's most remote wildlife destinations, and is accessible only by plane. Note that the park is best accessed from the NWT.

Split between the Northwest Territories and Nunavut, Victoria Island has a town in each: Ulukhaktok in NWT and the Inuit Cambridge Bay in Nunavut, where local Aboriginal people traveled each summer for char fishing, and caribou- and seal-hunting. The town today is a service center for locals and visitors along the Arctic coast. Polar bears, musk ox, wolves, and Arctic birds live nearby.

9

Banks Island and Victoria Island

🔁 🖈 1 800 661 0788

Located in the Arctic Ocean, Banks Island is one of the bigger members of the Canadian Arctic Archipelago, and home to the largest herds of musk ox in the world. The animals dwell in **Aulavik National Park**, on the sparse

Aulavik National Park

⊘ 🅰 Sachs Harbour 📞 (867) 777 8800 🕓 Daily, weather permitting

10

Baker Lake

🔁 📞 (867) 793 2456
🌐 bakerlake.ca

Geographically, Baker Lake lies at the center of Canada and is the country's only inland Inuit community. Located at the source of the Thelon River, in Nunavut, the area has always been a traditional summer gathering place for the Inuit. Its Inukitut name is Qamani'tuaq, meaning "where the river widens." Today, Baker Lake is an important center for Inuit art, especially textiles.

Heading westward, at the **Thelon Wildlife Sanctuary** visitors can see herds of musk ox in their natural habitat and glimpse other indigenous animals and birds.

Thelon Wildlife Sanctuary

🅰 186 miles (300 km) W of Baker Lake 📞 (867) 975 7700 🕓 Daily

> Its Inukitut name is Qamani'tuaq, meaning "where the river widens." Today Baker Lake is an important center for Inuit art, especially textiles.

→

A caribou calf grazing amid the bright fall colors in Baker Lake

INUIT ART AND CULTURE

As descendants from the Thule who emerged from coastal Alaska around 1000 AD, the Inuit are a 65,000 strong group of Aboriginal Canadians who now live in small, rural communities spread out across Northern Canada. Semi-nomadic for centuries, the Inuit are skilled fishers and trappers. This hunting lifestyle has created a distinct culture for the Inuit, one that is closely tied to their unforgiving landscape and harsh environment. And it is this hardship of northern life that has promoted artistic achievement throughout Inuit communities.

CARVINGS AND PRINTMAKING

Inuit carvings have been prized by Europeans as desirable art objects ever since they came into contact with the Inuit in the 16th century. Made in stone, ivory, and antler, these carvings were originally produced to depict animal spirits and mythical figures, and to amuse children. Inuits continue to carve and polish these works entirely by hand. In the 1950s, various other art forms, including printmaking, were adopted by the Inuit community. Prints and carvings, especially, are now highly sought after by art collectors.

← Tiny ivory carving, which was originally used to adorn Inuit clothing

ANIMAL SPIRITS

Set on the very fringes of the habitable world, the Inuit traditionally guarded against the threat of starvation with a supernatural belief system based on the respect of the animals they hunted. Their myths promote the belief that every living creature has a soul, and that a village shaman could commune with, and appease, the spirits in control of the hunt and the weather.

↑ Intricate Inuit soapstone
carving of a polar bear

INUKSUIT

For centuries, Inuit communities have built inuksuit, manmade stone landmarks across Northern Canada to help them navigate and mark hunting grounds and places of veneration. In recent years, these structures have become cultural icons: one was even adopted as the logo for the 2010 Winter Olympics.

MUSIC

Traditional music is very important to Inuit culture. Drum dancing plays a key role in most of life's great events: births, weddings, a successful hunt, and honoring a person who has died. Another form of music, throat singing, is usually performed by two women facing one another to recount a legend, life event, or myth.

TOP 3 PLACES TO SEE INUIT ART

Winnipeg Art Gallery
This art museum holds the world's largest public collection of contemporary Inuit art. Much of it will be on display in the new interactive Inuit Art Center *(p164)*.

Art Gallery of Ontario
The J.S. McLean Centre for Canadian Art has a superb collection of historic and modern pieces *(p182)*.

Musée des Beaux-Arts de Montréal
The Inuit art collection here contains pieces from past and present, and shows how Inuit culture draws on ancient legends and modern changes to traditional ways of life *(p246)*.

↑ Inukshuk silhouetted
against a sunset in the
Northwest Territories

NEED TO KNOW

Canadian Pacific Railway Train, Banff

BEFORE YOU GO

Forward planning is essential to any successful trip. Be prepared for all eventualities by considering the following points before you travel.

AT A GLANCE

CURRENCY
Canadian Dollar ($)

AVERAGE DAILY SPEND

SAVE	SPEND	SPLURGE
$125	$275	$500 +

BOTTLED WATER	COFFEE	BEER	DINNER FOR TWO
$1.75	$2.50	$7.50	$80 +

ESSENTIAL PHRASES (QUEBEC)

Hello	Bonjour
Goodbye	Au Revoir
Please	S'il vous plaît
Thank you	Merci
Do you speak English	Parlez-vous
I don't understand	Je ne comprends pas

ELECTRICITY SUPPLY

Standard voltage is 110 volts. Power sockets are type A and B, fitting two- or three-pronged plugs.

Passports and Visas

Citizens of all US, EU, and British Commonwealth countries do not require visas for stays of up to six months. For up-to-date visa information specific to your home country, visit the visa section of the **Canadian Government** website, and check with the nearest Canadian Consulate, Embassy, or High Commission before travel.
Canadian Government
w cic.gc.ca/english/visit/visas.asp

Travel Safety Advice

Visitors can get up-to-date travel safety information from the UK Foreign and Commonwealth Office, the US State Department, and the Australian Department of Foreign Affairs and Trade.
AUS
w smartraveller.gov.au
UK
w gov.uk/foreign-travel-advice
US
w travel.state.gov

Customs Information

An individual is permitted to carry the following within Canada for personal use:
Tobacco products 200 cigarettes or 50 cigars.
Cannabis 30g of cannabis within Canada; you cannot carry any cannabis across the border.
Alcohol 5 liters of alcoholic beverages with 24–70 percent alcohol. There are no restrictions on alcoholic beverages containing 24 percent alcohol or less.
Cash If entering or leaving Canada with more than $10,000 in cash (or the equivalent in other currencies) it must be declared to the customs authorities.

Insurance

It is important to take out insurance covering health problems, accidents, trip-cancellation and interruption, as well as theft and loss of valuable possessions.

Vaccinations

No inoculations are required to visit Canada.

Money

Major credit and debit cards are accepted almost everywhere, while prepaid currency cards and American Express are accepted in some shops and restaurants. ATM machines are widely available. US currency is accepted in Canada, but you will get a better rate exchanging US dollars at a bank.

Reserving Accommodations

Canada offers a variety of lodgings, from luxury five-star hotels to budget hostels. Camping, Motorhomes or RVs, and Airbnb are popular alternatives. In the summer months (June to September), accommodations are snapped up fast, and prices are often inflated.

Provincial Sales Tax (PST) must be paid on accommodations (and on goods and other services) and it varies from province to province, as does an additional accommodation tax (sometimes called Destination Marketing Fee). The Goods and Services Tax (GST) charge of 5 percent is standard nationwide. These taxes are usually paid on top of the advertised rates.

A comprehensive list of accommodations to suit any budget can be found on **Destination Canada**, Canada's official tourism site.
Destination Canada
w destinationcanada.com

Travelers with Special Needs

Nearly all public buildings provide wheelchair facilities with ramps and wide doors. However, some lodgings in historic buildings may not have these facilities so always check in advance.

Accessibility information for public transportation and travel are available from the **Canadian Transportation Agency**, which also provides an online guide for disabled visitors traveling by air. The **Canadian Institute for the Blind** also offers helpful information and advice.

Most transportation agencies can accommodate people with disabilities if you make your needs known at the time of booking. **VIA Rail** provide special assistance on their

trains, but you must contact them in advance. Car rental agencies offer hand-controlled vehicles and vans with wheelchair lifts at no additional charge.
Access to Travel
w accesstotravel.gc.ca
The Canadian Institute for the Blind
w cnib.ca
The Canadian Transportation Agency
w otc-cta.gc.ca
VIA Rail
w viarail.ca

Language

English and French are the official languages of Canada. New Brunswick is the only officially bilingual province, but French is widely spoken in the east, and the local tongue is known as "Québécoise". You will hear more Chinese languages and less French spoken in the west.

Closures

Mondays Some museums and tourist attractions are closed for the day.
Sundays Most shops and businesses are open for limited hours.
Public holidays Banks, schools, government offices, and some beer and liquor stores close all day. A handful of shops and attractions close early or all day.

PUBLIC HOLIDAYS	
Jan 1	New Year's Day
Mar/Apr	Good Friday
Mar/ Apr	Easter Monday
Before 25 May	Victoria Day
Jul 1	Canada Day
1st Mon in Sep	Labour Day
2nd Mon in Oct	Thanksgiving Day
Nov 11	Remembrance Day
Dec 25	Christmas Day
Dec 26	Boxing Day (except Quebec)

GETTING
AROUND

Whether you are taking a short city trip or leisurely touring the country, discover how best to reach your destination and travel like a pro.

AT A GLANCE

PUBLIC TRANSPORT COSTS

VANCOUVER

$2.95

Single bus and metro journey

TORONTO

$3.25

Single bus and metro journey

MONTREAL

$3.25

Single bus and metro journey

SPEED LIMIT

MULTI-LANE HIGHWAY	2-LANE HIGHWAYS OUTSIDE CITIES
110 km/h (65 mph)	**80** km/h (50 mph)

URBAN AND SUBURBAN AREAS	RESIDENTIAL STREETS
60 km/h (35 mph)	**40** km/h (25 kmph)

Arriving by Air

Canada's three largest international airports are Toronto, Montreal, and Vancouver. Air Canada is the country's major carrier, with WestJet as their main competitor. Several domestic airlines are reasonably priced on popular routes such as Porter Airlines, which serves the Atlantic Provinces, Ontario, and Quebec. Air North serves Alberta, BC, NWT, and the Yukon. Toronto Pearson Airport is close to several major transit routes.

All of Canada's international airports are well-served by bus, rail, and taxi services, or rented cars. Smaller airports depend more on taxis to surrounding areas. The table opposite lists popular transport options to and from Canada's main international airports.

The **Union Pearson Express (UP Express)** speeds passengers to Union Station, downtown Toronto, with trains leaving every 15 minutes. Alternatively, GO bus routes 40 and 34 leave every 30 minutes from a number of locations.

In Montreal, most people take a taxi to downtown. The 747 bus line service runs 24 hours a day, 7 days a week, between the Montréal-Trudeau airport and downtown Montreal.

Vancouver's rapid transit rail, the Canada Line, connects the airport to downtown Vancouver in 30 minutes. Accessible from both international and domestic terminals, the Canada Line operates from 5am to 1am. Should you require transport when it's not running, a taxi will cost less (due to light early morning traffic) than the usual fare.

All airports have both long- and short-stay parking facilities and offer a wide selection of rental car companies.

Union Pearson Express (UP Express)
W upexpress.com

Train Travel

VIA Rail *(p381)* is Canada's national passenger rail network and connects most of the country, with stops in all major cities. It is the only company to offer cross-Canada travel from Halifax to Vancouver. However, it doesn't extend

GETTING TO AND FROM THE AIRPORT

Airport	City Distance	Fare	Public Transport	Journey time
Toronto	18 miles (29 km)	$60	Taxi	30–60 mins
				(longer in snow)
		$12 approx	UP Express	25 mins
		$3	Airport Rocket bus	70 mins
		$70	Limo	30–60 mins
Montreal	12 miles (20 km)	$10	747 Express	45–60 mins
		$40 flat	Taxi	30 mins
		$55	Limo	30 mins
Vancouver	9 miles (15 km)	$9 ($4 to YVR)	Canada Line	30 mins
		$40	Taxi	20 mins
		$75	Limo	20 mins

to Newfoundland, Prince Edward Island or the Northwest Territories. On long distance VIA Rail routes there are two main classes of travel available, Economy and Business, and a variety of Sleeper classes.

VIA Rail also offers a number of routes to explore. For instance, The Ocean travels from Montreal along the Saint Lawrence River through New Brunswick to Halifax, Nova Scotia. Ontario–Quebec connects the big cities along the Quebec-Windsor Corridor. You can even hop aboard the 1950s stainless steel Canadian for a four-night, three-day trip adventure right across Canada.

VIA Rail offers discounts for groups, families, and senior-citizens. It also has flat-rate CanRAil passes, where you can travel between Quebec and Ontario for 21 consecutive days or across Canada for 60 consecutive days.

Regional Train Travel
Privately run regional train companies offer numerous additional journeys, although timetables are seasonal. The upscale **Rocky Mountaineer** connects Vancouver and Calgary, and stops at a number of BC and Alberta towns traversing the Canadian Rockies, including a separate trip from Vancouver to Whistler. **Ontario Northland** operates the seasonal Polar Bear Express on Hudson Bay, and the **Algoma Central Railway** accesses northern Ontario wilderness spots. Ontario also operates some passenger rail services. The service is most

efficient between Montreal and Toronto. Vancouver's SkyTrain and Canada Line connects bus and ferry services, all run by Translink.
Algoma Central Railway
🅦 translink.ca
Ontario Northland
🅦 ontarionorthland.ca
Rocky Mountaineer
🅦 rockymountaineer.com

International Train Travel
Both **Amtrak** and VIA Rail run three routes that link the US and Canada – terminating at Montreal, Toronto, and Vancouver. Customs inspections occur at the Canada-US border and not upon boarding.
Amtrak
🅦 amtrak.com

City Transportation
The **Toronto Transit Commission (TTC)** runs the public transportation system in Toronto, while the **Société de Transport de Montréal (STM)** runs the transit system in Montreal. Both cover subway systems, streetcars, buses, and commuter trains. Vancouver has an efficient monorail system, Calgary has a light-rail service called the CTrain, and Ottawa has a similar system called the O-Train.
Toronto Transit Commission (TTC)
🅦 ttc.ca
Société de Transport de Montréal (STM)
🅦 www.stm.info

Bus Travel

Buses are typically the most economical way to get around Canada, but often not the most convenient.

Long Distance Bus Travel

Greyhound Canada runs across Eastern Canada, and offers one route between Vancouver and Seattle. Smaller bus lines run along the Trans-Canada Highway, such as **Rider Express**, which offers bus service from Winnipeg to Vancouver. **Wilson's Transportation** runs an express service between Vancouver and Kamloops, and provides charter buses on Vancouver Island, and cross-ferry transport between Vancouver and Victoria.

Greyhound Canada
w greyhound.ca
Rider Express
w riderexpress.ca
Wilson's Transportation
w wilsonstransportation.com

Taxis

Taxis are plentiful in Canada's major cities, and are usually metered. They can either be flagged down or pre-ordered by phone. Uber also operates in Toronto and Montreal (but not yet in Vancouver).

Driving in Canada

A great way to explore Canada is by car, especially when visiting a remote country area. Canada's highway network is excellent and well maintained. However, city-center traffic congestion means that visitors to the major cities of Toronto, Vancouver, Montreal, and Ottawa may find that public transportation is quicker and cheaper than driving.

Vehicle Rental

Many international car rental companies have offices at city airports and downtown, and rentals are easily arranged before arriving in Canada. When picking up your rental car, you may be asked to show your passport and return airline ticket. Most rental companies offer GPS for a nominal fee, and child seats with advance notice.

Car2Go operates in Toronto, Montreal, Calgary and Vancouver. Costing $35 to join and then 41 cents per minute, or $15 per hour to use

---

JOURNEY PLANNER MAP

Banff
Calgary
Vancouver

Ottawa
Montreal
Toronto
Charlotte-town
Halifax
Niagara Falls

••• Direct car routes

Area of the main map

This map is a handy reference for traveling between Canada's main cities and tourist towns by car. The times given reflect the fastest and most direct routes available on each route.

Halifax to Charlottetown	3 hrs
Halifax to Montreal	12 hrs
Montreal to Toronto	5.5 hrs
Toronto to Niagara Falls	1.5 hrs
Toronto to Ottawa	4.5 hrs
Calgary to Vancouver	10.5 hrs
Banff to Vancouver	9 hrs

the vehicle, you locate a car with your smartphone app. You can park and leave them anywhere within designated areas.

The RV (recreational vehicle or motor home) rental business is mostly based in the west, with specialized agencies in Calgary, Edmonton, Whitehorse and Vancouver. **Canadreams Campers** has rentals in eight cities.
Car2Go
W Car2Go.com/CA
Canadreams Campers
W canadream.com

Parking
The majority of cities and towns have paid on-and off-street parking with parking meters and designated car parks. Parking in the downtown core of major cities is expensive: for instance, parking from a meter in downtown Vancouver can cost up to $10 per hour. Some meters limit parking to two hours. Illegally parked drivers run the risk of getting their vehicle towed with a fine.

Road Regulations
Everywhere in Canada you drive on the right-hand side of the road and traffic signs are in English, with French translations in the eastern provinces. Right turns on red (unless otherwise indicated) are allowed after coming to a complete stop in all provinces, except some places in Quebec. All vehicles must give way to emergency service vehicles, and traffic in both directions must stop for a school bus when signals are flashing. Pedestrians have the right of way at all intersections without stop lights and crosswalks.

Most provinces prohibit radar detection devices in vehicles and mobile phones may not be used while driving, with the exception of a "hands-free" system.

The **Canadian Automobile Association** is a great source for driving regulations and maps.
Canadian Automobile Association
W caa.ca

Insurance and Drivers' Licenses
Foreign drivers' licenses are valid and accident liability insurance is mandatory in Canada. Check with your insurer before your arrival to make sure you have sufficient coverage during your stay. Most of Canada requires that you carry at least $200,000 in liability insurance. US visitors should obtain a Canadian Non-Resident Inter-Province Motor Vehicle Insurance Liability Card, also know as a Yellow Card, from US insurance companies. The **Insurance Bureau of Canada** is a good resource to check and ensure you have adequate coverage.
The Insurance Bureau of Canada
W ibc.ca

Cycling

Cycling is a great way to get around the country during warmer months, and its popularity is on the rise. Most urban centers have dedicated bike lanes stretching hundreds of miles, and almost all cities allow bikes to be taken on public transportation. Some places, however, restrict bicycles during peak travel times, so check in advance.

Bicycle Hire
All major cities have shops that rent bikes, and some have tour guides available. Specialty bike shops also rent electric and mountain bikes. Vancouver, Montreal, and Toronto have bike-share programs with docking stations throughout the city, which allows cyclists to make one-way bike trips for a nominal fee. These programs use adjustable bikes, which are easy to ride for people of all abilities.
Montreal
W montreal.bixi.com/en
Toronto
W bikesharetoronto.com
Vancouver
W mobibikes.ca

Cycling Regulations
Regulations on the use of helmets vary across the country, so check in advance. The Maritime Provinces and BC have an all-ages helmet law that applies to cycling on roads. Vancouver also has a bylaw requiring helmets on most off-road paths. In Ontario helmets are not compulsory for adults over 18. Quebec and the Northern Provinces are lawless when it comes to bicycle helmets. Other large Canadian bike share systems differ by province.

Boats and Ferries

Across Canada, car ferries cross rivers, lakes, and oceans. Some ferry systems charge substantial fees, while others are free. **Marine Atlantic** is perhaps the biggest ferry operation on the east coast, and runs ships between Nova Scotia and Newfoundland. **BC Ferries** operates along the BC coast, including the gulf islands, and carries passengers from the mainland to Vancouver Island. During the summer months, it's a good idea to make a reservation if traveling from Vancouver (Tsawwassen or Horseshoe Bay) to Victoria (Swartz Bay), as ferry line-ups can take a few hours either way, despite it having the largest double-ended ferries in the world.
BC Ferries
W bcferries.com
Marine Atlantic
W marineatlantic.ca

PRACTICAL
INFORMATION

A little local know-how goes a long way in Canada. Here you will find all the essential advice and information you will need during your stay.

AT A GLANCE

EMERGENCY NUMBER

GENERAL
EMERGENCY

911

TIME ZONE
Canada spans six time zones: PST/MST/CST/EST/AST/NST. DST (Daylight Savings Time) is observed from the second Sunday in March to the first Sunday in November.

TAP WATER
Unless stated otherwise, tap water in Canada is safe to drink.

TIPPING

Waiter	15–20 percent
Hotel Porter	$2–3 per bag
Housekeeping	$3–5 per night
Concierge	$10–15
Taxi Driver	10–15 percent

Personal Security

Canada is one of the safest countries in the world. Most places are safe during the day and pickpocketing and muggings anywhere are rare. Theft is also rare in hotel rooms, but it's still a good idea to store valuables and important documents in the safe provided.

Health

A comprehensive range of treatment centers are available in Canada. For minor ailments, pharmacies offer a good source of advice and medicinal supplies, and walk-in clinics are available in all cities. In smaller communities, the emergency room of the closest hospital is the best option. Medical services are not free of charge in Canada, and it is important to take out health insurance prior to visiting.

There are risks associated with wilderness expeditions to the backcountry. Seek local advice about wild animals (including cougars), dangerous plants (including poison ivy), and insects (including mosquitoes), and always boil water that might be unsafe to drink. If you are bitten or scratched by an animal (domestic or wild), see a doctor immediately.

Smoking, Alcohol, and Drugs

Smoking is banned on all modes of transportation, but restrictions for other public places vary by province. Quebec allows smoking on outdoor patios but in BC and Alberta, it is banned in all public places and workspaces, including within 16 ft (5 m) of doors and windows.

Provinces across Canada have various provisions for regulating e-cigarettes and vaping products. Some cities ban vaping where smoking is banned, but others are less restrictive.

The legal limit for drivers in Canada is 80 mg of alcohol per 100 ml of blood or 0.08 percent BAC (blood alcohol content). This is roughly equivalent to a small glass of wine or a pint of regular-strength beer.

Recreational use of cannabis is legal in Canada, if you are 19 years of age or older. You

are limited to carrying up to 30 grams of dried cannabis in public, and smoking is permitted outside. Under the law, you are not allowed to smoke cannabis in enclosed public places and other common areas. While you can legally take cannabis from province to province, taking cannabis into another country can result in prosecution. Possession of illegal drugs may entail heavy fines and possibly jail time.

ID

There is no requirement for visitors to carry ID, but due to occasional checks you may be asked to show your passport. If you don't have it with you, you may be asked to present the original document within 24 hours.

Visiting Sacred Sights

Dress respectfully: cover your torso and upper arms. Ensure shorts and skirts cover your knees, and turn off your cell phone.

Cell Phones and Wi-Fi

Free Wi-Fi spots are generally available in main towns and cities, at major airports, libraries, and most hotels. Cafes and restaurants permit the use of their Wi-Fi on the condition that you make a purchase. For a list of Wi-Fi hot spots around Canada, visit the **Wi-Fi Freespot** website.
Wi-Fi Freespot
🅦 wififreespot.com

Cell Phones

Local SIM cards can be used in compatible phones and can be bought from local providers. US residents can usually upgrade their domestic cell phone plan to extend to Canada.

Pre-paid phone cards usually offer the best rates for international and long-distance dialing, and are sold in most drugstores and convenience stores.

Post

Canada Post handle most postal services in the country. Stamps can be bought from post offices, and some supermarkets, drug stores and even corner grocery stores. Allow three to four days when sending mail overseas. Parcels may take upward of two weeks.
Canada Post
🅦 canadapost.ca

Taxes and Refunds

A 5 percent Goods and Services Tax (GST) is levied on most goods and services. With the exception of Alberta, all provinces levy additional taxes (PST). Some provinces have HST (Harmonized Sales Tax) only, which combines taxes. There are also additional taxes on tourist lodging that vary by region (p381).

You may be eligible for a tax rebate under the Foreign Convention and Tour Incentive Program (FCTIP). More information is available from the **Revenue Agency** website.
Revenue Agency
🅦 canada.ca/en/revenue-agency

Discount Cards

The **Discovery Pass** offers unlimited admission for 12 months at over 80 Canadian National Parks that usually charge admission. Montreal's **Passeport MTL** gives access to 23 attractions in a 72-hour period. Toronto's **CityPass** offers 36 percent savings on admission to many attractions, and Vancouver and Ottawa offer 50 percent off entrance fees with **City Passport**.
CityPass
🅦 citypass.com/toronto
City Passport
🅦 citypassports.com
Discovery Pass
🅦 pc.gc.ca
Passeport MTL
🅦 passeportmtl.com

WEBSITES AND APPS

Destination Canada
Canada's official tourist website, www.canada.travel is full of useful tips.

Gas Buddy
For road trips around Canada, this app is a must. It locates gas stations near you, shows prices, sends price hike alerts, and notifies you about deals.

INDEX

Page numbers in **bold** indicate main entries.

PHRASE BOOK

IN EMERGENCY

Help!	Au secours!	oh sekoor
Stop!	Arrêtez!	aret-ay
Call a doctor!	Appelez un médecin!	apuh-lay uñ medsañ
Call an ambulance!	Appelez une ambulance!	apuh-lay oon oñboo-loñs
Call the police!	Appelez la police!	apuh-lay lah poh-lees
Call the fire department!	Appelez les pompiers!	apuh-lay leh poñ-peeyay

COMMUNICATION ESSENTIALS

Yes/No	Oui/ Non	wee/noñ
Please	S'il vous plaît	seel voo play
Thank you	Merci	mer-see
Excuse me	Excusez-moi	exkoo-zay mwah
Hello	Bonjour	boñzhoor
Goodbye	Au revoir	oh ruh-vwar
Good night	Bonsoir	boñ-swar
What?	Quel, quelle?	kel, kel
Why?	Pourquoi?	poor-kwah
Where?	Où?	oo

USEFUL PHRASES

How are you?	Comment allez-vous?	kom-moñ talay voo
Very well	Très bien	treh byañ
Pleased to meet you.	Enchanté de faire votre connaissance.	oñshoñ-tay duh fehr votr kon-ay-sans
Where is/are...?	Où est/sont...?	oo ay/soñ
Which way to...?	Quelle est la direction pour...?	kel ay lah deer-ek-syoñ poor
Do you speak English?	Parlez-vous anglais?	par-lay voo oñg-lay
I don't understand.	Je ne comprends pas.	zhuh nuh kom-proñ pah
I'm sorry.	Excusez-moi.	exkoo-zay mwah

USEFUL WORDS

big	grand	groñ
small	petit	puh-tee
hot	chaud	show
cold	froid	frwah
good	bon	boñ
bad	mauvais	moh-veh
open	ouvert	oo-ver
closed	fermé	fer-meh
left	gauche	gohsh
right	droite	drwaht
straight ahead	tout droit	too drwah
entrance	l'entrée	l'on-tray
exit	la sortie	sor-tee

SHOPPING

How much does this cost?	C'est combien s'il vous plaît?	say kom-byañ seel voo play
I would like...	je voudrais...	zhuh voo-dray
Do you have?	Est-ce que vous avez?	es-kuh voo zavay
What time do you open?	A quelle heure vous êtes ouvert?	ah kel urr voo zet oo-ver
What time do you close?	A quelle heure vous êtes fermé?	ah kel urr voo zet fer-may

TYPES OF SHOP

bakery	la boulangerie	booloñ-zhuree
bank	la banque	boñk
bookstore	la librairie	lee-brehree
cake shop	la pâtisserie	patee-sree
cheese shop	la fromagerie	fromazh-ree
chemist	la pharmacie	farmah-see
convenience store	le dépanneur	deh-pan-urr
department store	le grand magasin	groñ maga-zañ
grocery store	l'alimentation	alee-moñta-syoñ
market	le marché	marsh-ay
newsstand	le magasin de journaux	maga-zañ duh zhoor-no
post office	la poste, le bureau de poste	pohst, booroh duh pohst
supermarket	le supermarché	soo pehr-marshay

SIGHTSEEING

bus station	la gare d'autobus	gahr door-to-boos
cathedral	la cathédrale	katay-dral
church	l'église	l'aygleez
museum	le musée	moo-zay
train station	la gare	gahr
tourist information office	le bureau d'information	booroh duh infor-mah-syoñ
town hall	l'hôtel de ville	l'ohtel duh veel

EATING OUT

Have you got a table?	Avez-vous une table de libre?	avay-voo oon tahbl duh leebr
I want to reserve a table.	Je voudrais réserver une table.	zhuh voo-dray rayzehr-vay oon tahbl
The bill please.	L'addition s'il vous plaît.	l'adee-syoñ seel voo play
menu	le menu, la carte	men-oo, kart
wine list	la carte des vins	kart-deh vañ
breakfast	le petit déjeuner	puh-tee deh-zhuh-nay
lunch	le déjeuner	deh-zhuh-nay
dinner	le dîner	dee-nay
main course	le plat principal	plah prañsee-pal
appetizer, first course	l'entrée, le hors d'oeuvre	l'oñ-tray, or-duhvr

MENU DECODER

bread	le pain	pan
chicken	le poulet	poo-lay
coffee	le café	kah-fay
fish	le poisson	pwah-ssoñ
oil	l'huile	l'weel
onions	les oignons	leh zonyoñ
pork	le porc	por
potatoes	pommes de terre	pom-duh tehr
salt	le sel	sel
sausage, fresh	la saucisse	sohsees
seafood	les fruits de mer	frwee duh mer
snails	les escargots	leh zes-kar-goh
steak	le bifteck	beef-tek, stek
sugar	le sucre	sookr
tea	le thé	tay
water	l'eau	l'oh
red wine	le vin rouge	vañ roozh
white wine	le vin blanc	vañ bloñ

NUMBERS

0	zéro	zeh-roh
1	un, une	uñ, oon
2	deux	duh
3	trois	trwah
4	quatre	katr
5	cinq	sañk
6	six	sees
7	sept	set
8	huit	weet
9	neuf	nerf
10	dix	dees
11	onze	oñz
12	douze	dooz
13	treize	trehz
14	quatorze	katorz
15	quinze	kañz
16	seize	sehz
17	dix-sept	dees-set
18	dix-huit	dees-weet
19	dix-neuf	dees-nerf
20	vingt	vañ
100	cent	soñ
1,000	mille	meel

TIME

one minute	une minute	oon mee-noot
one hour	une heure	oon urr
one day	un jour	urr zhorr
Monday	lundi	luñ-dee
Tuesday	mardi	mar-dee
Wednesday	mercredi	mehrkruh-dee
Thursday	jeudi	zhuh-dee
Friday	vendredi	voñdruh-dee
Saturday	samedi	sam-dee
Sunday	dimanche	dee-moñsh

ACKNOWLEDGMENTS

The publisher would like to thank the following for their kind permission to reproduce their photographs:

Key: a-above; b-below/bottom; c-centre; f-far; l-left; r-right; t-top

123RF.com: ahkenahmed 13br; Olena Suvorova 152t.

Alamy Stock Photo: 917 Collection 294cr; Aerial Archives 290tr; AF archive / 20TH CENTURY FOX 62-3b; Aflo Co.; Ltd 157clb; age fotostock 145tr, 174-5b, 331tr, / Douglas Williams 84-5t, / Juan Carlos Muñoz 157cra; AGF Srl / Antonello Lanzellotto 229cra; Rubens Alarcon 193b; All Canada Photos 19cb, 28cr, 106bl, 109b, 205br, / Barrett & MacKay 32-3ca, 35tr, 40tl, 60-1b, 85cr, 164b, 324tl, / Ryan Creary 138clb, / Benjamin Dy 299cra, / Ron Erwin 148-9, 310-1b, 321tr, 321cra, 357clb,/ Henry Georgi 146tl, 325b, / Ken Gillespie 157crb, 176b, / Mike Grandmaison 226t, 303tr, / Chris Harris 66bl, / Jared Hobbs 141tl, / Stephen J. Krasemann 158cl, / Wayne Lynch 370-1, / Robert McGouey 32-3t, / David Nunuk 80-1t, / Steve Ogle 120cl, / Jason Pineau 368br, / David Purchase 347br, / Dave Reede 160-1b, 161cl, / Claude Robidoux 123tl, / Nick Saunders 161cr, / Stephen Shannon 126-7b, / Alan Sirulnikoff 138br, / TJ Watt 104-5b, / Ron Watts 346t; Archive Images 70-1t; Art Collection 4 56-7t; Art Directors & TRIP 373tl; Aurora Photos 146-7b; Bill Bachmann 322br; Jon Bilous 192tl; BiR Fotos / Stockimo 195b; Sabena Jane Blackbird 377tl; Kristina Blokhin 250tl, 281br; Ceri Breeze 141cr; Bill Brooks 184cr, 187bl, 197tl, 225br; William Brooks 220bl; Tawna Brown 65tl; Marc Bruxelle 49br, 249tl, 256b; canada 182-3t; canadabrian 323br; Lorne Chapman 195clb; Chronicle 204br; Citizen of the Planet / Peter Bennett 121tl; Mike Clegg 318-9t, 329br; Cosmo Condina 212b; Rob Crandall 266cra; Shaun Cunningham 98b; Ian Dagnall 34-5cb, 235t; Danita Delimont / Walter Bibikow 68cr, / Rob Tilley 242bl; dbimages 26cr, 44b, 58-9t; Dembinsky Photo Associates / Dominique Braud 299t; Design Pics 39cr, 170t, 290-1b, 294-5b, 356-7b, 358bl; Design Pics Inc / First Light / Henry Lin 184cra; doublespace-VIEW 20tl, 60tl, 178-9; Jason Doucette 161tr; Randy Duchaine 314tr; Entertainment Pictures 63br; Everett Collection Inc 62tl; EXImages 48-9t; eye35 134cra; eye35.pix 30cra; Steven Fines 89tl; Tony Florio 229t; FLPA 159tl; FOR ALAN 154-5t; FPW 172-3t; Alan Gallery 232tl; André Gilden 10-1b; Paul Christian Gordon 84bl; Bill Gozansky 340cr, 340bl; Sophia Granchinho 374-5t; Diego Grandi 248bc; Granger Historical Picture Archive 68br; Stéphane Groleau 251b; H. Mark Weidman Photography 4; HelloWorld Images 275tl; Stockimo 318bl; hemis.fr / Walter Bibikow 285cr, / Gregory Gerault 354br, / Camille Moirenc 13cr, / Bruno Perousse 246bl, / Philippe Renault 53cl, 53br, 245tl, 247cra, 285cra, 296tl, 296-7b, 297tr, 315cr, 315b; Historic Collection 309cr; Cindy Hopkins 346bl; Dave G. Houser 302bl; Aubrey Huggins 205bc; Bryn Hughes 18, 110-1; IanDagnall Computing 67bl; icpix_can 295cra, 295crb; Classic Image 204bc; imageBROKER 38bl, 59br, 205cb, 256tl; imageBROKER / Michael Runkel 217br; Ivy Close Images 66bc; Jukka Jantunen 369cra; Michael Jenner 173bl; Haiyun Jiang 274cl; John Elk III 123br, 124tl, 166clb; Inge Johnsson 10cla; Jon Arnold Images Ltd 171b, 253bl; JS Photo 42tc; Ken Gillespie Photography 165tr; Jim Kidd 280clb; Terrance Klassen 79tl, 174bl; Christian Kober 1 55cla; Art Kowalsky 252-3t, 293bl; Klaus Lang 291crb; Brian Lasenby 224-5t; Paul Andrew Lawrence 126tr; Lazyllama 328t, 999br; Cliff LeSergent 158-9b; Lyroky 204clb; Nino Marcutti 162-3t; Stefano Politi Markovina 36-7t, 83tl; Marshall Ikonography 64cra, 221t; Gunter Marx 87tr; Michael Matthews 101cra; mauritius images GmbH 23t, 230br, 270clb, 276-7, / Walter Bibikow 300br; Patti McConville 78bl; Megapress 59cb, 298bl; John Mitchell 255tr; Dawna Moore 272-3t; mooziic 70crb; Mountain Light / Galen Rowell 375b; Darlene Munro 225tr; National Geographic Image Collection / Brian J. Skerry 369br; Mark Newman 166-7t; NielsVK 216tr, 257tr, 356t; Nikreates 248clb, 268-9, 272bl; NiKreative 258cl; North Wind Picture Archives 66t, 67tl, 67tr, 68tl; Oleksiy Maksymenko Photography 237; philipus 196-7b, 205clb; Photo 12 204cb; PhotoV / Hisham Ibrahim 83ca; The Picture Art Collection 56b; picturelibrary 28cl, 52-3t; Pictures Colour Library 213tl; Melinda Podor 91t; Prisma by Dukas Presseagentur GmbH 101crb; 125b; 265br; 342-3t, / Heeb Christian 336cr; lev radin 71crb; Radius Images 282t; Rene Gauthier photography 89b; robertharding / Neale Clark 31tr, / Michael DeFreitas 330tl, / Michael Runkel 308-9t, 312-3t; Pierre Rochon 58bl; Rolf Hicker Photography 144tc,172cla, 232-3b; RosalreneBetancourt 10 198bl; Kay Roxby 46-7b; Russell Millner 369tr; Henryk Sadura 345t; rapisan sawangphon 86b; Science History Images 67cla; ScreenProd / Photononstop 63tr; Shawshots 70tl; sixshooter 81bl; Witold Skrypczak 106-7t, 119cr, 119bl; Keith J Smith 243t; Dmitry Smolyanitsky 210br; Jacek Sopotnicki 336t, 338-9t; SOTK2011 67bc; Mark Spowart 70bc; Spring Images 105cra; Pierre Steenberg 341; Harold Stiver 228-9b; Stock Connection Blue 101cr; StockFood Ltd. 45crb; Stocktrek Images; Inc. 24bl, 350-1; John Sylvester 24t, 332-3; Tetra Images / Henryk Sadura 313cr; P Tomlins 80br; Torontonian 28t, 64clb, 185; Universal History Archive / UIG 68bl; Universal Pictures / Entertainment Pictures 63cl; Francis Vachon 292clb; Vlad Podkhlebnik vladikpod 330-1b; Michael Wheatley 12clb, 44tr, 51tr, 51br, 57br, 72-3, 79tr, 83tc, 86clb, 88tl, 96bc, 100-1b, 101tc, 103clb, 116tr; 144b, 169tr; Jonny White 64cr; Wild Places Photography / Chris Howes 69tr; Robert Wyatt 37tr; YAY Media AS 354t; Colin D. Young 316-7t; John Zada 11br; Zoonar GmbH 108t.

© Art Gallery Of Ontario: Dean Tomlinson / Murray Frum Gallery 183br; / Phillip B. Lind 183cr, / Richard Barry Fudger Memorial Gallery 125 183crb.

Bisha Hotel Kost Restaurant via Iconink: 28br.

Bridgeman Images: Art Gallery of Ontario, Toronto, Canada 89/781 / Gift from the J.S. McLean Collection by Canada Packers Inc., 1990 / Skidegate, Graham Island, British Columbia 1928 Oil on canvas, 68.8 x 109.7 cm (27 1/16 x 43 3/16 in) by Emily Carr 183cra; Art Gallery of Ontario, Toronto, Canada 898 / Gift of Mr. and Mrs. Frank P. Wood, 1928 / Eve, c.1883 (marble) Overall: 76.2 cm, 105 lb. (30 in., 47.6 kg) by Auguste Rodin 182bl; Granger 68-9t; Private Collection / A Northern Canadian Lake (board), Thomas John Thomson (1877-1917) 57cla, / Look and Learn 247tl.

Canadian Museum of History and Canadian War Museum: 284-5b, 285tl, 285crb.

Canadian Tulip Festival: Steve Gerecke 64cl.

Celtic Colours International Festival: Corey Katz 64br.

The Commodore via Live Nation: 26crb, 48bl.

Depositphotos Inc: Bruno135 265tr.

Musée des beaux-arts de Montréal: Marc Cramer 246-7b.

Dreamstime.com: Alpegor 323t; Leonid Andronov 259br; Thomas Brissiaud 20cb, 200-1; Darryl Brooks 310tr; Elena Elisseeva 344-5b; Jacob Humphrey 344clb; Wangkun Jia 267cra; Chu-wen Lin 186; Christoph Lischetzki 264-5b, 267tl; Miroslav Liska 42bl, 156-7t; Maxbur 65crb; Meinzahn 54tl; Minnystock 96t; Outdoorsman 40bl; Tomas Pavelka 69bl; Norman Pogson 295tl; Robert Randall 10clb, 105tl; Jamie Roach 61cr; Ronniechua 142tr; Vismax 116-7b; Sara Winter 39br; Wwphoto 65cr.

Espace pour la Vie Montréal: Claude Lafond 254-5b.

Gardiner Museum: 192bl.

Getty Images: All Canada Photos / Ron Erwin 230tl, / Ken Paul 43br, / Michael Wheatley 101br; Victor Ovies Arenas 208-9b; Aurora Photos / Dan Rafla 17, 92-3; Bettmann 70bl; Aaron Black 51cla; Bloomberg / James McDonald 295cr; Marco Brivio 207t; by wildestanimal 366-7t; Matteo Colombo 8-9, 140-1b; CORBIS / Hulton-Deutsch Collection 161br; d3sign 8clb; Education Images / UIG / © The Henry Moore Foundation. All Rights Reserved, DACS / www.henry-moore.org 2019 Reclining Woman carved out of Green Horton stone 215cra; EyeEm / Brady Baker 34tl, / Nan Zhong 366br; Wei Fang 134-5b; ferrantraite 378-9; Nick Fitzhardinge 118-9; Gamma-Rapho / Louise Oligny 71br; Jesús M. García 142-3b; Raymond Gehman 372-3b; Hero Images 53tr; Hou 12t; ImagineGolf 11clb; INA / Philippe Bataillon 49cb; Eryk Jaegermann 168b; Naeem Jaffer 204-5; Kean Collection 69bc; KenCanning 41br; Jay Kerr 218-9t; laughingmango 46tr;

Jérémie LeBlond-Fontaine 369cr; Kjell Linder 133tc; LOOK-foto / Hermann Erber 372clb; Marko Stavric Photography 136-7; Richard McManus 369crb; MIXA Co. Ltd. 295br; MmeEmil 44clb; National Geographic Image Collection / Ian Mcallister 8cl, 31cla, 40-1b, / Pete Ryan 320-1b, / Sissie Brimberg 376cl; NHLI / Andy Devlin 13t; NurPhoto / Anatoliy Cherkasov 65clb, / Artur Widak 65cla; Pierre Ogeron 11t; Onfokus 265tl; Lauri Patterson 47cl; Pgiam 19tl, 128-9; Paul Bruch Photography 218br; Pierre Leclerc Photography 139; Posnov 343bl; Linda Raymond 45t; Joe Regan 326-7; Stanley Chen Xi, landscape and architecture photographer 37cla; Stocktrek Images / Alan Dyer 177tl; Manuel Sulzer 102t; Sungjin Ahn Photography 38-9t; lorenzo tombola 16c, 74-5; Toronto Star / John Boyd 184clb, / Reg Innell 184bc, / Boris Spremo 71tr, 71bc, / Andrew Stawicki 184cb; tulissidesign 41t; Vicki Jauron, Babylon and Beyond 36tl; Waitforlight 2-3; Michael Wheatley 30-1t; wichan yingyongsomsawas 282br; Alan V. Young 52bl.

Indigenous Tourism BC: 54-5b.

Ironworks Distillery: 47tr.
iStockphoto.com: aitzpurua 209tl; anouchka 26bl; benedek 99tr, 189tr, 227b; bgsmith 135tr; Bombaert 246cra; BrianLasenby 219cl; Marc Bruxelle 81crb; diegograndi 6-7; EddieHernandezPhotography 132br; fotoVoyager 188-9b; franckreporter 33tr; georgeclerk 22, 260-1; GibsonPictures 50b; gladassfanny 114-5t; moose henderson 36cra; Instants 292t; jamesvancouver 26t; JavenLin 190t; jimfeng 231t, 234bl, 321tl; kongxinzhu 90b; krblokhin 281tr; Steven Kriemadis 266-7b; Christophe Ledent 210t; LeonU 122b; marcduf 265cra; mericsso 359b; mfron 82-3b; MmeEmil 35tl; NicolasMcComber 286bl; NZSteve 364t; S. Greg Panosian 34tr; Leonardo Patrizi 50t; Pgiam 132-3t, 214-5b; s-eyerkaufer 30tl; Steve Schwarz 365cl; sharply_done 376-7b; SoumenNath 21, 238-9; studioworxx 42-3t; tomeng 32tl; UpdogDesigns 268bl, 349; Vladone 287t, 288-9, 301t; waterotter 359cl; zefart 204cl.

Manito Ahbee Festival via Neault Marketing Communication: Buio Assis 55cb.

Musée d'art contemporain de Montréal: François Maisonneuve 245cra; Sébastien Roy 245cla; Richard-Max Tremblay 244-5.

Musée National des Beaux-arts du Québec: Bruce Damonte 270b.

National Gallery of Canada / Musée des beaux-arts du Canada: 215tl, 215tr.
Niagara Wine Festivals: 47crb, 64cla.

Press Association Images: The Canadian Press / Adrian Wyld 184br.

Québec City Tourism: Francis Gagnon 271t.

Ripley's Aquarium of Canada: 194tl; Michael Hope 199tl.

Robert Harding Picture Library: Richard Cummins 316br; Michael Nolan 25, 338bl, 360-1; Michael Runkel 23bl, 304-5.

Shutterstock: HelloRF Zcool 222-3.

Wordfest Calgary : 61br.

World Ski & Snowboard Fest: Russell Dalby Photography 65tr.

Front flap: **Alamy Stock Photo:** Bryn Hughes bl; NielsVK cra; **Dreamstime.com:** Minnystock cla; Vismax t; **iStockphoto.com:** diegograndi c.

Cover images:
Front and spine: **Alamy Stock Photo:** Henk Meijer.
Back: **Alamy Stock Photo:** All Canada Photos tr; eye35 cla; HelloWorld Images c; Henk Meijer bc.

For further information see: www.dkimages.com

Penguin
Random
House

Main Contributors Lisa Voormeij, Donna Dailey, Mike Gerrard, Jane Mundy, Bruce Bishop, Eric and Katherine Fletcher, Paul Franklin, Sam Ion, Helena Katz, Philip Lee, Ffion Llywd-Jones, Cam Norton, Lorry Patton, Sandra Phinney, Geoffrey Roy, Michael Snook, Donald Telfer, Paul Waters

Senior Editor Alison McGill

Senior Designer Laura O'Brien

Project Editor Sophie Adam

Project Art Editors Ben Hinks

Designer Van Anh Le

Factchecker Pamela MacNaughtan, Jane Mundy, Candice Walsh

Editors Alice Fewery, Lucy Sara-Kelly, Zoe Rutland, Rachel Thompson, Danielle Watt

Proofreader Stephanie Smith

Indexer Helen Peters

Senior Picture Researcher Ellen Root

Picture Research Tim Draper, Sumita Khatwani, Harriet Whitaker

Illustrators Joanna Cameron, Gary Cross, Chris Forsey, Paul Guest, Claire Littlejohn, Robbie Polley, Kevin Robinson, John Woodcock

Cartographic Editor Casper Morris

Cartography ERA-Maptec Ltd, Simonetta Giori, Suresh Kumar, Reetu Pandey

Jacket Designers Maxine Pedliham, Bess Daly Simon Thompson

Jacket Picture Research Susie Peachey

Senior DTP Designer Jason Little

DTP Coordinator George Nimmo

Producer Samantha Cross

Managing Editor Rachel Fox

Art Director Maxine Pedliham

Publishing Director Georgina Dee

First edition 2000

Published in Great Britain by Dorling Kindersley Limited, 80 Strand, London, WC2R 0RL

Published in the United States by DK Publishing, 1450 Broadway, 8th Floor, New York, NY 10018

Copyright © 2000, 2019 Dorling Kindersley Limited
A Penguin Random House Company
19 20 21 22 10 9 8 7 6 5 4 3 2 1

A CIP catalog record for this book
is available from the British Library.

A catalog record for this book is available
from the Library of Congress.

ISSN: 1542 1554
ISBN: 978 0 2413 6532 8

Printed and bound in China.

www.dk.com

**The information in this
DK Eyewitness Travel Guide is checked regularly.**
Every effort has been made to ensure that this book is as up-to-date as possible at the time of going to press. Some details, however, such as telephone numbers, opening hours, prices, gallery hanging arrangements and travel information, are liable to change. The publishers cannot accept responsibility for any consequences arising from the use of this book, nor for any material on third party websites, and cannot guarantee that any website address in this book will be a suitable source of travel information. We value the views and suggestions of our readers very highly. Please write to: Publisher, DK Eyewitness Travel Guides, Dorling Kindersley, 80 Strand, London, WC2R 0RL, UK, or email: travelguides@dk.com